Tall Stories?

Tall Stories?

2 millennia of brochs

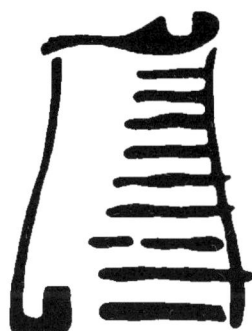

Edited by
Val E Turner
Rebecca A Nicholson
Steve J Dockrill
Julie M Bond

Shetland Amenity Trust
Lerwick
2005

Tall Stories?
2 millennia of brochs

ISBN 0 9543246 6 8

Published by Shetland Amenity Trust 2005

Printed by Shetland Litho
Gremista, Lerwick
Shetland, ZE1 0PX

Contents

Continued overleaf

List of Contributors

IAN ARMIT
Department of Archaeology
Queens University Belfast

BEVERLEY BALLIN SMITH
GUARD
Department of Archaeology
University of Glasgow
Glasgow

CATHY M. BATT
Department of Archaeological Sciences
University of Bradford
Bradford

IAN BLYTHE
3 Knipe Close
Huntingdon
Cambridgeshire

JULIE M. BOND
Department of Archaeological Sciences
University of Bradford
Bradford

RUBY CERÓN CARRASCO
Department of Archaeology
University of Edinburgh
Edinburgh

MIKE CHURCH
Department of Archaeology
University of Edinburgh
Edinburgh

DAVE COWLEY RCAHMS
John Sinclair House
Bernard Terrace
Edinburgh

STEPHEN J. DOCKRILL
Department of Archaeological Sciences
University of Bradford
Bradford

NOEL FOJUT
Historic Scotland
Longmore House
Salisbury Place
Edinburgh

SIMON GILMOUR RCAHMS
John Sinclair House
Bernard Terrace
Edinburgh

DENNIS HARDING
Department of Archaeology
University of Edinburgh
Edinburgh

RICHARD HINGLEY
Dept of Archaeology
University of Durham
Sadler Street
Durham

EUAN W. MACKIE
"Fairhills",
Station Road,
Old Kilpatrick,
West Dunbartonshire

J. G. MCDONNELL
Department of Archaeological Sciences
University of Bradford
Bradford

JACQUI MULVILLE
Department of Archaeology
University College Cardiff
Cardiff

REBECCA A. NICHOLSON
Department of Archaeological Sciences
University of Bradford
Bradford

J. N. GRAHAM RITCHIE
50/1 Spylaw Road
Edinburgh

IAN SIMPSON
Department of Environmental Sciences
University of Stirling
Stirling

NIALL SHARPLES
Department of Archaeology
University College Cardiff
Cardiff

IAN TAIT
Shetland Museum
Shetland Islands Council
Lower Hillhead
Lerwick
Shetland

JENNIFER THOMS
Orkney College
East Road
Kirkwall
Orkney

VAL E. TURNER
Shetland Amenity Trust
Garthspool
Lerwick
Shetland

List of Figures, Tables and Plates

Preface

"TALL STORIES?" began life as a conference held in Lerwick in July 2000. It was conceived as a celebration, both of the "inspirational stone towers" which have stood for around 2000 years and of the work underway at Old Scatness Broch. The Old Scatness project was then in its 6th year. It is a partnership between Shetland Amenity Trust and the University of Bradford. It combines cutting edge scientific research excavation with comprehensive field survey, a full environmental programme and an equally important public access to heritage project. Old Scatness provides a fitting bench mark for broch studies at the turn of the millennium and is the subject of several papers in this volume.

The conference gathered together the leading broch protagonists for wonderfully good humoured debate in which the full spectrum of views were represented. Indeed, the 40 or so people who accompanied Prof. Dennis Harding and Dr. Euan Mackie to Clickhimin for an impromptu guided tour on the final evening, now talk of the on site "Battle of the Brochs" as the stuff of legend.

All the papers in this volume arose from the conference, although two were not presented at the time. Graham Ritchie's introductory chapter has been added. The 100+ audience comprised interested parties who were not archaeologists and so Ian Armit responded to my request for an informal presentation about terminology which is included here. Ian Blythe is a former military man who spoke from the floor, initially in response to a throw away remark from Niall Sharples. The ensuing discussion provided a clear example of how and why we, as archaeologists, need to engage with specialists in the real world (architects, drystone dykers, and people with first hand experience of agriculture, fishing, economics and, indeed, war) if we are to come anywhere close to grasping how ancient peoples thought and behaved. I was therefore gratified when Ian offered a paper to this volume from his very different understanding of the evidence.

It is to my shame that four years have elapsed since then for a variety of reasons. All the authors have had their papers returned for checking after copy editing by Rebecca Nicholson this year. Several took the opportunity to update or even rewrite parts of their papers. So this volume still represents the current state of play as it goes to print.

Inevitably there are a number of people whose names do not appear elsewhere in this volume but whose contribution to the success of the conference, and to the production this book, should not be underestimated. Thanks are due to Lerwick Methodist Church, particularly Joan Robertson and George Anderson, for providing a comfortable venue and with an appreciated sound system (Joan made the black out specifically for the occasion); to Catrina Carter for slaving over a hot computer keyboard and, together with Rebecca Nicholson, making my life considerably easier; Davy Cooper for providing a sounding board, for scanning illustrations and for design work for the cover; Mark Donaldson, Sumburgh Hotel, and Tom Dawson for practical assistance during the conference; Jimmy Moncrieff for his enthusiasm and encouragement; and, most importantly, Biddy Simpson who took on the bulk of the conference organisation and worked so tirelessly throughout it that she wrote off her car a few days later – probably as result of pouring all her energies into making it such a resounding success.

Finally I would like to thank all my colleagues in the Old Scatness team and the sponsors who have enabled the conference and the project to happen. The conference itself was supported by Shetland Islands Council's Millennium Fund and Shetland Amenity Trust. Between 1995 – 2004 the Old Scatness project has been sponsored by: BP Exploration Operating Company, EC Objective 1 Programme, European Union (European Agricultural Guidance and Guarantee Fund), Historic Scotland, Pilgrim Trust, Robert Kiln Trust, Scottish Hydro Electric Plc, Scottish Natural heritage, Shetland Amenity Trust, Shetland Enterprise Company, Shetland Islands Council, Shetland Islands Council (Charitable Trust), University of Bradford, Heritage Lottery Fund, Shetland Islands Council Development Trust.

Val Turner
Lerwick & Old Scatness
December 2004

*Professor Dennis Harding enthrals and
entertains delegates as he puts his interpretation
of Clickhimin to participants on the
final evening of the Conference.*

Brochs: A Long View

J. N. GRAHAM RITCHIE

SIR WALTER SCOTT knew a Pictish fortress when he saw one. On Tuesday 9 August 1814 he: "Went ashore and see the very ancient castle of Mousa, which stands close on the sea-shore. It is a Pictish fortress, the most entire probably in the world. In form it resembles a dice-box, for the truncated cone is continued only to a certain height, after which it begins to rise perpendicularly – or rather, with a tendency to expand outwards. The building is round and has been surrounded with an outer wall, of which hardly the slightest vestiges now remain. … To give a vulgar comparison, it resembles an old ruinous pigeon-house." (*Journal of a voyage in the Lighthouse Yacht to Nova Zembla and the Lord knows where in the summer of 1814.*)

In his day impression was given by analogy and metaphor, and thus we have a broch as a dice-box and a pigeon-house, descriptions that may well not strike a chord today. Yet nomenclature is at the heart of the archaeological debate. The words that have been useful in the past, 'broch', 'dun', 'wheel-house', may on the one hand be cast aside as the straight-jacketed world of a woolly past, and the buzz of the more generalised and forward-thinking 'Atlantic round-house' of current protagonists introduced. There are both theoretical and generational approaches in play and we should respect both.

It is easy to say that you do not know what a broch is, but I have a pretty good idea. Even if they are not all Mousa, they are there in the countryside, whatever you call them. The circular wall-base may suggest traces of an intra-mural gallery. Of course sometimes you may not be sure, but by analogy with other structures or settlement mounds a long period of building-history that may have included a broch-like structure seems to be indicated. Field-survey can only be subjective.

In terms of western and north-western Iron Age archaeology the experience of the present writer began, as a member of staff of the Royal Commission on the Ancient and Historical Monuments of Scotland, in the Mull of Kintyre and moved northwards towards Shetland only later. Thus 'duns' to me really do exist, I have planned them from Kintyre to Ardnamurchan and beyond. Of course this is not to imply that we really know the date of such sites, nor that they are *not* 'Atlantic round-houses'. In that sweep of Atlantic Scotland from Kintyre to Shetland the imbalances of field-work and excavation since about 1950 have produced polarised attitudes to the interpretation of the scanty evidence that makes any overview difficult. The survey-work of the Commission in Argyll in the 1960s to 80s identified and planned many stone-walled structures, which were categorised as 'duns', and there was also a small number of classic 'brochs', including Dun Mor Vaul on Tiree and Tirefour on Lismore. During this period too responsibility for the depiction of ancient monuments on Ordnance Survey mapping fell to the Commission and thus an interest in crisp nomenclature was vital. The description of sites on maps, for example, is dependent not only on archaeological correctness, but also on space. Thus '*Dùn an*

Duin, Atlantic round-house' is unlikely to come into favour with map-makers; *brochs* and *duns* may yet survive. This is the sort of term the map-user and visitor expects, and the archaeologist has a duty today to this much broader constituency in terms of nomenclature. However valuable archaeologically the new nomenclature may be as indicating modern thinking (and I accept that there is a good case for it), it may take a long time to make any impact on those who actually fund the subject. The present author's only contribution to such nomenclature, however, is not really one to be proud of and began as a joke, but, as I bit the top of a jelly-baby, the similarity in shape with Pictish houses was all too apparent, the joke was passed on and sometimes even appears in print.

Several papers in this volume make mention the report by John Hamilton on *Jarlshof* (1956), and the comparison with what has been discovered at Old Scatness is certainly exciting; however there are a number of interesting aspects about Hamilton's book that have not fully been examined. This was the first, the flagship, volume of the Ministry of Works Archaeological Reports, and it was remarkable that the site chosen for monograph treatment was one so remote from London. But Hamilton had to be tactful, for at the time of writing the earlier excavators, A O Curle, J S Richardson and V G Childe, were still alive. In fact much of the excavation of Jarlshof had taken part before Hamilton's own work and his skill was to draw this material seamlessly together. Hamilton is most judicious in his discussion of what had gone before his work of 1949-52, his work was 'concerned with the stratigraphical sequence of deposits underlying the Viking house floors and the elucidation of the history of the settlement as a whole' (Hamilton 1956, 7). Larger scale excavations were possible outside the broch after the removal of an outhouse of 'Jarlshof' itself, and this allowed the plan and sections

published as Fig. 22. The monograph is thus the result of a long process of discovery and exploration to very different standards, and this is sometimes forgotten by readers of Hamilton's account. The broch, the two wheelhouses and the courtyard wall were excavated by the landowner, John Bruce, between 1897 and 1905, with a short account in the *Proceedings of the Society of Antiquaries of Scotland* (Bruce 1907). Frequently overlooked is the unusually full description of these remains in the Royal Commission on the Ancient and Historical Monuments of Scotland account of this part of the site prepared in 1935 and published in 1946, along with a plan and section that identifies the sequence of building (RCAHMS 1946, iii, 28-33). The various campaigns of excavation on both the earlier periods and Viking settlements are outlined fully by Hamilton. The importance of stratigraphy and levelling was identified by Hamilton as one of the vital aspects of his work on the site and he was fortunate in the collaboration of his Ministry of Works colleague, a recently graduated architect, John Reid. Reid supervised the overall planning of the site anew and created the survey grid that appears on the Master Plan in the back-pocket of the publication by the consolidation of the plans of earlier work along with what could be seen on the site as preserved, not always an easy task. Our appreciation of the site as published by Hamilton tends to mask the fact that that it had been examined by so many people in previous seasons, in Curle's case recording the work year by year, with annual plans. Hamilton again had recourse to the skills of his architectural colleagues to tie the levels together and produce period plans and reconstructions of the Viking settlements. The presentation of the *Jarlshof* volume has much to do with the period clarity of the fold-out plans and reconstruction views of Viking settlement: periods I – VII. These plans were prepared by John Reid, and the reconstructions were

BROCHS: A LONG VIEW

undertaken by Ian Begg, a college contemporary who joined in the work, in consultation with Hamilton. Both were to become distinguished conservation architects in Scotland in their own right, Reid having worked at Nimrud in between! The *Jarlshof* volume was to become a 'monument' in itself.

The Ministry of Works Archaeology Reports followed the tradition of the Society of Antiquaries of London Research Reports and in the Foreword to *Jarlshof* the Minister underlines the importance of publication of the results of excavation. The Minister has a charming description of the excavation as disclosing 'an intimate picture of village life in the Shetland Islands from the Stone Age to Viking times.' A touch of *The Archers of the North*. Hamilton's monograph was well received in reviews by Grahame Clark and Ralegh Radford, for example with phrases such a 'a complex task well discharged' and 'a full and lucid report' (Radford 1957). Clark (1957) is critical at Hamilton's reticence about 'the social units involved at the different phases of the occupation' (and interestingly he complains about the mean paper used).

Hamilton's work at Clickhimin between 1953 and 1957 is in contrast to that at Jarlshof, for it was far more comprehensive and followed rather more limited earlier work (Hamilton 1968). There is a clearer strategy of excavation with Interior and Exterior Panels or trenches, cross-sections, and more detailed sections, which I assume were drawn originally by Hamilton himself. As at Jarlshof he worked with Shetland men under the charge of the foreman, Mr Gilbert Sinclair of Clavel. There are again reconstruction illustrations, but these are not attributed. Perhaps mindful of Clark's criticism, the discussion is wide and discursive.

From a historical point of view Hamilton's *Addendum* (1968, 184) is interesting as the results of excavations on Skye and Tiree were beginning to be published and thus work on brochs took on a much wider dimension than

before. The present conference takes the discussion many stages further, not only because in Old Scatness in Shetland we have a site with a clear and correctly evolving excavation strategy, but also because the important work in the Western Isles has been closely integrated. The incremental nature of archaeological knowledge should not be underestimated. We should be aware both of the detail and intricacies of modern analysis and of the endeavours of our predecessors in the presenting information in the style of the times. The archaeological interpreter has a duty to try to assess not only the published information, but also the way that it is presented.

Several papers mention the likelihood of wooden structures within the stone framework, inevitably linked to the problems of roofing. It is worth recalling that A. O. Curle, the excavator of much of Jarlshof, was the first to identify the presence of a timber ring in a broch. In 1920 he was supervising the final stage of the Office of Works excavation at Dun Troddan, in Glen Elg, in western Inverness-shire, and it reads as though a good deal of the upper layers of the interior had already been removed. The floor levels remained to be excavated and recorded. He found a small pit about 0.6m (2 feet) in diameter lined with slabs and some 0.5m (1 foot 9 inches) deep. The significance of this discovery did not dawn on him at once, but 'after a night's reflection', he drew out a circle based on the centre of the broch and found ten other pits based on this circumference (Curle 1921, 90-1). He made the connection with the scarcement ledge and envisaged a timber structure in the interior of the broch. Something that has always surprised the present writer is why, if a timber interior was such an integral part of broch construction, there were not socket holes in the stonework. It may be that two distinct specialisms were involved and that the interior designs were a more individual matter to be considered after the stonework was completed. The analogy might be with a block of flats today with identical layouts, but with the interior design left to the individual owners. For brochs this would allow a greater degree of difference in the use of the interior space. The stone would be readily available, but as Fojut shows the timber might be more difficult to obtain. Thus experimentation with the most practical use of restricted space may imply internal rebuilding even in the early phases of broch use, which may be difficult to identify, as so few original floor levels are known. If the internal timber-work had been to a standard plan, surely there would be more trace in the surviving stonework. Equally, there may have been many styles of broch roofing.

The papers in this volume outline the great advances in broch studies in recent years, in excavation strategies, in environmental integration, and in setting monuments in wider theoretical frameworks. Our antiquarian forebears would have been delighted.

BIBLIOGRAPHY

Bruce, J. (1907) Notice of the excavation of a broch at Jarlshof, *Proceedings of the Society of Antiquaries of Scotland* 47 (1906-7), 11-33.

Clark J. G. D. (1957) Review of J. R. C. Hamilton (1956) "Excavations at Jarlshof, Shetland", *Proceedings of the Prehistoric Society* 23, 240-1.

Curle, A. O. (1921) The broch of Dun Troddan, Gleann Beag, Glenelg, Inverness-shire, *Proceedings of the Society of Antiquaries of Scotland* 55 (1920-1), 83-94.

Hamilton, J. R. C. (1956) *Excavations at Jarlshof, Shetland*. Ministry of Works Archaeological Reports, no. 1. Edinburgh, HMSO.

Hamilton, J. R. C. (1968) *Excavations at Clickhimin, Shetland*. Ministry of Works Archaeological Reports, no. 6. Edinburgh, HMSO.

Radford, C. A. Ralegh (1957) Review of J. R. C. Hamilton (1956) "Excavations at Jarlshof, Shetland", *Antiquaries Journal* 37, 226-7.

RCAHMS (1946) Royal Commission on the Ancient and Historical Monuments of Scotland *Inventory of the Ancient and Historical Monuments of Orkney and Shetland*, Edinburgh, HMSO.

Scott, Sir W. (1814) *Journal of a voyage in the Lighthouse Yacht to Nova Zembla and the Lord knows where in the summer of 1814*. Edited by W. F. Laughlan (1982). Hawick, Byway Books.

The Atlantic Roundhouse:
A Beginner's Guide

Ian Armit

CLASSIFICATION is a tedious necessity in the analysis and understanding of prehistoric structures. Even if we try not to impose classifications consciously we inevitably do it subconsciously. Since the late 1980s a number of researchers working in Atlantic Scotland have found it helpful to use a new terminology in the study of the structures variously known as brochs, duns, galleried duns, island duns, etc. First published in 1990 this has become known as the 'Atlantic roundhouse' terminology (Armit 1990). Although it has been used in academic circles for some years now, there has never been an easily accessible summary for a wider audience. Following an impromptu explanation delivered at the *Tall Stories* conference, the author was asked by Val Turner to set out the system in the present volume.

This short paper begins by outlining the problems with the conventional terminology that have bedevilled research in this field over many years. It then sets out the Atlantic roundhouse terminology and shows how it accommodates rather than supersedes the best elements of the traditional view.

THE OLD TERMINOLOGY

There are at least three basic problems with the traditional *academic* use of the term 'broch'.

1. *People mean different things by the term 'Broch'*

The conference which gave rise to this volume provided many examples of the problems with the traditional terminologies. Within a single session, for example, three speakers used the term 'broch' to refer to quite different groups of structures:

i) Euan MacKie used the term 'broch' to refer to a relatively narrow class of monumental roundhouse which he regards as demonstrably tower-like (MacKie this volume). MacKie regards these 'brochs' as quite distinct in their origins from other roundhouses which happen to share particular architectural traits such as intra-mural galleries and scarcements.

ii) David Cowley used the term 'broch' rather more loosely to refer to monuments identified principally through field survey, where the degree of original architectural complexity is rarely identifiable (see also Cowley 1999). This follows the conventional usage of the National Monuments Record for Scotland and the Ordnance Survey, where attribution as a 'broch' is based substantially on an impression of monumentality, as compared to, say, a hut circle (Cowley *pers. comm.*). Cowley thus included Crosskirk as an example of a 'broch' in Caithness, even though the construction methods of that structure would preclude it from acceptance as a 'broch' under MacKie's more stringent definition.

iii) Beverley Ballin Smith, in her presentation, described the sequence of excavated roundhouses at Howe in Orkney as 'brochs', even though most, especially 'Broch 1' would again fall foul of MacKie's criteria due to their structural peculiarities (see also Ballin Smith 1994) as well as most 'looser' definitions in customary use.

This is not to criticise the individual speakers, each of whom used the term entirely appropriately within the context of their own conference contributions. It is simply to highlight how quickly it becomes impossible to have meaningful dialogue when the same terminology is applied in different ways by different researchers. How can we examine such issues as the social role of these buildings, their chronology and structural evolution, and their relationships with other building traditions, if every researcher has in mind an overlapping but distinct group of sites, widely variable in time, place and construction?

2. *Sites which do not quite fit*

Perhaps even more problematic than the variable descriptions of what exactly constitutes a 'broch' is the tendency to exclude from archaeological consciousness all those structures which fail to live up to one's own particular definition. No satisfactory definition or classification system has yet been devised to give meaning to terms like 'dun', 'galleried dun', 'island dun', etc. The various 'dun' epithets effectively consign many hundreds of buildings to a typological dustbin from which they seldom re-emerge. Thus large numbers of Iron Age roundhouses in Atlantic Scotland, which clearly relate structurally to 'brochs' and share landscapes with them, have been left out of archaeological interpretations.

Worse still, it has become clear from both field survey and excavation, that the old division between 'brochs' and 'duns' is an artificial one, with the tower-like 'brochs' representing just one end of a spectrum of drystone building forms (e.g. Armit 1988; 1992; 1996). Once these structures have collapsed and/or been robbed to near their foundations any such typological niceties become entirely irrecoverable. It is a sad but simple truth that for the great majority of Iron Age roundhouses in Atlantic Scotland we have no way of telling if they were once tower-like 'brochs' or simple 'duns'. How then can we possibly make estimates about the numbers and densities of 'brochs' and thus build interpretations of their economic functions and social roles?

This is not, as is sometimes assumed, a problem peculiar to the Western Isles. Whereas in the Western Isles it has tended to be field survey that has highlighted the deficiencies of the conventional terminologies, in Orkney it has been excavation that has unearthed the problematic structures. For example, what, under the traditional terminology, are we to call a structure like 'Broch 1' at Howe (Ballin Smith 1994)? It clearly shares many traits of traditional 'broch' architecture, but peculiarities such as its paired and open-ended 'guard-cells' preclude any conventional tower-like form. Because such terms as 'dun' are rarely invoked in Orkney, we presumably have to regard it as some kind of aberrant 'broch-like' structure. But Howe is not alone in its stubborn refusal to fit the old terminology. What about Bu, Crosskirk and the rest? Indeed the great majority of Northern 'brochs', including some classic examples, are classed as such only through habit. Jarlshof, for example, fails to meet MacKie's criteria for acceptance (i.e. it has neither evidence for an upper gallery nor a void or gap over the door lintel, *c.f.* MacKie 1965, 103) and probably dates significantly earlier than the traditional 'broch' period of the 1st century BC/AD (Armit 1991, 193).

3. *The terminology divorces 'brochs' from the wider traditions of roundhouse architecture*

The third problem may at first seem minor, but it does have important implications. Under the traditional terminology, 'broch' relates to nothing else in Iron Age Britain or indeed anywhere else. There is no point of contact in the classification or terminology to tie these great stone roundhouses of Atlantic Scotland into wider interpretations of life in Iron Age Britain and beyond. This has contributed to a parochialism in the study of these buildings which is all the more ironic for its association with some of the wilder forms of diffusionism. Rarely has there been any attempt to set 'brochs' within the extraordinary, long-lived and wide-ranging phenomenon of roundhouse architecture which characterises Britain from at least the Middle Bronze Age to the Roman period. Any new terminology can help matters only if it lays stress on the context of 'broch' architecture within the wider background of British prehistory.

THE ATLANTIC ROUNDHOUSE TERMINOLOGY

The Atlantic roundhouse terminology reflects the basic unity underlying the range of stone-built roundhouses in northern and western Scotland. It set out to recognise and accommodate the wider range of structural forms and the greater time-depth revealed by modern excavation and field survey.

Fig. 1 sets out the Atlantic roundhouse terminology as a 'nested' system. In other words, the general category of Atlantic roundhouse contains within it a smaller sub-category of complex roundhouse, which in turn contains a sub-category of broch towers (see note 1). These can be defined as follows:

Atlantic Roundhouse: a regional manifestation of the wider tradition of substantial roundhouse-building in later prehistoric Britain. These structures are characteristically massive-walled drystone roundhouses, which would have been highly visible in the Iron Age landscape (see note 2). They need not be strictly circular, but they must retain a regularity of shape sufficient to allow roofing. The class is sufficiently distinct that scattered examples found in regions outside Atlantic Scotland (e.g. the 'southern brochs') are easily identifiable (see note 3).

Complex Roundhouse: an Atlantic roundhouse displaying one or more elements of architectural complexity ('broch architecture') such as intra-mural cells, galleries, stairs, or scarcements. Known examples are very varied and include excavated sites such as Crosskirk (Fairhurst 1984), Dun Bharabhat (Harding and Dixon 2000) and 'Broch 1' at Howe, (Ballin Smith 1984), which were clearly never of any great height and others such as Jarlshof (Hamilton 1956) where an original tower-like superstructure is possible but unknowable.

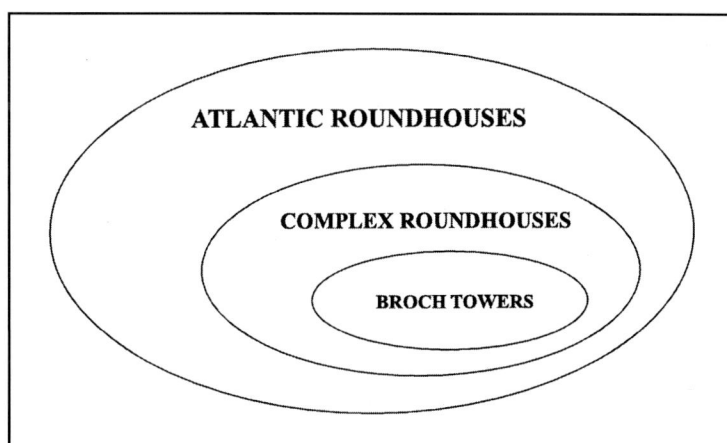

Fig.1 *The Atlantic Roundhouse Terminology.*

Broch Tower: a specialised form of complex roundhouse with hollow-walled, tower-like construction. This would most commonly be indicated archaeologically by the survival of a first floor gallery, or by voids above the entrance lintel indicative of a massive superstructure (e.g. Loch na Beirgh, Harding and Gilmour 2000). The definition is in essence the same as that used by MacKie to define 'brochs' (1965).

The Atlantic roundhouse tradition is thus envisaged as a vernacular architectural form which developed in the North and West of Scotland from around 700 BC to the early centuries AD. Some Atlantic roundhouses were fairly simple with no obviously significant architectural features beyond those used to define the class in general. Examples might include the early Orcadian roundhouses, such as Bu (Hedges 1987) and Pierowall (Sharples 1984), but also many potentially later simple roundhouses on the western seaboard. Others, as noted above, had elements of architectural complexity, the earliest of these complex roundhouses dating perhaps to around 400 BC (Armit 1991). Due to the vagaries of preservation, however, it is seldom possible to determine the height which most of the complex roundhouses attained and it will be impossible ever to determine the proportion of complex roundhouses that originally stood as broch towers. The terminology thus reflects the realities facing the archaeologist in the field, where levels of preservation may be sufficient to ascribe a site to the broad Atlantic roundhouse class, but not always sufficient for a more detailed attribution.

Broch towers can be seen in this context as a specific manifestation of the Atlantic roundhouse tradition, and their origins, social role and functions should be interpreted within that wider context, arguably as an elite form of architecture which emerges from a broader vernacular tradition. They appear to be restricted both regionally (e.g. the very small numbers in Argyll) and chronologically (although ongoing work at Old Scatness may suggest a fairly early emergence) relative to the overall distribution of Atlantic roundhouses (although see Gilmour this volume for an alternative view).

Other sub-groups within the Atlantic roundhouse tradition may yet emerge. For example, the presence of presumed timber-lacing in the roundhouse wall at Langwell (Nisbet 1974), and the clay-cored wall construction of Crosskirk (Fairhurst 1984) may hint at as yet dimly understood regional variants.

CONCLUSIONS

The Atlantic roundhouse terminology sets the traditional classification of 'brochs' within a wider classificatory system which draws in the many closely related buildings previously dismissed as miscellaneous duns and broch-like structures. It accommodates earlier terminological distinctions in that MacKie's (1965, 103) criteria for recognition of a given site as a 'broch' are more or less identical with the definition of a broch tower as defined here. While Dr MacKie would probably disagree with the implication enshrined in this terminological scheme that broch towers (his 'brochs') are an integral part of the wider Atlantic roundhouse tradition, the scheme itself does not contradict his own usage of the term.

The term 'broch' will obviously not go away. It will remain the popular descriptor for variously defined collections of Atlantic roundhouses, as is perfectly reasonable given its original derivation from the Old Norse for a 'strong place' (Ritchie 1988, 9) and its liberal distribution as a place-name element describing sites of a wide range of chronology and form (e.g. the Brough of Birsay). However, in *academic* usage it would be preferable for 'broch' to be restricted to sites which would be classed as 'broch towers' as defined above, the latter term being preferable in indicating that a precise meaning is intended.

The Atlantic roundhouse terminology explicitly sets the roundhouses of Atlantic Scotland within the wider roundhouse-building traditions of prehistoric Britain. Atlantic roundhouses can be seen as a regional variant of 'substantial roundhouses' (cf. Hingley, 1992) of which further variants might include ring ditch houses in southern and eastern Scotland, and many of the crannogs in the Central Highlands and elsewhere. One clear way forward for studies of the Atlantic Scottish Iron Age is surely in comparative studies with areas such as these.

ACKNOWLEDGEMENTS

I would like to thank Dave Cowley, Steve Dockrill, Dr Noel Fojut, Dr Simon Gilmour, Catriona Leask, Dr Euan MacKie and Professor Ian Ralston for their comments on preliminary drafts of this paper. Responsibility for the ideas contained remains my own.

NOTES

1. The Atlantic roundhouse terminology is a system for classification and description. It need not imply any particular evolution of structural forms. There is no assumption, for example, that complex roundhouses need have existed before broch towers could be built.

2. Buildings are not biological entities that can be defined with absolute precision. Instead they are the products of human agency; tradition, practicality and contingency merge with symbolism and ostentation, in their construction. It is thus impossible to divide Atlantic roundhouses absolutely from other structural forms, particularly given their wide distribution in time and space. The key to the Atlantic roundhouse terminology, therefore, like any archaeological classification, is its utility. The terminology can be used to provide a technical language to describe and discuss a range of Iron Age structures in Atlantic Scotland, retaining scope for the definition of sub-groups. It is not intended (and cannot hope) to have universal applicability.

The relationship between Atlantic roundhouses and other structural forms, for example wheelhouses, should be seen in this light. Wheelhouses have traditionally been defined on the basis of their internal spatial organisation and not on the basis of their overall structural form (as is the case with Atlantic roundhouses, even under the traditional terminological schemes). As the two structural forms are defined by different sets of criteria, it is unsurprising that there can be no clear line drawn between them. The vast majority of wheelhouses are not free-standing, above-ground structures; they are instead revetted into sand-hills or earlier buildings. They are clearly not, therefore, Atlantic roundhouses and their construction marks a radical break from traditions of Atlantic roundhouse construction (Armit, this volume). The small minority of wheelhouses which are free-standing (e.g. Allasdale in Barra) generally do not have the massive drystone walls associated with Atlantic roundhouses. There is no *a priori* reason, however, why a single structure could not be both a wheelhouse **and** an Atlantic roundhouse, since the two types are defined by different criteria (although no such structure has yet been identified).

3. There are of course structures outside Atlantic Scotland (the 'ring-forts' of Perthshire, for example) which are indistinguishable morphologically from simple Atlantic roundhouses: whether we choose to extend the terminology to such monuments is really a question of utility. As a reasonably coherently defined group,

both geographically and structurally, there seems little to be gained by describing the Perthshire 'ring-forts' as Atlantic roundhouses, although the relationship between these two groups of buildings is nonetheless worthy of future research.

BIBLIOGRAPHY

Armit, I. (1988) Broch landscapes in the Western Isles. *Scottish Archaeological Review* 5, 78-86.

Armit, I. (1990) Broch-building in Northern Scotland: the context of innovation. *World Archaeology* 21 (3), 435-445.

Armit, I. (1991) The Atlantic Scottish Iron Age: five levels of chronology. *Proceedings of the Society of Antiquaries of Scotland* 121, 181-214.

Armit, I. (1992) *The Later Prehistory of the Western Isles of Scotland.* British Archaeological Reports, British Series No. 221, Oxford.

Armit, I. (1996) *The Archaeology of Skye and the Western Isles.* Edinburgh, Edinburgh University Press.

Ballin Smith, B. (1994) *Howe: four millennia of Orkney prehistory.* Society of Antiquaries of Scotland Monograph Series, No. 9.

Cowley, D. C. (1999) Squaring the circle: domestic architecture in later prehistoric Sutherland and Caithness. *Northern Archaeology* 17/18, 67-75.

Fairhurst, H. (1984) *Excavations at Crosskirk Broch, Caithness.* Society of Antiquaries of Scotland Monograph Series, No. 3.

Fojut, N. (1981) Is Mousa a broch? *Proceedings of the Society of Antiquaries of Scotland* 111, 220-8.

Hamilton, J. R.C. (1956) *Excavations at Jarlshof.* Edinburgh, HMSO.

Harding, D. W. and Dixon, T. N. (2000) *Dun Bharabhat, Cnip: An Iron Age Settlement in West Lewis, Volume 1: the structures and material culture.* Calanais Research Series, no. 2, University of Edinburgh, Department of Archaeology.

Harding, D. W. and Gilmour, S. (2000) *The Iron Age settlement at Beirgh, Riof, Isle of Lewis, Excavations 1985-95, Volume 1,* Calanais Research Series No. 1, University of Edinburgh, Department of Archaeology.

Hedges, J. W. (1987) *Bu, Gurness and the brochs of Orkney, Vol. 1-3.* British Archaeological Reports, British Series, 163-5. Oxford.

Hingley, R. (1992) Society in Scotland from 700 BC to 200 AD. *Proceedings of the Society of Antiquaries of Scotland* 122, 7-53.

MacKie, E. W. (1965) The origin and development of the broch and wheelhouse building cultures of the Scottish Iron Age. *Proceedings of the Society of Antiquaries of Scotland* 31, 93-146.

Nisbet, H. (1974) Langwell: Tor a 'Chorcain. *Discovery and Excavation in Scotland 1974,* 59-60.

Ritchie, J. N. G. (1988) *Brochs of Scotland.* Aylesbury, Shire Books.

Sharples, N. M. (1984) Excavations at Pierowall Quarry, Westray, Orkney. *Proceedings of the Society of Antiquaries of Scotland* 114, 75-126.

Scottish Brochs at the Start of the New Millennium

EUAN W. MACKIE

*I*T WOULD not be fair to review the modern archaeology of the Scottish brochs without recognising the fundamental importance of the excavations in Shetland, on behalf of the then Ministry of Works, undertaken by John Hamilton in the years immediately after the Second World War. It may not be generally realised that, with his work at Jarlshof and Clickhimin in the late 1940s and early 1950s, Hamilton was the first person ever to excavate a broch complex in the modern stratigraphical manner pioneered in southern Britain by Mortimer Wheeler in the 1920s and 1930s. Before that time most sites had been excavated 'like potatoes', in Wheeler's memorable phrase, and the finds from them are little more than unstratified heaps of artefacts which are housed mainly in the Royal Museums of Scotland.

Even though at both Clickhimin and Jarlshof the brochs themselves had been cleared out much earlier, the results were epoch-making. *Excavations at Jarlshof, Shetland* was published in 1956 and, by describing in detail and illustrating at a large scale, the stratigraphical sequences he uncovered, Hamilton was able to reconstruct the long history of the site and to isolate the point at which the broch had appeared. For the first time the finds from each layer were described separately. It was purely an historical accident that the new work took place just before radiocarbon dates were widely available so that there are still some uncertainties about the absolute chronologies of both sites. The Jarlshof report changed everything and everyone who wished to explore a broch had a new standard of scientific excavation to follow. In view of this it is all the more remarkable that, within the last 20 years, two large scale broch excavations have been published without any adequate section drawings at all.

Reverting to a more general theme, broch archaeology may fairly be said to be in a peculiar situation at present. For the last 25 years almost all the work in this field has consisted of the excavation of individual sites, often by teams from the south. With the exception of Noel Fojut's ground-breaking work in Shetland (Fojut 1983) almost no systematic (by which is meant statistical) studies have been published about how the buildings relate to the landscape, or which compare the architecture of sites throughout the Atlantic province. Arthur MacGregor's work on the finds from the broch of Burrian, Orkney (MacGregor 1974) and Sally Foster's on post-broch bone pins and combs (Foster 1990), both studies done in the late 1970s and early 1980s, are notable exceptions and Andy Heald is now working on the bronze spear butts (Heald 2001). Apart from that, nothing has been published comparing in detail the large quantities of unpublished broch pottery and artefacts from old excavations in Scottish museums.

Some good work has been carried out in the last 30 years, especially in the excavation of individual brochs and wheelhouses, and also in the collection by John Hedges and his team of great quantities of information about the Orkney brochs (Hedges 1997). I have recently published a detailed descriptive Corpus of all known brochs from data I have been gathering since the 1960s and this will help progress towards a more reliable general picture of the dry stone buildings and associated material cultures all over Atlantic Scotland (MacKie 2002a). Wonderfully detailed new pictures of individual sites are emerging from skilled excavation but, because of this backwardness of material cultural studies (Smith 2002), it is very difficult to know how typical these sites are of the general population. There has therefore been a long standing tendency for each excavator to assume that the discoveries at his or her site have at last solved the 'problem of the brochs' (Hamilton 1965; Fairhurst 1984, 173; Parker Pearson and Sharples 1999, 345).

For these reasons I aim to try to answer some basic questions about these structures by looking at the submerged mass of unpublished information as well as at modern research. I shall concentrate on analysing three aspects of the primary evidence to build up what I hope will be a reliable picture of the basics of broch archaeology. I shall look first at architecture, second at dating and third at material culture.

ARCHITECTURE AND STRUCTURAL EVOLUTION

The essentials of broch architecture

The question of what exactly a broch is, other than a thick-walled, circular structure about 18m in diameter with various chambers and galleries in the wall, has featured prominently in writings on the subject for the last twenty years but I do not wish to get bogged down here in detailed typological arguments. In essence there seem to be two views at present.

The first view is the relatively new concept of the *variable structure with a long chronology* which maintains that the term 'broch' should be subsumed within a broader category of 'Atlantic Roundhouses'. This category covers the wide variety of stone roundhouses constructed in the maritime province from the 7th century BC or earlier right down perhaps to the 5th AD (though the lower limit is unclear). The second is the much older view of the *homogeneous structure with a short chronology* which holds that there is a class of hollow-walled broch towers, sufficiently distinct from everything else to mark them out as a dramatic innovation in Scottish prehistory. These were built over a relatively short period, say from the late 2nd or 1st centuries BC to perhaps the end of the 1st century AD. This idea was generally accepted before about 1975 (MacKie 2000).

The traditional hollow-walled broch tower of course exists and it should have at least one raised intra-mural gallery, either on top of a ground-level one (the ground-galleried broch) or on a solid wall base (the solid-based broch). Since the purpose of such a feature seems to be to achieve a high, strong yet light stone wall, there are likely to have been at least three or four such raised galleries linked together by a stone stair inside the wall. Also invariably associated with these features is the narrow, lintelled entrance passage, with massive door-checks between a third and two-thirds of the way down it, and a chamber over the entrance, open only to the interior. Thus most of the lintels covering the passage can be flat and fairly thin, since there is no stonework on top of them, but the outer one is massive in order to support the high outer wall face. As far as I know these 'voids' over internal openings do not occur in any other Iron Age structure in Britian. There is always a ledge or scarcement on the inside wall face, usually between 1.8 and 3.6m above the primary floor, with often an opening at this level leading out from a landing in the intra-mural stair. This suggests that access to a raised wooden internal floor was needed from inside the wall.

Although they vary in detail, this combination of features, together with the massive wall base and circular plan, is remarkably consistent in all the brochs which survive to a height greater than about 2m throughout Atlantic Scotland. Even in those less well preserved examples where no upper gallery survives, the size and proportions are consistent (Graham 1947). These features are not random architectural elements which the builders could 'pick and mix' at whim. Since they combine lightness with strength, they are essential for a high, hollow drystone wall to be constructed, even if 'high' can mean anything between about 7.6m (25 ft) and 15.25m (50 ft).

The other consistently occurring feature, the ledge or scarcement on the inside wall face, teaches us that the elaborate internal woodwork was just as much a part of the hollow-walled broch as the stone shell. Angus Graham's fieldwork for the Royal Commission in the 1940s found evidence that the stone ledge supported a level raised wooden floor rather than a lean-to roof; the ledge inside Caisteal Grugaig above Loch Alsh, Western Inverness-shire, is sited on a rocky slope and is too close to the rock on the uphill side to have held a roof (Graham 1949). The intra-mural stair, leading up to a first floor landing with a big doorway opening on to the ledge, is exactly what one would expect if there was a massive, ring-shaped upper wooden floor resting on it.

Unfortunately relatively few brochs have been systematically excavated down to their primary floor levels. Most of those which have yielded a ring of massive post holes, concentric with the main wall and about 1.8m in from it (MacKie 1995, 153). This makes it highly likely that every hollow-walled broch had a complex, two or even three storey wooden roundhouse inside it, perhaps with the main fireplace on the ground in the centre. I am not convinced by the theory of a complete raised

wooden floor with a fire resting on it (drawing reproduced in MacKie 2000, fig. 1); too many central hearths have already been found on the ground to make this plausible. A ring-shaped floor or balcony is surely more likely. The main roof was probably near the top of the wall but the details of its construction will remain unclear until a full-size broch is reconstructed. Alan Braby's reconstruction of Dun Carloway, Lewis, offers a good working hypothesis (see Fig 55, Fojut, this volume).

Are brochs architecturally homogeneous?

One fundamental question which the brief survey above does not answer is what proportion of all known and suspected 'brochs' do these elaborate and specialised hollow-walled towers form? In 1947 Sir Lindsay Scott advanced the view that structures with the high galleried wall, the true 'broch towers', are a minority among many other, much lower buildings with similar ground plans (Scott 1947). Some have now taken this further and claim that it is pointless to single out the towers as a class and that typological (by which is meant architectural) studies are a hindrance to progress, but I doubt the wisdom of dismissing a whole class of important evidence in this way. If homogeneity can be demonstrated across material cultural boundaries this could be explained by the presence of a caste or class of professional builders, a potentially valuable insight into Iron Age society.

The best way of examining the enormous quantity of architectural evidence (which is, I believe, in favour of the theory of structural homogeneity) would be to go on a six or eight week tour for a detailed examination of about 130 sites all over the Atlantic province. In the absence of that, five strands of evidence will be considered here.

(a) *The distribution of architectural features.* A table of the visibility of architectural features in both excavated and unexcavated sites, compiled from my own observations (MacKie 1995, 146), shows those which seem essential for the building both of the high galleried wall and of the complex wooden roundhouse inside this stone shell. They are: at least one upper gallery, a chamber above the entrance, voids in the inner wall face and a raised scarcement on it, and an intra-mural stair. These are distributed more or less uniformly throughout 130 sites. It is difficult to interpret this pattern in any other way than by concluding that the vast majority of the ruins are the stumps of hollow-walled drystone towers.

(b) *Careful demolition of brochs in the Iron Age and later.* Very important to the argument is clear evidence, in a few well understood brochs, for the deliberate and careful demolition of their high walls in the Iron Age and while the structures were still being lived in. This was first noticed at Dun Mor Vaul on Tiree in 1963 and it was concluded there that, after several centuries of occupation, the high drystone wall was inevitably getting a bit shaky and unstable so that it had to be reduced to a modest height. The rubble was taken right off the site (MacKie 1974). Midhowe in Orkney is another clear example as is Clickhimin in Shetland (MacKie 1995, 144; 2002, sites HY33 1 and HU44 1). Further evidence is likely to appear as more brochs are properly excavated.

One conclusion from this discovery is that it is no longer possible to argue, as Sir Lindsay Scott did in 1947, that a low broch mound with a relatively small amount of rubble in and around it must mean that the structure was never very high; masses of material could have been taken away during the Iron Age itself. Another interesting conclusion from the

discovery of deliberate demolition, if it proves to be widespread, may be that the tall tower was not essential for defence. Prestige and display may have been at least as important in building high brochs, a conclusion which has been derived from the entirely different topographical evidence collected in Shetland by Noel Fojut (1982).

To Iron Age demolition we might add the abundant historical evidence available which shows that a number of brochs have been drastically reduced in height by stone robbery over the last four centuries. It is thus fair to conclude, as did Joseph Anderson many years ago (1883, 184-86), that such robbery occurred earlier too and that vast numbers of brochs are now mere stumps compared with what they once were.

(c) *Badly built low 'brochs'.* As the result of several important discoveries in Orkney since the early 1970s we now know that there was a significant tradition of massive stone roundhouses in those islands in the early Iron Age, apparently long before any hollow-walled brochs were built. It is also clear from the extremely important, excavated, multi-period site at Howe in Orkney (Ballin Smith ed. 1994), and from Crosskirk on the north coast of Caithness (Fairhurst 1984), that late forms of this local roundhouse tradition were built with very broch-like features, such as a massive wall and an intra-mural stair. The fundamental difference seems to be that they were not high towers. No traces of the galleried wall were found on their 12 ft (4m) high, solid wall heads and these huge foundations contained large amounts of clay, an entirely unsuitable foundation for a high stone tower. This is particularly clear at Howe where the gigantic low 'broch' of Phase 7 was founded on the remains of the clay mound of a Neolithic chambered tomb and showed several signs of instability and partial collapse because of this (MacKie 1998).

It might be argued that there were first floor wall galleries at Howe and Crosskirk but at a slightly higher level and that they had therefore been destroyed long ago. Against this idea is the fairly low broch mound at Carn Merk near Westerdale in Caithness where in the 1950s a trench was cut across the wallhead, immediately exposing an upper gallery 3ft deep (MacKie forthcoming, site ND15 9).

When we compare the jerry-built 'broch' at Howe with, for example, Gurness and Midhowe – sophisticated, solid stone, hollow-walled brochs not far away – we can surely conclude that the Howe structure, like Crosskirk, was an unskilled copy of a new style of drystone tower which had recently arrived in the island. The dating evidence suggests that none of these buildings can plausibly be put back before the first or second centuries BC. The broch-like structure of Phase 6 at Howe is dated in the report to the early Iron Age, but the evidence does not really support this (MacKie 1998); at Crosskirk the report is vague about the stratigraphy but there too an early Iron Age date seems very unlikely (MacKie forthcoming, site ND07 2: see also 'Dating' section below).

    (d) *The Hebridean Semibrochs*. Another line of argument strongly favouring the idea that the high galleried wall was part of a connected group of highly successful Iron Age structures, quite distinct from all the other stone roundhouses of the period, is the existence of a class of what Sir Lindsay Scott called 'non-circular brochs' and which I have called semibrochs for many years (MacKie 1965). These are strongholds with exactly the same high, hollow wall as the brochs but not forming a complete circuit; the open side is usually defended by a high cliff and a relatively low wall. In a few cases the high wall is a simple, gently curving one, cutting off the neck of a cliff promontory. One can argue about the status of one or two of the sixteen definite and probable sites in this class but there is no doubt that they exist; the D-shaped one near Glenelg is a good example, as is the promontory semibroch on Barra Head at the southern tip of the Outer Hebrides. There is a small amount of evidence that the four or five promontory semibrochs belong to the early Iron Age (MacKie 2002, 364).

Two semibrochs have been excavated, namely Dun an Rhiroy in Wester Ross (MacKie 1980) and Dun Ardtreck on Skye (MacKie 2002). Whilst the evidence is not strong enough to place them before the 1st or 2nd centuries BC with any confidence, it is overwhelmingly against the old idea that they were part of a larger class of buildings called 'galleried duns' belonging to the post-broch, late Iron Age period (MacKie 1992). Evidence that they appeared in pre-broch times exists at the Clickhimin broch site; there the so-called 'forework' is almost identical to a promontory semibroch but is attached to the remains of a galleried wall which runs under the nearby solid-based broch (MacKie 2002a, site HU44 1).

It has been suggested that semibrochs could be alternatives to the broch tower (Harding 1984) although, since both the convenience of their locations and their defensive capacity is much less, it is hard to see why. On the other hand they could be prototypes, the immediate forerunners of the broch towers. Four distribution maps have been published which seem to tell a clear story of an increasingly successful building technique changing over time and space (MacKie 1992, figs. 1-4). Initially there are a few promontory semibrochs, the simplest and presumably the earliest form of the high, hollow wall: four in the Western Isles and one in Shetland. The much larger number of D- and C-shaped semibrochs is essentially in the same area: Skye and adjacent regions. The ground-galleried brochs occur in even larger numbers, again concentrated in the Western Isles though with a few in Orkney and Shetland, while the usually more massive, solid-based brochs are overwhelmingly concentrated in the Northern Isles and the North-East mainland.

These maps imply that the class of hollow-walled stronghold is a distinctive and specialised one which began in a small way in the Western Isles (probably in the 7th or 6th centuries BC) and gradually improved, undergoing phenomenal success and expansion when the broch tower form was developed a few centuries later.

When we look at broch material culture (below) we see overwhelming evidence, if the pottery and artefacts form a reliable guide, that the spread of the broch form of this architectural tradition occurred, apparently quickly, and across clear cultural boundaries. Thus we may be seeking only the expanding activities of a class of increasingly successful professional builders who invented their new structure in the Western Isles and took it up north. Of course if this picture is true it does mean that the broch as a structure is an import in the Northern Isles and that the early Iron Age roundhouses there did not have much if anything to do with its architectural development until a relatively late date. However since the broch can now be seen to be a hybrid structure, an amalgamation of semibroch defence architecture and the widespread British Iron Age wooden roundhouse tradition, the Orkney stone roundhouses could have contributed something of the latter (see Addendum).

(e) *Gurness and Midhowe in Orkney*. Before deciding whether brochs form an homogenous class of buildings or are part of a larger and more diverse class of Iron Age stone roundhouses there is one final piece of evidence to review – that from the important sites which have been claimed as proof of the second hypothesis. One is Gurness in Orkney about which there have been extensive discussions. John Hedges used the site as crucial evidence for his view that not only was there direct continuity between the simple Orcadian stone roundhouses of the 7th century BC and the hollow-walled brochs of a much later period, but also that the brochs themselves were a more diverse class of structures than had been supposed hitherto (Hedges and Bell 1980). Hedges believed that the mass of stone cubicles inside and surrounding Gurness (and, by logical extension, inside and surrounding the almost identical Midhowe broch on Rousay) were all original design features. If so this would allow their direct descent, for example, from the early Iron Age Bu roundhouse. The older view was that these internal stone slab features and the stone settlements outside were all later additions to the original broch towers (RCAHMS 1946, 2, no. 263; MacKie 2002a, site HY32 2).

Our understanding of both these Orkney ground-galleried brochs is hindered by the old fashioned way in which they were excavated in the 1930s, and because, in order to make spectacular displays, the primary floor levels in both remain hidden. Yet at both these conserved and protected sites the architectural evidence suggests that each broch was originally a tall tower within outer fortifications, probably with an interior free of stonework and containing a two-storey wooden roundhouse, and probably without an extensive stone village outside it (MacKie 1995). The addition of the stone slab structures inside and outside each seems to have occurred after the partial demolition of both brochs and marks a return to more indigenous early Iron Age traditions of Orkney settlement. The old dichotomy in Orkney between the new hollow-walled tower and the ancient local Orkney stone roundhouse thus remains firmly in place. The excavation of primary floor levels at one of these sites would certainly advance the argument and support one or the other hypothesis decisively (MacKie 1995, ill. 5).

How widely can the definition of brochs be stretched?

There are two more sites which reinforce the argument that brochs are structurally homogeneous and, to some extent, culturally homogeneous when compared with the radically different mainland cultures. The site at Dun Lagaidh on Loch Broom was thought to be a broch (sitting on a ruined vitrified fort) when it was first planned by Calder and Steer (1949). However it proved to be a solid-walled dun of Argyllshire type, with guard cell, a narrow intra-mural stair (of distinctly non broch type), at least one intra-mural wall face and a curious entrance passage with two sets of door-checks (MacKie 1977, figs. 4 & 5, pls. II & IV-X). There is no sign whatever of a high galleried wall. Moreover the scanty finds inside reinforce the impression that this was the stronghold of an aristocratic chief, probably from south-west Scotland, who had come north; he rode a horse with an iron three-link bridle bit and had a fine beaten bronze cauldron which was repaired on site at one stage. No broch has yet revealed such signs of fine metalwork in its primary levels; the cultural gap between the Atlantic towers and Dun Lagaidh is enormous. Yet structurally the building is not much further away from a hollow-walled broch than for example, Dun Cuier on Barra, which is generally classified as an Atlantic Roundhouse. Using only architectural criteria, Dun Lagaidh should surely also be classified as an Atlantic roundhouse and would, following the primary publication, almost certainly have been classed as a complex one (a hollow-walled broch) if it had not been excavated.

The same applies to the strange 'vitrified dun', also sitting on a ruined hillfort, at Langdale in Strath Oykel in South-East Sutherland, at the edge of the broch province there. Helen Nisbet found that, before its destruction by fire and the consequent vitrification of much of its timber-laced wall core, this circular, thick-walled dun must have looked very like a low broch, especially from the outside from where one would not have been able to see the ends of the wooden beams in rows in the inside wall face. The resemblance is increased by the fact that there were post-holes for a massive wooden roundhouse inside it (Nisbet 1996). This structure is a late element (from about the 3rd century BC) in the late Bronze Age and early Iron Age mainland complex of timber-framed hillforts, again culturally a world away from the Atlantic province. Yet it too should surely be included among the Atlantic Roundhouses if their present all embracing definition is held to.

One could also point to the hundreds of duns in Argyllshire, some of which have been shown to be of Late Iron Age date; the few brochs stick out like sore thumbs among them (RCAHMS 1980; 1989). However I rest my case; the theory of the broch as a variable structure is untenable without constantly moving the goal posts of definition.

Dun Cuier

Finally in the context of this discussion about what exactly a broch is we must look again at Dun Cuier in Barra, the arguments over which have been rumbling on for some years. This broch-like building was excavated by Alison Young in the 1950s but she concluded that it was not a broch at all but a round, thick-walled dun with a gallery in the wall (which she thought, because it was full of contemporary earth and rubbish, had served as insulation) and which she believed (due to the artefact assemblage) had been occupied only in the mid or late 1st millennium AD, centuries after the 'Age of the Brochs' (Young 1956).

Some years ago Ian Armit argued that this was a misinterpretation, and that Dun Cuier was really a Middle Iron Age broch which was subsequently cleared out and re-occupied much later and once it had become a ruin (Armit 1988). This re-interpretation really began as a test of his prediction that the number of brochs in the Outer Isles had been greatly underestimated in the past. Dun Cuier is vital to this new view because the excavator's interpretation implies that there could be a class of late duns in the Outer Isles, perhaps a large one, which would undermine the idea that most of these ruined mounds were really brochs. Also if it is a broch it is a slightly aberrant one and would support the 'brochs are variable structures' argument. What is interesting about Dun Cuier is how the new interpretation has been adopted by some despite the contradictory evidence (e.g. Harding 1997, 126). The site must therefore be considered again briefly here.

In the first place the structure does indeed look superficially like a broch, having a circular plan with appropriate dimensions, a thick wall, an intra-mural gallery running all the way round and a scarcement ledge on the inside wall face. However the design of the entrance passage is unusual for a broch; I have seen well over a hundred in both excavated and untouched sites and not one has this curious design of a single door-check right at the inner end of the passage. We do not know from Young's report how much of the mural gallery was exposed, or how much of the primary inner wall face could be seen after the interior had been excavated, but she records no signs of an intra-mural stair, basic to broch design, or a door from it to the interior. The only way to be sure about this would be to re-excavate the whole of the gallery.

The material culture found on top of and within the primary deposits inside (pottery, bone combs and pins) is all of late Iron Age type; a few middle Iron Age sherds were found in the deposits in the mural gallery. The pottery in the interior now takes its name from this site, Dun Cuier ware, and we know from Alison Young's excavations on Middle Iron Age wheelhouse that it occurs there in secondary levels 2 or even 3 feet above the primary floors with their Middle Iron Age pottery and artefacts (Young and Richardson 1960). Now we also have the evidence from the long series of stratified deposits and related C-14 dates from Dun Vulan in South Uist where Dun Cuier ware is independently allocated a time span from the 6th - 9th centuries AD, a period which agrees perfectly with the associated bone pins and composite combs found at Dun Cuier which were originally dated by historical means (Parker Pearson and Sharples 1999). The fact is that, irrespective of the precise stratigraphical position of the secondary wall face inside Dun Cuier, no trace was found of a primary floor level with Middle Iron Age pottery and artefacts in it; the pale sand underneath the dark floor level and resting on the rock contained only Late Iron Age material. One cannot legitimately assume a completely vanished primary floor level in order to re-date a site.

DATING THE BROCHS

Pinning down the time span when the hollow-walled brochs were built and used is at the heart of the controversy between the two general hypotheses being considered here. One of the reasons that many people have found the new idea of the brochs as variable structures with a long time span so attractive is that it seems to break free of the diffusionist constraints of the 1950s and 1960s which, so the argument goes, have distorted the chronology of the towers by refusing to abandon the idea that they were the products of refugees from the south fleeing from the activities of Julius Caesar in the 1st century

BC. The analogy is sometimes drawn with Sir Mortimer Wheeler's pre-war dating of what was then called the Iron Age B cultures of southern England which, for reasons which seemed good at the time (apparent links between south English B pottery and that from Brittany), he dated as starting in 56 BC. This was the year when Caesar's Roman forces destroyed the ships of the powerful sea-faring Veneti in Brittany in a naval battle, after which refugee chiefs and warriors and their families may well have come to southern Britain and strongly influenced the local cultures there.

However later archaeological correlations, followed by C-14 dates, showed that the southern Iron Age 'B' cultures started several centuries earlier in the south, probably in the 5th Century BC (Harding 1974, chaps. 10 and 13). The '56 BC hypothesis' had indeed badly distorted south English Iron Age chronology for quite a few years in the 1940s and 1950s. So it was naturally very tempting from the 1970s onwards for those who thought that broch archaeology needed to be freed from out-dated 1960s thinking to deduce that the same applied in Scotland; in other words that the brochs had been given a low dating primarily because of similar diffusionist assumptions. Thus if these assumptions were abandoned the towers should spring back naturally several centuries into the early Iron Age.

Dating brochs before radiocarbon

Before the first radiocarbon dates were obtained for an excavated broch in the early 1960s the only clear evidence for how old these buildings were came from Roman finds. As V.G. Childe explained (1946) the clearest evidence came from a handful of brochs in the Scottish mainland which, it was assumed, were among the last to be built because they are far away from the main concentrations in the far North and North-West. Since Torwoodlee in South-East Scotland had much late 1st century

Roman pottery inside it seemed that this final phase of broch building had been completed by the late AD 70s, when the Romans arrived in southern Scotland (Curle 1892). Later it was found that Torwoodlee was actually built on top of Roman material (Piggott 1951), as was Leckie in Stirlingshire (MacKie 1985; 1989), but the chronological argument remained much the same. What obviously could not be assessed reliably from this data is how long before AD 100 brochs had begun to be built. It might indeed have been several centuries earlier though Childe preferred a shorter time span. This was because he considered that many of the artefacts found inside brochs were so similar to their equivalents in the Iron Age cultures of south-west England in the immediately pre-Roman Iron Age that they indicated a clear connection so that an equivalent date for the brochs in the 1st centuries BC and AD was indicated. Thus by the standards and assumptions of fifty years ago, immediately before the radiocarbon era, there was perfectly good archaeological evidence that the brochs were not being built much before the end of the first millennium BC.

Radiocarbon dates

Dun Mor Vaul was the first broch to show that radiocarbon dates might support this older view. Not only did Antonine Roman finds not appear on the site below the top of the primary floor level, showing that the broch had been there for some time before the 2nd century AD, but of two radiocarbon dates for the construction levels the reliable one also implied a date in the 1st or 2nd centuries AD (MacKie 1974; 1997). Likewise dates for older occupation levels, clearly stratified below the broch, supported this by being several centuries earlier. Thus the approximate 1st century BC date for the building Dun Mor Vaul suggested in the 1974 report was based firmly on the sequence of radiocarbon dates and was supported by the stratified Roman finds. This date was later refined in the same report to the middle part of the 1st century BC by 'diffusionist' assumptions, based on what still seemed to me at the time to be strong resemblances between the broch-builders pottery and some vessels in southern England. The general resemblance between the artefacts of the two areas, emphasised by Childe, also seemed plausible.

It is instructive in this context to recall that in the 1960s the Scottish timber-framed hillforts were also given a late first millennium BC date because of diffusionist assumptions concerning connections with southern England (Stevenson 1966). However in 1965 Stuart Piggott put forward the idea that they began much earlier, in the late Bronze Age (Piggott 1965). Comparable hillforts of that date were known from Switzerland among other places. In 1967 the author, convinced by Piggott's arguments, excavated a Scottish vitrified hillfort (Finavon in Angus) to test this hypothesis. The resulting radiocarbon dates strongly supported Piggott's case for a long chronology and started a revolution in the dating of Scottish hillforts (Alexander 2002). A new 'local development' scenario was proposed suggesting that the origins of the Pictish people lay in the prehistoric populations of the same area (MacKie 1969).

Returning to the Atlantic Province, it was of course quite possible that the dates from Dun Mor Vaul would turn out to be not typical and that the beginning of the 'Age of Brochs' would steadily move backwards as more radiocarbon dates accumulated from new excavations. However the great majority of the radiocarbon dates for material clearly linked with primary broch floor levels, and from a few linked with actual broch construction levels, have tended to fall into the 1st centuries BC and AD (MacKie 1995; Parker Pearson and Sharples 1999). There is a handful which might be earlier but there is usually a doubt about the reliability of these (see Addendum).

For example, the early date from Crosskirk was from within the thin primary floor level, but only slightly below its surface. This surface included 2nd century AD Roman material as well as material which gave another, appropriately late C14 date. The first may therefore be wrong (Fairhurst 1984, 160-63). In addition there was late Bronze Age occupation on the site so early carbonised wood might have been lying about (Fairhurst 1984, 108-10: MacKie forthcoming, site ND07 2). The one absurdly early date from the construction level of Dun Mor Vaul was contradicted by later dates from stratigraphically earlier levels (MacKie 1997).

One broch-like site which has been claimed as disproving the short chronology is Dun Bharabhat in Harris, where what looks like an early Iron Age date was obtained from material under the 'Atlantic roundhouse' wall; the building itself must have been built later. Two dates were obtained from charred timber which burned at the end of a secondary occupation of the interior and fell approximately in the 3rd and 2nd centuries BC. More recently Church has shown that these timbers were of driftwood and the actual date of the fire could have been a long time after that (Church 2002).

The great majority of certain dates recently reviewed by Parker Pearson and Sharples (1999, 355) seem to fall at around the turn of the 1st millennia BC and AD. This could be strong independent evidence in favour of some kind of impact in the Western Isles of a few influential refugees fleeing from the political and military upheavals of the late 2nd and the 1st centuries BC in North-West Gaul and Southern England. However whether this explanation is accepted or not, at the beginning of AD 2000 most of the reliable dating evidence for hollow-walled brochs was consistent with this view rather than a much earlier appearance of the towers (but see Addendum).

MATERIAL CULTURE

Contrast between the Mainland an the Atlantic Province

When considering Iron Age material culture in Scotland one is struck immediately by the fundamental difference between the pre-Roman artefacts of the North Mainland (broadly from the Forth/Clyde valley up to Caithness) and those of the coastal and island zones of the far North and North-West. Throughout the mainland zone the various monumental buildings (hillforts, vitrified hillforts, brochs and other massive high status constructions which may reasonably be assumed to have belonged to tribal elites) tend to produce a fairly uniform and rather simple material culture which includes plain, gritty, urn-shaped pottery vessels, jet armlets, jet ring pendants and occasionally bronze pins and brooches. Many of the finds that bear out this view are in the National Museums of Scotland and have never been properly published; in such cases their museum numbers are given here.

Here are some examples of such sites in the Southern part of the zone. The broch at Torwood, Stirlingshire, produced gritty pottery (GM 26 & 29), stone cups and lamps (GM 13 & 14) and a stone whorl (GM 17). The small timber-framed hillfort at Sheep Hill, Dunbartonshire gave the gritty pottery and jet armlets together with probable fragments of moulds for late Bronze Age axes and a sword (MacKie 1976, fig. 3 & pl. 1). The timber-framed hillfort at Finavon in Angus gave the thick gritty pottery (HH 400-403), a jet pendant (HH 396) and a decorated stone whorl (HH 395) (Childe 1935). The unburned timber-framed hillfort at Castle Law, Abernethy produced the gritty pottery (GP 55), a deep stone cup (GP 18), a jet pendant (GP 27), a decorated jet armlet (GP 28), an Early Iron Age iron ring-headed pin (Curle 1910, fig. 3), a La Tène I bronze fibula (GP 30) and a Middle Iron Age bronze spiral finger ring (GP 29) (Christison 1899).

This kind of plain gritty pottery, sometimes known as Dunagoil ware, has been shown to go back to the late Bronze Age by the finds in the earliest level in the Covesea cave, Morayshire. There a rim sherd of a true Dunagoil urn (HM 191) was found among the 'flat-rimmed ware' together with the bronze armlets and the gold-plated ring money which typologically dates the earliest occupation of the cave to perhaps towards the end the 8th century BC (Benton 1931). The pottery was also found in the lowest levels, apparently with socketed bronze axes associated with a small dwelling, at Traprain Law (Burley 1958); the excavation of the dwelling was described by Cree and Curle and a note with one large gritty urn reads "close to a Late Bronze Age dwelling, from the lowest level" (Curle 1922, 206 ff.). As mentioned the ware was found with late Bronze Age mould fragments at Sheep Hill in West Dunbartonshire.

The same simple early Iron Age assemblage turned up in Caithness at that strange site called the Wag of Forse which produced the same pottery (HD 718, etc.) and jet armlets (HD 717) (Curle 1941; 1946; 1948). There is a closed assemblage of similar pottery from the pre-broch levels at Crosskirk on the north coast of Caithness which almost certainly dates to the late Bronze Age (Fairhurst 1984). This includes one of the rare finer vessels of the gritty pottery style, with a slightly out-turned lip decorated with shallow finger impressions immediately below it. An almost identical jar came from Sheep Hill on the Clyde (MacKie 1976, fig. 2). Evidently, and despite the variety of structures, there was some sort of underlying cultural unity in this huge mainland province in the second half of the first millennium BC. This simple material culture contrasts sharply with that found in the maritime Atlantic province. There, brochs and allied sites tend to produce large quantities of finely made, smooth, hard-fired pottery in several distinct styles some of which are elaborately decorated. With the pottery is consistently found a diverse array of bone, antler and stone tools, all of which will be considered shortly in a little more detail.

Despite this generally sharp contrast there are some clear signs of overlap between the Atlantic and mainland material cultures. At Dun Mor Vaul on Tiree for example the mainland gritty pottery was found side by side with fine Atlantic wares in the pre-broch levels, with lesser quantities in later horizons, and a fine jet ring pendant was also found in the broch floor (MacKie 1974). A mainland gritty urn came from Midhowe broch in Orkney, as also did a completely different, fine, black-burnished Everted Rim jar of Atlantic type (MacKie 2002: site HY31 1). Several Caithness brochs have produced the gritty pottery too; there is large such vessel from one of the poorly excavated sites at Keiss (GJ 203).

In fact it is among the brochs on the flat plain of Caithness and along the eastern coastal zone of Sutherland that a transitional zone is most apparent. Although the brochs there were nearly all excavated many years ago the finds give us a vital clue to the nature of the whole broch phenomenon. What follows has already been described in more detail (MacKie 2000).

If one plots the main diagnostic finds from a selection of excavated sites, from the Orkney brochs, through Crosskirk on the north coast of Caithness and down to Carn Liath near Golspie (near the 'frontier' of the broch zone at the Dornoch Firth), one sees a clear though gradual transition from typical Atlantic assemblages in the north (with abundant fine pottery and masses of bone implements) to others in the south-west which exhibit the impoverished mainland culture with no Atlantic traits at all. Neither Carn Liath nor Kintrodwell for example seem to have produced any fine pottery or bone implements but they did give a fair number of jet armlets and some rotary querns some of which show

distinctive mainland, not Atlantic, characteristics (MacKie 2002, fig. 2 and table 1).

A good example of a mainland Iron Age artefact which also helps to define this 'frontier zone' is the handled stone cup or lamp. This is widespread in Aberdeenshire and occurs in the brochs of the Golspie area (Steer 1956). It is found in few mainland brochs further north, with only one or two known from Orkney and Shetland. The decorated stone spindle whorl may prove to be a similar phenomenon (one, mentioned earlier, comes from the Finavon timber-framed hillfort) although its frequency and distribution have still not been researched and plotted.

In the past Caithness and Sutherland have been included in the Atlantic province because of the large numbers of brochs, but we can now say confidently that the buildings by themselves do not define a cultural province. A study of the material cultural rather than the buildings shows that the north-eastern tip of Scotland is, as one might expect from its geographical position, a transitional zone between the maritime Atlantic regions and the mainland to the South. This interesting phenomenon is completely obscured if we consider only the monumental stone buildings, which give the illusion of uniformity. The evidence only comes to light if the material from these old excavations is sought out and studied.

The peer/polity hypothesis

This North-Eastern mainland area seems to be a excellent example of the relevance of Colin Renfrew's peer/polity interaction hypothesis in explaining certain types of changes in the archaeological record (Renfrew and Cherry 1996; MacKie 2000). Broadly it suggests that two neighbouring political groups, which we might term 'tribes' for convenience, with quite radically different traditions but approximately of the same power and status can exchange ideas and technologies (perhaps even craftsmen) while retaining political and social integrity. Thus major innovations in the archaeological record can in some circumstances be explained without any disruptions like significant numbers of immigrants.

The brochs of, on the one hand, flat Caithness with their strong Atlantic connections and, on the other, South-East Sutherland (and perhaps over all the mountainous areas inland north of the Dornoch Firth) with their mainland culture, seem to be an excellent example of this. They surely prove beyond a doubt that this sophisticated Iron Age drystone tower was not culturally diagnostic by itself but was an ingenious invention, immensely attractive to people of power and influence because of its strength, its architectural sophistication and spectacular appearance, and which was built for such people by specialist builder/craftsmen, perhaps for a variety of purposes and in a variety of social contexts.

The maritime zone

Throughout the maritime zone there is finely made pottery in abundance, but with very distinct regional styles. In the Inner Hebrides for example there are two distinct ceramic traditions, first recognised at Dun Mor Vaul in Tiree, one of which probably goes back to the late Bronze Age in the 7th or 8th centuries BC. This is Vaul ware, the indigenous Iron Age pottery of Tiree, which comes in two vessel forms decorated with geometric patterns in incised lines. The other tradition is a cordoned jar with a sharply everted rim and often ornamented below this with concentric arches of channelled lines. This version is usefully called the Clettraval sub-style of Everted Rim ware (MacKie 1997). The pottery found in the brochs of Orkney and northern Caithness is quite different, much of it consisting of plain pots which look

like storage jars. Shetland broch pottery is different again (MacKie 2002).

Some Shetland brochs seem to show fundamental differences in material culture even when they are only a few miles apart. The broch horizon at Jarlshof produced a large number of cutting and chopping tools of slate with little evidence of iron-working (even though this was a prominent feature of the early Iron Age village on the site). Clickhimin broch, twenty miles to the north and presumably inhabited at about the same time, had no stone chopping tools and signs of iron-working (Hamilton 1956; 1968).

This evidence from the regional pottery styles as well as from other differences must surely also mean that the brochs were introduced to a variety of local cultures in some way, and one or two further cultural 'boundaries' which seem to confirm this will be indicated.

Yet in the maritime zone there is also a large number of what one might call 'universal broch artefacts' which are found everywhere (except, as noted, in the Highland Caithness and the Sutherland brochs). They include bone and antler objects like long-handled combs, 4-sided rectangular dice, bone pommels for sword and dagger handles, buttons made of human femur-heads, bridle cheek-pieces made of antler tines, and a variety of awls and other simple tools.

The disc-shaped rotary quern seems one of the most significant stone artefacts found in brochs all over the maritime zone. It is fundamentally different to the beehive and bun-shaped querns of the Southern Scottish mainland in that it is adjustable; the lower stone is completely perforated, presumably for the long spindle on which the bridge or rind in the upper stone sits (MacKie 1989). Judging from recent Highland examples this spindle rested on a wooden frame below the quern table which was moved up and down to fractionally adjust the distance between the upper and lower stones to give coarser and finer degrees of grinding. The adjustable quern is also quite different from the pre-Roman quern tradition of western Germany, England, France and parts of Iberia and so far similar pre-Roman adjustable querns have been located by the author only in Iberia and perhaps in Brittany and Ireland. Other 'universal broch' artefacts include glass beads, particularly the small yellow ring-bead, and bronze ornaments like spiral finger rings and ring-headed pins with a projecting head.

The situation in the maritime zone is thus quite distinct from that in South-East Sutherland. We seem to have clear regional groups of material culture, indicated mainly by the pottery styles, but running across all these is some kind of cultural unity indicated by the hollow-walled brochs themselves and by a fair number of other artefacts. I also suspect that the introduction of new iron tools and weapons will prove to be important here, in addition to potentially new techniques of cultivation and stock-breeding, marked for example by the iron-shod ard and efficient metal shears for clipping sheep. It is difficult not to draw the preliminary conclusion that the first appearance of the brochs and the 'universal' artefacts in them signifies some new social, perhaps political, unity over maritime Scotland, caused perhaps by the appearance of a new ruling class with access to new equipment.

Frontier zones among the brochs

Two clear further examples of cultural 'frontier zones' in the west support the idea that the broch as a building is not culturally diagnostic. The first occurs in the long and rugged North-West coast running from Inverness-shire through Ross and Cromarty to Sutherland and Cape Wrath. This coastal strip has a few brochs and broch-like buildings scattered along it, mostly quite well preserved because of their isolation. The rugged and

sterile mountainous terrain of the mainland, which comes right down to the sea, implies that these brochs are on the fringe of the main area of distribution, on Skye and the Outer Hebrides.

Loch Broom is the longest sea loch in the North-West and the well preserved Dun an Ruigh Ruaidh on its southern shore could be a partly destroyed broch or a D-shaped semibroch (I support the latter view). Whichever view is correct it is clearly a Hebridean building, an outlier from that maritime broch zone. When Rhiroy was excavated in 1968 and 1978 it also revealed in the primary floor the ring of massive post-holes and the central paved hearth, which we associate with hollow-walled towers (MacKie 1980). However the associated aceramic material culture was extremely poor and lacked all the types typically found in the Hebridean brochs: decorated pottery, bone tools and so on. There were stone pounders and discs, several stone whorls or beads, a fragment of a jet armlet and two atypical rotary querns, at least one of which has clear links with a particular form of the bun-shaped series of the southern mainland (Mackie 2002b). Here again we see how a sophisticated Atlantic building was adopted by a completely distinct mainland culture; the contrast with the abundant maritime material culture found in the structurally similar D-shaped Dun Ardtreck not far away in Skye is complete.

A second 'frontier zone' may exist among the elaborate material culture of the Hebridean islands and is more subtle. When Dun Mor Vaul broch in Tiree was excavated in the 1960s an exceptionally clear correlation was found between the building of the broch and the appearance of a new pottery style (Everted Rim ware). The pottery in the earlier levels was the quite different 'native' pottery, incised line-decorated Vaul ware (MacKie, 1997) and it was therefore assumed that this would be found to be the usual state of affairs among brochs in the Western Isles. However the report on the partial excavation of Dun Vulan broch in South Uist shows, although the interior could not be fully explored in this rescue excavation, that the pottery associated with the construction of the tower is a plain gritty ware, quite unlike the cordoned Everted Rim ware found at Dun Mor Vaul (Parker Pearson and Sharples 1999). It is also quite unlike the elaborately decorated native Vaul ware found in the earlier levels in Tiree. Until the primary occupation floor in the interior of Dun Vulan or a neighbouring broch is explored there must obviously be some reservations about this statement, but it seems reasonable at the moment to accept it. This discovery suggests that at least some brochs in the Outer Isles were built by people possessing no Everted Rim ware; indeed that pottery only appears at a later stage at Dun Vulan, as also at the Sollas wheelhouse in North Uist (Campbell 1992). Here again we seem to have a very rapid adoption of the hollow-walled broch by indigenous communities, followed some time later by the adoption of fashionable new artefacts like Everted Rim pottery.

Exactly the same thing can be seen at Dun Ardtreck on Skye (MacKie 2002c). This badly ruined, probable D-shaped semibroch was violently destroyed by fire and then demolished; much of the equipment in use inside it just before the destruction was found partially incinerated on the floor, and this included large parts of at least four pots. All of these were Vaul ware vases; not a trace of Everted Rim ware was found in the original occupation, although it appeared on the site later. The elaborate broch-like building was apparently erected in the 1st or 2nd century BC for an indigenous local culture although, to make matters more complex, this community did have some middle Iron Age material, for example adjustable rotary querns and perhaps small glass beads. At both Dun Vulan and Dun Ardtreck there is again the impression that the

sophisticated hollow-wall building style spread rapidly among pre-existing communities, and that brochs were surely therefore put up by a class of professional builders. It will be fascinating to see, when its primary floor level is excavated, whether the broch at Traigh na Berie in western Lewis shows a similar phenomenon.

CONCLUSIONS

Four important aspects of Scottish Atlantic Iron Age archaeology, as it is at the turn of the millennium, have been considered above in some detail and a fifth alluded to briefly. From this I draw the following reasonably firm conclusions on which, if no dramatically contradictory evidence turns up, future research could be based.

1. *There is a large class of 'traditional' hollow-walled brochs.* Detailed analysis of the buildings seems to show fairly clearly that in their essential architecture brochs are an homogeneous group of buildings with a plausible set of prototypes to spring from. Whether the term 'complex Atlantic roundhouse' should be used to cover these hollow-walled brochs is a moot point; the high probability that the towers were devised to contain complex wooden roundhouses is a strong point in favour, provided that the uniqueness of the hollow-walled brochs is not doubted. If the term is so used there can surely be no justification for excluding wheelhouses from the more general classificatory term.

2. *Most hollow-walled brochs are probably not much older than the 1st or 2nd centuries BC.* Reliable radiocarbon dates for the construction of the hollow-walled brochs, and for their early use, are quite numerous now and clearly cluster in a relatively short time span, from the later

2nd century BC to the 1st AD. The stratification of Roman finds from brochs tend to support this picture (but see 'Addendum' below).

Thus most independent dating evidence does not conflict with the old theory that there was at that time a period of close contact of some kind between Atlantic Scotland and regions further south and south-west and that such cultural hybridisation may have had something to do with the invention of the broch tower in the north. However the plausibility of this idea depends on a proper understanding of the 'exotic' broch artefacts which have not been discussed in detail here (see 'Addendum').

3. *The Atlantic Iron Age material culture (ca. 600 BC to AD 500) is quite distinct from that of the Scottish mainland.* The major difference is in the pottery which is much more plentiful, as well as better made and decorated, than any other contemporary ceramic tradition in the whole of north Britain. A wide range of bone tools and artefacts are also hardly known elsewhere in Scotland and the rotary quern is a completely different type to that in use in the Southern mainland. The fact that this distinctive material culture is found in a maritime zone is suggestive.

4. *Brochs are not culturally diagnostic and may have been the creation of a specialist class.* The evidence that hollow-walled brochs are not culturally diagnostic within the Atlantic province seems overwhelming. They clearly were adopted by a variety of local cultures (judging by the pottery) and at least once crossed the major boundary between Atlantic Scotland and the completely distinct mainland Iron Age area. This could well mean that the hollow-walled towers were constructed by a class of professional builders for local chiefs, probably for reasons of prestige as much as of defence.

5. *The 'universal' broch artefacts still have to be plausibly explained.* There has not been space to explore this theme adequately here but it is of great importance and there is plenty of evidence to review. A whole range of new artefacts appear at about the same time as, or just before, the brochs and inaugurate the middle stage of the Iron Age sequence all over Atlantic Scotland. Understanding what this means is of first importance.

The conclusions outlined above, allowing for modification in detail with future discoveries, should provide a foundation from which brochs studies can progress henceforth.

ADDENDUM, JANUARY 2004

In the three and a half years that have elapsed since the Lerwick conference continuing work at the broch of Old Scatness in Southern Shetland has produced some dating evidence from a variety of techniques which may prove to be an exception to the chronological scenario outlined in Section 3 above. A group of buildings which post-date the broch there, and which includes an aisled "wheelhouse", has been tentatively dated to the period 400-100 BC (Dockrill 2002: MacKie 2002: site HU31 4). More detailed publication of the chronology of Old Scatness will be warmly welcomed.

In addition I undertook in 2002, while writing the final version of the entry for that site in my 'Corpus of Brochs', a detailed re-assessment of Hamilton's 1968 account of his work in the pre-broch levels at Clickhimin (MacKie 2002a: Site HU31 4). It had previously seemed to me that Hamilton's dating of the structures and deposits of the first 'ring-fort' there to about 400 BC was much too early; for example the small yellow ring beads in the earliest fort midden (resting on beach deposits outside the wall) surely showed that they should be assigned to the start of the middle stage of the Atlantic Iron Age sequence and therefore not earlier than perhaps the later 2nd century BC.

However if one reads Hamilton's account carefully clues can be found hidden in the text that the earliest fort pottery did indeed occur side by side in that midden with the carinated wares of the early Iron Age settlement; using the evidence from the contemporary sites in Orkney this settlement must surely belong to the 6th century BC at the latest. Hamilton of course claimed that the first ring-fort followed immediately after the Early Iron Age settlement but the evidence for this was not set out clearly and the bead evidence referred to, seemed to contradict it. The absence of rotary querns from the early fort levels could also support this Early Iron Age date, as indeed could the diagnosis of the pre-broch 'blockhouse' as a promontory semibroch; these structures seem likely to belong to the early Iron Age in Skye (MacKie 2002c, 364).

Thus both old and new evidence from Shetland may be pointing to a very early arrival in the South Mainland there of elements of what is later defined as the Middle Iron Age material culture, notably the form of Everted Rim pottery with internal rim fluting, sometimes known as the Clickhimin sub-style. If this is the case the appearance of this pottery becomes much more nearly contemporary with the period of the Urnfield (late Bronze Age) wares in Western France from which, Hamilton thought, it was probably derived (Hamilton 1968, 92, 162). So far these early dates for a 'proto middle Iron Age' material culture have not been replicated anywhere outside Shetland. We may surely anticipate some surprising new discoveries at Old Scatness.

BIBLIOGRAPHY

Anderson, J. (1883) *Scotland in Pagan Times: the Iron Age*. Edinburgh, David Douglas.

Alexander, D. (2002) An oblong fort at Finavon, Angus: an example of the over-reliance of the application of science. In Ballin Smith, B. and Banks, I (eds.) *In the Shadow of the Brochs: the Iron Age in Scotland*, 45-54. Stroud, Tempus.

Armit, I. (1988) Broch landscapes in the Western Isles. *Scottish Archaeological Review* 5, 78-86.

Ballin Smith, B. (ed.) (1994) *Howe. Four Millennia of Orkney Prehistory*. Society of Antiquaries of Scotland Monograph Series no. 9. Edinburgh.

Ballin Smith, B. and Banks, I. (eds.) (2002) *In the Shadow of the Brochs: the Iron Age in Scotland*. Stroud, Tempus.

Benton, S. (1931) The excavation of the Sculptor's Cave, Covesea, Morayshire. *Proceedings of the Society of Antiquaries of Scotland* 65, 177-216.

Burley, E. (1958) Metalwork from Traprain Law. *Proceedings of the Society of Antiquaries of Scotland* 89 (1955-56), 118-226.

Calder, C. S. T. and K. A. Steer (1949) Dun Lagaidh and four other prehistoric monuments near Ullapool, Ross and Cromarty. *Proceedings of the Society of Antiquaries of Scotland* 83 (1948-9), 68-76.

Campbell, E. (1992) Excavations of a wheelhouse and other Iron Age structures at Sollas, North Uist, by R J C Atkinson in 1957. *Proceedings of the Society of Antiquaries of Scotland* 121 (1991), 117-73.

Childe, V. G. (1935) Excavation of the vitrified fort of Finavon, Angus. *Proceedings of the Society of Antiquaries of Scotland* 69 (1934-35), 49-80.

Childe, V. G. (1946) *Scotland Before the Scots*. London, Methuen.

Christison, D. (1899) On the recently excavated fort on Castle Law, Abernethy, Perthshire. *Proceedings of the Society of Antiquaries of Scotland* 33 (1898-99), 13-33.

Church M. (2002) The archaeological and archaeobotanical implications of a destruction layer in Dun Bharabhat, Lewis. In Ballin Smith, B. and Banks, I (eds.) *In the Shadow of the Brochs: the Iron Age in Scotland*, 67-75. Stroud, Tempus.

Coles, J. M. (1960) Scottish Late Bronze Age metalwork: typology, distributions and chronology. *Proceedings of the Society of Antiquaries of Scotland* 93 (1959-60), 16-134.

Cree, J. E. and Curle, A. O. (1922) Account of the excavations on Traprain Law during the summer of 1921. *Proceedings of the Society of Antiquaries of Scotland* 56 (1921-22), 189-260.

Curle, J. (1892) Notice on two brochs recently discovered at Bow, Midlothian, and Torwoodlee, Selkirkshire. *Proceedings of the Society of Antiquaries of Scotland* 26, 68-84.

Curle, A. O. (1910) Notice of some excavations on Bonchester Hill, Roxburghshire. *Proceedings of the Society of Antiquaries of Scotland* 44 (1909-10), 225-36.

Curle, A. O. (1941) An account of the partial excavation of a wag or galleried building at Forse, in the parish of Latheron, Caithness. *Proceedings of the Society of Antiquaries of Scotland* 75 (1940-41), 23-39.

Curle, A. O. (1946) The excavation of the wag or prehistoric cattle-fold at Forse, Caithness. *Proceedings of the Society of Antiquaries of Scotland* 80 (1945-6), 11-24.

Curle, A. O. (1948) The 'Wag' of Forse, Caithness: Excavations of 1947-48. *Proceedings of the Society of Antiquaries of Scotland* 82 (1947-8), 275-85.

Dockrill, S. J. (2002) Brochs, economy and power. In Ballin Smith, B. and Banks, I (eds.) *In the Shadow of the Brochs: the Iron Age in Scotland*, 153-162. Stroud, Tempus.

Fairhurst, H. (1984) *Excavations at Crosskirk Broch, Caithness*. Society of Antiquaries of Scotland Monograph series no. 3. Edinburgh.

Fojut, N. (1983) Towards a geography of Shetland brochs. *Glasgow Archaeological Journal* 9, 38-59.

Foster, S. (1990) Pins, combs and the chronology of later Atlantic Iron Age settlements. In Armit, I. (ed.) *Beyond the Brochs: Changing Perspectives in the Scottish Atlantic Iron Age*, 143-174. Edinburgh, Edinburgh University Press.

Graham, A. (1947) Some observations on the brochs. *Proceedings of the Society of Antiquaries of Scotland* 81, 48-99.

Graham, A. (1949) Notes on some brochs and forts visited in 1949. *Proceedings of the Society of Antiquaries of Scotland* 83 (1948-9), 12-24.

Hamilton, J. R. C. (1956) *Excavations at Jarlshof, Shetland.* Edinburgh, H.M.S.O.

Hamilton, J. R. C. (1965) The mystery of the brochs solved at Clickhimin. *Illustrated London News*, 247, no. 6580, 33-5.

Hamilton, J. R. C. (1968) *Excavations at Clickhimin, Shetland.* Edinburgh, HMSO.

Harding, D. W. (1974) *The Iron Age in Lowland Britain.* London, Routledge and Kegan Paul.

Harding, D. W. (1997) Forts, duns, brochs and crannogs: Iron Age settlements in Argyll. In Ritchie, J. N. R. (ed.) *The Archaeology of Argyll*, 118-140. Edinburgh, Edinburgh University Press.

Harding, D. W. (1984) The function and classification of brochs and duns. In Miket, R. and Burgess, C. (eds.), *Between and beyond the Walls: essays on the prehistory and history of Northern Britain in honour of George Jobey*, 206-220. Edinburgh, John Donald.

Harding, D. W. and Dixon, T. N. (2000) *Dun Bharabhat, Cnip: an Iron Age settlement in West Lewis. Vol. 1; the structures and material culture.* Calanais Research Series Number 2: University of Edinburgh, Dept. of Archaeology.

Heald, A. (2001) Knobbed spear-butts of the British and Irish Iron Age: new examples and new thoughts. *Antiquity* 75, 689-95.

Hedges, J. W. and Bell, B. (1980) That tower of Scottish prehistory: the broch. *Antiquity* 54, 87-94.

Hedges, J.W. (1987) *Bu, Gurness and the brochs of Orkney.* 3 vols. British Archaeological Reports, British series 163. Oxford, Oxbow Books.

MacGregor, A. (1974) The Broch of Burrian, North Ronaldsay, Orkney. *Proceedings of the Society of Antiquaries of Scotland* 105 (1972-74), 63-118.

MacKie, E. W. (1965) The origin and development of the broch and wheelhouse building cultures of the Scottish Iron Age. *Proceedings of the Society of Antiquaries of Scotland* 31, 93-143.

MacKie, E. W. (1969) Radiocarbon Dates and the Scottish Iron Age. *Antiquity* 43, 15-26.

MacKie, E. W. (1974) *Dun Mor Vaul: an Iron Age broch on Tiree.* Glasgow, Glasgow University Press

MacKie, E. W. (1976) The vitrified forts of Scotland. In Harding, D. W. (ed.) *Hillforts: Later Prehistoric Earthworks in Britain and Ireland*, 205-232. London, Academic Press.

Mackie, E. W. (1977) The vitrified forts of Scotland. 205-32 in D.W. Harding, ed., *Hillforts: later prehistoric earthworks in Britain and Ireland.* London, Academic Press.

MacKie, E. W. (1980) Dun an Ruigh Ruaidh. *Glasgow Archaeological Journal* 7, 32-79.

MacKie, E. W. (1985) The Leckie broch, Stirlingshire; an interim report, *Glasgow Archaeological Journal* 9, 60-72.

MacKie, E. W. (1989) Leckie broch,impact on the Scottish Iron Age. *Glasgow Archaeological Journal* 14, 1-18.

MacKie, E .W. (1992) The Iron Age semibrochs of Atlantic Scotland: a case study in the problems of deductive reasoning. *Archaeological Journal* 148 (1991), 149-81.

MacKie, E. W. (1995) Gurness and Midhowe brochs in Orkney: some problems of misinterpretation. *Archaeological Journal* 151 (1994), 98-157.

MacKie, E. W. (1997) Dun Mor Vaul revisited: fact and theory in the re-appraisal of the Scottish Atlantic Iron Age. In Ritchie, J. N. G. (ed.) *The Archaeology of Argyll*, 141-180. Edinburgh, Edinburgh University Press.

MacKie, E. W. (1998) Continuity over three thousand years of northern prehistory: the 'tel' at Howe, Orkney. *Antiquaries Journal* 78, 1-42.

MacKie, E. W. (2000) The Scottish Atlantic Iron Age; indigenous and isolated or part of a wider European world? In Henderson, J. (ed.). *The Prehistory and Early History of Atlantic Europe: papers from a session held at the European Association of Archaeologists Fourth Annual Meeting in Goteborg 1998*, 99-186. British Archaeological Reports International Series No. 861. Oxford, Oxbow Books.

MacKie, E. W. (2002a) *The roundhouses, brochs and wheelhouses of Atlantic Scotland c. 700 BC to AD 500: architecture and material culture. Part 1: the Orkney and Shetland Isles.* British Archaeological Reports British Series No. 342. Oxford, Oxbow Books.

Mackie, E. W. (2002b) Two querns from Appin. *Scottish Archaeological Journal* 24.1, 85-92.

MacKie, E. W. (2002c) Excavations at Dun Ardtreck, Skye, in 1964 and 1965. *Proceedings of the Society of Antiquaries of Scotland* 130 (2000), 301-411.

MacKie, E. W. (forthcoming) *The roundhouses, brochs and wheelhouses of Atlantic Scotland c. 700 BC to AD 500: architecture and material culture. Part 2: the mainland and the western islands, with a general discussion.*

Nisbet, H. (1996) Excavation of a vitrified dun at Langwell, Strath Oykel, Sutherland. *Glasgow Archaeological Journal* 19 (1994-95), 51-74.

Parker Pearson, M. and Sharples, N. (1999) *Between Land and Sea: Excavations at Dun Vulan, South Uist.* Sheffield, Sheffield University Press.

Piggott, S. (1951) Excavations in the broch and hill-fort of Torwoodlee, Selkirkshire, 1950. *Proceedings of the Society of Antiquaries of Scotland* 85 (1950-51), 92-116.

Piggot, S. (1965) *Ancient Europe.* Edinburgh, Edinburgh University Press.

Renfrew, C. and Cherry, J. F. (eds.) (1996) *Peer Polity Interaction and Socio-Political Change.* Cambridge, Cambridge University Press.

RCAHMS (1946) *Twelfth Report with an Inventory of the Ancient Monuments of Orkney and Shetland. Three vols.: 1 Report and Introduction: 2 Orkney: 3 Shetland.* Edinburgh, The Royal Commission on the Ancient and Historical Monuments for Scotland.

RCAHMS (1980) *Argyll vol. 3: Mull, Tiree, Coll & Northern Argyll.* Edinburgh, The Royal Commission on the Ancient and Historical Monuments for Scotland.

RCAHMS (1989) *Argyll volume 6: Mid Argyll and Cowal: Prehistoric Sites and Early Historic Monuments.* Edinburgh, The Royal Commission on the Ancient and Historical Monuments for Scotland.

Scott, Sir L. (1947) The problem of the brochs. *Proceedings of the Prehistoric Society* 13, 1-36.

Scott, Sir L. (1948) Gallo-British colonies; the aisled round-house culture in the north. *Proceedings of the Prehistoric Society* 14, 46-125.

Smith, A. (2002) Artefacts of the Iron Age of Atlantic Scotland: past, present and future. *Antiquity* 76, 808-12.

Steer, K. A. (1956) An Early Iron Age Homestead at West Plean, Stirlingshire. *Proceedings of the Society of Antiquaries of Scotland* 89 (1955-56), 227-49.

Stevenson, R. B. K. (1966) Metal work and some other objects in Scotland and their cultural affinities. In Rivet, A. L. F. (ed.) *The Iron Age in Northern Britain*, 17-44. Edinburgh, Edinburgh University Press.

Young, A. (1956) Excavations at Dun Cuier, Isle of Barra, Outer Hebrides. *Proceedings of the Society of Antiquaries of Scotland* 89 (1955-56), 290-328.

Young, A. and Richardson, K. M. (1960) A Cheardach Mhor, Drimore, South Uist. *Proceedings of the Society of Antiquaries of Scotland* 93 (1959-60), 135-73.

The Atlantic Scottish Iron Age: External Relations Reviewed

D. W. HARDING

PRESUMPTIONS OF PREVIOUS RESEARCH

THE EXTERNAL relations of the Atlantic Iron Age, as represented in both structural and material types, have been studied in modern times by a succession of distinguished scholars, so that it might appear improbable that any new light could be cast upon the scene by a further review. Yet they were all constrained by the methodological and chronological frameworks of their time, and by the lack of a well-defined sequence for Atlantic Scotland, in terms of either structural evidence or material culture, with which external assemblages might be compared.

Gordon Childe (1935; 1946) ensured for a couple of generations the predominance of south-western connections by underlining parallels with the Somerset Lake Villages, and set the pattern of interpretation by seeing weaving combs as evidence for migration of southern communities into Atlantic Scotland. Sir Lindsay Scott (1948) followed Childe's lead, extending the origins of his south-western colonists to include Brittany, and thus linking the whole edifice to the historical horizon of the first century BC and the catalyst of Caesar's conquest of the Veneti. In the 1950s and 60s, the work of J. R. C. Hamilton also assumed south-western colonists, at least as far as Orkney (1968, 48ff), though he inferred that 'settlers penetrating into the relatively barren islands of the Shetland group were unaccompanied by their womenfolk' from the fact that their innovative ceramic styles were rapidly subsumed into local fashions. One need not be an ardent feminist to ponder the implications of this analysis. Hamilton toyed with the idea that these introductions could have taken place at an earlier time, on account of continental Urnfield affinities of some individual pottery fashions, like internal rim fluting, but such a radical revision of the conventional dating gained little support. MacKie (1971, 47) too recognised some possible parallels with Urnfield pottery styles, but has retained very firmly the first century BC horizon for his English migrants, invoking the parallel historical catalyst of refugees displaced by the Belgic invaders which are alluded to by Caesar (de Bello Gallico, V, 12), though never yet satisfactorily identified in the archaeological record.

With the general discrediting of the invasion hypothesis as a simplistic explanation of cultural innovation, Lane (1987) systematically discounted all the artefactual and ceramic connections with southern Britain which had previously been claimed, not because the evidence was insufficient or implausible, which in some instances it certainly was, but almost on principle as an anti-diffusionist reaction. Clarke's work, by contrast (1970; 1971), though anti-diffusionist by basic disposition, tried to analyse the extent and significance of material types from Atlantic Scotland, including apparently or demonstrably exotic types. Other than Clarke's papers, now thirty years past, no serious attempt has been made to evaluate the material culture of Atlantic Scotland in the context of the later prehistory of Britain and Ireland in Atlantic Europe, without prejudice to whatever relationships might subsequently be inferred. The outcome is that there is no consensus regarding the external relationships of the Atlantic Scottish Iron Age in terms of its material culture. MacKie (1995, 662; 2000) has recently published a convenient summary and restatement of his earlier case for southern migrants, while most other authorities either regard the Atlantic Iron Age as essentially locally-generated or regard the entire debate as relatively unimportant compared to issues of social, economic or cosmological reconstruction.

Chronology continues to be a vexed issue, but one which is central to any meaningful analysis of relationships between different regions. The minority view, which still sees southern migrants of the first century BC as the probable catalyst for broch construction, at least has a rational, if improbable, basis for believing in a first century BC horizon. Without the historical framework there is no particular case for such a late dating of complex Atlantic roundhouses, and whilst it is true that radiocarbon dates do not yet (2001) demonstrate beyond doubt that they have their origins nearer the middle than the end of the first millennium BC, progressively accumulating evidence seems likely to endorse this conclusion, notwithstanding the problems of calibration. Taking refuge in the architectural typology argument- that earlier sites are not galleried and therefore not 'true' brochs- will not avail for sites like Dun Bharabhat in the west or the Howe, Crosskirk nor Old Scatness in the north. No-one is insisting that all complex Atlantic roundhouses should have early origins, nor that some of the developed broch towers might not be relatively late in the series. Whilst these may not be as early as sites such as Bu, it becomes increasingly improbable nevertheless that they

should be divorced from the sequence of monumental buildings that preceded them. For this reason especially it is important that some greater resolution should be introduced into the material cultural sequence, and in particular into the pottery sequence for the second half of the first millennium BC.

Along with the dating of Atlantic roundhouses, a parallel nettle which needs to be grasped is the dating of forts in Atlantic Scotland. Hamilton dated the fort construction at Clickhimin to the Early Iron Age because at the time of excavation in the 1950s, and even into the 60s when the report was published, forts were regarded as diagnostically Iron Age, when the material culture associated with the fort and pre-existing farmstead at Clickhimin do not demand such an interpretation. Fort-construction elsewhere, on the Continent, in Britain and in Ireland, is now regularly seen as a phenomenon of the later Bronze Age, a period in which over large parts of Europe a concatenation of circumstances led to a variety of expressions in the archaeological record which may be read as the product of social or political disruption. In Argyll the fort at Dunagoil may well have its origins in the late Bronze Age, even if much of its material assemblage belongs to a later horizon; in the Western Isles preliminary radiocarbon dates may point to the same possibility for some of the promontory or cliff-edge forts of Lewis. A late Bronze Age phase was claimed at Clickhimin, within the complex of cellular structures on the north-west side of the site, though seemingly more on the basis of analogy with the courtyard houses at Jarlshof (Hamilton 1956) rather than through any diagnostically late Bronze Age material from the structures themselves. In fact, in the presently-restored state of the site these look more like part of the post-broch cellular complex around the site's western circuit than survivals from the late Bronze Age, which if authentically primary have remained remarkably intact despite the obvious depredations of later building episodes which are manifest elsewhere on the site. But in terms of dating, there is no compelling reason for denying a possible Late Bronze Age phase in the occupational sequence (*pace* Fojut 1998).

CERAMIC SEQUENCES AND THEIR AFFINITIES

In the light of these considerations, how might we regard the material assemblage of the Atlantic Iron Age in general, and the Hebridean Iron Age in particular, in relation to its neighbours to south and east, and through the Western Seaways? Past assessments of ceramic connections between Atlantic Scotland and southern Britain have been too frequently based on one-off claims of similarity or derivation for form or decorative motif with alleged parallels from a variety of quite disparate regions and dating horizons in southern Britain, which have therefore been easy to ridicule methodologically. If we could establish for Atlantic Scotland a well-documented sequence of pottery styles and other associated artefact types spanning the period from the later Bronze Age to the Pictish period, then an objective comparison with other parts of Atlantic Europe might prove instructive. But while that remains an incomplete objective we can at least avoid the more facile sins of individual trait-chasing and try to consider demonstrable classes of material for want of full associated assemblages. Simply suggesting comparison between Atlantic Scotland and southern Britain is liable to induce anti-diffusionist neurosis in some, even if the exercise of comparison is undertaken without prejudice to possible explanations of perceived similarities or dissimilarities.

One reason for undertaking such a comparison is that Atlantic Scotland and southern Britain at least have in common the distinctive fact that their Iron Age cultures display a rich and varied ceramic tradition, though rather less so in the Northern Isles than in the Western Isles, so that the two regions should not be lumped together uncritically. Those of neighbouring regions, by contrast, conspicuously do not. Western, central, and eastern Scotland, together with the Borders, do not have an abundant ceramic assemblage, and what pottery there is displays a crudity of fabric and manufacture and simplicity of form that suggests a wholly separate tradition. Northern England from the Trent to the Tyne is certainly not aceramic, but assemblages are mostly late pre-Roman Iron Age or even Roman native, and are again limited to basic forms with little ornamentation beyond occasional simple plastic decoration. Wales falls essentially into the same category, while Ireland is almost totally aceramic. It is hardly surprising therefore that southern Britain is the obvious quarry for those seeking 'parallels' for some of the more distinctive Atlantic Iron Age pottery; the problem at issue is simply the single-track interpretation which has invariably been prompted by any perceived similarities.

SOUTHERN BRITAIN: WESSEX AND BEYOND

Any attempt to synthesise the principal elements in the southern British ceramic assemblages of the later Bronze Age and Iron Age runs the risk of over-simplification, though past studies of regional groups and styles could equally be accused on the other extreme of failing to see the wood for the trees. Here we are concerned only with late Bronze Age-early Iron Age groups on the one hand, and middle-later Iron Age groups on the other: the latest, wheel-thrown pottery of south-eastern England is here discounted as a separate tradition not directly relevant to Atlantic Scotland.

The later Bronze Age tradition, divided by Barrett (1980) into decorated and plain ware assemblages, are nevertheless difficult to characterise for lack of truly distinctive forms or styles. Only the Early All Cannings Cross group, as defined by Cunliffe (1974; 1991) but even more abundantly represented at Longbridge Deverill Cow Down in Wiltshire, has such distinctive forms and styles. Pre-eminent among these are fine ware jars, often with haematite slip, decorated with deeply-incised geometric designs or punched infilling, commonly filled with white chalk paste, and smaller haematite-coated bowls bearing horizontal furrowing or rilling and frequently with omphalos or dimple base. The earliest of these bowls are in form not unlike bipartite bowls from south-eastern and eastern England from an equally early horizon, though the Wessex examples sometimes have a short everted rim to give an overall form comparable to the unique Welby bronze vessel. Slightly later are the campanulate variety of Cunliffe's All Cannings Cross-Meon Hill group. The continental affinities of the All

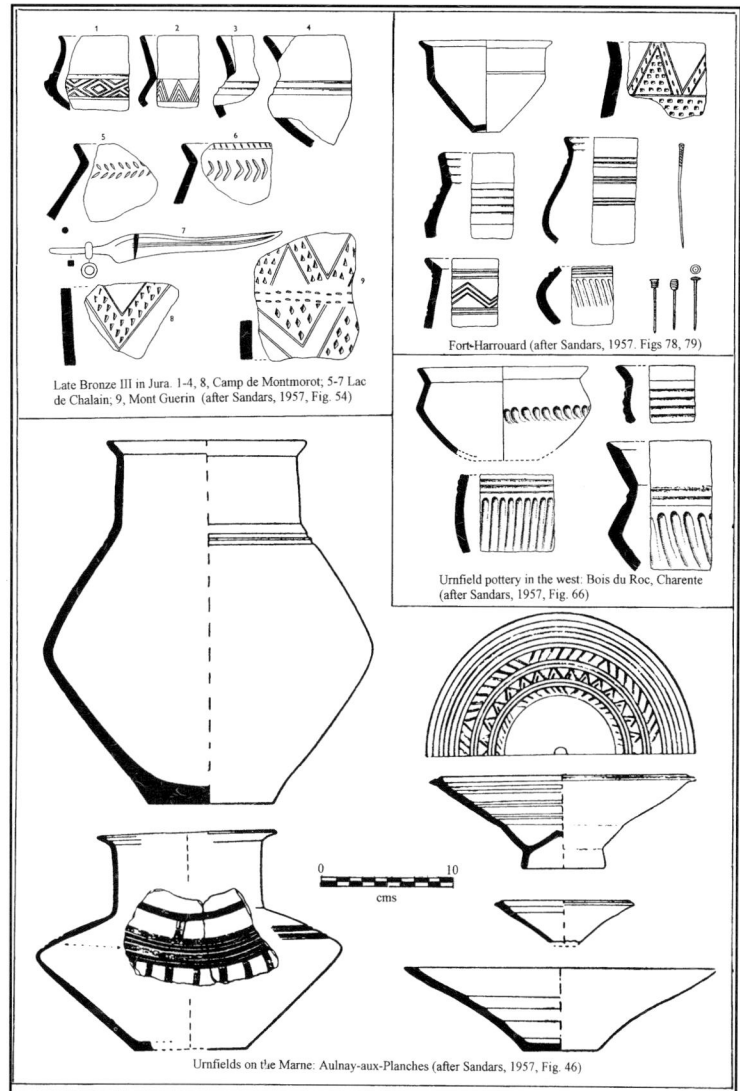

Late Bronze III in Jura. 1-4, 8, Camp de Montmorot; 5-7 Lac de Chalain; 9, Mont Guerin (after Sandars, 1957, Fig. 54)

Fort-Harrouard (after Sandars, 1957. Figs 78, 79)

Urnfield pottery in the west: Bois du Roc, Charente (after Sandars, 1957, Fig. 66)

Urnfields on the Marne: Aulnay-aux-Planches (after Sandars, 1957, Fig. 46)

Fig.2 *Late Bronze Age Urnfield Assemblages from eastern France. (after Sandars, 1957)*

Cannings series are unquestionably late Urnfield, with Sandars' best parallels in eastern France (Fig. 2), dating hardly later than the early eighth century (I am indebted to Dr Brendan O'Connor for his comments on late Urnfield chronology at the conference). In the comparison of the All Cannings assemblage with late Urnfield, it is important that both deeply incised geometric ornament and furrowed bowls, with both everted and taller rims, are found in association in late Bronze 3 Urnfield contexts in the Doubs and Jura (Sandars 1957, figures 53 and 54) but the two most recurrent late Urnfield forms, the cylinder-neck jar and the splay-sided bowl, are conspicuously absent in Britain, not to

mention the distinctive metalwork types of the Urnfield culture. Even among the decorative repertory there are notable absentees in the British assemblages, such as vertical fluting. In acknowledging the undoubted connection Cunliffe (1991) did not consider it necessary to invoke actual population movement, though he carefully did not rule it out. The highly selective introduction of certain ceramic styles, not to mention the absence in Britain of the Urnfield funerary mode, makes colonisation extremely unlikely.

Alongside these distinctive groups, coarse ware jars in southern Britain conform to a fairly standard shouldered form, formerly described as 'situlate' because of their presumed derivation from metal bucket prototypes, in which rows of finger-tipping, diagonal slashing or similar plastic decoration is frequently applied to rim or shoulder. In eastern England, at West Harling (Clark and Fell, 1953) and Staple Howe (Brewster, 1963) notably, applied cabled cordons fulfil the same role.

Within such a broad class of pottery there are naturally wide variations, but it remains a recognisable fact that by the middle Iron Age, represented most clearly at Little Woodbury and Maiden Castle (though there wrongly described by Wheeler (1943) in the Hawkes (1959) terminology as Iron Age A rather than B) slacker body-profiles come to predominate, and there is a marked decline in plastic ornament. Other coarse jar forms include barrel-shaped or incurving-rim jars, generally undecorated. These rather nondescript forms are in fact quite distinctive for their recurrent and widespread distributions. The middle Iron Age in southern Britain, however, is much better known for its fine pottery ('smooth, dark ware' to use the phrase coined by Brailsford (1948) at Little Woodbury), and for its variety of decorated wares. If any one form is dominant, it would be the ill-named 'saucepan pot', though regional groups like the globular ('goldfish') bowls of the south midlands, dumpy omphalos jars in the south-east or necked bowls in the south-west are distinctive. Decoration, generally applied with a shallow-tooled technique, includes a greater range of curvilinear designs, though they are still generally repetitive rather than freestyle in execution. Different regional fashions in motif or technique of application can be highlighted, such as swags or interlocking swags in the south midlands, 'eyebrow' or arcaded ornament in the south-east, 'duck-stamped' ornament in the south-west and the Welsh Marches.

Most frequently cited as a potential source by parallel-hunters since Childe have been the assemblages from the twin 'lake villages' of Glastonbury (Bulleid and Gray 1911, 1917; Coles and Minnitt 1995) and Meare (Bulleid and Gray 1948; Gray and Bulleid 1953; Gray and Cotton 1966; Coles 1987), with their wider associations in the south-west and Brittany. The Breton series begins in early La Tène, by the fourth century BC, and though chronological definition within the 'lake-village' assemblages has proved far from straightforward, it is clear that simply citing parallels from Glastonbury is no longer an endorsement of a first century BC date. In fact the Glastonbury style frequently uses basketry hatching to create, through a distinctively but not exclusively insular technique, an interplay between foreground and background. This is characteristic of early La Tène art on metalwork on the continent, is far more sophisticated than most developed regional styles on pottery in southern Britain, and evokes no echoes in Atlantic Scotland whatsoever. Equally, there are distinctive and recurrent pottery forms in the south-west, like the saucepan pot and the necked bowl, from which ornamental traits cannot simply be detached in order to provide parallels for ceramic innovations elsewhere. In sum, Glastonbury and Meare have been greatly over-rated as a source for stylistic comparisons, largely because for half a century they were principal among the only major assemblages available.

Finally, though the late Iron Age wheel-thrown pottery of the south-east is hardly pertinent to the present discussion, reference should be made to the broadly contemporary wares of central-southern and south-western England, in which the use of bead-rims has frequently been seen as diagnostic of 'Wessex B' or 'C'. Durotrigian bead-rim bowls are, indeed, distinctive, but they are also part of a package which in the south-west includes, for example, countersunk handles, so that any single trait divorced from its package should not be made to bear undue significance as an indicator of migrants.

ATLANTIC SCOTLAND AND PROBLEMS OF SEQUENCE

Reviewing past attempts at comparison between Atlantic Scottish and southern British Iron Age pottery it is abundantly clear that too often southern comparanda have been cited from regional and chronological groups which are totally disparate and unrelated, as well as not necessarily being representative of their respective assemblages. From the Atlantic Scottish standpoint it is also probable that material from quite a wide chronological span has been conflated for want of greater definition in the sequence. The first millennium AD sequence, that is, from the decline of the monumental complex Atlantic roundhouses down to the Norse period, is now being clarified as a consequence of recent excavations on post-Atlantic roundhouse settlements (Harding 2000), but the first millennium BC sequence remains to be given greater resolution.

INCISED ORNAMENT AND THE PROSPECT OF AN EARLY HORIZON

Topping (1987) considered the case, previously advanced by Young and others, for regarding incised-decorated pottery styles in the Hebridean Iron Age as an indication of an early horizon, as would be implied if it was regarded as contemporary with similar styles of the late Bronze Age or earliest Iron Age in southern England reviewed earlier. His conclusion was that the case could not be sustained, since incised ornament at Dun Mor Vaul, for example, occurred throughout that site's chronological

sequence, from the second half of the first millennium BC. Faced with this evidence we can only draw one of three conclusions, either that incised decoration has a long currency, and that, if it first appears in the Hebrides by 500 BC or even earlier, it nevertheless continues much later, or that the later occurrences are residual, rubbish-survivals from earlier deposits incorporated into later, or that different sets of material from different horizons have been conflated together through the lack of subtlety of archaeological classification, in effect we are not comparing like with like, even though we imagine them to be the same.

The third option (c) is perhaps more likely in the case of comparison of vessel form (the characterisation of which in the case of hand-made wares is notoriously subjective) than of

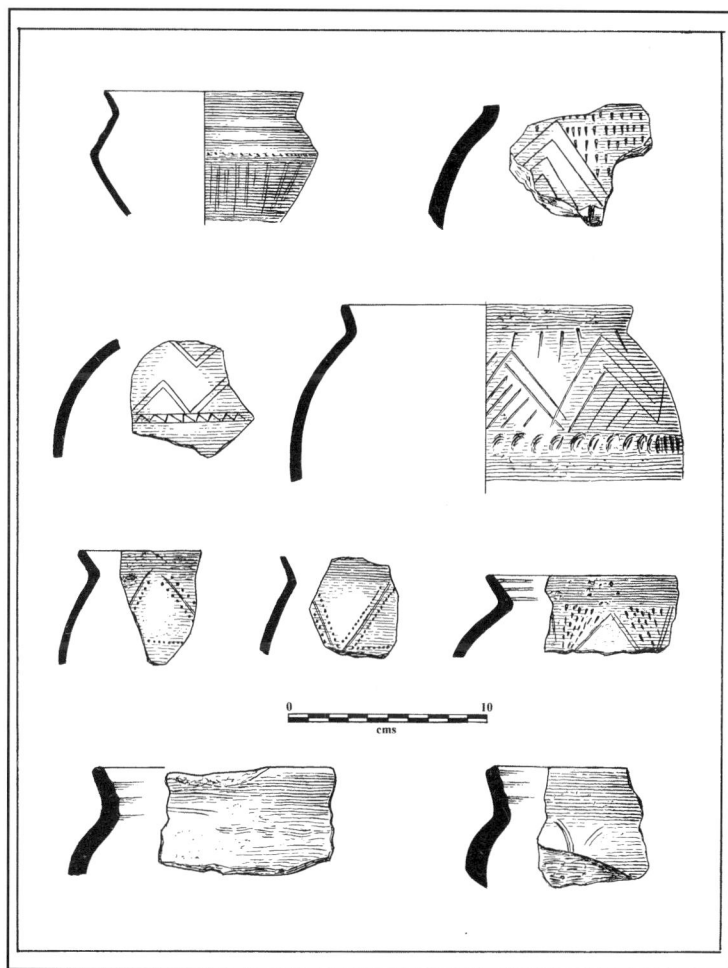

Fig.3 *Beirgh, Riof, Isle of Lewis: pottery from Phase 10 and exterior occupation. (drawings: D. W. Harding)*

decoration, which should be more amenable to definition. Nevertheless, some differences are apparent in decoration between sharply incised and impressed designs which could be significant in that it is with the former rather than the latter that comparisons with southern England might most clearly be drawn. With regard to (b) some of the Dun Mor Vaul sherds, for example, do indeed look rather worn, but this could be said as much of those from early contexts as from later. If (a) proved to be the case, then incised ornament could not be regarded as diagnostically early in itself, but its continuation into a later period would certainly explain why it has proved so hard to define the pottery of the earlier phase.

Both Beirgh (Fig. 3) and Dun Mor Vaul (Fig. 4) have geometric incised ornament, and both have external furrowing, though the latter is not demonstrably early at Dun Mor Vaul. Both also have internally-fluted rims, though again not yet demonstrably 'pre-broch' or 'pre-Clettraval', though at Dun Mor Vaul examples did occur in context Iota, attributed to the early broch occupation. At Beirgh incised wares, a single example of a furrowed bowl and an example of a vessel with exaggerated internal rim-bevel could all be paralleled at All Cannings Cross (Cunnington 1923). This is what would have been First A under Hawkes' ABC scheme (Hawkes 1959), but which we have noted would now be regarded as Late Bronze Age and dated to the eighth-seventh centuries. The principal concentration of incised-decorated pottery at Beirgh came from the lowest level of the exterior occupational sequence, the absolute dating of which has yet to be established, but there is at present no basis for believing that this context could be as early as the southern British antecedents.

Plastic ornament is also in evidence widely in the Hebridean Iron Age, particularly the use of applied cabled cordons, which, if it appears in early, first millennium BC horizons (e.g. Bharabhat, Harding 2000, Fig. 8), certainly continues in modified and sometimes distinctive forms in the post-broch, 'Cellular' occupational phases at Beirgh (Harding 2000, Fig.10). Simple finger-tipping is less common, though rows of diagonal stabs or slashes are known. Though these decorative techniques are certainly applied to coarse wares, they are not exclusively so, and plastic ornament including cabling is found combined on finer ware

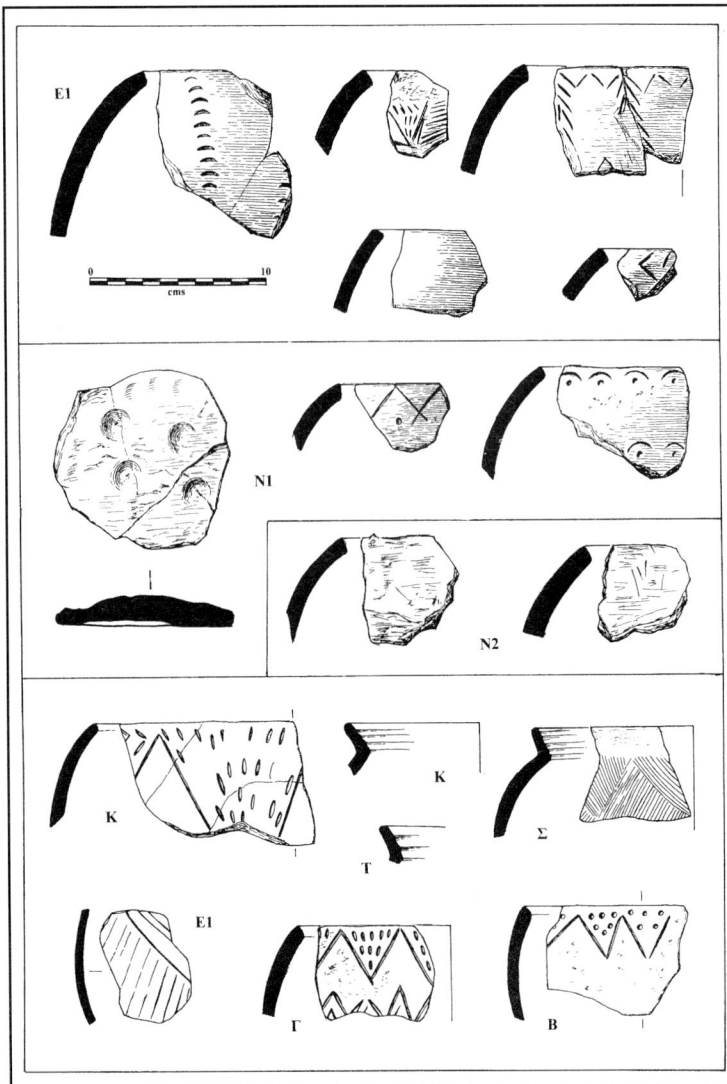

Fig.4 *Pottery from Dun Mor Vaul. (drawings, upper panels by D. W. Harding; lowest panel redrawn by DWH after Mackie, 1974.)*

vessels with geometric, incised or other forms of impressed ornament, by contrast with southern Britain where the two styles are almost mutually exclusive.

One type which has tantalised scholars in the past is the internally-fluted rim, which is represented at both Dun Mor Vaul and Beirgh, though not notably in early contexts, but which is more especially found in the fort and broch phases at Clickhimin (Fig. 5). Hamilton was not the first to note its similarities to Urnfield pottery, though interestingly perhaps it does not occur (in multiple fluted form at any rate) at All Cannings Cross. The yawning chasm, however, between an Urnfield date and the generally-accepted date of the Atlantic Scottish examples has always proved an insuperable barrier to effecting any meaningful link between the two. I have suggested earlier that the Early Iron Age dating of the Clickhimin fort or any demonstrably antecedent homestead should be reviewed, but until these can be shown to have their origins in the Late Bronze Age the discrepancy in dating remains. Recognising this, several authorities have turned instead in their search for parallels to the internally-grooved wares of late Iron Age of south-western Britain and Brittany, which provided the re-assurance of support for a late and compressed chronology for monumental building in Atlantic Scotland (MacKie 1995; 2000). Realising that one of the problems of pottery studies is that no two observers will ever agree that like is like, or unlike unlike, I have to declare nevertheless that I do not see the slightest similarity between broad, internal rim fluting and the fine rim grooving of south-western vessels. Furthermore, as indicated earlier, the associated forms and decorative styles of the south-west, as Childe acknowledged (1935),

have little or nothing in common with Atlantic Scotland. Citing the apparent survival of internal rim fluting on late Hallstatt cremation jars from Brittany (MacKie 1995, incorrectly referenced to Giot, Briard and Pape, *Protohistoire de la Bretagne*, 1979, 231ff; title corrected in MacKie 2000) hardly bridges the gap in chronology. Despite his later and uncharacteristic recantation, I believe Wheeler was on the right lines when he identified the internally-grooved rim as a device for retaining a lid (1943, 216); his subsequent (Wheeler and Richardson 1957, 58) preference for a metalworking skeuomorph might be appropriate for the south-western internal grooving, but only underlines the difference between the latter and internal fluting. If we regard this feature as essentially functional, then its recurrence at different periods in different regions need occasion no great surprise. But the use of furrowed fluting, as opposed to a deep, internal bevel (as, for example, at Beirgh and at All Cannings Cross) still seems to be a very particular variation on the theme, presumably to accommodate lids of

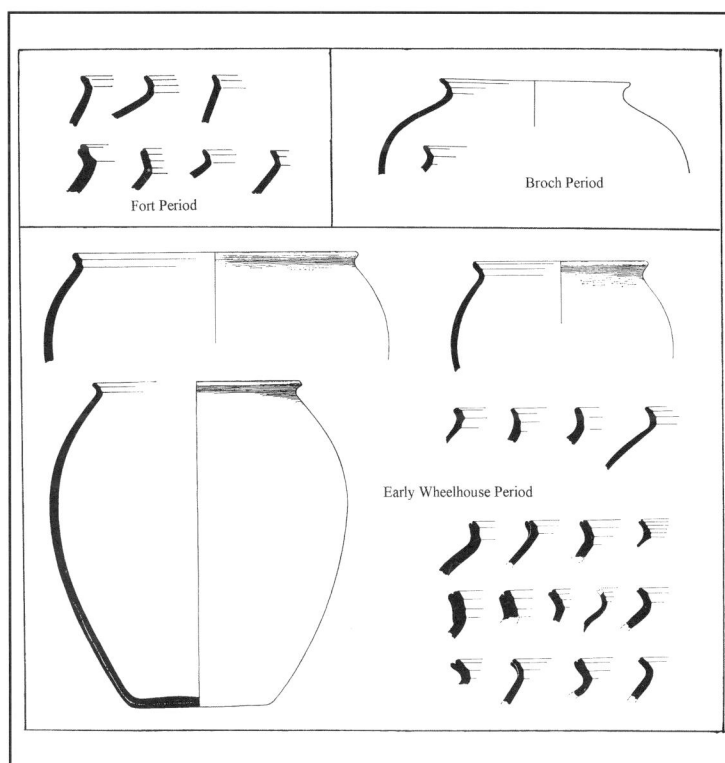

Fig.5 *Clickhimin, Shetland: fluted pottery (after Hamilton, 1968).*

different sizes, and perhaps implying the need to achieve a good, airtight seal.

Internally-decorated bases are another form for which an early origin has been considered (Topping1987); at Bharabhat they certainly occur in the early occupation, but at Beirgh apparently continue well into the post-broch sequence, a pattern which appears to be true also of Dun Mor Vaul (MacKie 1974). In the Northern Isles, decorated bases of a rather different, spiral style appear in the fort phase at Clickhimin, alongside internally-fluted rims, both of which continue there into the period of wheelhouse occupation. This, too, then could be a style which begins early, but cannot be regarded as diagnostically early.

BHARABHAT AND VAUL WARE

In the pre-occupation with dating the origins of complex Atlantic roundhouses it is easy to overlook the fact that MacKie (1974) identified at Dun Mor Vaul a pottery assemblage for which he acknowledged an early dating, starting from the middle of the first millennium BC (Fig. 4). Incised geometric ornament was present from contexts Epsilon and Eta, along with 'Vaul' ware, that is plain, coarse ware jars and vessels in harder fabric with incurving rims. This assemblage is not unlike that from Dun Bharabhat on Lewis (Harding 2000, Fig. 8; Harding and Dixon 2000), where the early occupation is also represented by coarse ware jars, finer incurving-rim jars and incised geometric ornament, and the radiocarbon dates from which would be compatible with that main phase of occupation in the second half of the first millennium BC. Dun Mor Vaul remains an important element in the equation, not least because its ceramic assemblage is really hardly typical, at any rate, of mainland Argyll, and for its ceramic affinities we therefore need to look to the outer islands.

The currency of incurving-rim jars in Atlantic Scotland would appear to coincide or overlap with the use of jars of not dissimilar barrel-profile in southern Britain, but the form is so basic that any connection is likely to be coincidental. Again function may be a factor in design, the 'hole-mouth' shape being plainly not intended for pouring. In general the southern British examples are plain, coarse ware vessels, whereas those from the Hebridean Iron Age are finer and frequently decorated. Simple designs may have a widespread distribution and currency, but the apparent similarity in form between the coarse ware jars from Jarlshof and Clickhimin and the classic middle Iron Age jars of the Little Woodbury, Maiden Castle, Hunsbury or Breedon-on-the-Hill series is quite striking. These forms are the common denominator of southern British Iron Age pottery of the second half of the first millennium BC, and there is no reason why a similar tradition should not have characterised Atlantic Scotland at broadly the same time.

THE BEIRGH-VAUL MIDDLE IRON AGE SERIES

The principal ceramic types of the middle Iron Age series were identified by MacKie at Dun Mor Vaul as comprising notably everted rim vessels, and everted rim vessels with applied cordons, including those distinguished by so-called Clettraval ornament of shallow-tooled or finger-impressed arcades, together with the continuation of incised ornament and decorated bases. These were dated from around the turn of the millennia. In general terms, the Beirgh sequence (Harding and Gilmour 2000) follows a similar pattern, though the chronology requires further fine-tuning. Earlier forms undoubtedly continued in use in west Lewis too, like the decorated bases and incised decoration. But the proliferation of decorative motifs, almost in some cases symbols, which are not found in Southern Britain in this period underlines the independent character of the Hebridean middle Iron Age.

I have no wish here to resurrect at length the vexed debate about the claimed derivation of the arcaded style of ornament on 'Clettraval ware' from southern Britain (MacKie 2000, 105 with earlier references). Arcaded ornament, among a variety of related ornamental motifs, occurs in several regions of southern Britain in the later Iron Age, including on bead-rim bowls in Wessex and on dumpy omphalos jars in the south-east. Nowhere to my knowledge does it occur on everted rim vessels with applied girth cordons, other than in the Hebridean Iron Age. The fabric, form and decoration of these vessels may be novel at Dun Mor Vaul, but their local manufacture has never been disputed.

SUMMARY OF POTTERY ANALYSIS

If the undoubted similarities with some Urnfield pottery styles do not demand explanation in terms of wholesale population movement into Southern Britain, there is really no reason to require such a radical explanation for a further extension of such styles to Atlantic Scotland. Though they may have persisted longer in the Atlantic west than in the south, it does strain credulity to insist on a half-millennium time-lag before their introduction. And though some might believe that the levels at Dun Mor Vaul published as pre-broch were more probably early broch, it is not necessary to open that debate in order for the Vaul sequence, and the evidence from Bharabhat, to fit in with the mid-first millennium BC currency of some ultimate Urnfield ceramic styles being transmitted along the Western Seaways. Pointing to some similarities in pottery styles is not to attribute the entire repertory to southern influence; much of what characterises the early material at Dun Mor Vaul is not really like transitional Late Bronze Age- earliest Iron Age pottery from Wessex, or if there are similarities they are at such a 'common denominator' level that they hardly signify beyond the level of an

Atlantic continuum. The use of finger-impressed ornament and even applied cabled cordons I would be inclined to put in this category; the latter are found in many quite different cultural contexts, and might easily be a ceramic skeuomorph of rope tied around the rim for suspension, or for closing the mouth of a duffle-bag or kit-bag of leather or textile.

Whether there is a distinct change in pottery traditions in the middle Iron Age in the Hebrides generally, as has become an article of faith for Dun Mor Vaul, is arguable. Everted rim bowls appear at Bharabhat without the distinctive arcaded ornament, perhaps suggesting progression rather than radical change. Plainly we need more well-stratified sequences, of which Beirgh holds out an obvious prospect, within the core area of the regional distribution.

The later ceramic sequence in the Hebrides, exemplified particularly clearly, but not exclusively, at Beirgh through its Cellular to later Pictish period, has been dealt with elsewhere (Harding 2000), and need only be summarised briefly here. Incised or impressed decoration continues into the post-Atlantic roundhouse phases, but rapidly disappears in the Cellular phase of settlement, though applied cables continue and even diversify in their styles. By the later Pictish-period, plain wares are ubiquitous, as has been noted on a number of occasions elsewhere.

METALWORK AND OTHER TYPES AND THE ATLANTIC SEAWAYS

Any modern review of non-ceramic artefacts from Atlantic Scotland and their external affinities must begin with David Clarke's paper 'Small Finds in the Atlantic Province: Problems of Approach' in *Scottish Archaeological Review* (1971, 27-54). This seminal study was written in the context of the decline of the 'invasion hypothesis' as an invariable explanation of cultural innovation and change, so that it rejected the assumption that any type which had parallels in the southern British Iron Age must have derived therefrom. More importantly perhaps in terms of methodology it warned against using 'exotic artefacts' to define or date local cultural assemblages for the very reason that they were not representative. There was, however, a problem of definition, and the term 'exotic' seems to have been used in two distinct senses. Samian pottery is exotic in the sense of demonstrably 'foreign' or 'introduced from abroad'; spiral rings or ring-headed pins are not necessarily exotic in that sense, though they had too often been treated as such. The projecting ring-headed pin is sufficiently distinct from southern ring-headed pins to be regarded as a native type, and when Clarke used the term 'exotic' of these (1971, 32) he was warning against the use of the 'abnormal or special' in preference to 'the mass of material' or 'normal' which characterised local cultural assemblages. Clarke examined critically the derivations then fashionable for both spiral rings and ring-headed pins. He effectively showed that the former had too long a currency and too wide a distribution for any single source to be identified for Scottish Iron Age rings, and though attempts have been made to retain spiral rings as an introduction (MacKie 1995; 2000) Clarke's point remains essentially valid. As regards ring-headed pins, there are more players on the board than the Scottish-southern English polarisation would suggest, as we shall argue below.

Bone Dice (Fig. 6)

Clarke's other major contribution of that time, 'Bone Dice and the Scottish Iron Age' (1970, 214-32), examined the distribution of parallelepiped bone dice in Britain,

Ireland and continental Europe, and concluded that MacKie's claim that Scottish examples were 'clear imports from southern England' as part of a Wessex B package was unwarranted. Lane reinforced this point (1987) by citing Caulfield's recognition of differences in the mode of numerical display between the English and Scottish examples. Though there are differences of opinion in terms of origins and relationships, by common consent parallelepiped dice in Scotland are dated to the early centuries AD, rather than very much earlier. Examples from Ireland are hardly earlier (Raftery 1984, 247-8) and some apparently continued in use on Early Christian settlements including the crannog sites of

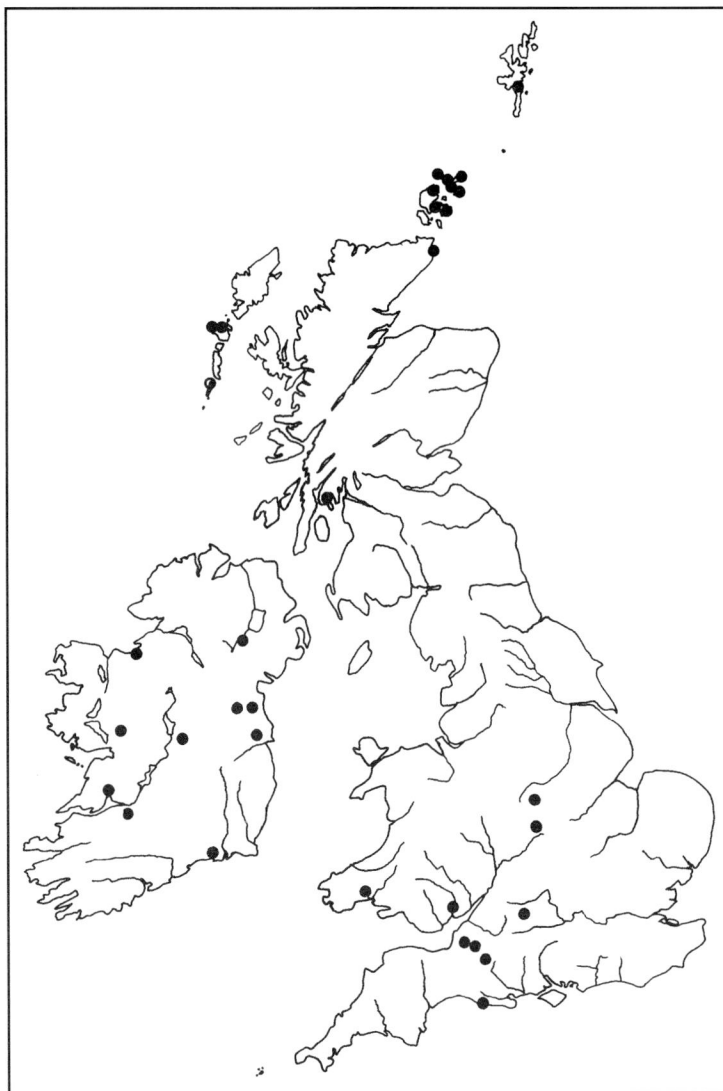

Fig.6 *Distribution of parallelepiped bone dice (after Clarke, 1971 and Raftery, 1984).*

Lagore and Ballinderry. In fact, the southern British distribution is hardly representative of mainstream Iron Age culture in Wessex or the south-east. Centred on Glastonbury and Meare, they are absent altogether from Danebury, and the late Iron Age princes of the south-east, whose gaming-pieces occur regularly among funerary furniture, were evidently addicted to other board games. The concentration in Orkney is still outstanding, and the relationship between the different groupings in the overall distribution is far from clear.

Glass Beads

Much the same could be said of glass beads with inlaid spiral designs. Apparently earliest in the series is Guido's Class 10 (Guido 1978), the distribution of which (Fig. 7) is repeatedly said to be south-western England, but which in reality are represented in the south-west only at Meare, South Cadbury and Maiden Castle, with others in Wales, south-west Scotland and Ireland superficially similar but not necessarily from the same source. Based on radiocarbon dates, the Meare beads are assigned to the fourth and third centuries BC, a conclusion which is also consistent with the evidence of their chemical analyses (Henderson 1987). The assumed primacy of Meare in the distribution has been conventionally inferred not only from their early date, but also from the fact that the West Village yielded evidence for glass bead production. It was hardly surprising therefore that both Jope (Jope and Wilson 1957) and Guido should have regarded the burial group from 'Loughey', Co Down, which included a necklace of eight 'Meare-type' spiral-ornaments

beads with sixty-eight further opaque yellow glass beads, as the grave-goods of an immigrant from central-western England. In fact, Henderson's analyses have shown that the Loughey beads were almost certainly not made at Meare, but more probably were the product of a Northern Irish workshop. The presence of a purple glass armlet and Nauheim-derivative brooch in the Loughey grave may even indicate direct connections with Continental Europe in the later first century BC. This date would also satisfy the evidence from Granagh, County Galway, so that the Irish series really need not be closely related to those from Meare in either production or date. If the Meare group is no longer seen as the catalyst

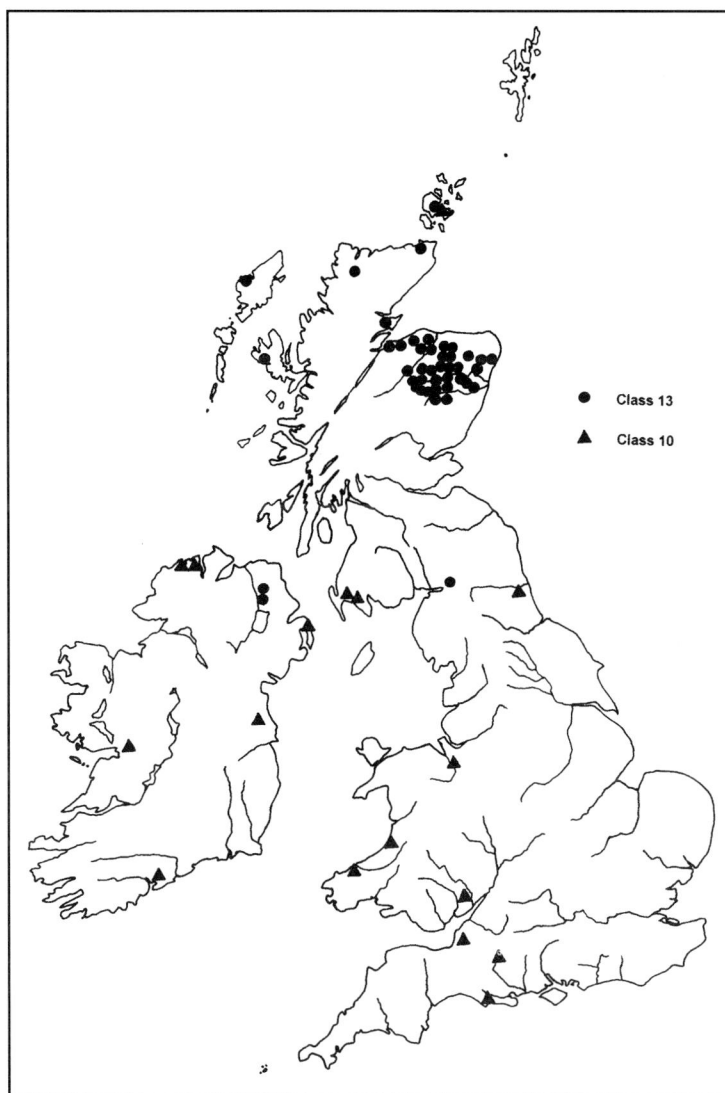

Fig.7 *Distribution of spiral-ornamented glass beads of Class 10 and Class 13 (after Guido, 1978, with additions).*

for the Irish spiral-ornamented beads, is there any reason for insisting on such a relationship for the Scottish, which for the most part are manifestly different even from inspection?

Class 13 spiral-decorated beads differ in being slightly more angular and without the colourless matrix of Class 10, which, according to Guido, the Scottish tribesmen might have preferred, had they had the technical competence of their southern neighbours (1978, 85). The dense concentration in Aberdeenshire, Banff, Moray and Nairn (Fig. 7) leaves little doubt that this was the product of local manufacture, but the apparently late associations have in the past lead inevitably to the inference that these were derived from the southern British Class 10. The rather heterogeneous Class 14 annular beads (which Lane (1987, 53) appears to equate with Class 13, since Guido makes no claim of southern origin for Class 14) concentrate in much the same region and sometimes occur in association with spiral-ornamented beads of Class 13 and smaller yellow beads of Class 8. There are outliers in the north and west, and in Northern Ireland, of both Class 13 and Class 14, which Guido regarded as essentially the same, notwithstanding their divergence of decoration (1987, vi) in an overall pattern which invites interpretation as the product of a regional centre in the north-east around the first century AD. Among those outliers the Bharabhat Class 13 bead on the basis of calibrated radiocarbon dates might be rather earlier than current estimates for the series in Scotland, underlining the fact that late dating is frequently induced by the absence of clearly defined criteria for earlier beginnings. The north-eastern concentration in

distribution perhaps invites endorsement of a later date, by analogy with the similar concentration in massive armlets and related bronzes, but in fact the two distributions are complementary rather than coincidental, almost all the beads lying north of the Dee.

It is worth noting that the sparse distribution of Class 10 beads as a representative type of the southern British Iron Age stands in marked contrast to another variant of spiral-ornamented bead, namely Class 6 which is distinguished by having multiple spirals on low bosses. In Southern Britain its distribution (Fig. 8) is also exactly complementary to that of Class 10, with the notable exception of Meare and Maiden

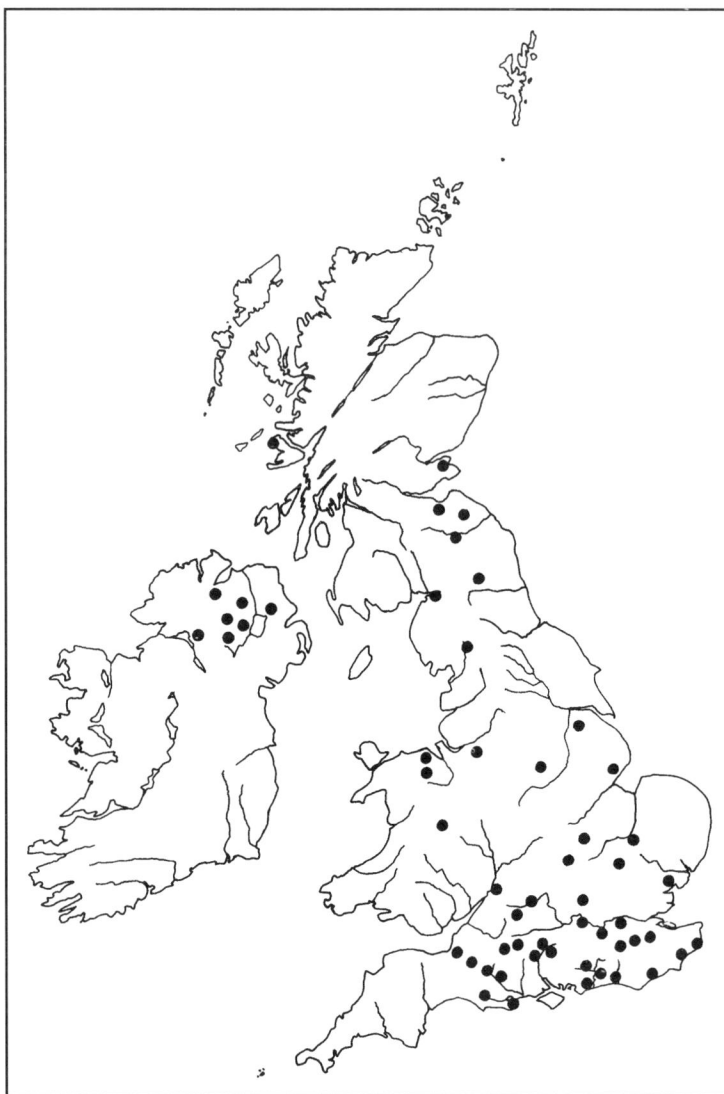

Fig.8 *Distribution of spiral and boss-ornamented glass beads of Class 6 (after Guido, 1978, with additions).*

Castle, where both types occur, and its currency was apparently rather later, around the second and first centuries BC. These are the beads which should have triggered Scottish derivatives if the catalyst for the latter were English migrants of the first century BC. In effect, there are several variant regional groups of spiral-ornamented glass beads in the later first millennium BC in Britain and Ireland, and as a candidate for a single origin, even if such were necessary, Class 10 looks less than convincing.

Small, annular yellow glass beads (Guido's Class 8) have also been introduced into the debate, and are certainly worth considering, not least because their distribution (Fig. 9), with the exception of an unstratified find from Roman Silchester, is again decidedly not representative of Wessex or south-eastern England. In fact, there are more find-spots in the Hebrides than there are in southern England and Wales combined. Once again, Meare features in the schedules as a significant production centre of the fourth-second centuries BC, whilst Culbin Sands in Morayshire was evidently another, possibly in the first or second centuries AD (Henderson 1991). At Bharabhat they occur in both primary and secondary occupation, in the latter likewise with the spiral-ornament variety. On the other hand, they occur on forts and native settlements of the Roman period in the hinterland of Hadrian's Wall, so that they cannot be regarded as diagnostic of an early horizon, and *disjecta membra* must certainly be expected in later contexts. Apart from this late group, their distribution is decidedly western, both in Scotland and in southern Britain.

Long-handed combs (Fig. 10)

Long-handled combs of bone or antler have also been invoked to support southern migrants into Atlantic Scotland since Childe first argued that the introduction of weaving must have meant the presence of 'womenfolk' as part of a community migration from the south-west, rather than the product of trade or other factors. Setting aside the issue of function- whether combs were indeed used in the weaving process or any specialist part of it (Tuohy 1999) the Atlantic Scottish combs are now widely recognised as rather different, both in construction and ornament, from the southern British. Whilst they may well be treated as cognate

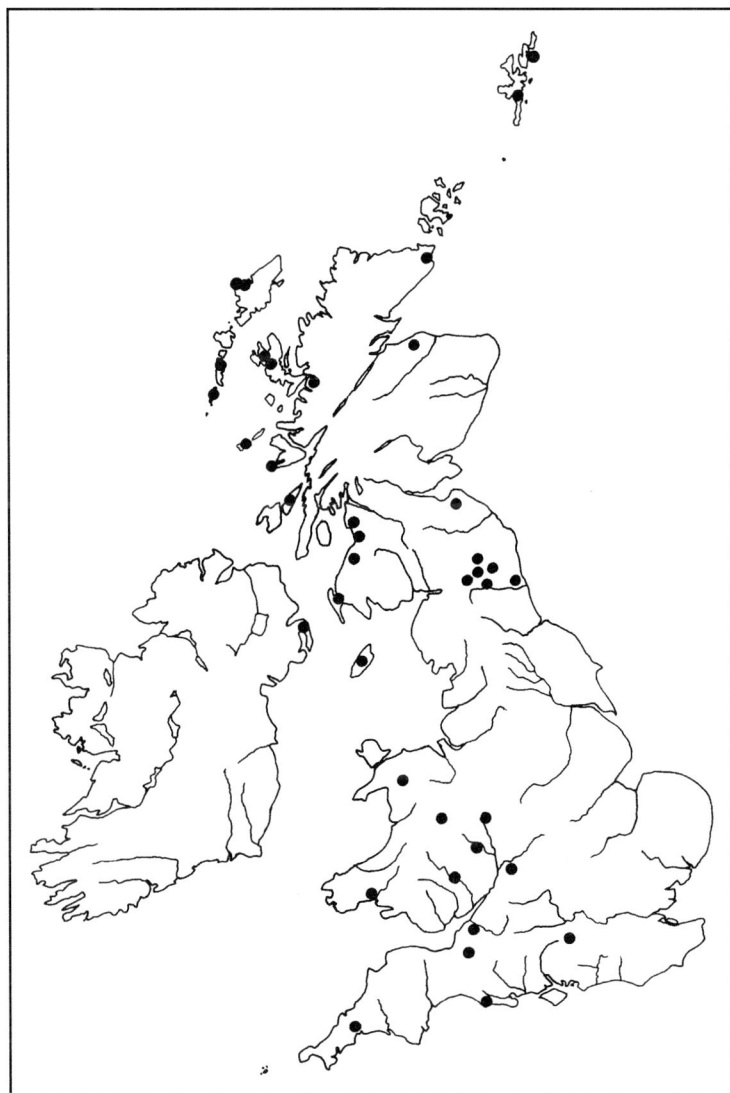

Fig.9 *Distribution of yellow glass beads of Class 8 (after Guido, 1978, and Lane, 1987, with additions).*

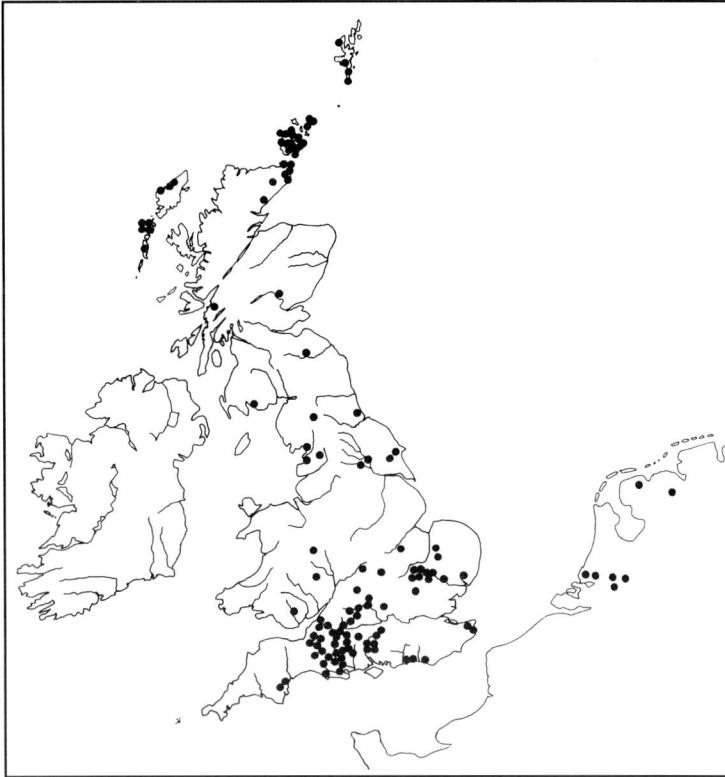

Fig.10 *Distribution of antler and bone combs (after Tuohy, 1999).*

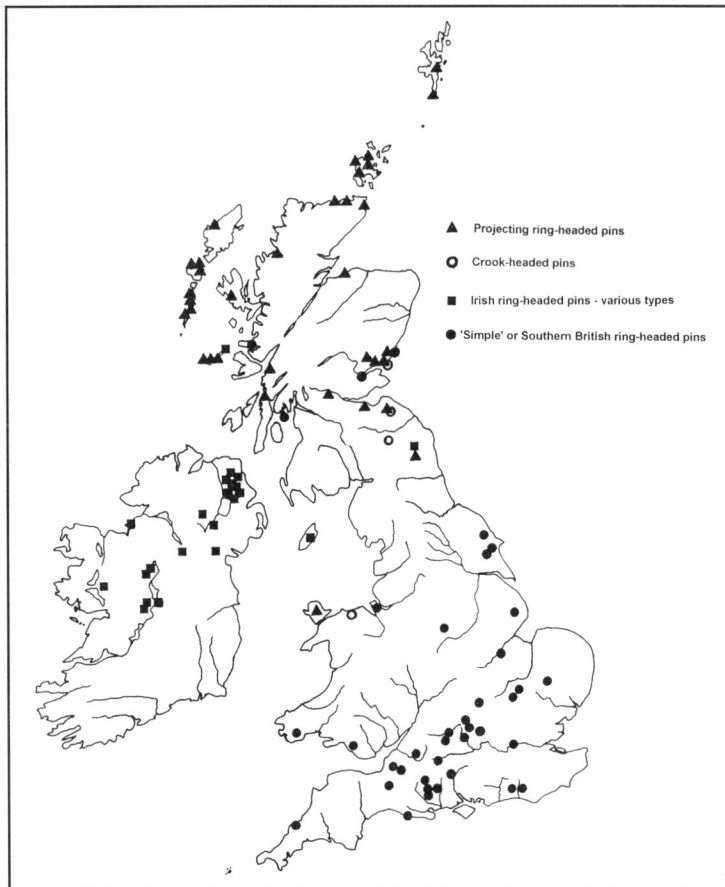

Fig.11 *Distribution of ring-headed and related pins (after Dunning, 1934, Clarke, 1971, and Raftery, 1984, with additions).*

groups, therefore, there is no compelling reason for regarding any one group within the British or northern European distributions as derivative from another. The absence of examples from Ireland is notable, and the paucity of finds from the south-west and from Wales is equally striking. In fact, the distribution has a bias towards the southern North Sea basin rather than the Western Seaways, perhaps serving as a timely reminder that the Irish Sea route is not the only artery of sea-borne access into Atlantic Scotland.

Ring-headed pins (Fig. 11)

Ring-headed pins, though not revisited by Lane in his case against English migrants, have nevertheless been invoked at various times as part of the diffusionist package, and their regional variants are worth re-examining. Essentially an insular (British and Irish) type, rather than one representative of Continental La Tène, generations of scholars have looked for Continental antecedents, if indirectly through the swan's neck pins of the late Bronze Age, which, though represented only in modest numbers in Southern Britain and Scotland, with even fewer in Ireland, do nevertheless compare sufficiently strikingly to Continental analogies to warrant their consideration as part of a wider north-western European phenomenon. The majority of ring-headed pins are of bronze, and following Dunning (1934) have generally been recognised in two variants, one made of bent wire, the other cast. The latter, which technically is amenable to more complex embellishment of the ring-head or stem than the simple wire form, has been conventionally regarded as a later development, though there seems to be no *a priori* reason why it should not have been simply a more professionally-produced version of a simple domestic type. In Southern Britain the distribution of ring-headed pins is principally south and east of the Jurassic Ridge, which with the possible exception of south-west England may reflect no more than the concentration of research.

While there are ring-headed pins analogous to Southern British examples north of the border, Scottish ring-headed pins also include different variants. Dunning noted the crook-headed type, in which perhaps rightly he saw Irish connections, though few Irish archaeologists today would concur with his derivation of the very distinctive Irish series from the Scottish (1934, 286). The other distinctive form, not treated specifically by Dunning, was the projecting ring-headed pin, represented either by the artefacts themselves or their alleged impressions in pottery. These are almost exclusively Scottish in distribution and decidedly Atlantic Scottish at that. Their origins, from other regions of Britain, or from antecedent types in Scotland or other regions of Britain, have exercised archaeologists for many years. The three prevailing options, that they were derived from English involuted pins (on which the head is likewise turned at ninety degrees to the stem, but which also have the involuted or humped stem, of course, which the Scottish pins do not), that they derived from Scottish sunflower pins, or that they are simply a Scottish variant of the ring-headed pin tradition, were each examined by Clarke (1971, 28ff), who concluded that 'one could be forgiven for believing that none of them provides even an approximation to the truth'. Faced with the inadequacy of the evidence,

one might despairingly concur, but the fact is that the three options are not alike, in that the first two require demonstration, whereas the last might be regarded as the *status quo* until demonstrated otherwise. Why a distinctive Scottish variant of ring-headed pin, cognate with but not necessarily derivative from other regions, on the same model as has been proposed for beads, cannot be accepted is unclear. Inter-relationships between the different regions of Britain and Ireland may be expected. There are certainly odd examples of Irish ring-headed pins in northern Britain, and at least one projecting ring-headed pin in northern Ireland, and via the Western Seaways we might anticipate connections with southern and south-western Britain too. But the imperative for a transmission from south to north of a type which is demonstrably not of direct Continental origin anyway, can only be grounded in a now discredited model of unilinear cultural diffusion. In any event the origin or affinities of the Scottish pins cannot be divorced from the issue of chronology. Recent research (A. Heald, pers. com.) has underlined the fact that the great majority of Scottish pins, where dating is reasonably assured, belong to the Roman period, and neither pins nor moulds can confidently be dated earlier than the first century BC. This is true even of Dun Mor Vaul, where it was the presence in earlier contexts of pottery with ring-impressions presumed to have been made with a pin that sustained the idea of an earlier currency for the artefact type. This being the case, then the Scottish pins with projecting head turned at ninety degrees to the stem seemingly appeared centuries after the appearance of their southern counterparts with non-projecting heads in the same plane as the stem, which by the end of the first millennium BC had developed rather different characteristics anyway. This analysis hardly seems to afford a sound basis for proposing a particular relationship between the two.

Spiral finger-rings

Little can be added to what previous commentators have observed regarding spiral finger rings (Clarke 1971; Lane 1987), which cannot be regarded as chronologically or culturally diagnostic, since they apparently are found in virtually identical form from the Middle Bronze Age to the mid-first millennium AD. Where they do occur in demonstrably Iron Age contexts, as at Maiden Castle, their associations have suggested a late dating in the first centuries BC and AD, though the example from Pimperne, Dorset (Harding, Blake and Reynolds 1993, Fig. 26) was unquestionably from an earlier horizon. The Irish examples, though hardly definitive chronologically, would also satisfy a late currency around the turn of the millennia. The distribution of the type is concentrated into regional clusters. In the south they occur from Dorset to the south midlands, but hardly in the south-east, and even at Danebury there were no unequivocal examples. In the north there is a significant distribution from southern Scotland to Argyll, but relatively few in the Hebrides, so that as an index of southern migrants into that region they are hardly convincing.

Querns

Once regarded as an innovation in the Hebrides which was prompted by direct contact from southern England (MacKie 1971, 54) the discoid rotary quern is now recognised as 'completely different' from the 'La Tène' querns of England, southern Scotland or northern Ireland (MacKie 2000, 106), and following a suggestion by Caulfield, connections with Brittany and the Iberian peninsula have been postulated. The Irish distribution may not argue for the disc quern as a non-La Tène type, but a case could be made for regarding it as an Atlantic variant. As regards inter-regional connections, it is true that trade in heavy items like quernstones

seems less than convincing (though broken stones would make effective ballast for ships plying the Western Seaways), and there are other plausible mechanisms for the transmission of technological innovations like the adjustable quern. For the purposes of the present debate, however, the key point is that once again we are unable to identify a consistent series of types with a broadly compatible southern distribution or chronology to sustain the diffusionist explanation. No-one is arguing for cultural isolation; on the contrary, the evidence suggests a far more complex set of inter-relationships, in which the role of the seaways was plainly crucial.

CONCLUSIONS

Many other material types which are representative of Atlantic Scotland need to be studied, and their distributions plotted, before we shall be able to evaluate adequately the complex network of relationships which were in evidence during the later first millennium BC and early first millennium AD along the Western Seaways and the southern North Sea basin. Much closer evaluation of their chronology will also plainly be necessary, since the probability is that some variations within the classic types, including those discussed above, have been conflated and compressed into the short chronology hitherto prevailing for the Atlantic Iron Age, when in reality they may prove to belong to rather different phases within a much longer time-span. As it stands, however, it has to be admitted that the majority of non-ceramic types appear relatively late in the Atlantic Iron Age, and the material assemblage of the earlier Iron Age does not display the variety which is characteristic of the middle and later Iron Ages (Harding 1995). Fieldwork is already affording some illumination of the currency of key types, such as door-knob spearbutts and associated types of the first half of the first millennium AD

(Heald 2001), but more evidence will be required to establish the range of types current in the second half of the first millennium BC.

What is already apparent is that the picture is not a simple one of an Irish Sea zone in which a variety of types are equally represented in all the adjacent regions. Some types, like long-handled combs and pottery, are virtually absent from Ireland; others, like dice and certain types of bead, occur on both sides of the water. Among the beads the Class 6 spiral-ornamented variety, hardly represented in western Britain though densely distributed in the south and south-east, nevertheless are present in an enclave in Ulster. This pattern might suggest that specific areas across the Western Seaways may have exploited reciprocally their own political or diplomatic liaisons, or negotiated with their favoured suppliers of imported goods, and not necessarily just between immediately neighbouring regions, throughout later prehistory and into the early historic period. There is of course no reason to exclude kinship ties or population movement from this model, which is not the same as reviving the older unilateral A to B diffusionism. Such interaction was presumably commonplace long before it impinged upon the historical record, which is one reason why the identification through archaeological distributions, either of site-types or diagnostic artefacts, of Dalriadic Scots, in Northern Ireland or Argyll has always proved to be a fruitless exercise.

BIBLIOGRAPHY

Barrett, J. (1980) The pottery of the late Bronze Age in lowland England, *Proceedings of the Prehistoric Society* 46, 297-320.

Brailsford, J. W., 1948. 'Excavations at Little Woodbury, Wiltshire (1938-39). Part II', *Proceedings of the Prehistoric Society*, 14, 1-23.

Brewster, T. C. M., 1963. *The Excavation of Staple Howe*, Scarborough, East Riding Archaeological Research Committee.

Bulleid, A. and Gray, H. St George, 1911. *The Glastonbury Lake Village*, Vol. 1, Taunton, Glastonbury Antiquarian Society.

Bulleid, A. and Gray, H. St George, 1917. *The Glastonbury Lake Village*, Vol. 2, Taunton, Glastonbury Antiquarian Society.

Bulleid, A. and Gray, H. St George, 1948. *The Meare Lake Village*, Vol. 1, Taunton, printed privately at Taunton Castle.

Childe, V.G. (1935) *The Prehistory of Scotland*, London, Kegan Paul.

Childe, V.G. (1946) *Scotland before the Scots*, London, Methuen.

Clark, J. G. D. and Fell, C. I., 1953. The Early Iron Age Site at Micklemoor Hill, West Harling, Norfolk, and its Pottery, *Proceedings of the Prehistoric Society*, 19, 1-40.

Clarke, D.V. (1970) Bone dice and the Scottish Iron Age, *Proceedings of the Prehistoric Society* 36, 214-32.

Clarke, D.V. (1971) Small finds in the Atlantic Province: problems of approach, *Scottish Archaeological Forum*, 3, 23-43.

Coles, J. M., 1987. *Meare Village East: The Excavations of A. Bulleid and H. St George Gray 1932-1956*, Somerset Levels Papers No 13.

Coles, J. M., and Minnitt, S., 1995. *'Industrious and Fairly Civilised': the Glastonbury Lake Village*, Somerset Levels Project and Somerset County Council Museums Service.

Cunnington, M. (1923) *The Early Iron Age Inhabited Site at All Cannings Cross Farm, Wiltshire*, Devizes, George Simpson.

Cunliffe, B. W. (1974;1991) *Iron Age Communities in Britain*, 1st ed. 1974, 3rd ed. 1991, London, Routledge.

Dunning, G. C. (1934) The swan's neck and ring-headed pins of the Early Iron Age in Britain, *Archaeological Journal* 91, 269-95.

Fojut, N. (1998) How did we get here? Shetland studies to 1995. In Nicholson, R. A., and Dockrill, S. J., (eds), *Old Scatness Broch, Shetland: Retrospect and Prospect*, 1-41. University of Bradford/Shetland Amenity Trust/ NABO.

Giot, P-R., Briard, J., and Pape, L. (1979) *Protohistoire de la Bretagne*, Rennes, Ouest France Université.

Gray, H. St George and Bulleid, A., 1953. *The Meare Lake Village*, Vol. 2, Taunton, printed privately at Taunton Castle.

Gray, H. St George and Cotton, M. A., 1966. *The Meare Lake Village*, Vol. 3, Taunton, privately printed at Taunton Castle.

Guido, M. (1978) *The Glass Beads of the Prehistoric and Roman Periods in Britain and Ireland*. London, Report XXXV of the Research Committee of the Society of Antiquaries of London, Thames and Hudson.

Hamilton, J. R. C. (1956) *Excavations at Jarlshof, Shetland*. Edinburgh, HMSO.

Hamilton, J. R. C. (1968) *Excavations at Clickhimin, Shetland*. Edinburgh, HMSO.

Harding, D. W. (1995) *Atlantic Scotland and the Western Seaways*, (Paper presented to Tenth International Congress of Celtic Studies, Edinburgh, 1995). University of Edinburgh, Department of Archaeology.

Harding, D. W. (2000) *The Hebridean Iron Age: Twenty Years' Research*, University of Edinburgh Department of Archaeology, Occasional Paper 20.

Harding, D. W., Blake, I. M. and Reynolds, P. J. (1993) *An Iron Age Settlement in Dorset: Excavation and Reconstruction*, University of Edinburgh, Department of Archaeology, Monograph No 1.

Harding, D. W. and Dixon, T. N. (2000) *Dun Bharabhat, Cnip: An Iron Age Settlement in West Lewis, Vol. 1, Structures and Material Culture*. University of Edinburgh Department of Archaeology, Calanais Research Series, No 2.

Harding, D. W. and Gilmour, S. M. G. (2000) *The Iron Age Settlement at Beirgh, Riof, Isle of Lewis, Excavations 1985-95, Vol.1, The Structures and Stratigraphy*. University of Edinburgh Department of Archaeology, Calanais Research Series, No 1.

Hawkes, C. F. C. (1959) The ABC of the British Iron Age, *Antiquity* 33, 170-82.

Heald, A. (2001) Knobbed spearbutts of the British and Irish Iron Age: new examples and new thoughts, *Antiquity*, 75, 689-96.

Henderson, J. (1987) The Iron Age of 'Loughey' and Meare: Some Inferences from Glass Analysis, *Antiquaries Journal* 67, 29-42.

Henderson, J. (1991) Industrial Specialization in Late Iron Age Britain and Europe, *Archaeological Journal*, 148, 104-48.

Jope, E. M., and Wilson, B. C. S. (1957) A burial of the first century AD near Donaghadee, County Down, *Ulster Journal of Archaeology*, 3rd series, 20, 73-95.

Lane, A. (1987) English migrants in the Hebrides: Atlantic Second B revisited, *Proceedings of the Society of Antiquaries of Scotland* 117, 47-66.

MacKie, E. W. 1(971) English migrants and Scottish brochs, *Glasgow Archaeological Journal* 2, 39-71.

Mackie, E. W. (1974) *Dun Mor Vaul: an Iron Age broch on Tiree*, Glasgow, University of Glasgow Press.

MacKie, E. W. (1995) The early Celts in Scotland. In Green, M. J. (ed), *The Celtic World*, 654-670. London, Routledge.

MacKie, E. W. (2000) The Scottish Atlantic Iron Age: Indigenous and Isolated or Part of a Wider European World? In Henderson, J., (ed) *The Prehistory and Early History of Atlantic Europe*, British Archaeological Reports International Series 861, 99-116. Oxford, BAR.

Raftery, B. (1984) *La Tène in Ireland. Problems of Origin and Chronology.* Marburg, Vorgeschichtlichen Seminars Marburg, Sonderband 2.

Sandars, N. K. (1957) *Bronze Age Cultures in France,* Cambridge, Cambridge University Press.

Scott, Sir Lindsay (1948) Gallo-British colonies: the aisled roundhouse culture in the north, *Proceedings of the Prehistoric Society* 14, 46-125.

Topping, P.G. (1987) Typology and Chronology in the later prehistoric pottery assemblages of the Western Isles. *Proceedings of the Society of Antiquaries of Scotland* 117, 67-84.

Tuohy, T. (1999) *Prehistoric Combs of Antler and Bone.* British Archaeological Reports, British Series 285, Oxford, BAR.

Wheeler, R.E.M. (1943) *Maiden Castle, Dorset.* Oxford University Press, Report No XII of Research Committee of the Society of Antiquaries of London.

Wheeler, R .E. M., and Richardson, K. M. (1957) *Hillforts of Northern France.* Oxford University Press for the Society of Antiquaries of London.

Old Scatness: The First Millennium AD

Stephen J. Dockrill, Julie M. Bond & Cathy M. Batt

THE EXCAVATION of a multi-period settlement mound at Old Scatness in the South Shetland Mainland (Fig. 12) has a unique archaeological research potential. The archaeological sequence identified at Old Scatness consists of a broch and wheelhouse together with Pictish, Norse and Post-Medieval settlement. Settlement continuity at Old Scatness from the Broch period to the 20th century allows research themes of cultural and economic continuity, adaptation and change to be studied within a broad research framework. This paper focuses on three areas forming the research core to the excavation and provides a structural overview of the archaeological evidence for the Iron Age so far.

The mid and late Iron Age settlement at Old Scatness is not archaeologically unique, as it is mirrored by evidence from the past excavations at the nearby site of Jarlshof (located at the head of the Sumburgh peninsula several kilometres to the south of Old Scatness (see Fig. 51, Turner, this volume). However, the Jarlshof excavations took place before the dawn of environmental and scientific archaeology and the resulting evidence is limited. Old Scatness has the potential to supplement comparable data missing from these earlier excavations at Jarlshof (Hamilton 1956) allowing a complete re-evaluation for this 'type site' and the surrounding landscape.

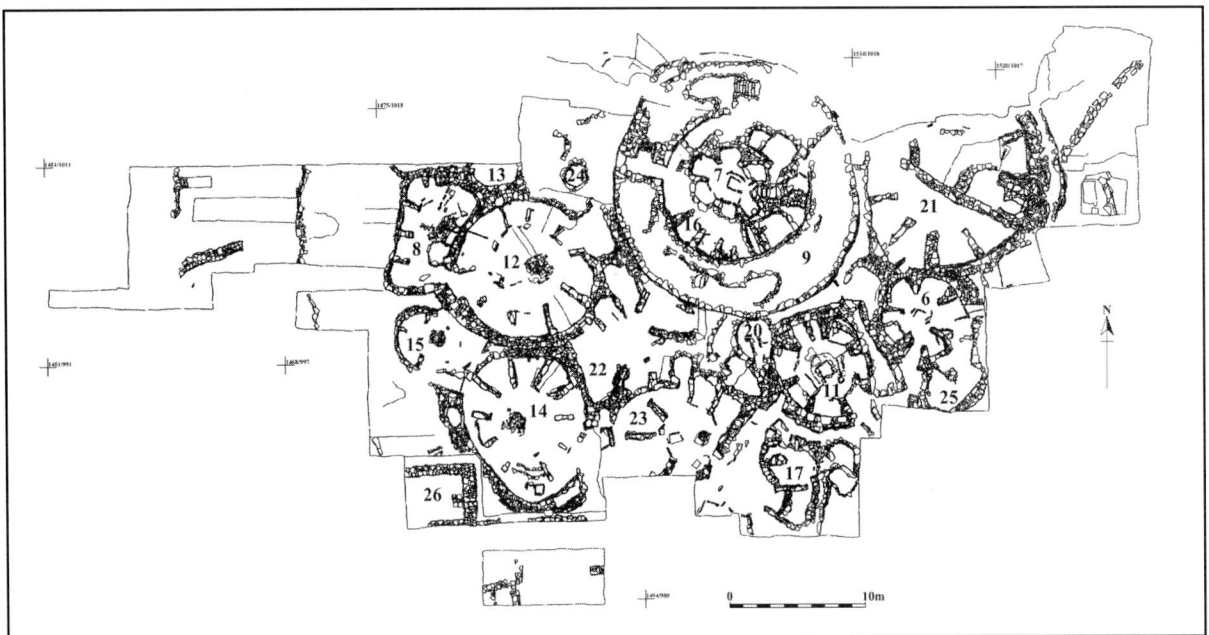

Fig.12 *Plan showing Late Iron Age structures.*

THE RESEARCH AGENDA

Three major research objectives are at the heart of the Old Scatness excavation programme, the first of which is the need to develop a reliable absolute chronology for the site. The second objective is to examine the site's economy within that chronological framework. The third research theme, resulting from the full analysis of the cultural and economic evidence, is a refined understanding of Broch and later Iron Age society and an understanding of the Pictish to Norse transition. Within this framework we may go some way towards answering questions of economy, society and past lifestyles and how these developed through time at Old Scatness. Elements of this research, such as the exploitation of resources and the surrounding landscape, as well as the analysis of the structures within a tight absolute chronological framework, are significantly enhancing the evidence presented at Jarlshof and our understanding of the North Atlantic Iron Age as a whole.

Old Scatness represents an integrated research project driven by questions about economy and society, and owes its origins to the wider multi-disciplinary approach to archaeological excavations begun by Renfrew with his excavation campaign in Orkney in the early seventies (Renfrew 1985, 5). Central to Renfrew's new approach to research was the application of both radiocarbon dating to provide a chronological framework and environmental archaeology to reconstruct past environments and economies (*ibid.*). Today these are central features of modern excavation research designs, but they were unavailable to excavators in the earlier twentieth century. Sites such as Jarlshof were excavated using local labourers to empty the structures. Stratigraphic and contextual recording for artefacts lacked the rigour made possible by today's understanding. In a modern excavation, such as Old Scatness, the manipulation of large volumes of contextual information concerning the stratification sequence and artefacts is facilitated by computerised management of data. Added to this, the integration of disciplines within today's archaeology has the potential to add significantly to our existing knowledge. It is within an integrated multi-disciplinary research framework that the excavation of Old Scatness is being undertaken. The project is a partnership between Shetland Amenity Trust and members of the Department of Archaeological Sciences, University of Bradford.

A QUESTION OF TIME

The establishment of an integrated absolute chronology for Old Scatness is essential in order to provide a framework for the excavated data that will allow interpretation and understanding of questions surrounding the site's past inhabitants and their cultural identity. Evidence for either continuity or for social or economic change on such a multi-period site requires a viable and tested chronological framework in which the evidence may be examined. Although the aim of establishing an absolute chronological framework occurs on all modern high calibre excavations, the sampling in many cases is often reflective, with radiocarbon samples being selected during post excavation work. At Old Scatness the dating programme is based on the integration of techniques, requiring the generation of research questions in the field and sampling during the excavation process.

Three scientific dating methods have been employed so far; archaeomagnetic dating of *in situ* fired structures such as hearths by Dr C. Batt and Z. Outram (University of Bradford), accelerator radiocarbon dating of carbonised plant remains (barley grains) from secure depositional events and surfaces, and lastly optically stimulated luminescence (OSL) dating of the last exposure to light of quartz grains within the stratigraphic sequence. At site level a collaborative project with researchers at the University of Oxford is targeting the midden depositional sequences and, at an off-site, level OSL investigations of wind blown sands and buried soils forms a focus of research by Simpson and Turner (University of Stirling) and Burbidge (formerly University of Wales).

The research nature of this project gives a time depth (from 1995-2003 under present funding) that facilitates such methodological integration. Such a luxury is not available to many projects, especially those contracted in response to rescue/developmental threat. The application of this combination of methods to targeted chronological problems has shown great potential in not only the validation and reinforcement of dates produced by a single method but perhaps more importantly in the production of a more precise chronology with the application of Bayesian statistics to date sequences (Buck *et al.* 1996; Batt 1998).

An accurate chronological framework is essential in furthering any reassessment of material from other sites such as Jarlshof, which were excavated before the rigorous stratigraphic recording and three-dimensional location of artefacts that are associated with archaeological practice today.

THE ECONOMIC EVIDENCE

As with the need to establish a chronological framework in which to study the archaeological data, there is the need to understand the site's economy in terms of arable cultivation, animal husbandry, hunting, fishing and use of terrestrial, marine and intertidal resources. These elements are essential to the understanding of the site's stability and viability as a settlement focus over time, together with awareness of the past lifestyles of the inhabitants. The absence of economic data on so many early broch excavations, including that of Jarlshof, makes this a key feature of the Old Scatness

excavation programme. Data interpretation and understanding is being facilitated by comparative investigations of the economic material from archaeological contexts from Old Scatness with information available from historic and ethnographic records.

Particular emphasis has been placed on understanding the surrounding soils and the importance of infield arable cultivation. This work on the cultivated soil sequence (in association with Prof I.A. Simpson, University of Stirling) has identified a sequence spanning the late Neolithic/Early Bronze Age through to the early 20th century. Stratigraphic data and the use of radiocarbon and OSL have suggested a chronology for these soils. Characterisation of these soils using conventional thin-section micromorphological analysis provides evidence for continuity in the addition of soil amendments and infield management, but with a significant change in the nature of the manuring strategy over time. In the Neolithic and Bronze Age the soils are characterised by the application of domestic wastes with substantial volumes of ash (Simpson *et al.* 1998, 111). A significant change occurs within the Early Iron Age soils surrounding the settlement, with a move to animal manures (*ibid.*).

Cultivation in the Iron Age at the Old Scatness site appears to be based on the "infield" area created by the earlier occupants of the site. The continued focus of settlement and surrounding infield results in the infield becoming an important resource in its own right and crucial to the settlement's viability. This form of agriculture ensured high yields in normal circumstances over relatively small acreages because of the fertility and soil structure obtained by the manuring strategy and intensive soil management (in terms of cultivation and weeding). The crop best suited to cultivation in the infield is six-row barley, which dominates the carbonised plant assemblages from the site. The occurrence of the black or Shetland oat in the Iron Age samples represents the cultivation of a plant which favours poorer sandy soils and may represent the utilisation of these soils. An expansion of the infield area appears to have taken place during the Late Iron Age and Norse phase of the site (Simpson *et al.* 1998, 122). Bond, Nicholson and Simpson present a more comprehensive review of the economic evidence from Old Scatness in this volume.

A QUESTION OF STATUS

In Hingley's review of the Scottish Iron Age, broch sites are seen as representing substantial houses in the North Atlantic region whose owners control and maintain power through the manipulation of subservient communities by the control of services and agricultural production (Hingley 1992, 24-5). Within such a framework, awareness of the economic resource is an essential ingredient to the understanding of Iron Age society and status. Economic wealth in a rural community underlies the wealth seen within the material culture through trade and exchange and craft specialisation (perhaps embodied in the specialist broch builder or metals-smith). Material culture provides a framework for viewing wealth and status in terms of prestige artefacts such as metalwork. McDonnell has argued that the presence of iron working and copper alloy working on broch sites (both in the Broch phase and most importantly in the post-Broch phases) form an important indicator of status (McDonnell 1998, 159-160 and this volume).

The questions of social hierarchy and status are also bound up with the control of both natural and agricultural resources. For example, if an 'elite' central storage model is envisaged barley could be collected as tithe, providing a bankable resource which may be stored in times of surplus and redistributed to the underlying or 'client' population during poor years, or it might be used as a tradable commodity (Dockrill 1998, 77). Such a system would have the potential to provide security for the 'client' population in times of stress and would reinforce the power-base and wealth of the broch elite. It is significant that Old Scatness is situated within one of the most fertile areas in Shetland and the importance of this area to agricultural production is perhaps demonstrated by the density of brochs within the South Dunrossness region of Shetland. These issues of status and the control of economic wealth are discussed in greater detail within the paper 'Brochs, economy and power' (Dockrill 2002, 153-162).

The intensive study of the site of Old Scatness and surrounding landscape is providing new insights into the available economic resource as well as providing evidence for activities such as metal working and artefacts representing trading contacts. The integration of this evidence is beginning to allow a better understanding of Iron Age society and its changes through the first millennium AD.

THE ARCHAEOLOGICAL SEQUENCE AT OLD SCATNESS

The second part of this paper discusses the archaeological evidence, focusing on the Iron Age structural sequence at the Old Scatness site. As such this is an interim statement based on the analysis and conclusions drawn in the main from the first six years of the project (but up-dated at the end of the 2003 season). A further account of the structural sequence may be found in Dockrill (2003, 82-94). All of the scientific dates quoted below are calibrated and are calculated to 95% confidence.

THE EARLIEST EVIDENCE

The earliest evidence for human activity on the Old Scatness site is provided by a layer of cultural sediment containing struck quartz dating to the late Neolithic / Early Bronze Age. This is sealed by a quartz sand which forms a 'natural' stratigraphic marker across the site. This sand deposit is sealed by a red midden under the north face of the broch and elsewhere by a reddish soil with visible carbon inclusions. Micromorphology of the soil indicates the anthropogenic influence behind the creation of this deposit, as it has an exceptionally high ash-midden content (Simpson *et al.* 1998, 116). The interpretation of this soil as a cultivated arable infield is supported by at least two sets of ard marks (Plate 2) formed by the use of a primitive plough. The deposit is associated with thick poorly fired pottery containing coarse rock, schist or siltstone temper that suggests a Late Bronze Age context. Both radiocarbon and OSL dating also indicates a Late Bronze Age / Early Iron Age date for this soil.

It is interesting that Lamb identified a "brown" soil with ard cultivation sealing sand at the nearby site of Sumburgh Airport (Downes and Lamb 2000, 8). The question arises as to whether the brown soil identified at Old Scatness is part of the same infield system? If so, what was the nature of the early settlement? The Sumburgh house forms comprise two adjoining structures representing possibly a 'homestead' of a single household or family unit. Was the primary settlement a dispersed cluster of such 'homesteads' as seen in the west mainland of Shetland at sites such as Stanydale, Gruting School and the Scord of Brouster, with each settlement being associated with an arable infield? If so, is there a pre-broch sequence of occupation for the Old Scatness site? At present the excavated evidence is unable to answer these questions.

THE BROCH PERIOD

Although the pre-broch deposits forming the mound have yet to be excavated, the circuit of the broch, some 18.5 metres in diameter, has been exposed by excavation (Fig. 12 and Plate 1). It must be remembered that the broch (Structure 9) is not at base or ground level at

every point and as these structures have external battered walls, the ground level diameter will be consequently greater. The broch wall varies in width between 3.5 to 3.8 metres. The outer wall and inner walls of the broch have been defined, although partial collapse of the inner wall on several segments of the broch has limited investigation of both galleries and the remains of intramural corbelled cells in the 2000 excavation season. In 2002 a ground floor cell on the northern circuit of the broch revealed an internally blocked passage leading into the broch and an intramural stairway leading clockwise from the ground floor level to the first floor. An intramural stairway leading up in a clockwise direction from a first floor level was identified during the 2000 season, rising from a gallery over the west facing entrance passage. Below the lintels forming the first floor level over the entrance passage, the door jambs and bar holes of the inner broch door were identified. In 2003 the entrance of the broch at ground floor level and an outer door with *in situ* pivot and threshold stones were discovered. The passageway was found to extend at least a metre beyond the broch's outer wall. The slight curvature seen within the northern wall of this outer passage way suggests a slight funnel-like form to the corridor leading to the broch door. A massive triangular lintel above the entrance provides a visible statement of monumentality, together with structural support. A crawl-way leads from the gallery at second floor level over the passageway beyond the inner door. Spaced lintels set on edge allow observation into the underlying passage. This would have provided the opportunity for the broch occupants to vet the entry of individuals within the passage beyond the internal door. This crawl-way might also allow an offensive opportunity against any would be attacker in the restricted entrance passage below.

Excavation in 2003 between four of the piers of the secondary structure (Structure 16) within the southern arc of the broch interior revealed a scarcement ledge at first floor level.

The construction of the broch wall is characterised by a high standard of craftsmanship. Outer and inner walls consist of large faced blocks varying in size from around 0.75m to 0.5m. The junctions between these stone blocks are tightly closed and the horizontal coursing is maintained by the use of thin packing stones to level the faced wall stones where necessary. The standard of walling associated with the broch surpasses that seen in later structures and might imply the use of a craft specialist.

The broch construction

The excavation of the north face of the 1975 cutting allowed the broch construction to be examined in detail between 2001 and 2003. The broch was constructed over midden on the north face and over a flag raft on the northeast arc and the northwest arc. The flag raft appears to have been used in order to disperse the weight of the tower. The initial wall construction over the midden appears to have subsided, requiring reinforcement by large orthostats running parallel to the broch wall, which at this point contained a rubble fill. This feature appears to provide a buttress-like support to the brochs foundation. The flag raft either side of this stretch of walling overlies the buried soil to the northeast and peat to the northwest. At this point the wall of the broch on the northwestern side is a course wider in diameter and is keyed into the original northern circuit. This increase in diameter appears to be intentional and may have provided a greater weight distribution over the softer peat. This zone of paving was covered with yellow clay, as was a curved wall concentric with the broch. Here the application of clay seems to have been to act as a sealant for the underlying peat. Initial radiocarbon and OSL dates suggest a date for construction between 400 and 200BC. Further

dating samples were taken in 2003 and it is hoped that a higher precision date for the broch construction might be achieved. The underlying peat dates from 400BC–90 cal. BC (Context 5205, Lab. ref. GU-11105).

A second blocked entrance within this northern circuit may have been a constructional feature allowing direct access to the staircase, however the destruction in 1975 within this zone limits interpretation.

The ditch

The defensive nature of the broch is reinforced by the presence of a stone-revetted ditch, some 8m wide, at the western base of the mound. This feature was identified on both the magnetic and earth resistance survey conducted before the commencement of the excavation. Excavation confirmed that the sharp western edge of this anomaly, identified within both data sets, represents the contrast between the ditch infill and the infield soil sequence discussed earlier together with the underlying sand. The unstable nature of this sand appears to have necessitated the use of a drystone revetment for the ditch, which is near-vertical on the western edge. The primary infilling of the ditch contained cattle bones many of which were from 'beef age' cattle. The presence of beef cattle might be seen as an indicator of wealth and status, which could be associated with 'feasting' within a chiefdom society. The butchery marks on the bone indicate the use of a substantial iron cleaver. Radiocarbon dating of the bone indicates a date between 390 and 110 cal. BC (Context 305, Lab. ref. GU-11106).

Projection of the rampart from truncated tips behind the mound suggests that the distance from the ditch floor to rampart top might have been in excess of 6m. This would have presented a formidable barrier to any potential attacker and reinforces the monumentality and status of the settlement, complementing the monumental architecture of the broch.

THE POST-BROCH SEQUENCE

Excavations from 1997 to 2003 have revealed that an extensive post- broch settlement existed around the remains of the broch tower in what can be considered as being contemporary with the late use of the broch through the Middle (200BC-200 cal. AD) and Late Iron Age period (conventionally dated to 200-800 cal. AD). This settlement shows clear evidence of modification and growth and shift in focus with no visible indicators of abandonment.

The aisled roundhouses

A substantial complex of structures west of the broch tower provide a secondary sequence to that of the broch. This structural sequence is centred on an aisled roundhouse (Structure 12) some 10m in internal diameter. Internal evidence indicates the presence of radial piers with some evidence for corbelling of the inner wall on the northern side of the structure. A central hearth was replaced by a sequence of off-centre hearths, set within a kerbed zone in the southeast quadrant of the structure. A flagged walkway ran between this hearth service zone and the piers in the southern section. The cells, which were created by the radial piers were flagged by several layers of horizontally laid tabular stone. Rather than representing a number of re-surfacing events this layering suggests a structured approach to raise the height of the cells.

There is strong evidence for later modification within the structure. An original western entrance appears to have been blocked. As part of the secondary refurbish-ment a rectangular cell was added to the northeast circuit of the building and the aisled piers on this side and on the southern arc were infilled. A doorway to the southeast, which survives complete with *in situ* lintel, appears to relate to a secondary phase of use for this building. Evidence here suggests that the wall was reconstructed straight rather than corbelled, to facilitate the insertion of an upper mezzanine level supported by the piers. Access to this higher level was gained by the infilled original entrance to the east where the blocking incorporated a series of steps. Rebuilding of the western wall facilitated the insertion of the specialist building, Structure 8.

The abandonment of Structure 12

Structure 12 abandonment occurs with the collapse of the inner wall face and pier on the northeast half of the north wall. The destruction seems to have been caused by the collapse of an orthostat forming a pier-head into a void created within an underlying structure presumably contemporary with the broch construction. This shift lead to a major structural collapse, evidenced by the *in-situ* rubble and flags that had been left uncleared.

The cultural infilling

Structure 12's infill is of ash midden sealing rubble. The upper depositional sequence of the ash midden tips suggests both a primary and structured deposition rather than mixed material that may have been moved several times around the site. The use of roofless discarded buildings as receptacles for ash midden is replicated across the site. Infilling from this building appears to occur from the east, with the final tips of material sealing the walls of the structure and butting the broch wall. This material has produced a good range of carbonised plant material and the micro-environment created by these deposits has facilitated the survival of bone. The material contains domestic midden but a significant proportion of the material originates as ash residues from fuel burning. Dating of carbonised barley from two tip layers from this sequence produced AMS radiocarbon dates suggesting deposition somewhere between 86BC to 216 cal. AD (42BC-216 cal. AD: Context 1728, Lab No AA-3426, GU8379) and 86BC-127 cal. AD (Context 1729, Lab no AA-34525, GU8380). These early dates have been supported by provisional OSL dates on quartz inclusions (Rhodes *pers. comm.*).

The surrounding structures

A second aisled roundhouse (Structure 14, Plate 3) adjoining the southern wall of Structure 12 has a slightly smaller diameter of some 9m. Structure 14 indicates substantial structural preservation with internal wall 'cupboards', a scarcement ledge and at least eight drystone supporting pillars forming radial spokes. The coincidence of the surviving height of both these radial supports and of the level of the scarcement ledge strongly suggests the presence of an upper floor level to this structure. This construction technique is paralleled within the aisled roundhouse at Jarlshof (Hamilton 1956, 200). The partial obscuring of one of the internal wall 'cupboards' by one of these piers may indicate that these represent a secondary refurbishment of the structure (again paralleled by the Jarlshof aisled roundhouse).

One piered bay of this structure was heavily modified, being transformed into a cell with an entrance linking this cell to an amorphous structure to the northeast. The rest of Structure 14 was backfilled with midden. This amorphous building is also linked to the late phase of Structure 12, with the south-eastern entrance of Structure 12 leading into this later structure. Substantial collapse of this amorphous structure and the walling in the vicinity of the Structure 12 entrance indicates subsidence, presumably into earlier structures underlying this complex.

To the south of the central roundhouse, a second adjoining building (Structure 15) appears to cut Structure 14. This sub-circular building some 5m in diameter, although robbed has three piers surviving and a central hearth. The hearth surround is formed by the use of flat beach pebbles placed upright in the floor. An entrance to the passageway to the north (which also leads into the west entrance of Structure 12) was blocked during the life of this building. This phase appears to be associated with a secondary floor surface associated with Structure 14.

Adjoining the western wall of the central roundhouse (Structure 12) is a piered sub-rectangular building (Structure 8). This structure appears to be different to the others discussed, with short rectangular piers ending in orthostats dividing the long axis of the structure into three approximately equal zones on the western side. A degree of symmetry exists on the eastern wall, afforded by piers and orthostatic divisions. Centrally placed along the east wall is a rectangular drystone box constructed by walling and orthostats, with a central opening in the stone shelf which forms the top of the structure and a flue-like hole at the base, suggesting an oven (Plate 4). This oven is adjacent to a large hearth area situated to the north and against the east wall. Perhaps significantly, clay rendering can be seen on the walling. There is also the suggestion of a linking blocked entrance into the larger roundhouse (Structure 12). This building appears to have a specialist function in terms of the position of the large hearth and the oven-like structure. One possibility is that this represents a specialised cooking area adjacent to the large roundhouse Structure 12. Alternatively it is possible that this area might be associated with some specialised processing such as grain drying or the processing of fish oil.

The presence of a sub-circular structure (Structure 13) to the north of the large central 'roundhouse' (Structure 12) provides a degree of symmetry in the building layout of the settlement. Although only the north facing circumference and part of the midden fill of this structure has been examined, as the majority of the structure lies under the main north /south section which bisects both the broch and the mound, this building has proved to be of particular interest. In the wall on its internal south and south-west arc are a group of 9 wall 'cupboards' in three tiers. Some of the upper cupboards have lost their capping due to later disturbance but the lower structures are complete. On the eastern internal wall face of the same structure a thin layer or 'skim' of yellow clay has been applied to the stone wall-face. This clay, as with that recorded in Structure 8, appears to be a form of rendering to the face and is not associated with any attempt at sealing the junctions between the dry stone courses.

Excavation since 2000 has clearly identified that both Structure 15 and Structure 8 are secondary buildings to Structures 14 and 12 respectively. These new structures are associated with major alterations within the original buildings that echo changes seen within the aisled roundhouse at Jarlshof.

Radiocarbon dates for late occupation surfaces from Structures 8 and 15 suggest an early date for this building complex. Structure 8 has an AMS radiocarbon date between cal. 342BC-0AD (Context 1818, Lab. ref. AA-37259, GU-8873) and Structure 15 a date of cal. 348BC-2BC (Context 1909, Lab. ref. AA-37257, GU-8875). These buildings are significantly higher within the stratigraphy than the projected ground surface associated with the broch. The collapse of some of these structural elements may be due to subsidence probably associated with settlement /collapse of earlier buildings, possibly contemporary with the building of the broch. These early dates for Structure 8 and 15, together with those for the midden infilling of Structure 12, further support an origin for the Old Scatness broch earlier than the accepted 100BC-100AD date for broch construction.

Long piered structures

The broch appears to have been standing higher than at present during this settlement phase, as rubble associated with the robbing of the broch wall overlies the depositional sequence infilling Structure 12. There is clear evidence for the later refurbishment of the broch (Structure 16), which might be contemporary with other long piered structures present at Old Scatness: either the modified Structure 12 or the slightly later Structure 21. A secondary internal wall face was added to the south-eastern face of the broch. It is unclear whether the addition of this wall was just a structural re-lining or whether it facilitated the addition of other structural features.

East of the broch evidence for further large piered structures are present; these structures, (Structure 17, Structure 21, Structure 23 and Structure 25) reflect a settlement phase for the early centuries AD (in between the structural sequence described above and the wheelhouse sequence discussed in detail below). These structures again show a high degree of modification and the use of long piers in their later developments. It has not been possible to fully excavate all of these structures, but one (Structure 21) is worthy of specific comment here. Structure 21 is subdivided into two elements by a dividing wall similar to that found within the aisled roundhouse at Jarlshof. This building displays clear evidence for an upper mezzanine floor, with the collapse of one of the flooring flags together with an external staircase.

A corn-dryer forms one of the last additions to the structure, the bowl of which contained carbonised grain from its last usage. The kiln element of the dryer was found to be associated with a small flagged room, which incorporated the north face of the dividing wall. The flag surface appeared to be heat cracked. The zone to the south of this corn dryer seems to have been used for midden dumping in this late phase.

Evidence for metalworking, with finds of over 40 moulds including those of pins and penannular brooches, is associated with the late midden infill within this building. Midden infilling this structure has produced an AMS radiocarbon date of 222AD-530AD (Context 0579, Lab. ref AA-34533, GU8370).

PICTISH WHEELHOUSES AND CELLULAR BUILDINGS

Outside the broch in the south eastern part of the excavation area two wheelhouse structures survive. The area to the south of the broch is dominated by a large sub-circular building (Structure 11) with an internal diameter of some 6m and seven structural piers. These piers differ from those identified in Structure 12, being triangular in shape and having a strong suggestion of corbelling which mirrors the corbelled radial cells seen at the near complete Jarlshof W2 (Hamilton 1956 Fig 22). The primary floor associated with the triangular piers has a horseshoe kerbed hearth zone containing a rectangular stone set hearth. Dating evidence obtained from the primary and subsequent hearths, using both AMS radiocarbon and archaeomagnetic methods, suggest that this building was occupied during the 9th and 10th centuries AD (Dockrill *et al.* 2002). It is assumed that this evidence relates to the re-use of the structure; since the stone-lined hearth is sunken this may cut through what are likely to be earlier floor deposits associated with the triangular piered primary floor.

The surrounding cells within the piers would have been set at a higher raised level to the central service area. A smaller cell (Structure 20) provides an inner sanctum opposite the entrance.

In 2002 a finely incised carving of a bear was found on the underside of a dressed flag. It is possible that this carving may have been part of an orthostat pier terminal opposite the entrance. The carving is clearly of quality status and reflects the continued wealth of the site within the Pictish period.

This wheelhouse shows evidence for an extended period of use and modification. The triangular piers clearly postdate the circumference walling of this building, the stonework of which shares the same characteristics as that of the dividing wall of

Structure 21, suggesting that the structural shell is being utilised for a period in excess of seven hundred years. Two blocked entrances on the southern circumference again are indicative of the long use of this building.

A second wheelhouse (Structure 6), some 5m in diameter with 6 radial triangular piers, has been excavated to its primary floor surface. This building was inserted into a larger earlier structure and reuses several wall elements of this earlier structure. As with the examples at Jarlshof, the piers terminate with an upright orthostat. There is clear evidence that these piers, like those in Structure 11, represent corbelled cells similar to W2 at Jarlshof (Hamilton 1956, 67-68). (An experimental reconstruction of a corbelled wheelhouse using the ground plan of Structure 6 in the 2000 season illustrated the possibilities available with corbelling techniques). The entrance to Structure 6 is on the south-western side of the structure and is connected by a passageway running off to the south west. At least four floor surfaces have been identified, each of which is associated with a central hearth. The earliest hearth has produced an archaeo-magnetic date of 500-750 cal. AD (Context 1248, Lab. no. OSB14). The secondary floor has produced an AMS radiocarbon date of cal. 664AD-891AD (Context 1146, Lab ref. AA-34528, GU-8377) and an archaeo-magnetic date of 750-850 (Context 1175, Lab no. OSB12). Two further AMS radiocarbon dates for the third phase of the structure suggest occupation between cal. 695AD-981AD at (Context 890, Lab ref. AA-34530, GU8375) and 642AD - 890AD at (Context 872, Lab. ref. AA34531, GU8374). The last phase of this structure is associated with the construction of an inner wall between the piers on the north-west of the structure and a later layer of paving laid in the cell formed between these piers. AMS radiocarbon dating for barley from this phase provides a date of cal. 663AD and 890AD (Context 838, Lab ref. AA-34533,

GU8372). When processed, taking into account stratigraphic order, this sequence of dates will produce a refined absolute chronology for the development and occupation of this building.

A third piered building form (Structure 17) is partially visible within the excavation area to the south of Structure 11. An east-west passageway leading into Structure 6 separates these two buildings.

To the north a multi-cellular semi-subterranean structure characteristic of Pictish architecture (Structure 5, Plate 5) was found to have been added to an earlier complex of cells and corridors lying under the main north/south section. These new cells appear to have been inserted into earlier deposits, with large tabular blocks set upright at the base of the structure providing a foundation course for the inner drystone face lining the subterranean element of the structure. During construction the builders incorporated part of an *in-situ* pier of an earlier building. The subsequent weight of Structure 5's walling caused it to crack over this pier. Evidence for the wall above the subterranean element of Structure 5 does not survive, although traces of a reddish soil halo around the structure might be used to argue for the presence of a turf jacket type construction with an inner stone facing. A stone alignment on the north-east side provides a concentric "halo" for part of Structure 5 which could be interpreted as representing the footings for roof timbers.

The larger cell of Structure 5 contained a central hearth defined by a horseshoe arrangement of small upright stones or orthostats which butt two larger inward facing orthostats set each side of the entrance. Curiously, if these two uprights are contemporary they would funnel anyone entering the cell directly into the hearth. One of the hearth-stones was found to have been inscribed with a carving of a boar. This stone may have a symbolic positioning or meaning.

An archaeomagnetic date for the hearth suggests a date between 600AD and 850AD at 95% confidence (Batt 1998, 130). The entrance-way from the passage was blocked before the building was abandoned.

This building is characteristic in construction and conforms to type with a number of examples in the Northern Isles which form a figure of 8 shape (Ritchie 1985, 193-8). This form of structure is considered as being characteristic of Pictish culture within the Northern Isles, dating to a period within the later half of the first millennium AD (conventionally 600-800). What is significant about the Old Scatness structure is its infill, which contains artefacts that are diagnostic of the early Norse period, suggesting that the site contains an unbroken sequence of settlement crossing the archaeologically significant interface between the Pictish and Norse cultures.

Structure 5 appears to have been part of a larger settlement complex, which included a tertiary cellular building (Structure 7, Plate 6) constructed within the broch. The building is formed by single faced walls and contains 5 cells divided from the central area by either low walls or orthostats. A hearth similar to that found in Structure 11 dominates the central area. To the east a short passage leads from the centre of Structure 7 to a doorway (with an *in situ* lintel) through which a sub-rectangular cell was formed against the relined broch wall. This 'clover-leaf' style structure is connected to the passageway to Structure 5 by a curving stepped entrance passage running to the east. Halfway along this passage an orthostat formed a door block, while an associated whale-bone pivot survived *in-situ*. Evidence derived from the walling and rubble contained within this structure strongly suggests that this building may have been corbelled. Two AMS radiocarbon dates are available for the late use of Structure 7; they are cal. 688AD-924AD (Context 2248, Lab. ref. AA-37256, GU-8876) and cal. 444AD-659AD (Context 2290, Lab. ref. AA-37255, GU-8873).

Two further cellular building elements (Structures 19 and 20) are located on the western edge of Structure 11. These two structures appear to cut the original form of Structure 11. Structure 19 has a similar orthostatic lower course paralleling the construction method seen in Structure 5. A central hearth has provided an archaeo-magnetic date of cal. 780AD-880AD (Context 1304, Lab no.OSB16) and a radiocarbon AMS date of cal. 662AD-881AD (Context 1304, Lab. ref. AA-37258, GU-8874). The structure adjoins a passage to the southeast which runs to the southwest and a spur which runs southwest against the south external walls of Structure 11 and Structure 17.

THE PICTISH/NORSE INTERFACE AND NORSE SETTLEMENT

A large number of artefacts (loom weights, steatite bowl fragments and spindle whorls) within the upper fill of Structure 11 have provided a significant Norse assemblage. These artefacts are associated with native pottery forms (see below for further discussion). There was no observable evidence for either a stone-walled or post-constructed Norse structure, although disturbance by later activity may have removed traces of the latter. The artefacts appeared to be confined within Structure 11 with many being associated with a floor surface constructed on this infill and contained within the structure. A central long hearth associated with this floor has produced an archaeomagnetic date of cal. 850-960 AD at (Context 1127, Lab. no. OSB11). Two AMS radiocarbon dates for carbonised barley have produced the following result; cal. 781AD-1018AD (Context 786, Lab ref. AA-345343, GU8371) and cal. 692AD-982AD (Context 1111, Lab. ref. AA34529, GU83676). A significant proportion of artefacts from the floor appear to be early Norse in character rather than a native use of steatite.

Unpublished postgraduate research by Bradford student Amanda Forster has indicated that the carinated steatite bowls from these deposits have direct parallels to those from graves in southern Norway which are thought to date between 750 and 850 AD (*pers. comm*). In the Western Isles "platter ware" is seen as ceramic form of a 'bakestone' and has been used to characterise Norse settlement; steatite bakestones found at Old Scatness perform the same function and again may represent an artefact associated with early Viking settlement rather than one associated with a native tradition.

Viking artefacts associated with the final phase of Structure 6 suggest a usage contemporary with the late floor seen in Structure 11. Fish and animal bone found on and above the flag surface suggest that the building may have been utilised as a smoke house or "skeo" during this late period of use.

The infilling of the characteristic Pictish multi-cellular building (Structure 5) described above provides evidence for steatite artefacts that can be considered to be diagnostic of the Norse period. These included a steatite line sinker whose closest parallel is with a Late Viking example from Rogaland in southern Norway, dating to 900 - 1000 AD (Foldøy 1995, 149). These artefacts at Old Scatness appear with a distinctive thin walled form of pottery with a barrel shaped body and a simple rounded rim form. The appearance of this ceramic form is repeated in other excavation contexts containing steatite, suggesting that native ceramic traditions survived into the Early Norse period. Similar forms of pottery appear at Jarlshof within the uppermost levels of Hut 2, the latest multi-cellular structure identified by Hamilton (1956, 88-91).

Norse presence on the site is further supported by preliminary analysis of the botanical remains. Flax (argued as being a crop whose appearance within the archaeological record of the late first millennium is in many cases associated with Norse agricultural intensification; Bond 1994) also appears in the midden infill of the Pictish structure.

Although there is no surviving structural evidence for Early Norse buildings within the excavated areas, the evidence points to a strong Norse presence on the site. Perhaps more important is the evidence for surviving "native" traditions of pottery, in a period generally regarded as being near aceramic with steatite vessels taking on many of the functions of ceramics. These ceramics may in some instances be redeposited, however the integration of complete vessels within contexts with steatite artefacts from this early phase suggests an alternative explanation.

Three interpretative models are possible to explain this evidence. The first is that there are trade contacts with the Viking world and the settlement is essentially Pictish. Alternatively the steatite may form an expansion of a late Iron Age tradition, however the strong typological parallels to forms from the Viking homeland undermine this. A third model for Viking colonisation seems most likely. Old Scatness must still be seen as a status site in the Pictish period and as a prime economic farming unit would be a rich acquisition for Early Norse colonisation. Steatite working might represent a male activity and might explain the Norwegian parallels if incoming colonists undertook this craft. The cultural interaction between native Shetlander and Norse incomer suggested by the artefact assemblage might be explained by the taking of native brides and the interaction with local (free or slave) workforce.

CONCLUSION

This description of the Iron Age at Old Scatness has concentrated on the structural sequence with the post excavation analysis being very much in progress. The Iron Age phases described here provide a significant chronological framework for the first millennium AD both for Shetland and North Atlantic Britain as a whole. The structural sequence at Old Scatness provides a key to understanding the development of building forms in North Atlantic Britain. The aisled roundhouses represented by Structures 12 and 14 provide an important link to the wheelhouses of the Western Isles in both architectural style and chronology. The move from large circular building forms to smaller wheelhouses and cellular building forms raises a number of interpretive issues. A number of new questions can be asked of the data; for example, is the change in size driven by outside influence and fashion representative of social change, or was there a need to change building style because of a scarcity of timber? The roofing of smaller structures would require smaller timbers to span the buildings, and potentially other smaller structures could be corbelled.

The evidence suggests that Old Scatness is a high status settlement throughout the Iron Age period and the changes in architectural style in the centuries following the monumental broch construction do not reflect a decline in social standing. The high status nature of the settlement in the Pictish period is emphasised by the quality of the Pictish bear symbol stone found in 2002. The economic resources remain and intensify in this period, as does the evidence for metallurgy, suggesting no devaluation in status. Old Scatness and Jarlshof were perhaps among the richest farming estates throughout the Iron Age in Shetland and as such both seem to have been prime targets for Viking settlement.

BIBLIOGRAPHY

Batt, C. M. (1998) Magnetic moments in the past. In Nicholson, R.A. and Dockrill, S. J. (Eds.) *Old Scatness Broch, Shetland: Retrospect and Prospect*, 127-138 Bradford, Bradford Archaeological Sciences Research 5 / North Atlantic Biocultural Organisation Monograph 2.

Bond, J. M. (1994) *Change and Continuity in an Island System; the Palaeoeconomy of Sanday, Orkney*. Unpublished Ph.D. Thesis, University of Bradford.

Buck, C. E., Cavanagh, W. G. and Lintton, C. D. (1996) *Bayesian Approach to Interpreting Archaeological Data*. Chichester, John Wiley and Sons.

Burbidge C, I., Batt, C. M., Barnett, S. M. and Dockrill S. J. (in press) The potential for dating the Old Scatness Site, Shetland, by Optically Stimulated Luminescence. *Archaeometry.*

Dockrill, S. J. (1998) Northern Exposure: Phase 1 of the Old Scatness Excavations 1995-8. In Nicholson, R. A. and Dockrill, S. J. (eds.) *Old Scatness Broch, Shetland: Retrospect and Prospect*, 59-80 Bradford, Bradford Archaeological Sciences Research 5 / North Atlantic Biocultural Organisation Monograph 2.

Dockrill, S. J. (2002) Brochs, economy and power. In Ballin Smith, B. and Banks, I (eds.) *In the Shadow of the Brochs: The Iron Age of Scotland*, 153-162. Stroud, Tempus.

Dockrill, S. J., Bond, J. M. and Turner, V. E. (2002) *Old Scatness Broch and Jarlshof Environs Project: Field Season 2001*. Interim Report No. 7. Bradford, Shetland Amenity Trust/ University of Bradford

Dockrill, S. J. (2003) Broch, wheelhouse, and cell: redefining the Iron Age in Shetland. In Downes, J. and Ritchie, A. (eds.) *Sea Change: Orkney and Northern Europe in the Later Iron Age AD 300-800*. Balgavies, Angus, the Pinkfoot Press.

Downes, J. and Lamb, R. (2000) *Prehistoric Houses at Sumburgh in Shetland: Excavations at Sumburgh Airport 1967-74*. Oxford, Oxbow Books.

Foldøy, O. (ed.) (1995) *Finds of Rogaland: from Ice Age to Middle Ages*. The Museotec at the Archaeological museum in Stavanger. Stavanger, Arkeologisk museum I Stavanger.

Hamilton, J. R. (1956) *Excavations at Jarlshof, Shetland*, Ministry of Works Archaeological Reports No.1. Edinburgh, Her Majesty's Stationary Office.

Hingley, R. (1992) Society in Scotland from 700BC to AD200. *Proceedings of the Society of Antiquaries of Scotland* 122, 7-53.

McDonnell, J. G. (1998), Irons in the fire - evidence for ironworking on broch sites. In Nicholson R. A. and Dockrill, S. J. (Eds.) *Old Scatness Broch, Shetland: Retrospect and Prospect*, 150-162 Bradford, Bradford Archaeological Sciences Research 5 / North Atlantic Biocultural Organisation Monograph 2.

Renfrew, C. (ed.) (1985) *The Prehistory of Orkney*. Edinburgh, Edinburgh University Press.

Ritchie, A. (1985) Orkney in the Pictish Kingdom. In Renfrew, C. (ed.) *The Prehistory of Orkney*, 183-209. Edinburgh, Edinburgh University Press.

Simpson, I. A., Dockrill, S. J. and Lancaster, S. J. (1998) Making Arable Soils: Anthropogenic Soil Formation in a Multi-period Landscape. In Nicholson, R. A. and Dockrill, S. J. (eds.) *Old Scatness Broch, Shetland: Retrospect and Prospect*, 111-126, Bradford, Bradford Archaeological Sciences Research 5 / North Atlantic Biocultural Organisation Monograph 2.

Orcadian Brochs:
Complex Settlements with Complex Origins

BEVERLEY BALLIN SMITH

INTRODUCTION

VERY FEW nucleated Middle Iron Age settlements with defences have been excavated to their foundations or below. The only one that has in Orkney is the broch at Howe Farm near Stromness (Ballin Smith 1994) where, due to exceptional circumstances and with the availability of public finance, the Iron Age structures were excavated to destruction as part of a rescue strategy and not as a research excavation (Fig. 13). The complexity of the structural history at this site only came to light through the controlled archaeological destruction of the broch. An exceptionally rich amount of information was generated about the buildings and the very human history of their development, but the story did not begin with the Iron Age. The Howe project presented an opportunity to take the history of the site back further, to its origins as a Neolithic funerary monument some 2000 years before the advent of brochs. The sheer perseverance of our Iron Age ancestors to continue to build on what we would term a 'brown-field' site, to produce their own monumental architecture on the foundations of their Neolithic ancestors', is an epic story which has not had the impact it deserves.

It is the aim of this paper to stress, that by preserving a complex site by consolidation, a complex site at what we is generally believed is to be one point in time, we may in fact be losing 50% of the information that the site has to give. To attain a more wide-ranging picture of these complex broch sites it is necessary to undertake more exploratory research, with greater basic questioning about the origins of both the broch and the site itself, as was recently achieved at Scalloway in Shetland (Sharples 1998). It is the opinion of this author that other Howes exist in the Northern Isles, and probably also in Caithness, and that the information gained in the latter part of the 20th century should be applied to future Iron Age research excavations. It is quite obvious that not all sites will produce the detailed prehistory found at Howe; this phenomenon

Fig.13 *Aerial view of Howe, during excavation of the Phase 7 Broch 2 and settlement. The earlier Phase 6 Broch 1 can be seen within the walls of Broch 2. The settlement is surrounded by a clay and stone rampart. Copyright Charles Tait.*

Plate 1. *Aerial photograph showing the Iron Age phase of Old Scatness. (page 56)*

Plate 2. *Late Bronze Age/Early Iron Age ard marks cutting the site 'natural', a marine sand. (page 56)*

Plate 3. *Structure 14 showing radial piers. (page 59)*

Plate 4. *Hearth and 'oven-like' structure in Structure 8. (page 59)*

might be one particular to Orkney because of the nature of the geology, and not every complex Iron Age site will be a Howe. Although the evidence for pre-broch use of sites is present in the various Atlantic regions of Scotland, this area of research has been hardly explored. In order to progress research into the Early and Middle Iron Age periods of the North of Scotland, a gathering and testing of basic information is required looking at the transition between the Bronze and Iron Ages and that of Iron Age settlement studies in particular.

CHALLENGING ASSUMPTIONS (THE EVIDENCE FROM HOWE)

The fact that a broch mound or site has, in our minds and experiences, always existed, does not mean to say it has always existed in the form in which we see it.

The Orcadian broch (Fig. 14)

Broch towers have always appealed to the researcher and the archaeologist. The shear monumentality of the building, whether it survives a few or many metres in height attracts the attention and imagination of the archaeologist. It is the most obvious structure

to have been investigated, often at the expense of surrounding or overlying buildings, and has dominated broch studies for over six decades (Callander and Grant 1934, Richardson 1948). The confined interior surrounded by a relatively clearly defined circular wall has been the easy target of the excavator. Limits to excavation were naturally set by the walls of the structure itself. Following the boundaries of that wall downward and along was not as problematic as following thinner and more ephemeral walls of other structures on the same site, such as those found at Gurness. We know more about broch towers than any other domestic dwelling on Middle Iron Age sites, and yet we probably know less about them than we think. We know a lot about their physical make-up, but little about their actual construction, virtually nothing about their foundations and even less about the sites they were erected on.

The excavations at Howe have been instrumental in questioning the validity of what we see and the validity of what we assume to be the case in broch studies. At Howe, the excavation methodology employed included the total removal by hand of all the Iron Age structures under modern scientific analytical conditions. Had it not been for this strategy the sequence of events on the one site, incorporating the multiplicity of brochs or substantial roundhouses and the exposure of the underlying Neolithic structures, may never have come to light.

The number of floors encountered within the broch tower initially posed serious questions about the chronology of the use of the structure. This was because the floors were not expected in the numbers in which they appeared. Although floors later than the construction of the broch towers are on display at the brochs of

Fig.14 *The Broch of Gurness. The monumental tower surrounded by its settlement and ditches, overlooking Eynhallow Sound and the Island of Rousay. Copyright Beverley Ballin Smith. From the south-west.*

Midhowe and Gurness, the complexity of the sequence found at Howe is presently unparallelled. Without the constraints of the politics of leaving archaeology on display to the general public, it was possible to excavate to the bottom of the broch interior, through all the floor levels, to the base of the walls and to analyse the full sequence of events. It was recognised that two of the lowest excavated floors were stratigraphically earlier than the exposed broch walls, and a sub-floor chamber was identified as having partly originated in the Neolithic period. Unlike our 1930s predecessors (Richardson and Craw at Gurness, and Callander and Grant at Midhowe) the excavation of the broch interior did not cease at the floor that was considered the lowest or the most informative for the public display. It was possible to pursue the information further to the end and get literally to the bottom of that broch's story. The assumption of a fairly simple interior stratigraphic sequence was no longer the case.

Another general assumption concerns the form and architecture of confronted us with the brochs themitselvesf. The last broch at Howe, termed *Broch 2*, had no intra-mural gallery at ground level, it had no scarcement to speak of, and, there was no well. A first floor landing and staircase existed, even an additional staircase springing from the floor of the interior was found, as at Gurness, but this structure which was very much a broch did not fit MacKie's hypotheses for a true broch (MacKie 1965, 100, and also MacKie 2002 for a revised classification). The structure was basically low and squat and may not have attained any great height compared with the elegance of Mousa, even though (following the formula given by Fojut 1981) its the percentage of the overall diameter taken up by the wall-base of Howe *Broch 2*, at about 63%, is actually very close to the figure of 64.5% given for Mousa (*ibid.*).

The assumption that at Howe there was a single round structure on the site was also shattered during the dismantling of *Broch 2*. Beneath this lay *Broch 1*, a thinner-walled structure with opposing mural staircases with landings and a cell at either side of the entrance (Fig. 15). Again, it did not conform to MacKie's broch hypothesis, but no matter whether we call it a broch or a roundhouse, what is important was its explicit relationship to an earlier structure, a roundhouse found beneath it, and its clear stratigraphic relationship to its successor, *Broch 2*. It is this sequence of superimposed similar structures on the one site which must be put into perspective in broch studies. Apart from Howe no other broch site has been tested for this type of complexity. The evidence from Howe challenges our assumptions, in that the standing broch now visible might not have

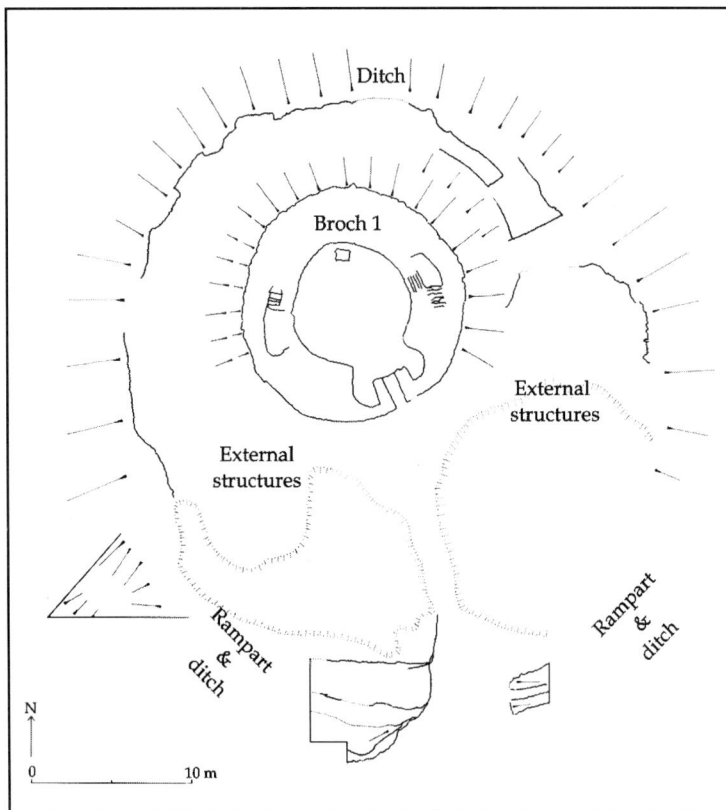

Fig.15 *Plan of the Phase 6 Broch 1 at Howe with the northern ramparts and ditch.*

been the earliest on the site. This information has generated a reassessment of broch studies and the understanding of broch development on Orkney and possibly the Northern Isles in general (see current work at Old Scatness, Shetland and Minehowe, Orkney).

The defences

Ever since the beginnings of brochs research, archaeologists have concentrated on examining the broch tower at the expense of surrounding structures. However, this research usually also took in the

Fig.16 *An aerial view of the Broch of Gurness showing the tower, the surrounding buildings and ramparts, and reconstructed later Iron Age buildings on the right. Copyright Charles Tait.*

defensive features of a site, exemplified by the monumental ditches and ramparts surrounding the settlement at the broch of Gurness (Fig. 16). Ramparts and ditches are both prominently defined and negatively contained features, often with clear boundaries. Like the broch itself they were features which may not have been complicated to excavate. One hypothesis put forward by MacKie (1998, 22) is that a true broch (a hollow-walled tower) had an outer wall and ditch. However, one need only look with a little more detail at the Broch of Gurness defences to realise that the outer ditch is largely a product of the 1930s excavations and as such did not exist during the Middle Iron Age. What is accepted now as an Iron Age feature was not the case in prehistory (however, MacKie 2002, 230, still accepts the third ditch as a prehistoric feature).

Broch 2 at Howe, although not a hollow-walled tower was encircled by a single, but prominent, yellow clay rampart which remained visible but unexcavated until the last seasons of the project. Until part of the rampart was excavated it had always been assumed that it and its ditch were contemporary with *Broch 2* and its settlement.

Investigation of this feature revealed it to be much more complex than first thought. It was not only earlier than expected but it was contemporary with the roundhouse. It was later modified during the construction and use of *Broch 1*, and again during *Broch 2*. In fact its origins went back much further, to the first ditches and banks created during the Late Bronze Age/Early Iron Age occupation of the site. It even incorporated human material from the Neolithic period, when the earliest structure beneath the brochs, a Maeshowe-type chambered tomb, was partly dismantled and the interior cleared out.

The question remains: can we assume that substantial roundhouses (whether hollow-walled brochs or not) and defences are contemporary on Orkney? Without further detailed analysis of monuments on display such as Gurness and Midhowe, and the exploration of unexcavated sites such as Green Tulloch and Wattenan South, Caithness (Mercer 1981; 1985) which are known to have a complex series of structures and defences, we may never understand fully the complex relationship between the broch and its surroundings in these northern regions.

Buildings within the defences

That settlement often surrounded the broch tower has long been known and is exhibited at sites such as the brochs of Gurness and Midhowe in Orkney, and Clickhimin in Shetland etc. However, it is the picture of the lone tower, symbolised by Mousa, which persists (Hedges and Bell 1980). It would appear from records of the time (see below) that the excavation of what were often fragile buildings of the Middle and Later Iron Ages, surrounding and overlying the broch towers, was fraught with confusion as their archaeological complexities were difficult to unravel. In contrast to the broch, the lack of solid boundaries to these structures, as well as the additional complications of the presence of collapsed and rebuilt walls, made their excavation exposure and interpretation problematic. The problem was compounded by unsophisticated archaeological excavation techniques. Archive documents, as well as displays of public monuments, provide an inadequate explanation of their form, their dating and the sequence of these buildings. This is, best exemplified by the plans of the Broch of Lingro, excavated in 1870-71 (Hedges 1987, III, 135). It has always been assumed that the more ephemeral structures were constructed later than the broch tower, especially as at Gurness (MacKie 1995: 2002, 229) where such structures are clearly later than the defences (see below). Our inadequate reading of limited evidence may lead us to false assumptions and hypotheses. Only with further archaeological investigation will new evidence be added to the present sum of our knowledge.

The excavation of Howe produced the first systematic excavation and analyses of a complex series of buildings lying around the base of a broch tower. During the archaeological investigation, each series of structures was found to be contemporary with each roundhouse / broch structure on the site. That is to say, that for every broch or roundhouse there were contemporary associated buildings lying within the surrounding defences, but only through careful archaeological destruction was this evidence exposed. The latest series of buildings, the best preserved, was contemporary with *Broch 2* and exhibited evidence for precise planning within the confines of the defences, and also design in the interior features provided for each structure (Ballin Smith 1994; see also MacKie, 1988, 22-24) (Fig. 13). Earlier buildings were less well preserved and the understanding of their form and function was limited. It would have been extremely difficult to test the accepted assumptions about the relationship of these buildings to the broch, and their function, without destructive and invasive archaeological techniques.

Tests need not be as totally destructive as at Howe, but the partial or total removal of the external structures was necessary in this case for thorough scientific investigation.

External structures at broch sites have long been neglected or avoided. Without an understanding of the detailed inter-relationship between them and the broch or roundhouse, and the defences, in forming a cohesive broch settlement complex, the story of the site would only be half told. The intricacies of the stratigraphic building sequence found at Howe may be exceptional, or commonplace, but this needs to be tested at other sites.

Assumptions of limits

The excavations at Howe also challenged the implied assumption that the nucleated broch settlement stopped at its defensive boundaries, or just outside the causeway through them. Although the results from that excavation were slight due to destruction by ploughing, the existence of Middle and Late Iron Age structures lying beyond the defences, but linked to the nucleated settlement, were proven (Ballin Smith 1994, 82, 84-89).

The exploration of areas external to the immediate settlement has been taken one stage further by the excavations at Old Scatness, with the examination of the soils and the fields around the site (Simpson *et al.* 1998). With a more holistic approach to broch studies, where hypotheses can be tested, a more complete picture of the settlement-scape of the Middle Iron Age will emerge.

CHALLENGING PERCEPTIONS

Our modern excavations of brochs have come a long way from the explorations of the 19th century by wealthy individuals and antiquarians. Long gone is recording of the excavation of brochs by letter (the main site records apart from plans) as occurred at sites simultaneously dug such as Gurness in the Orkney Mainland and the Broch of Midhowe in the island of Rousay lying across Eynhallow Sound. Correspondence was exchanged between Richardson and Craw who were digging at Gurness and Callander and Grant working on Midhowe in the 1930s. From their letters it would seem that the aim of their excavations was to expose the contents of two large mounds which were being eroded by the sea for the recovery of relics (Hedges 1987, II, 2). During the '*clearing out*' of the structures it became apparent that it was feasible to consolidate and display the monument, and this idea was reinforced by the good preservation of the Broch of Gurness and the possibility of constructing a site museum to house some of the finds. This aim was furthered by the removal of some later structures from the upper levels of the broch settlement; these were later rebuilt and redisplayed outside the site museum. This was possibly the first time archaeological reconstruction on this scale had been attempted in Scotland.

Nowhere in the excavation s archives of Gurness and Midhowe (held at the National Monuments Record for Scotland, Edinburgh) was there an implicit strategy to recover information about the brochs' foundations, the earliest history of the sites, or to delve deeper

into the complexities of structural analysis. Indeed, in Hedges' account of the history of the works at Gurness there is a strong suggestion that structures '*were stripped of unnecessary adhesions*' (Hedges 1987, II, 2) thereby simplifying the story of the site as it was excavated. Research by Hedges and this author into the site records suggests that a large complex of later structures existed above the broch settlement of which only fragments of three or four buildings remain visible today (see also Ballin Smith 1993, 96). The site archives also reveal that complex stratigraphy was reached beneath the floors of House 5 (at the back of the stone rampart to the ditch) and an earlier hearth and fragmentary floor were found above the well structure in the centre of the broch. These features, potentially extremely important for the understanding of earlier events on the site, to this day have never been fully explored or understood.

Our perception and understanding of the site of Gurness is therefore influenced by the excavator's aims, the excavation methodology, the surviving site archives as they exist, the removal and consolidation of structures and the modern day presentation of the site. What information is available to us as researchers is captured primarily at one moment in time, a moment of time of the excavator's and consolidator's making. We are confronted with an inadequate picture where the full history of the site is not known. Gurness is undoubtedly one of the most spectacular Iron Age monuments on display to the public in Scotland, but how accurate is its story which is depicted?

Modern research excavations of broch sites are limited and self-limiting in many ways. Funding and time are the main factors. The size of the structure of the nucleated broch settlement makes excavation extremely costly, both in terms of time as well as money, which is why to date only the excavations at Old Scatness in Shetland can be compared to the results and evidence provided by the Howe project.

Preservation or conservation?

A major factor influencing the excavation of Iron Age monumental nucleated structures today is the opportunity for the preservation and conservation of the site, as in the example of Old Scatness (Dockrill *et al.*, this volume). At Howe, there were not sufficient funds available for an extremely costly conservation exercise to consolidate *Broch 2* and its associated structures. Indeed, it was never considered a prime aim of the project. Apart from the fact that over half the site story history of the site would have been left unexplored and therefore untold if the site had not been fully excavated, the only opportunity to test the assumption that the structures that were exposed were roughly contemporary was by further excavation. It can also be argued that the stone structures were not worth preserving. Once buried Stromness flagstone is re-exposed to the weather it has the unfortunate habit of fracturing along its bedding planes, which sunlight, and wind and rain encourage. What appears to be solid lumps of stone in the summer can be reduced to a pile of small slivers of rock over a winter. The settlement structures were encapsulated in a mound of small pieces of shattered rock.

The sequence of events at Howe is preserved by record alone, except for the Neolithic features which lie concealed below the field surface, covered with the clay of their own Maeshowe-type tomb mound. The almost totally destructive nature of this archaeological project means that the Iron Age structures cannot be revisited in order to test the results and findings. It was an exercise that to all intents and purposes is not to be applauded or repeated (too often). Not only is the archaeological resource depleted, (whether significantly or otherwise, is not known) but the excavators and the funding body, presumably also the landowner, are left with the dilemma

of whether total destruction was a complete act of vandalism or whether it was necessary, in this instance, for the recovery of evidence and the search for knowledge. This author remains convinced that for this particular site, with the story it encapsulated, there was no alternative, apart from not excavating in the first place. How, with all its stratigraphic complexities, could the settlement mound at Howe have been sampled and the story understood? No doubt certain parts of the excavation could have been sampled but the details of the site story would have remained a mystery.

It is part of the Old Scatness project strategy that the site will be preserved and consolidated once the later Iron Age and Norse settlement is completely excavated (Moncrieff 1998, 47). At Old Scatness information concerning the Bronze Age origin and use of the site has already been published (Simpson *et al.*, 1998, 111; Dockrill 1998, 62). It would appear that, as at Howe, the history of Old Scatness goes back further than the Iron Age. If this is so, where will the consolidation begin, or in fact end? Will it be possible to gain a coherent picture of the origins of this settlement which will illuminate the stratigraphic sequence implied at the nearby site of Jarlshof?

In his summary of Shetland Iron Age studies, Fojut (1988, 12) lists a number of research themes which he suggests still need further exploration. Included are:

- The nature of pre-broch activity on major settlement sites.
- The date of the first broch-like structures in Shetland and the north in general.
- The nature of the transition from pre-broch to broch-period society.

Exploring some of these themes at Old Scatness is still a possibility, and they may be part of the overall research agenda, but there is a dichotomy: to excavate or to consolidate? Excavation may provide some of the answers and allow further research, but it is this author's opinion that consolidation will inhibit, to a large degree, both.

CONCLUSION: POLITICAL AND ECONOMIC FACTORS

It has been argued here that our perception of sites on public display may be may be incomplete and inaccurate. Our understanding of these sites is limited by the lack of opportunity for further scientific research into them. We have much to thank our archaeological predecessors for in exposing such magnificent monuments, which have undoubtedly been considered as giving us a reliable history of our ancestors' achievements. However, it is this author's contention that they generally pose a hindrance to modern scientific research and the furtherance of public knowledge.

Political as well as economic factors also greatly influence the amount of excavation, recovery of information, the preservation and conservation of complex sites which is possible. If one monumental broch and settlement is on display to the public, why preserve another for display in the same county or island group? This manner of thinking was part of the decision not to preserve the Iron Age structures at Howe.

Today, public funding of such large excavations is rare (the excavation of the Old Scatness Broch is in receipt of funding from at least 11 large organisations including regional, national and international authorities) and private funding difficult. Funding of even minor fact-finding excavations of nuclear sites for research purposes is also rare. Modern investigations of large complex Iron Age sites are largely confined to coastal monitoring which at best will give an isolated horizontal picture which will be hard to link with the vertical history of the site. Developer funding is a rare occurrence because there are usually ways of avoiding large structures, a strategy which is reinforced due to the real fear of initiating a project requiring a bottomless pot

of money for archaeological research. Sampling of large broch sites can hardly be recommended, as health and safety issues would prevent excavation of deep stratigraphy in narrow confined trenches or on eroding and often unstable cliff faces.

Archaeological fieldwork studies of brochs are therefore limited to the very rare expensive excavation such as Howe and Old Scatness, to coastal monitoring, or to limited surface investigations. The latter approaches will restrict our knowledge and confine our research. In the single example of Howe, a number of important archaeological assumptions about broch and broch research have been challenged, simply because of the exposure of new evidence. But Howe is only one site, and it is in Orkney. It is important for the archaeological community to consider that other archaeologically complex sites will exist in other areas, as is shown by the work at Old Scatness. The interpretation of the results at Howe will never be fully assimilated into generally accepted archaeological hypotheses without further targeted research of broch sites on display and the occasional complete excavation of a complex Iron Age settlement. We have a duty, not only to ourselves and the next generation of archaeologists, but also to the furtherance of broch and Middle Iron Age studies, to seek out the complexities of these sites, challenge the assumptions of the immediate past, question our perception of monuments on display, and above all to bring the whole story into the public domain.

BIBLIOGRAPHY

Ballin Smith, B. (1993) The Broch of Gurness. In Batey C. E., Jesch J. and Morris C. D. (eds.) *The Viking Age in Caithness, Orkney and the North Atlantic*. Edinburgh, Edinburgh University Press.

Ballin Smith, B. (ed.) (1994) *Howe, four millennia of Orkney Prehistory*. Edinburgh, Society of Antiquaries of Scotland Monograph Series 9.

Callander, J. G. and Grant, W. G. (1934) The Broch of Midhowe, Rousay, Orkney. *Proceedings of the Society of Antiquaries of Scotland 68* (1933-34), 444-516.

Dockrill, S. J. (1998) Northern exposure: phase I of the Old Scatness excavations 1995-8. In Nicholson R. A. and Dockrill S. J. (eds.) *Old Scatness Broch, Shetland: Retrospect and Prospect*, 59-80. University of Bradford / Shetland Amenity Trust / North Atlantic Biocultural Organisation.

Fojut, N. (1981) Is Mousa a broch? *Proceedings of the Society of Antiquaries of Scotland* 1981, 220-228.

Fojut, N. (1998) How did we end up here? Shetland Iron Age studies to 1995. In Nicholson, R. A. and Dockrill, S. J. (eds.) *Old Scatness Broch, Shetland: Retrospect and Prospect*. University of Bradford / Shetland Amenity Trust / North Atlantic Biocultural Organisation, 1-41.

Hedges, J. W. and Bell, B. J. (1980) That tower of Scottish prehistory: the broch. *Antiquity* 54, 87-94.

Hedges, J. W. (1987) *Bu, Gurness and the Brochs of Orkney. Part II Gurness*. British Archaeological Reports, British Series 164. Oxford, BAR.

Hedges, J. W. (1987) *Bu, Gurness and the Brochs of Orkney. Part III The Brochs of Orkney*. British Archaeological Reports, British Series 165. Oxford, BAR.

MacKie, E. W. (1965) The origin and development of the broch and wheelhouse building cultures of the Scottish Iron Age. *Proceedings of the Prehistoric Society* 31, 93-143.

MacKie, E. W. (1995) Gurness and Midhowe brochs in Orkney: some problems of misinterpretation. *Archaeological Journal* 151 (1994), 98-157.

MacKie, E. W. (1998) Continuity over three thousand years of northern prehistory: the 'tel' at Howe, Orkney. *The Antiquaries Journal* 78 (1998), 1-42.

MacKie, E. W. (2002) *The Roundhouses, Brochs and Wheelhouses of Atlantic Scotland c. 700 BC to AD 500: Architecture and Material Culture. Part 1: the Orkney and Shetland Isles.* British Archaeological Reports British Series 342. Oxford, Oxbow Books.

Mercer, R. J. (1981) *Archaeological Field Survey in Northern Scotland, Vol II*. 1980-1981. University of Edinburgh, Department of Archaeology Occasional Paper No.7.

Mercer, R. J. (1985) *Archaeological Field Survey in Northern Scotland, Vol III*. 1982-1983. University of Edinburgh, Department of Archaeology Occasional Paper No.11.

Moncrieff, J. (1998) Old Scatness: the vision for the future. In Nicholson, R. A. and Dockrill, S. J. (eds) *Old Scatness Broch, Shetland: Retrospect and Prospect*, 42-48. University of Bradford / Shetland Amenity Trust / North Atlantic Biocultural Organisation.

Richardson, J. S. (1948) *The Broch of Gurness, Aikerness, West Mainland, Orkney*. Edinburgh, Ministry of Works Official Guide.

Royal Commission on the Ancient and Historical Monuments of Scotland (1946) *Orkney and Shetland*. Volume 3 Shetland. Edinburgh, HMSO.

Sharples, N. (1998) *Scalloway, a Broch, Late Iron Age Settlement and Medieval Cemetery in Shetland.* Oxbow Monograph 82, Oxford, Oxbow Books.

Simpson, I. A., Dockrill, S. J. and Lancaster, S. J. (1998) Making arable soils. Anthropogenic soil formation in a multi-period landscape. In Nicholson, R. A. and Dockrill, S. J. (eds.) *Old Scatness Broch, Shetland: Retrospect and Prospect*, 111-126. University of Bradford / Shetland Amenity Trust / North Atlantic Biocultural Organisation.

Complex Atlantic Roundhouses: Chronology and Complexity

SIMON GILMOUR

INTRODUCTION

RADIOCARBON dating of contexts recovered from Atlantic Scottish Iron Age sites reveals an interesting pattern of activity that suggests the construction of complex Atlantic roundhouses began as early as 400 cal. BC (Tables 1-7). This same data supports a three-fold sequence of development of Atlantic roundhouse structures detailed elsewhere (Gilmour 2000a), including the early construction of 'simple Atlantic roundhouses', the development of complex Atlantic roundhouses and finally their reorganisation and re-use accompanied by the construction of wheelhouses. This sequence of domestic structures is also apparent from their relative stratigraphies (Fig. 17). The fact that the same general pattern is visible chronologically as well as stratigraphically across a wide area has important implications for the understanding of Atlantic Iron Age societies. The Western Isles however, appear not to include 'simple Atlantic roundhouses', suggesting that complex Atlantic roundhouses were introduced to the islands as a developed concept.

Structural morphology in the Atlantic Scottish Iron Age has become a somewhat unfashionable, or at least questionable, route to understanding the societies that built drystone monuments. The contentious recognition of a broad group of 'Atlantic roundhouses' by Ian Armit was an attempt to break from a stultifying obsession with architectural detail in the classification of 'brochs' and 'duns' (e.g. Armit 1992; Armit this volume). I believe this classification, albeit a somewhat unwieldy terminology by comparison, was successful and aided the progressive dismantling of previous social models of Iron Age lifestyle and chronology that saw 'brochs' as the pinnacle of a hierarchy and heavy reliance on diffusion from outside Atlantic Scotland. This hierarchial model has recently been resurrected with 'true brochs' assuming pre-eminence over 'wheelhouses' (Parker Pearson *et al.* 1996; Parker Pearson and Sharples *et al.* 1999). Within the general term 'complex Atlantic roundhouse' Armit accedes to a special group of monuments that he calls 'broch towers' (Armit 1990b, 60). All of these terms are, however, still reliant on structural morphology; the identification of a 'true broch' expects certain architectural details to be present that can distinguish the site from other similar structures, and the recognition of a 'broch tower' requires "definite evidence of an upper gallery" (Armit 1990b, 60). However, many of these criteria cannot be resolved due to the nature of the evidence, collapse and re-use obscuring details and often the precise ground plan (*ibid.*, 50-53). The height of any given structure can, on present evidence, only be assumed, but the majority of complex Atlantic roundhouses do incorporate an intramural staircase. This feature indicates that at least a first floor existed at these sites. Only Mousa in Shetland has access via an intramural staircase to the wall-head, and it requires an abnormally large wall-base percentage to do so (Fojut 1981). If it is agreed that intramural staircases led to upper floors within the stone casement

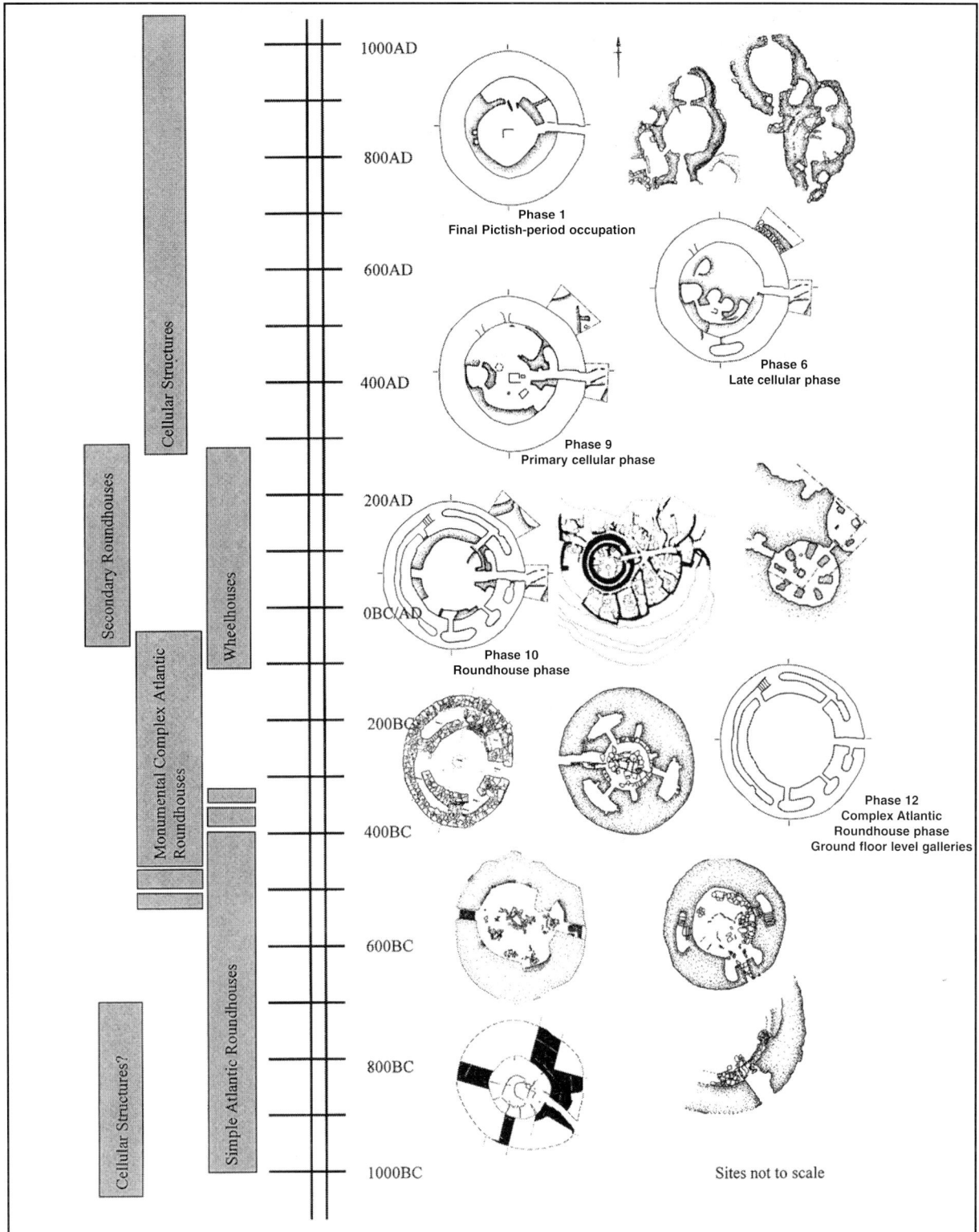

Fig. 17 *Chronological Table: Loch na Beirgh figure of eight building (Harding and Gilmour 2000), Bostadh beach figure of eight buildings (after Neighbour and Burgess 1997), Loch na Beirgh cellular structures and secondary roundhouse (Harding and Gilmour 2000), Gurness complex Atlantic roundhouse (after hedges 1987ii), Cnip wheelhouse (after Armit 1996), Dun Bharabhat complex Atlantic roundhouse (Harding and Dixon 2000), Mousa complex Atlantic roundhouse (after Hamilton 1970), Loch na Beirgh complex Atlantic roundhouse (Harding and Gilmour 2000), Rahoy vitrified Atlantic roundhouse (after Childe and Thorneycroft 1938), Howe complex Atlantic roundhouse (after Ballin Smith 1994), Bu simple Atlantic roundhouse (Hedges 1987i), St. Boniface simple Atlantic roundhouse (after Lowe 1998).*

then we can conclude that complex Atlantic roundhouses were tall, multi-storeyed monuments.

This contrasts with the pre-cursors of complex Atlantic roundhouses, the 'simple Atlantic roundhouses', which by their very nature, have no intramural features and never incorporate intramural staircases. These buildings were probably single storey structures with only a ground floor, but would have stood out in the landscape by virtue of a prominent location and/or their stone construction and massiveness compared to other early semi-subterranean structures. I have argued elsewhere (Gilmour 2000a) that the structures following complex Atlantic roundhouses, including secondary roundhouses and wheelhouses (*infra*), are similarly single storey buildings in the main, although some small loft or upper structural space may exist at a few sites. Wheelhouses are mainly semi-subterranean structures, and even the few upstanding examples often have poorly defined outer walls that are frequently overgrown or subsumed within midden deposits. Certainly the later cellular structures that form the majority of mid- to late-first millennium AD settlement types are single storey, and often semi-subterranean. Complex Atlantic roundhouses are therefore different from their preceding and succeeding building types due to their height. This is to be expected since it is the construction of intramural cells and galleries that lightens the wall allowing a greater volume of stonework, and thus height, without greatly increased stress.

CHRONOLOGY

Dates for most simple Atlantic roundhouses in Northern Scotland fall into the notorious 'flat-spot' in the calibration curve for the first millennium cal. BC. This produces a somewhat false cut-off point at 410 cal. BC and stretches the dates over much of the early first millennium cal BC (Table 1). However, whilst perhaps obscuring a pattern of dates within the early first millennium they still suggest early construction and occupation of simple Atlantic roundhouses. It has been argued elsewhere (Gilmour 2000b) that similar structures exist in Argyll, for example at Rahoy, Morvern, although this still needs to be proven conclusively through modern excavation.

Mid- to late-first millennium cal. BC dates are rare (the grey band on tables 1-7 covers 500 cal. BC to 100 cal. BC), and I would argue that this is simply due to a lack of excavated primary deposits from complex Atlantic roundhouses. Some sites do produce these early dates, such as the *terminus post quem* and *terminus ante quem* assays from Dun Bharabhat, West Lewis (Harding and Dixon 2000) or the dating from the Howe, Orkney (Gilmour 2000a; Table 3), and Crosskirk, Caithness (Table 1). However, other contemporary dates are from either poor samples or are simply too few. Indeed, the calibration curve again has a relatively flat area running between 365 cal. BC and 100 cal BC that should allow dating of sites to this broad period. That dates can occur within this time period is amply illustrated by non-Atlantic roundhouse sites such as An Dunan, West Lewis, or Eilean Olabhat, North Uist (Table 2), and I shall return to these in due course.

An explosion of radiocarbon dates begins again from the first century cal. BC onwards, and especially in the early centuries of the first millennium cal. AD. These dates are retrieved from wheelhouses in the main, although contexts more closely associated with complex Atlantic roundhouses are also present. However, these latter have yet to be proven to represent primary complex Atlantic round-house deposits relating to construction and original occupation of the site and are arguably all from secondary contexts (e.g. Gilmour 2000a). The recent dates from secondary or even tertiary occupation at Old Scatness, Shetland, indicate that the complex

Atlantic roundhouse there must be earlier than the first century cal. BC (Dockrill *et al.*, 2000; and this volume).

There is a suggestion here that complex Atlantic roundhouses could have been built anytime between circa 400 cal. BC and the end of the first century cal. BC, considerably earlier than conventional 'brochology' would allow (Parker Pearson and Sharples *et al.* 1999, 359; MacKie 1965 etc.). This also suggests an overall longer time-span for their period of construction than the couple of centuries indicated by earlier models. Before we can answer any questions as to why these structures were built we must first be certain of how and when they were built, perhaps allowing some insight into who built them. A long development in the second half of the first millennium cal. BC, with the conceptual idea of monumental drystone roundhouses stretching even earlier, is a very different model to the short and late development of 'brochs' pursued elsewhere. This brings us again to classification problems, with some arguing that 'true brochs' were built only towards the end of this chronological period, presumably reflecting the progressive development of building techniques and an increase in tower-like proportions. However, this argument is based on a linear evolutionary principle that may be too simplistic; it takes no account of possible complexities inherent in the social infrastructure employed within any given period and area of Iron Age Atlantic Scotland.

Atlantic Iron Age societies may have been dynamic and fluctuating, suggesting that the scale, architecture and other evidence that could highlight differences in status for example, may only have been transitory or applicable to its period of original construction or time of deposition. It is perfectly possible that a site like Loch na Beirgh, West Lewis, may originally have commanded a very high status in any social system around the time of primary construction and use, perhaps early in the second half of the first millennium cal. BC (Harding and Gilmour 2000). However, this does not preclude subsequent shifts in status and perhaps even function, from generation to generation over the period of its lifetime. Even communal expression of monumentality need not assume that a structure has inherent status greater than any other contemporary structure. This same issue is relevant to the dating of complex Atlantic roundhouses; the chronology of construction and primary occupation will be relevant to any given structure's social or landscape context. This means that structures currently considered by some to be 'true brochs' could have been built as early, if not earlier than, other buildings thought not to have the full range of 'broch' attributes. For example, the relatively small scale of Dun Bharabhat (Harding and Armit 1990, Harding and Dixon 2000), and the complex entrance construction of 'broch 1' at Howe (Ballin Smith 1994), mean that many are happy to accept an early date for their construction and occupation. However, it is quite possible that sites like Loch na Beirgh (Table 6) and perhaps even Dun Mor Vaul, on Tiree (Table 3), could have been built just as early.

Similarly, if the contemporary dating between midden deposits at Dun Vulan and the Kildonan III wheelhouse in South Uist can be shown conclusively (Table 4) then there is good evidence here for differences in economic remains that could reflect social, status or perhaps even functional differences (Parker Pearson *et al.* 1996). However, the deposits at Dun Vulan do not appear to relate to the occupation of the complex Atlantic roundhouse in its primary form, but rather from some secondary activity in the unexcavated interior of the roundhouse (Gilmour and Cook 1998; Armit 2000). Further excavations could shed light on this earlier part of its history. The same problems of linking external middens with internal occupation may relate to the Kildonan III deposits which are dated by two radiocarbon assays, only one of which overlaps the end of the midden accumulation at Dun Vulan (Table 4). Indeed, the contemporary nature of complex Atlantic roundhouses and wheelhouses has yet to be proven; at every location where a wheelhouse can be stratigraphically related to an Atlantic roundhouse, the former are always secondary, sometimes by a considerable period of time (e.g. Eilean Maleit, North Uist (Armit 1999), Allt Chrisal, Ben Tangaval, Barra (Pouncet 2000), Old Scatness, Shetland (Dockrill 1998)).

Given the possible complexity of Atlantic Iron Age society it is probable that even those sites considered to be 'true brochs' could predate the first century cal. BC, perhaps by several centuries. I suggest here that complex Atlantic roundhouse construction and primary occupation could fill the 'gap' in radiocarbon dating evidence between the mid-first millennium cal. BC and the first century cal. BC (Tables 1-5). Furthermore, it is just as credible that those sites previously considered 'true brochs' or even 'broch towers' could have been built as early as those that are considered to be of lesser stature or status.

ARCHITECTURE AND CONSTRUCTION

Complexity in construction suggests knowledge of the techniques and ability to command the resources required. The site at Dun Bharabhat collapsed after construction, but this seems due to insubstantial foundations, a problem that could not be perceived through surface survey alone (the likely pre-development investigation method used in the Iron Age). The collapsed stonework from this site is substantial, providing the material from which a secondary structure was built into the roundhouse and tertiary cellular structures constructed outside. The tumble obscured the galleries and other architectural details prior to excavation prompting the suggestion it was a 'solid walled island dun', or 'simple Atlantic

roundhouse' (Harding and Armit 1990, 83; Harding and Dixon 2000, 3). In fact the lack of any positive evidence for the latter in the Western Isles has been used to argue that such structures may not exist in this area of Atlantic Scotland (Armit 1990b, 47 and 55). This raises interesting issues regarding the transmission of both the concept and structural understanding of complex Atlantic roundhouses to the Western Isles, especially if the only pre-cursors to the architectural style are to be found in the north of Scotland. However, simple Atlantic roundhouses may also exist in Argyll (Gilmour 2000b), providing a plausible background for the indigenous development of complex Atlantic roundhouses in this area too. How is this knowledge transferred to the Western Isles, and how does this impact on the local society? Did the construction of large monumental complex Atlantic roundhouses in drystone require fundamental changes to the social infrastructure of the Hebridean Iron Age, or was it easily adopted? The ability to construct one of these buildings would have required in-depth knowledge of the architectural concept, but was certainly not based on a single 'blueprint' since every site is different in its scale and constructional layout. Indeed, different sizes, constructional detail, location and perhaps even entrance orientation of the roundhouses themselves may have indicated various social or functional differences between sites of a similar period. Visiting a complex Atlantic roundhouse during its use may not have been enough to allow reproduction since many features such as the lintels tying walls together, weight relieving gaps above doorways, and the scarcement may have been obscured by textiles or wooden furnishings. Wooden floors for example, may have lined the dark intramural spaces (Parker Pearson and Sharples, *et al.* 1999, 32; Harding and Gilmour 2000, 56-57). This raises the possibility of 'architects' or a group of people who controlled the knowledge of complex construction. Only careful analysis of complex Atlantic roundhouse engineering might answer some of these questions, and some detail will surely be gained from further excavations at Loch na Beirgh where preservation of the remains is outstanding. Our current information base in the Outer Hebrides is seriously lacking any conclusive primary deposits relating to Atlantic roundhouse construction and occupation, except perhaps the truncated remains from Dun Bharabhat (Harding and Dixon 2000).

ATLANTIC ROUNDHOUSE LANDSCAPES

Several non-complex Atlantic roundhouse sites have dates relating to the second half of the first millennium cal. BC (Gilmour 2002). These include the small oval and revetted structure at Eilean Olabhat, North Uist (Armit *et al.* forthcoming) and the sub-rectangular islet site at An Dunan, West Lewis. The former is dated by AMS radiocarbon assays from residues on the associated pottery to between the fourth and first centuries cal. BC, and the latter to the same period through AMS assays from multiple seeds in sealed contexts (Table 2). Both sites are located within or on the edge of lochs, and another site in West Lewis, at Guinnerso, is similarly positioned next to a partially dried loch. The Guinnerso site includes a small, revetted structure associated with incised decorated pottery that may also date to the late first millennium cal. BC. Two structures in Skye, at Tungadale and Coile a'Ghasgain, have also been dated to this period (Armit 1996), but the latter has a radiocarbon date spread across the entire millennium (Table 2), making comparisons difficult. This site is a relatively small oval structure with an extended south-eastern entrance situated in the blacklands of Skye outside of good quality agricultural land, comparable perhaps to Guinnerso. Eilean Olabhat is located only a couple of hundred metres from a complex Atlantic roundhouse (Armit *et al.* forthcoming) but the function of this structure is unclear;

although several phases had no hearth they were very truncated, and at least one early phase had a large elaborate hearth perhaps suggesting some form of occupation. The site at An Dunan, in an inter-tidal zone, produced some incised decorated pottery along with the remains of cremated human teeth within a large central hearth that may indicate a mortuary function for the site rather than occupation. Guinnerso and Coile a'Ghasgain are so remote from quality land that it is hard to believe they were perennially occupied. All of these structures may form part of a contemporary landscape with complex Atlantic roundhouses, and in general seem to be non-domestic in nature, perhaps reflecting at most, seasonal occupation (Gilmour 2002). They are unlikely to represent a separate social class of occupant, but instead Coile a'Ghasgain and Guinnerso at least are indicative of transhumance carried out by complex Atlantic roundhouse dwellers. These small non-monumental buildings are important functional aspects of the complex Atlantic roundhouse economic (and presumably social) landscape, which in Lewis at least, may have revolved around the importance of red deer (Gilmour and Cook 1998).

At least some promontory sites in the Atlantic province may also be contemporary with complex Atlantic roundhouses. Their function remains obscure but it is doubtful many were occupied perennially and most may have been host to ritual assemblies, trade centres or other non-settlement occurrences (Gilmour 2000b). Of these some include a large stone-built 'blockhouse' structure that incorporates so many architectural similarities with complex Atlantic roundhouses it is hard to see them as anything but contemporary. In fact, the recent excavations at Scatness 'blockhouse', Shetland, highlighted its longevity of use including the dismantling to ground floor level and the construction of casement walls around the original walls

(Carter *et al.* 1995). This sequence of development is mirrored in complex Atlantic roundhouses.

REDUCING THE WALLS

Secondary structures are invariably built on complex Atlantic roundhouse sites after the walls have been carefully dismantled to a single storey, often incorporating the blocking of intramural staircases. The structural stability of the original walls suggests this was a symbolic act within the history of the site, suggesting important social changes. The contemporary construction of wheelhouses indicates a move back to single storey structures with little outward monumentality. Wheelhouses were an architecturally complex building type, potentially more difficult to build than a complex Atlantic roundhouse and invariably more unstable. Every example excavated to date incorporates evidence for later shoring and secondary works. The details of wheelhouse construction, including the slender piers, with careful facing and increasing width with height, the Y-lintels tying the inner wall to the piers and the corbelling of the surrounding cells, as well as the organic roofing of the central area, are difficult to reconcile over a long period of construction. Is it possible that such a complex yet decidedly homogenous and widespread construction could occur over several centuries at different times in different areas? Indeed, the shoring of 'aisled' wheelhouses during secondary works indicates that these buildings were inherently unstable, and makes it surprising that there are so few structural refinements to wheelhouses over time, such as the construction of buildings without the 'aisle' feature, if they were built over an extended chronology. Radiocarbon dates from several sites suggest they were built over a short period from the final century of the first millennium cal. BC to the early first millennium cal. AD, a period covering perhaps only two to three hundred years. This could allow detailed traditions to be passed orally

through generations. Re-use of wheelhouses is characterised by cellular structures comparable to those that re-use the secondary buildings inside complex Atlantic roundhouses (Gilmour 2000a). Again secondary roundhouses, such as that within the complex Atlantic roundhouse walls at Loch na Beirgh (Harding and Gilmour 2000, 56), and wheelhouses (Sharples this volume) appear to have been deliberately dismantled prior to the development of cellular structures. The construction of a few free-standing wheelhouses in the southern isles of the Outer Hebrides and circular 'wags' in Northern Scotland (Baines 1999) reflects the contemporary construction of secondary roundhouses within complex Atlantic roundhouses, including a similar organisation of internal space.

The structures discussed above, lacking the height of complex Atlantic roundhouses, highlight a return to the earlier simple Atlantic roundhouse style, with an integration of earlier semi-subterranean construction and a lack of attention to external visualisation or symbolism. It is from these structures that the majority of excavated and dated contexts, such as those at Dun Vulan, probably belong. Complex Atlantic roundhouses appear to have been an abnormal structure in the pedigree of Atlantic settlement types – a blatant expression of outward monumentality. Interestingly, there is perhaps an increase in midden material recovered from sites during post-complex Atlantic roundhouse occupation. This may be a factor of taphonomy, but might also reflect differences in economic strategy or social discourse enacted around boundaries. The portrayal of outward monumental symbolism seems to have waned; for example, complex Atlantic roundhouses in Orkney and Northern mainland Scotland were lowered in height and shrouded in external villages. In other areas structures congregate over and around the complex Atlantic roundhouses, for example

Plate 5. *Structure 5, a multi-cellular Pictish building. (page 62)*

Plate 6. *Structure 7, the 'clover-leaf' style cellular building within the broch. (page 62)*

Plate 7. *Culswick Broch: entrance from outside, showing skilled construction in an intractable granite. (page 152)*

Plate 8. *Eastshore, Virkie: one of several Shetland brochs halved by the slowly rising sea-level. A storm beach lies within what was the inner courtyard, and a portion of the inner wall face can be seen, with less substantial later walling. (page 155)*

the wheelhouses at Jarlshof (Hamilton 1956) and structures at Old Scatness, Shetland (Dockrill 1998). It is during this increased activity around complex Atlantic roundhouse shells that large external middens develop, perhaps reinforcing a lack of concern for outward appearances. Concentration appears to have focussed on the interiors of structures, with particular attention being paid to division of space. In addition, wheelhouses graphically illustrate the focus of internal monumentality, and, with secondary roundhouses, incorporate increased use of stone furnishings. That there was a significant re-organisation of Iron Age society at this time is clear, and this may have been connected with a lack of timber for constructional elements, whether through loss of access or a decline in the available woodland.

SEQUENCING THE COMPLEXITY

Since every site so far excavated has produced very similar, if not identical, sequences of structural types, it is hard to believe that there is no chronological contemporaneity associated with specific building types across a wide area. There is a clear development from simple Atlantic roundhouses, to complex Atlantic roundhouses, to the re-establishment of single storey roundhouses and wheelhouses, invariably followed by a sequence of cellular structures (Gilmour 2000a). It seems implausible to believe that such a sequence would be independently enacted at almost every Atlantic Iron Age site over significantly different chronological spans. Construction of buildings as well-designed as complex Atlantic roundhouses or as intricate as wheelhouses is unlikely, in my view, to have occurred over an extended period ranging from the mid-first millennium BC well into the mid-first millennium AD (*contra* Parker Pearson and Sharples *et al.* 1999, 359; MacKie 1989). The main problem in resolving these issues is still a distinct lack of excavated primary deposits relating to complex Atlantic roundhouses across Atlantic Scotland, as highlighted by Euan MacKie in his analysis of Gurness and Midhowe (1994). This problem is most applicable to the Western Isles and Argyll where no conclusive primary deposits have been directly dated and few excavated, an interesting situation for a conference on 'brochs' in the year 2000, twelve years on from the last (Armit 1990a).

CONCLUSION

Although several models for the development, chronology and use of 'brochs' or 'complex Atlantic roundhouses', have been proposed, there is little conclusive evidence due to the lack of definite primary material excavated across Atlantic Scotland. This is a reflection of longevity inherent in the settlement pattern from the beginning of the Iron Age in Atlantic Scotland where sites have been used and re-used over the millennia, and some have even older origins, although perhaps not as settlement locations. Recognition of complexity in the social infrastructure operating at any given time in any given area should warn against broad generalisations, and yet there is a very definite commonality binding the Atlantic areas together, such as the recurrence of sequences of specific structural types on sites from Shetland to Argyll. Further excavations are required in the hope of identifying and dating well-preserved deposits that relate to the original occupation and use of buildings.

ACKNOWLEDGEMENTS

I would like to thank Ian Armit, Rebecca Jones and Catherine Flitcroft for reading drafts of this paper and providing invaluable comments and advice. Patrick Foster, John Pouncet, Dennis Harding and Marek Zvelebil kindly provided excavation information prior to publication. Responsibility for the views expressed here and any errors remains with the author.

BIBLIOGRAPHY

Armit, I. (ed.) (1990a) *Beyond the Brochs: Changing Perspectives on the Atlantic Scottish Iron Age*. Edinburgh, Edinburgh University Press.

Armit, I. (1990b) Brochs and Beyond in the Western Isles. In Armit, I. (ed.) *Beyond the Brochs: Changing Perspectives on the Atlantic Scottish Iron Age*, 41-70. Edinburgh, Edinburgh University Press.

Armit, I. (1992) *The Later Prehistory of the Western Isles of Scotland*. British Archaeological Reports British Series 221. Oxford, BAR.

Armit, I. (1996) *The Archaeology of Skye and the Western Isles*. Edinburgh, Edinburgh University Press.

Armit, I. (1999) Re-excavation of an Iron Age wheelhouse and earlier structure at Eilean Maleit, North Uist. *Proceedings of the Society of Antiquaries of Scotland* 128, 255-272.

Armit, I. (2000) Review of Mike Parker Pearson and Niall Sharples with Jacqui Mulville and Helen Smith (1999). *Between Land and Sea: Excavations at Dun Vulan, South Uist*. Sheffield Academic Press, Sheffield. *Antiquity* 74, 244-245.

Armit, I., Campbell, E. and Dunwell, A. (forthcoming) Excavation of an Iron Age, Early Historic and Medieval settlement and metal-working site at Eilean Olabhat, North Uist.

Baines, A (1999) Breaking the Circle: Archaeology and Architecture in the Later Iron Age of Northern Scotland. In Frodsham, P., Topping, P. and Cowley, D. (eds.) *'We were always chasing time.'* Papers presented to Keith Blood Northern Archaeology volume 17/18 (special edition), 77-85

Ballin Smith, B. (ed.) (1994) *Howe, Four Millennia of Orkney Prehistory*. Edinburgh, Society of Antiquaries of Scotland Monograph Series No. 9, Edinburgh.

Carter, S. P., McCullagh, R. P. J. and MacSween, A. (1995) The Iron Age in Shetland: Excavations at five sites threatened by coastal erosion. *Proceedings for the Society of Antiquaries of Scotland* 125, 429-482, fiche 2: c7-c14.

Childe, V. G. and Thorneycroft, W. (1938) The Vitrified Fort at Rahoy, Morven, Argyll. *Proceedings of the Society of Antiquaries of Scotland* 72, 23-43.

Dockrill, S. J. (1998) Northern Exposure: Phase 1 of the Old Scatness Excavations, 1995-8. In Nicholson, R. A. and Dockrill S. J. (eds.) *Old Scatness Broch, Shetland: Retrospect and Prospect* Bradford Archaeological Sciences Research 5, NABO Monograph No. 2, University of Bradford/Shetland Amenity Trust/North Atlantic Biocultural Organisation, 59-80.

Dockrill, S. J., Bond. J. M. and Turner V. E. (eds.) (2000) *Old Scatness Broch & Jarlshof Environs Project: Field Season 1999* Interim Report No. 5 (Data Structure Report), Bradford Archaeological Sciences Research 9. Bradford, Shetland Amenity Trust and University of Bradford.

Fojut, N. (1981) Is Mousa a broch? *Proceedings of the Society of Antiquaries of Scotland* 111, 220-228.

Gilmour, S. (2000a) First Millennia Settlement Development in the Atlantic West. In Henderson, J. C. (ed.) *The Prehistory and Early History of Atlantic Europe*, 155-70. British Archaeological Reports International Series 861. Oxford, BAR.

Gilmour, S. (2000b) *Later Prehistoric and Early Historic Settlement Archaeology of the Western Seaways: A study of the Western settlement record from Shetland to Brittany in the first millennia BC and AD*. Unpublished PhD Thesis, University of Edinburgh.

Gilmour, S. (2002) Mid-first millennium BC settlement in the Atlantic West? In Ballin Smith and Banks (eds.) *In the Shadow of the Brochs: The Iron Age in Scotland*, 55-66. Stroud, Tempus.

Gilmour, S. and Cook, M. (1998) Excavations at Dun Vulan: a reinterpretation of the reappraised Iron Age. *Antiquity* 72, 327-37.

Hamilton, J. R. C. (1956) *Excavations at Jarlshof, Shetland*. Edinburgh, HMSO.

Harding, D. W. and Armit, I. (1990) Survey and Excavations in West Lewis. In Armit, I. (ed.) *Beyond the Brochs: Changing Perspectives on the Atlantic Scottish Iron Age*, 71-107. Edinburgh, Edinburgh University Press.

Harding, D. W. and Dixon, T. N. (2000) *Dun Bharabhat, Cnip: an Iron Age settlement in west Lewis – Volume 1: The Structures and Material Culture*. Calanais Research Series 2. Edinburgh, Department of Archaeology, University of Edinburgh.

Harding, D. W. and Gilmour, S. M. D. (2000) *The Iron Age Settlement at Beirgh, Riof, Isle of Lewis, Excavations 1985-95 – Volume 1: The Structures and Stratigraphy*. Calanais Research Series 1. Edinburgh, Department of Aarchaeology, University of Edinburgh.

Hedges, J. W. (1987) *Bu, Gurness and the brochs of Orkney Part 2: Gurness*. British Archaeological Reports British Series 163. Oxford, BAR.

Lowe, C. (1998) *Coastal Erosion and the Archaeological Assessment of an Eroding Shoreline at St. Boniface Church, Papa Westray, Orkney*. Edinburgh, Sutton Publishing/Historic Scotland.

MacKie, E. W. (1965) The origin and development of the broch and wheel-house building cultures of the Scottish Iron Age. *Proceedings of the Prehistoric Society* 31, 93-143.

MacKie, E. W. (1989) Dun Cruier again. *Scottish Archaeological Review* 6, 116-118.

MacKie, E. W. (1994) Gurness and Midhowe brochs in Orkney: some problems of misinterpretation. *Archaeological Journal* 151, 98-157.

Marshall, P., Mulville, J., Parker Pearson, M. and Ingram, C. (1999) *The Late Bronze Age and Early Iron Age Community at Cladh Hallan, South Uist*. Unpublished Interim Report, Department of Archaeology and Prehistory, University of Sheffield.

Neighbour, T. and Burgess, C. (1997) Traigh Bostadh, (Uig Parish). *Discovery and Excavation in Scotland 1996*, Council for Scottish Archaeology, 113-114.

Parker Pearson, M. and Sharples, N. M. with Mulville, J. and Smith, H. (1999) *Between Land and Sea: Excavations at Dun Vulan, South Uist*. Sheffield, Sheffield Academic Press.

Parker Pearson, M., Sharples, N. M. and Mulville, J. (1996) Brochs and Iron Age society: a reappraisal. *Antiquity* 70, 57-67.

Parker Pearson, M., Sharples, N. M. and Mulville, J. (1999) Excavations at Dun Vulan: a correction. *Antiquity* 73, 149-152.

Pouncet, J. (2000) *Allt Chrisal, Ben Tangaval* unpublished report for Historic Scotland.

Table 1

Atmospheric data from Stuiver et al. Radiocarbon 40 1041-1083 (1998); OxCal v3.3 Bronk Ramsey (1999); cub r:4 sd:12 prob usp[chron]

Atlantic Seaways Radiocarbon Dates

Bu
GU-1228 2470±95BP
GU-1154 2460±80BP
  Quanterness
Q-1465 2570±85BP
Q-1464 2440±85BP
  Tofts Ness
GU-2183 2990±100BP
GU-2207 2510±140BP
GU-2288 2470±50BP
GU-2544 2470±50BP
  St Boniface
GU-3059 2830±50BP
GU-3271 2850±50BP
  Pierowall
GU-1580 2510±80BP
GU-1581 2425±60BP
  Howe phase 5
GU-1789 2405±70BP
  Bharabhat
GU2436 2550±50BP
GU2435 2100±50BP
GU2434 2010±50BP
  Crosskirk
SRR-267 1880±70BP
SRR-272 2050±50BP
SRR-271 2070±80BP
SRR-270 2100±100BP
SRR-268 2120±50BP
SRR-266 2380±50BP
SRR-269 2770±100BP
  Langwell
GaK-4862 2240±90BP
GaK-4860 2210±90BP
GaK-4861 2200±100BP
GX-3274a 1040±210BP
GX-3274b 2040±140BP

3000CalBC   2000CalBC   1000CalBC   CalBC/CalAD   1000CalAD   2000CalAD

Calibrated date

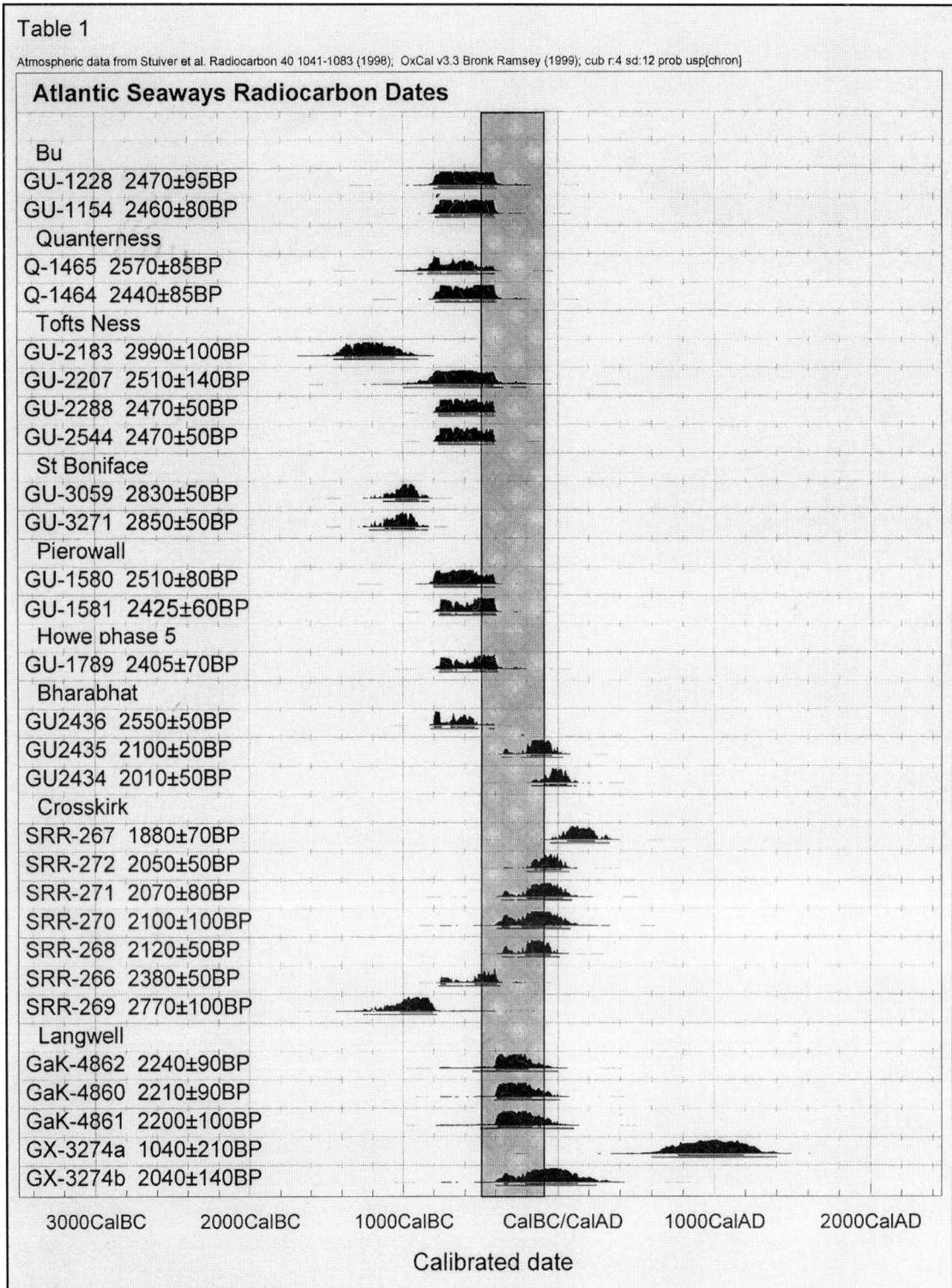

Tables 1-7 *Radiocarbon dates from sites in Atlantic Scotland.*

Table 2

Atmospheric data from Stuiver et al. Radiocarbon 40 1041-1083 (1998); OxCal v3.3 Bronk Ramsey (1999); cub r:4 sd:12 prob usp[chron]

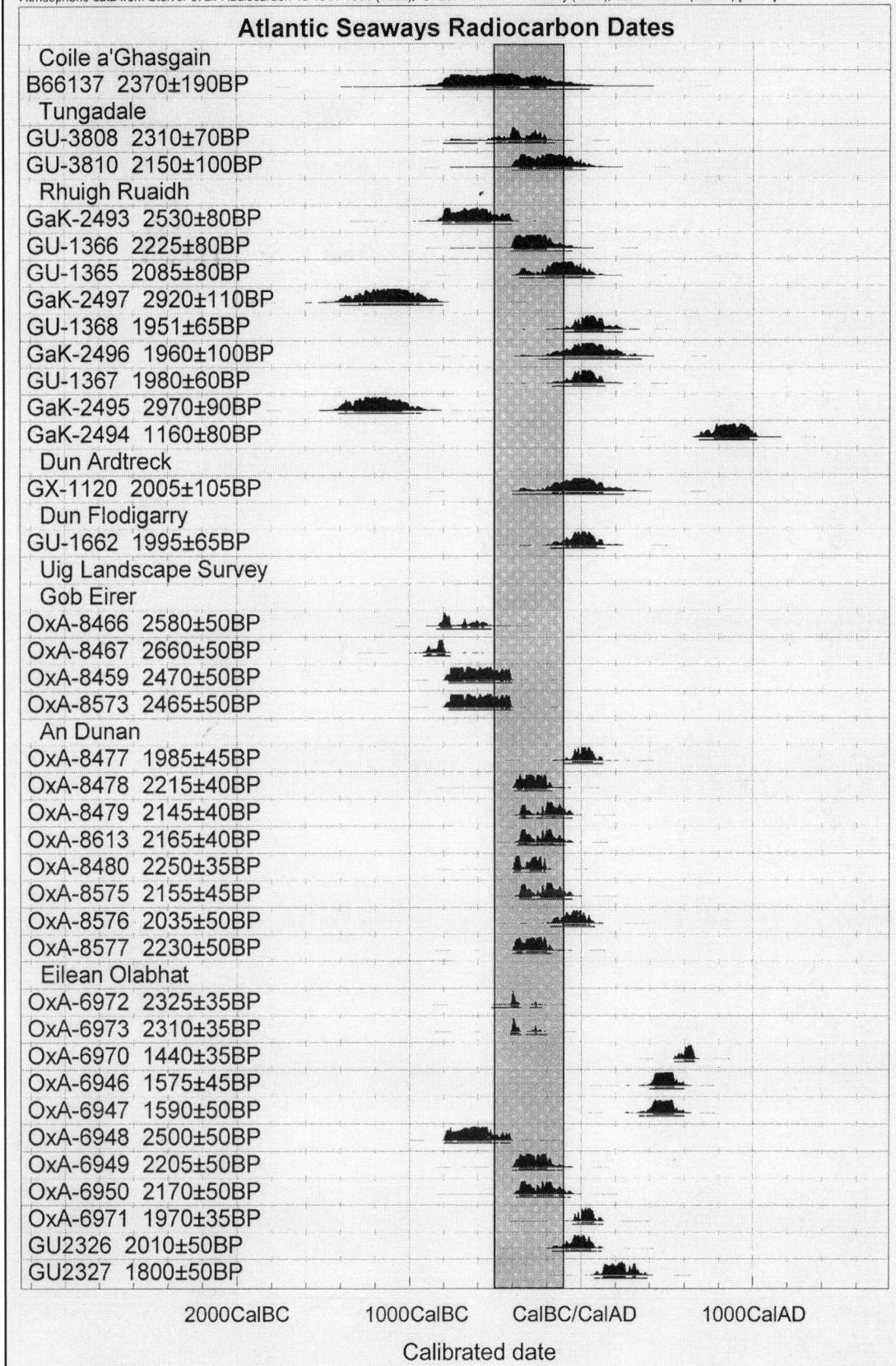

Atlantic Seaways Radiocarbon Dates

Coile a'Ghasgain
B66137 2370±190BP
Tungadale
GU-3808 2310±70BP
GU-3810 2150±100BP
Rhuigh Ruaidh
GaK-2493 2530±80BP
GU-1366 2225±80BP
GU-1365 2085±80BP
GaK-2497 2920±110BP
GU-1368 1951±65BP
GaK-2496 1960±100BP
GU-1367 1980±60BP
GaK-2495 2970±90BP
GaK-2494 1160±80BP
Dun Ardtreck
GX-1120 2005±105BP
Dun Flodigarry
GU-1662 1995±65BP
Uig Landscape Survey
Gob Eirer
OxA-8466 2580±50BP
OxA-8467 2660±50BP
OxA-8459 2470±50BP
OxA-8573 2465±50BP
An Dunan
OxA-8477 1985±45BP
OxA-8478 2215±40BP
OxA-8479 2145±40BP
OxA-8613 2165±40BP
OxA-8480 2250±35BP
OxA-8575 2155±45BP
OxA-8576 2035±50BP
OxA-8577 2230±50BP
Eilean Olabhat
OxA-6972 2325±35BP
OxA-6973 2310±35BP
OxA-6970 1440±35BP
OxA-6946 1575±45BP
OxA-6947 1590±50BP
OxA-6948 2500±50BP
OxA-6949 2205±50BP
OxA-6950 2170±50BP
OxA-6971 1970±35BP
GU2326 2010±50BP
GU2327 1800±50BP

2000CalBC   1000CalBC   CalBC/CalAD   1000CalAD

Calibrated date

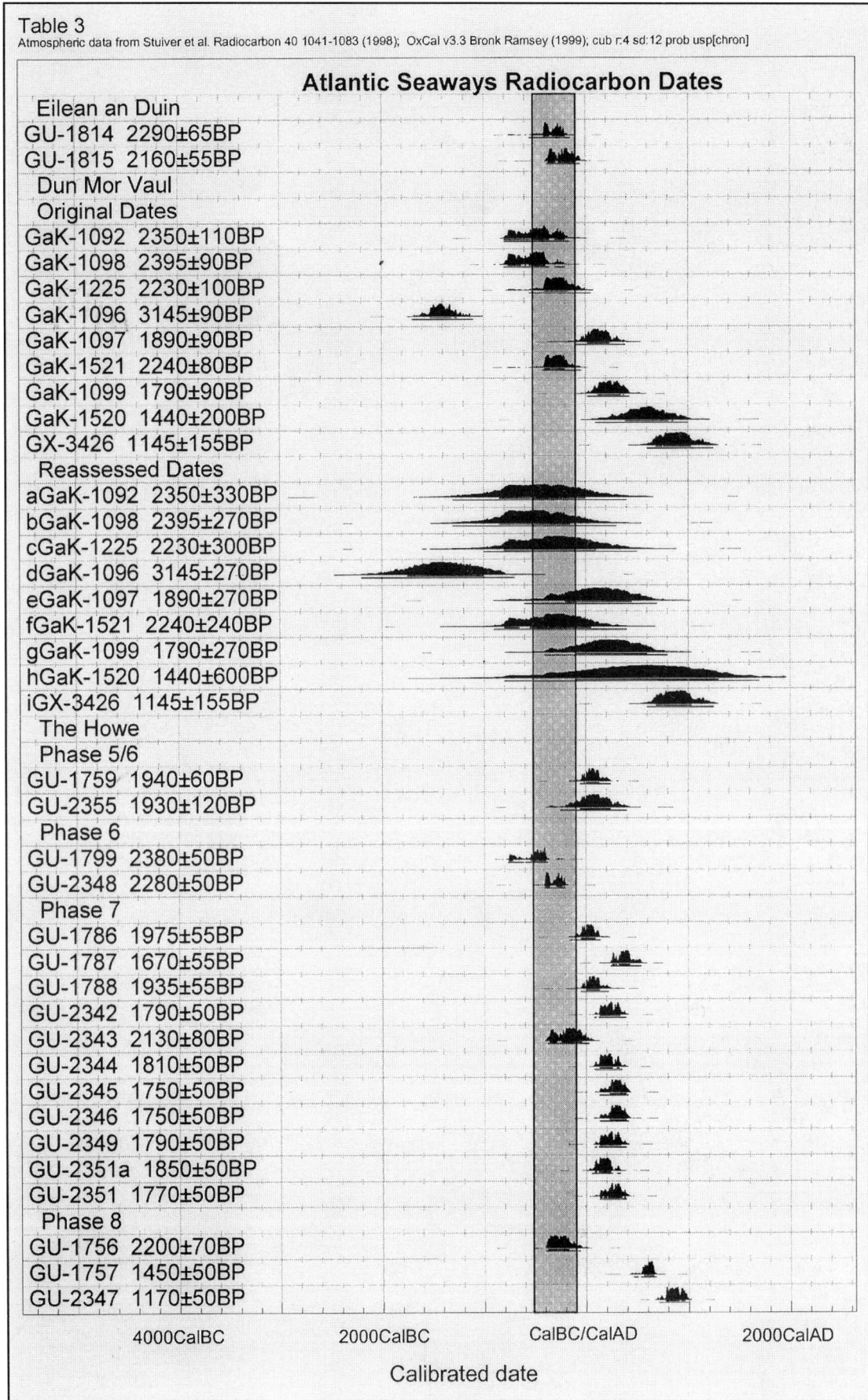

Table 3
Atmospheric data from Stuiver et al. Radiocarbon 40 1041-1083 (1998); OxCal v3.3 Bronk Ramsey (1999); cub r:4 sd:12 prob usp[chron]

Atlantic Seaways Radiocarbon Dates

Eilean an Duin
GU-1814 2290±65BP
GU-1815 2160±55BP
 Dun Mor Vaul
 Original Dates
GaK-1092 2350±110BP
GaK-1098 2395±90BP
GaK-1225 2230±100BP
GaK-1096 3145±90BP
GaK-1097 1890±90BP
GaK-1521 2240±80BP
GaK-1099 1790±90BP
GaK-1520 1440±200BP
GX-3426 1145±155BP
 Reassessed Dates
aGaK-1092 2350±330BP
bGaK-1098 2395±270BP
cGaK-1225 2230±300BP
dGaK-1096 3145±270BP
eGaK-1097 1890±270BP
fGaK-1521 2240±240BP
gGaK-1099 1790±270BP
hGaK-1520 1440±600BP
iGX-3426 1145±155BP
 The Howe
 Phase 5/6
GU-1759 1940±60BP
GU-2355 1930±120BP
 Phase 6
GU-1799 2380±50BP
GU-2348 2280±50BP
 Phase 7
GU-1786 1975±55BP
GU-1787 1670±55BP
GU-1788 1935±55BP
GU-2342 1790±50BP
GU-2343 2130±80BP
GU-2344 1810±50BP
GU-2345 1750±50BP
GU-2346 1750±50BP
GU-2349 1790±50BP
GU-2351a 1850±50BP
GU-2351 1770±50BP
 Phase 8
GU-1756 2200±70BP
GU-1757 1450±50BP
GU-2347 1170±50BP

4000CalBC   2000CalBC   CalBC/CalAD   2000CalAD

Calibrated date

Table 4

Atmospheric data from Stuiver et al. Radiocarbon 40 1041-1083 (1998); OxCal v3.3 Bronk Ramsey (1999); cub r:4 sd:12 prob usp[chron]

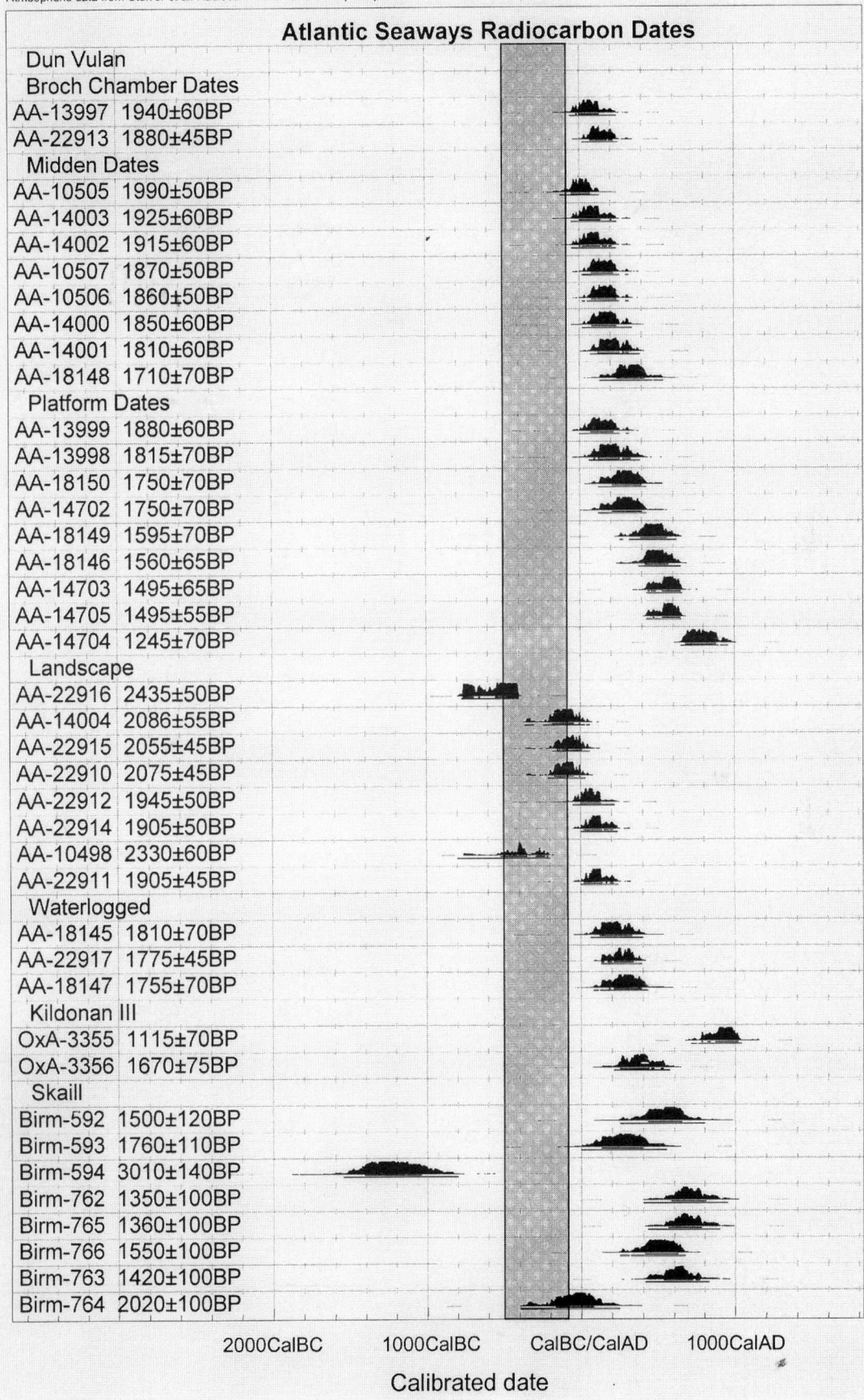

Atlantic Seaways Radiocarbon Dates

Dun Vulan	
Broch Chamber Dates	
AA-13997	1940±60BP
AA-22913	1880±45BP
Midden Dates	
AA-10505	1990±50BP
AA-14003	1925±60BP
AA-14002	1915±60BP
AA-10507	1870±50BP
AA-10506	1860±50BP
AA-14000	1850±60BP
AA-14001	1810±60BP
AA-18148	1710±70BP
Platform Dates	
AA-13999	1880±60BP
AA-13998	1815±70BP
AA-18150	1750±70BP
AA-14702	1750±70BP
AA-18149	1595±70BP
AA-18146	1560±65BP
AA-14703	1495±65BP
AA-14705	1495±55BP
AA-14704	1245±70BP
Landscape	
AA-22916	2435±50BP
AA-14004	2086±55BP
AA-22915	2055±45BP
AA-22910	2075±45BP
AA-22912	1945±50BP
AA-22914	1905±50BP
AA-10498	2330±60BP
AA-22911	1905±45BP
Waterlogged	
AA-18145	1810±70BP
AA-22917	1775±45BP
AA-18147	1755±70BP
Kildonan III	
OxA-3355	1115±70BP
OxA-3356	1670±75BP
Skaill	
Birm-592	1500±120BP
Birm-593	1760±110BP
Birm-594	3010±140BP
Birm-762	1350±100BP
Birm-765	1360±100BP
Birm-766	1550±100BP
Birm-763	1420±100BP
Birm-764	2020±100BP

2000CalBC   1000CalBC   CalBC/CalAD   1000CalAD

Calibrated date

Table 5

Atmospheric data from Stuiver et al. Radiocarbon 40 1041-1083 (1998); OxCal v3.3 Bronk Ramsey (1999); cub r:4 sd:12 prob usp[chron]

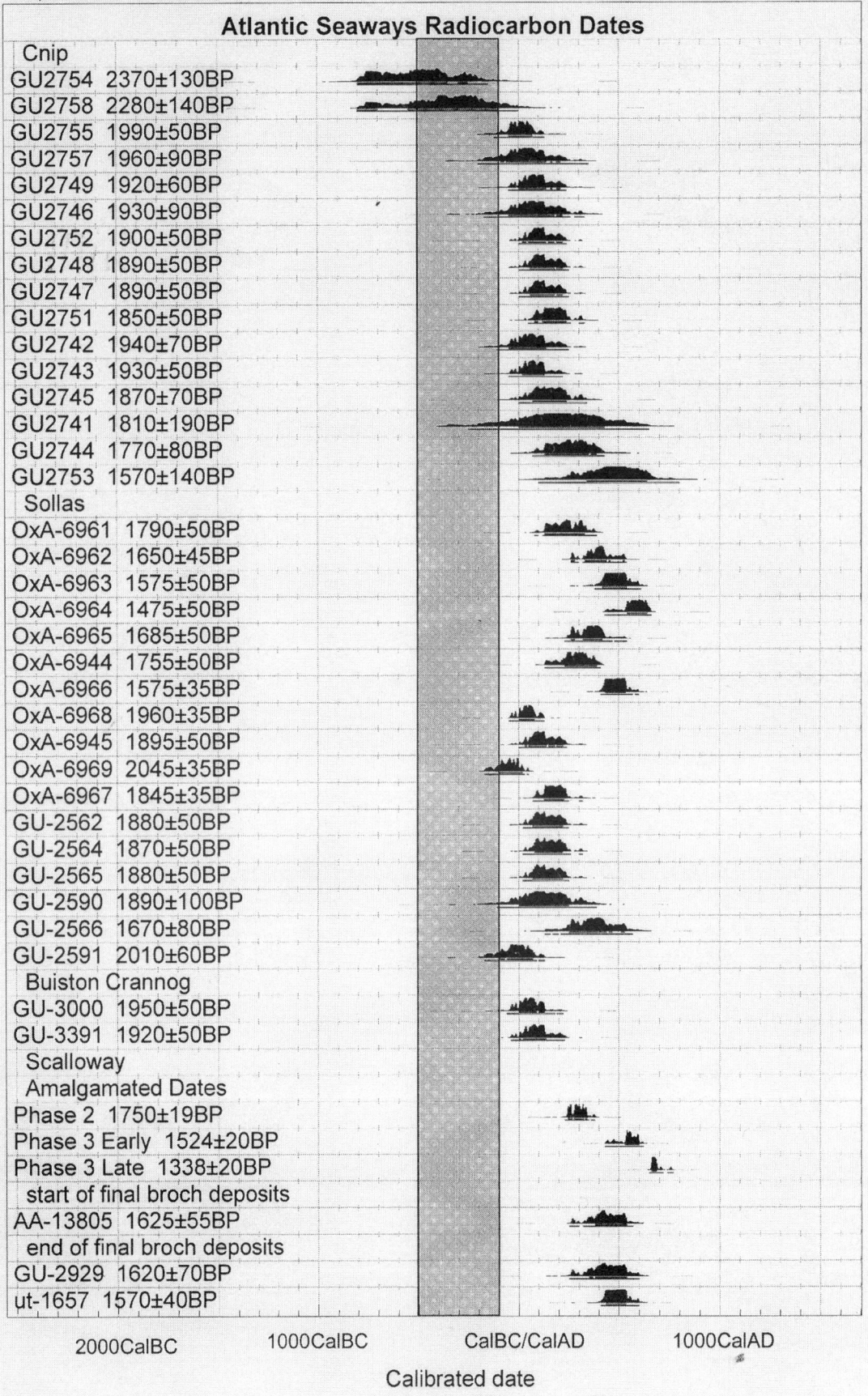

Atlantic Seaways Radiocarbon Dates

Cnip
GU2754 2370±130BP
GU2758 2280±140BP
GU2755 1990±50BP
GU2757 1960±90BP
GU2749 1920±60BP
GU2746 1930±90BP
GU2752 1900±50BP
GU2748 1890±50BP
GU2747 1890±50BP
GU2751 1850±50BP
GU2742 1940±70BP
GU2743 1930±50BP
GU2745 1870±70BP
GU2741 1810±190BP
GU2744 1770±80BP
GU2753 1570±140BP
Sollas
OxA-6961 1790±50BP
OxA-6962 1650±45BP
OxA-6963 1575±50BP
OxA-6964 1475±50BP
OxA-6965 1685±50BP
OxA-6944 1755±50BP
OxA-6966 1575±35BP
OxA-6968 1960±35BP
OxA-6945 1895±50BP
OxA-6969 2045±35BP
OxA-6967 1845±35BP
GU-2562 1880±50BP
GU-2564 1870±50BP
GU-2565 1880±50BP
GU-2590 1890±100BP
GU-2566 1670±80BP
GU-2591 2010±60BP
Buiston Crannog
GU-3000 1950±50BP
GU-3391 1920±50BP
Scalloway
Amalgamated Dates
Phase 2 1750±19BP
Phase 3 Early 1524±20BP
Phase 3 Late 1338±20BP
start of final broch deposits
AA-13805 1625±55BP
end of final broch deposits
GU-2929 1620±70BP
ut-1657 1570±40BP

2000CalBC   1000CalBC   CalBC/CalAD   1000CalAD

Calibrated date

Table 6

Atmospheric data from Stuiver et al. Radiocarbon 40 1041-1083 (1998); OxCal v3.3 Bronk Ramsey (1999); cub r:4 sd:12 prob usp[chron]

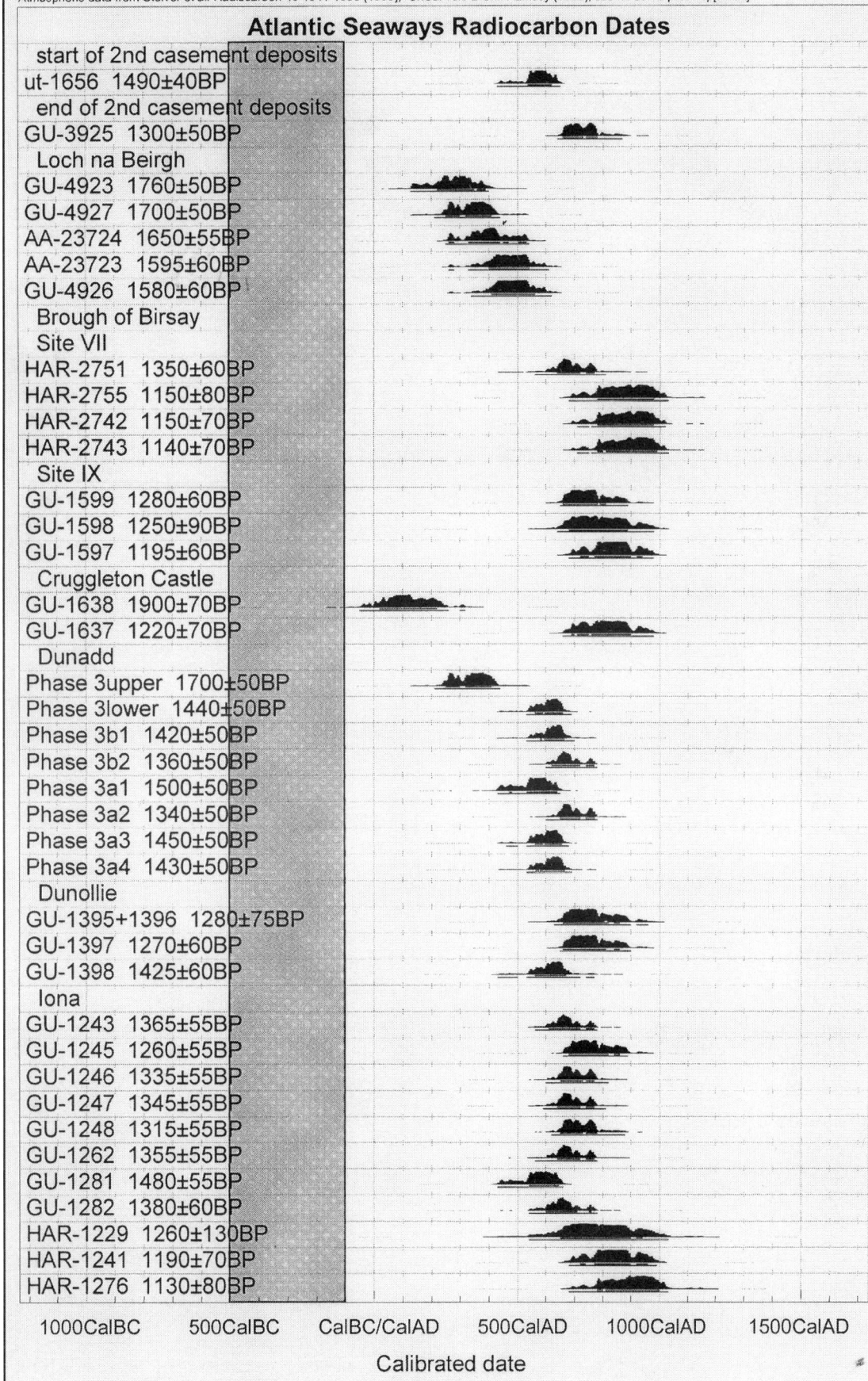

Atlantic Seaways Radiocarbon Dates

start of 2nd casement deposits	
ut-1656 1490±40BP	
end of 2nd casement deposits	
GU-3925 1300±50BP	
Loch na Beirgh	
GU-4923 1760±50BP	
GU-4927 1700±50BP	
AA-23724 1650±55BP	
AA-23723 1595±60BP	
GU-4926 1580±60BP	
Brough of Birsay	
Site VII	
HAR-2751 1350±60BP	
HAR-2755 1150±80BP	
HAR-2742 1150±70BP	
HAR-2743 1140±70BP	
Site IX	
GU-1599 1280±60BP	
GU-1598 1250±90BP	
GU-1597 1195±60BP	
Cruggleton Castle	
GU-1638 1900±70BP	
GU-1637 1220±70BP	
Dunadd	
Phase 3upper 1700±50BP	
Phase 3lower 1440±50BP	
Phase 3b1 1420±50BP	
Phase 3b2 1360±50BP	
Phase 3a1 1500±50BP	
Phase 3a2 1340±50BP	
Phase 3a3 1450±50BP	
Phase 3a4 1430±50BP	
Dunollie	
GU-1395+1396 1280±75BP	
GU-1397 1270±60BP	
GU-1398 1425±60BP	
Iona	
GU-1243 1365±55BP	
GU-1245 1260±55BP	
GU-1246 1335±55BP	
GU-1247 1345±55BP	
GU-1248 1315±55BP	
GU-1262 1355±55BP	
GU-1281 1480±55BP	
GU-1282 1380±60BP	
HAR-1229 1260±130BP	
HAR-1241 1190±70BP	
HAR-1276 1130±80BP	

1000CalBC   500CalBC   CalBC/CalAD   500CalAD   1000CalAD   1500CalAD

Calibrated date

Table 7

Atmospheric data from Stuiver et al. Radiocarbon 40 1041-1083 (1998); OxCal v3.3 Bronk Ramsey (1999); cub r:4 sd:12 prob usp[chron]

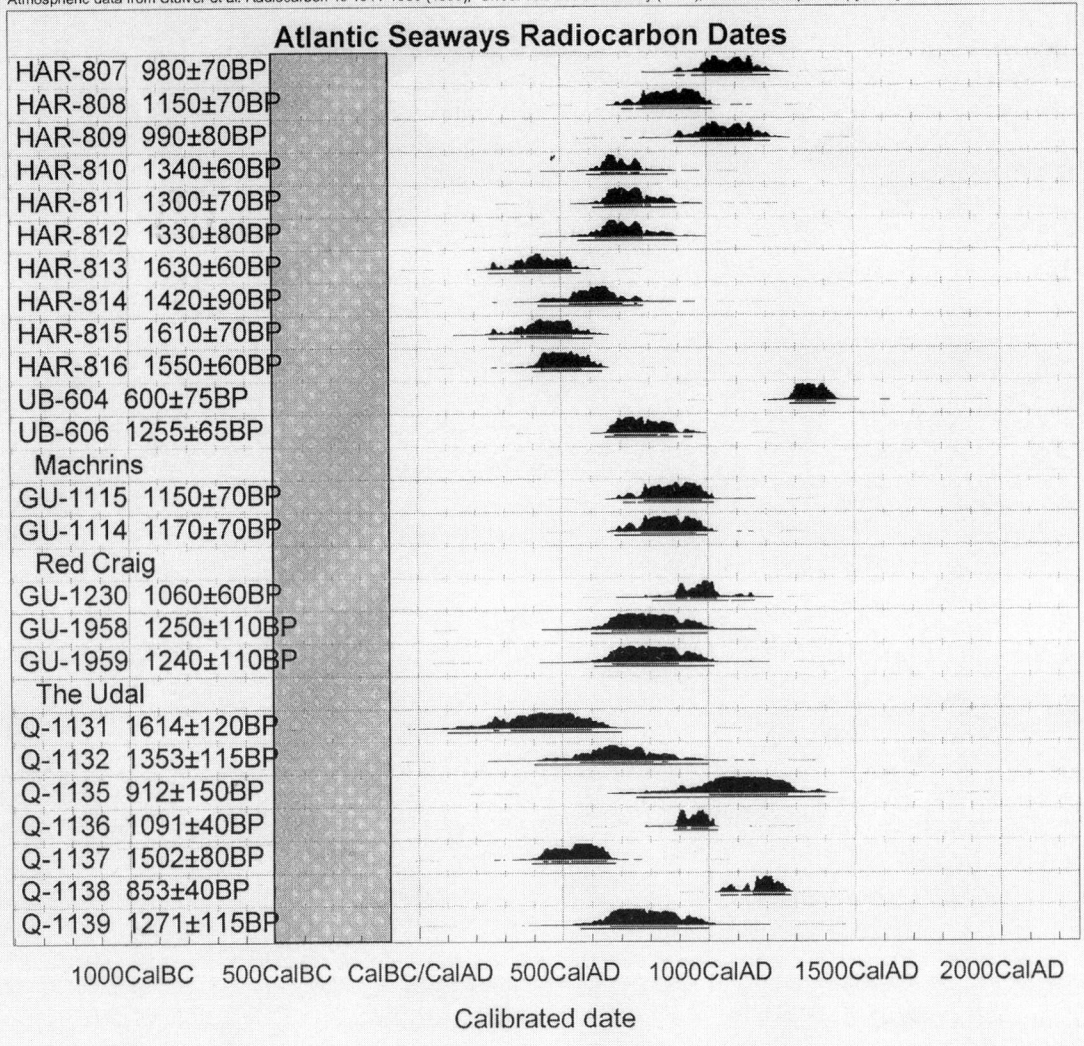

Atlantic Seaways Radiocarbon Dates

HAR-807	980±70BP
HAR-808	1150±70BP
HAR-809	990±80BP
HAR-810	1340±60BP
HAR-811	1300±70BP
HAR-812	1330±80BP
HAR-813	1630±60BP
HAR-814	1420±90BP
HAR-815	1610±70BP
HAR-816	1550±60BP
UB-604	600±75BP
UB-606	1255±65BP
Machrins	
GU-1115	1150±70BP
GU-1114	1170±70BP
Red Craig	
GU-1230	1060±60BP
GU-1958	1250±110BP
GU-1959	1240±110BP
The Udal	
Q-1131	1614±120BP
Q-1132	1353±115BP
Q-1135	912±150BP
Q-1136	1091±40BP
Q-1137	1502±80BP
Q-1138	853±40BP
Q-1139	1271±115BP

1000CalBC   500CalBC   CalBC/CalAD   500CalAD   1000CalAD   1500CalAD   2000CalAD

Calibrated date

96

Brochs as Markers in Time

RICHARD HINGLEY

INTRODUCTION – DISAGREEMENTS

THE PAST twenty years has been a dynamic period in the development of broch studies. A number of significant excavations have been carried out (for instance, the excavations at Howe [Orkney], Dun Vulan [South Uist], Loch na Berie [Lewis] and Scatness [Shetland]; see Ballin Smith 1994, Sharples 1998 and Parker Pearson and Sharples 1999) and excavation reports published (on Howe, Bu and Dun Vulan; see references above and Fairhurst 1984). A series of synthetic works has also been produced, with books and articles about the Scottish Iron Age published, for instance, by Ian Ralston, Ian Armit and Richard Hingley (see for instance Hingley 1992, Ralston 1996 and Armit 1997a). As a consequence of this work, much new material is available with which to study brochs and a series of new ideas about the origin and significance of these monuments has been generated.

Twenty years ago there was no clear consensus about the meaning of the term 'broch' and there has been an intensification and broadening of the debate in recent years. As the amount of evidence increases, so does the intensity of the debate. A variety of major areas of disagreement emerged during the broch conference in Shetland in July 2000 and these are derived from earlier discussions (see for instance Armit 1997b; 1997c and Sharples and Parker Pearson 1997). For instance, a debate exists over the meaning of the term 'broch' and the range of sites that should be included in the category if indeed it is a single category – alternative terms such as 'complex Atlantic roundhouse' and 'substantial roundhouse' were bandied around. Another area of contention is the date of the origin of broch architecture - do brochs originate in the mid or the late first millennium BC? In addition, what is the context of broch construction – do they form the homes of high-status families within a subservient community, or just one of the types of substantial roundhouse that categorise the Iron Age of the North?

I do not see this disagreement as problematic since I feel that it actually helps to create a lively subject. The past was a complex place to live in and our accounts should mirror this complexity rather than making the past appear simple and predictable. The definitions and approaches that we use should help us to understand changes in the nature of society through time and space. The architecture and the archaeology of the individual broch varied from place to place in Scotland. If the concept of the broch *is* meaningful, its meaning evidently varied between places and times and our work should allow for this variation. In fact, the more open debate and disagreement we have the better.

As well as the quantity of work that has been undertaken on brochs over the past twenty years, the period has also been a dynamic time in the development of the later prehistoric archaeology of Britain as a whole. The most influential book during this lengthy period has been Barry Cunliffe's *Iron Age Communities* (Cunliffe 1971; 1991). Although the value of this book has perhaps declined through time, as considerable quantities of additional material have been collected from excavation and fieldwork throughout Britain, there is as yet no comprehensive work to replace it. From the mid 1980s changes have occurred in the nature of the theory that is used to interpret later prehistoric archaeology, with the increasing influence of post-modernist philosophy on the subject. Approaches to the symbolic significance of Iron Age material culture and social space have become increasingly powerful in the south of Britain under the influence of a range of writers (for a useful summary of a variety of perspectives, see the papers in the volume edited by Gwilt and Haselgrove [1997]). In particular J.D. Hill produced a powerful perspective on structured deposition in later prehistoric Wessex (Hill 1995). Cosmological models for the organisation of social space have also become influential, particularly through the work of Mike Parker Pearson and Andrew Fitzpatrick (Parker Pearson 1996; Fitzpatrick 1997). These new approaches to later prehistory have created original perspectives about Iron Age settlement and material culture; some elements of them have been imported into the study of brochs, for instance by Armit, Hingley and by Parker Pearson and Sharples (Armit 1997b; Hingley 1992; 1996; Parker Pearson and Sharples 1999).

Recently the attention of a number of archaeologists has turned towards another topic relating to the symbolism of past material culture - the social biography of buildings and objects (see for instance, Gosden and Lock 1998; Bruck 1999; World Archaeology 1999). This perspective is sometimes taken to suggest that a conceptual parallel may have been drawn during later prehistory between the spirit of the object or structure and that of the individual or the community (Hingley 1997). This is an area of theory that I intend to study with regard to the architecture of the Scottish broch. In the spirit of my comment that debate and disagreement is valuable, I will make a number of suggestions in this paper that I

intend to provoke dissent and discussion. These relate to the meaning of broch architecture and the significance of brochs in the northern Iron Age. They focus on why later prehistoric communities in some areas built brochs and what these structures meant.

HOUSES FOR THE LIVING AND FOR THE DEAD

In 1996 I published an article in *World Archaeology* in which I suggested that some of the well-excavated substantial roundhouses in Atlantic Scotland appear to have been built out of the ruins of Neolithic chambered cairns (Hingley 1996). A relationship appears also to exist between later prehistoric houses and stone circles (partly explored in Hingley 1999). I suggested that during later prehistory people were actively engaged in the rebuilding of some of the ancient monuments that formed part of their ancestral landscapes. Therefore Iron Age people lived within a heavily-domesticated landscape of fields, areas of pasture and settlement. Within these inherited landscapes there were individual monuments built in ancient times, the most monumental of which were often the chambered cairns and stone circles. These monuments would have been, at one and the same time, both familiar and strange to the people who lived in these areas during later prehistory. They were familiar because they existed within the landscapes which people inhabited and lived their everyday lives. Communities would have had folk tales that explained the origin and history of various features in the landscape (Bruck and Goodman 1999, 8), including these inherited monuments. These accounts would have projected an idea of the considerable ancestry of these archaeological features and also perhaps have provided some mythical story of the origins of each structure (for a comparable situation in early historic Ireland see Rees and Rees 1961; Lynn 1993; and Raftery 1994, 180). At the same time chambered cairns and stone circles were also strange, in that they were physical remains derived from a bygone age.

During later prehistory people no longer built burial monuments for their dead (Hingley 1992). The remains of the dead sometimes occur in the settlements of the living. Occasional burials occur in the archaeological record but they are rare and it would appear that the majority of people were not buried in formal graves. People may have been exposed to the elements and their remains later collected for various types of ritual (see Bruck 1995 for a discussion of the late Bronze Age evidence). Pieces of people are sometimes found in domestic contexts – in the fills of pits, in the packing of drains and the filling behind walls – a particular association appears to occur in Atlantic Scotland between pieces of people and the entrances and drains of houses (Hingley 1996, 233; Parker Pearson and Sharples 1999, 139). It is likely that the presence of these human remains on domestic sites relates to ritual actions carried out within the household or community.

The monumental structures created during later prehistory were the houses of the living, not those of the dead, although the remains of the dead were sometimes incorporated into them. The ancient tombs in the later prehistoric landscape would have been known to people, and evidence suggests some physical intervention in the remains during later prehistory. A number of chambered tombs have produced later prehistoric artefacts (Fig. 18); and I have suggested that people were entering tombs, removing and curating the Neolithic deposits contained within them and, sometimes, leaving deposits of their own (Hingley 1996). Direct evidence for the removal and the curation of Neolithic and early Bronze Age burial deposits during later prehistory has yet to be located in Neolithic chambered cairns within Scotland, but there is some indirect evidence for this type of activity. A cist at Sand Fiold in Orkney (Dalland 1999)

was built with a hinge to allow access to the burial deposits after burial. The evidence from the very careful excavation and post-excavation of this site indicates a number of distinct burial events within the cist over a period of 1500 years or more. In one of these events, an urn from an earlier burial was repaired and bound. The latest phase of use of the cist appears to date to the later Bronze Age and the evidence from Sand Fiold indicates continued reuse of an earlier burial monument during later prehistory. If my arguments about the reuse of Neolithic chambered cairns during later prehistory are correct, further careful excavation of burial deposits within Neolithic chambered cairns in the future should produce comparable information to that from Sand Fiold.

I would argue, therefore, that Neolithic monuments were both familiar and unfamiliar to people in the later prehistoric period. They were well-known features of the landscape and were used in various ways; but they were also unfamiliar, as they had a timespan that was probably recorded in some form in folk tales and stories. I have also suggested that people at this time tried to draw upon the inspiration of the monumental architecture of the Neolithic chambered tomb in building their own domestic structures (for the details of this process, see Hingley 1996). Some general aspects of the architecture of Atlantic substantial roundhouses and also of souterrains were derived from a later prehistoric appreciation of the form of three thousand year-old monuments (Brothwell 1977; Hingley 1996). Perhaps the physical interventions into the monuments led to an understanding of their structure which was used in creating later prehistoric houses and settlements – a process that I have described as a type of prehistoric archaeological research (Hingley 1996, 242).

The best evidence comes from the detailed excavation of Howe (Orkney), where the people who built the substantial roundhouse

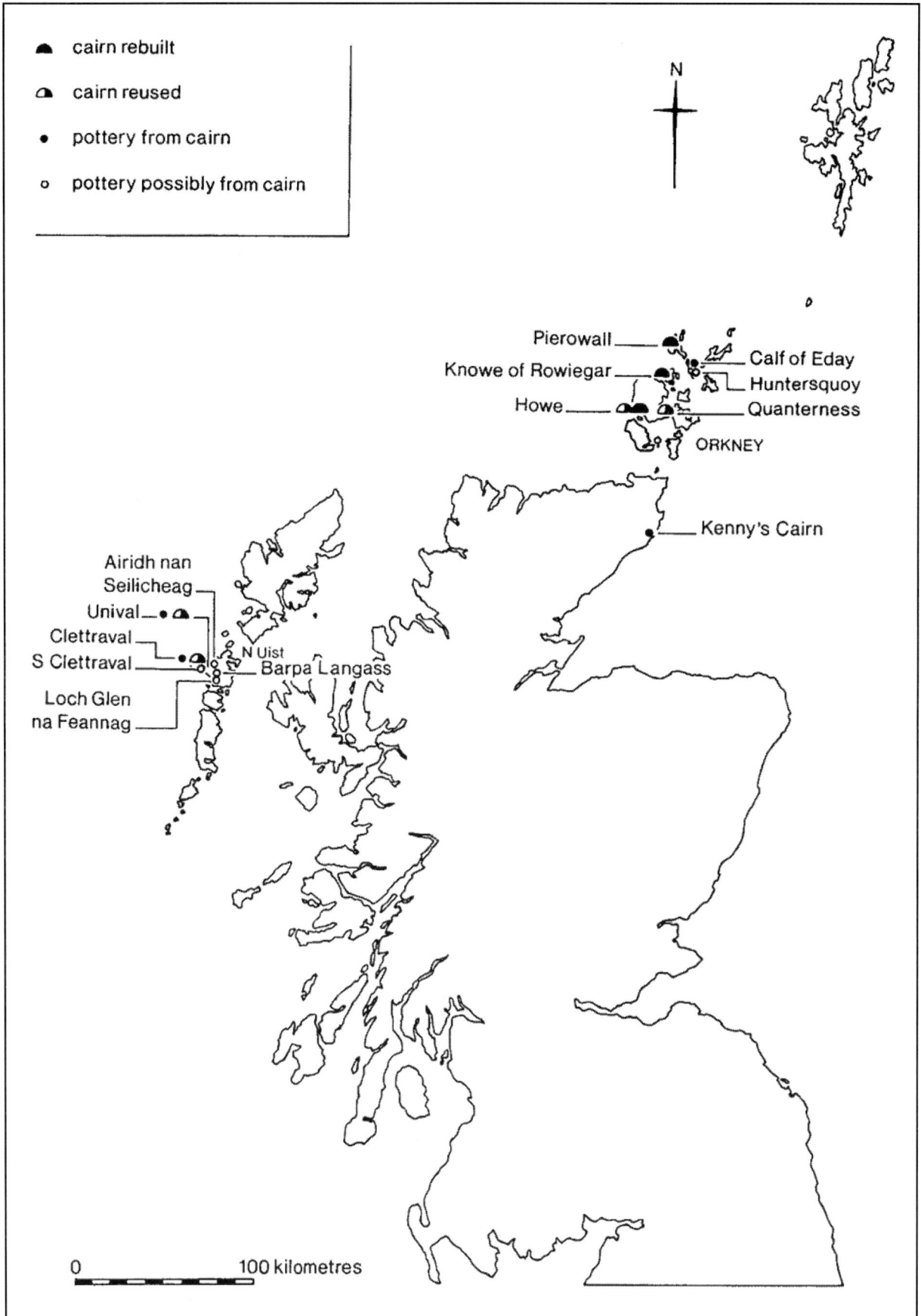

Fig.18 *The distribution of Neolithic chambered cairns in Atlantic Scotland which have (a) produced Iron Age pottery, or (b) were rebuilt as Iron Age roundhouses (reprinted from Hingley 1996).*

adapted the chambered cairn and incorporated its chamber into their own structure (Ballin Smith 1994; Hingley 1996). The roundhouse itself followed on from an earlier occupation which focused on control of access to the chamber (Fig. 19) I suggested in my 1996 paper that the household at Howe and those on a number of sites elsewhere had access to and curated the human remains and other cultural items within the Neolithic burial chamber (for more discussion of the individual sites see Hingley 1999). Not all brochs were built on top of Neolithic monuments (see for instance Sharples 1998), but very few have been excavated down to the earliest layers and it is currently unclear what percentage of brochs had a sequence comparable to that at Howe. The fact that not all brochs overlie Neolithic monuments does not, however, devalue the significance of the evidence for later prehistoric interventions into Neolithic monuments.

I have suggested that later prehistoric people curated and used the materials from the Neolithic burial deposits. The evidence from Howe and elsewhere suggests that control of these resources was important to certain households. People at this time may have controlled these remains, uncovered them from time to time and used them for certain acts within the community. Some of these acts of use may also have involved the deliberate conservation of the objects, as in the case of the urn from Sand Field. The use and control of these deposits may have derived from the fact that they had a particularly powerful role in acts of ritual at this time.

TEMPLES OR HOUSES?

It has also been suggested that brochs in general (or perhaps some particular brochs, for instance, Howe) might have functioned as temples – places of worship. The use of the human remains within the chamber of the tomb and the general idea of modifying a burial place into a domestic structure perhaps suggests to the modern mind the idea of ritual and religion. I do not feel, however, that this argument is helpful to the debate. Distinct ritual structures and buildings are generally rare in the later prehistoric period in the British Isles (Woodward 1992). In

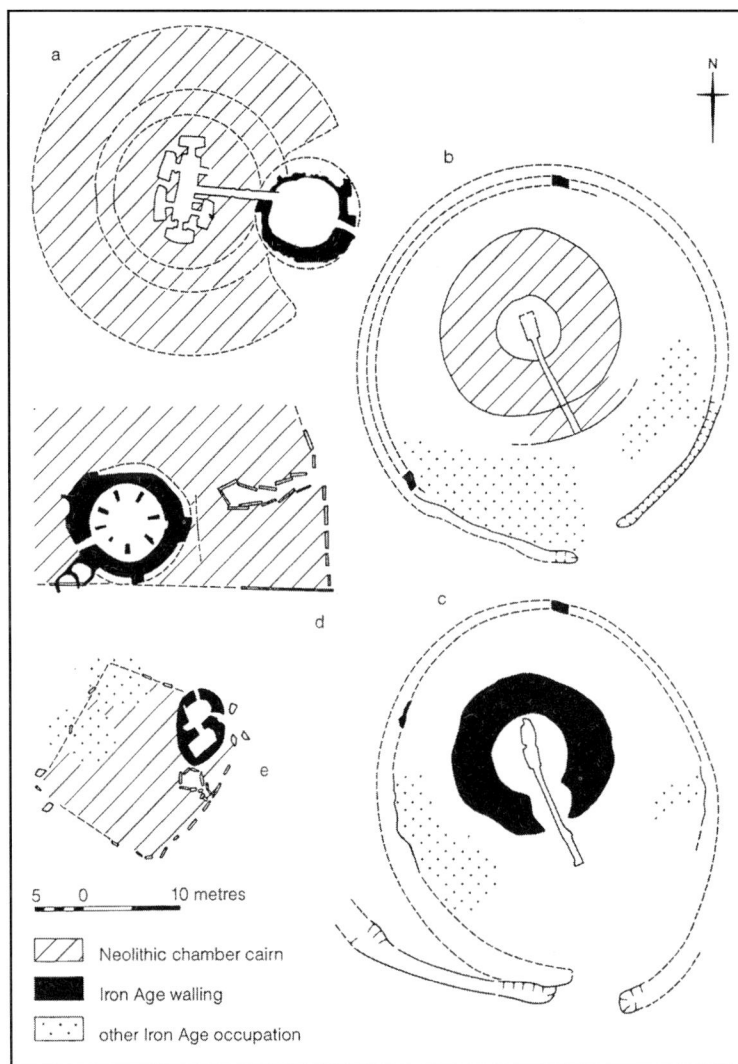

Fig.19 *Neolithic chambered cairns rebuilt during later prehistory (reprinted from Hingley 1996). a) Quanterness (Orkney; after Renfew 1979 and Davidson adn Henshall 1989); b) Howe Phase 3-4 (Orkney; after Ballin Smith 1994); c) Howe Phase 5 (after Ballin Smith 1994); d) Clettraval (North Uist; after Lindsay Scott 1934-5); e) Unival (North Uist; after Lindsay Scott 1948).*

addition, brochs contain many of the elements that are used to define domestic houses in Scottish later prehistory. They often contain hearths and were divided up into a number of rooms, often on a radial basis (Hingley 1992). Quantities of domestic material (broken pottery, animal bones and other food remains) are found during excavation. It is likely that ritual beliefs were a fundamental part of everyday life in Iron Age Scotland. The cycle of daily life will have been imbued with ritual and all actions will have had ritual dimensions. Brochs, like houses in many societies, were probably temples and houses at one and the same time, as few distinct places of worship existed - ritual was part of every day life (Hingley 1998).

The suggestion that houses in later prehistoric Scotland may sometimes have been built to maintain access to the bones of ancestors does not suggest a distinct ritual usage for the houses but an aspect of the domestic occupation. Perhaps particular groups, by living in a house which contained a significant earlier structure and also the human remains associated with that structure, were demonstrating power over others in their own community. The elaboration of the house at Howe may indicate the extension of the power of a particular household or group of households. An increasing control of access to the ancestors occurs through time on this site and this may demonstrate the escalating power of the household. This power may have been derived through physical control of access to the inherited structure of the chambered tomb and the human material within its chamber. In effect, by controlling more powerful rituals these households may have had effective control over others within the landscapes dominated by the brochs.

MARKERS IN TIME

In some cases during later prehistory people may have entered chambered cairns and used the materials within them; access to these inherited monuments may have been strictly controlled by a section of society at this time. On occasions, dominant households may have built brochs and substantial roundhouses to control access even more effectively, as appears to be the case at Howe (Fig. 19). By constructing a broch the household may also, in effect, have drawn upon the architectural remains of the chambered cairn as a source of inspiration for elements of their new house.

At the same time, I would argue that by their very nature brochs are monumental structures that have effectively acted to create markers in time and space. They are usually impressively sited in the landscape and are also highly monumental structures that use their monumentality to dominate their surroundings. The monumentality of the broch was a deliberate statement. Later prehistoric people lived in a landscape that contained ancient stone-built monuments. Tales within society will have attributed a great age to these chambered cairns and probably also have provided some idea about their origin. I have suggested that people dug into and explored these earlier monuments at this time, acquiring knowledge of the materials and techniques used to build them. People during later prehistory would also have a detailed knowledge of the character of buildings from their own experience of the structures that they erected and lived within. These factors all suggest that the builders of brochs were fully aware of the nature of building stone as a material that would survive an individual human lifetime. The architecture that was used to construct the brochs also appears to have been intended to create structures with long duration. The walls were thick and stable and constructed to last. There was presumably a deliberate intention at this time to build stable and long-lasting structures.

I would contend that knowledge encapsulated in folk memory allowed the creation of a conception of time that enabled the builders of brochs to build for the future (for the concept of prehistoric time see Gosden and Lock 1998 and Hingley 1999). Mythical history provided an ancestry for the chamber cairns and later prehistoric society drew the physical remains of these monuments into the landscape of the living. House-building was informed by this concept of 'history' (Hingley 1999). The creation of a broch was perhaps an active attempt by dominant households to create a marker in time around which the future could be focused. In some cases the broch actually used the remains of a chambered cairn in its construction and thereby drew the earlier structure into a new domestic context. At the same time, it was intended that the broch would have a future at the time of its construction.

I am not suggesting some evolved form of knowledge within later prehistoric society of past history, the present or the future. Our current understanding suggests, rather, a dominant cyclical view of time. It has been argued that the roundhouse of Iron Age Britain effectively created a cosmological calendar that helped to mark and define time (Fitzpatrick 1997; Oswald 1997; Parker Pearson 1996). This would help to define a series of elements as basically cyclical – including the day, the year, the human lifetime and perhaps the life of the household. Yet, although this general model has its uses, I would suggest that monumental architecture during later prehistory may incorporate a desire to fix the present moment using the inheritance of the past. Perhaps an idea existed during later prehistory of a different past in which life was lived in a different way. The excavation of chambered tomb chambers must have caused people to think about how the materials that they uncovered differed from those that existed within their own society. The nature of the sequence at Howe and other sites suggests that people were fully aware that the

power of the inherited monuments derived from their otherness. This realisation of a different past perhaps represents a tool which was used by broch-builders as part of their attempt to define their own communities by building substantial houses which served to project the unity of the household and its future identity.

Finally, it is of interest that the attempts by later prehistoric households to create markers in time has actually had an effect over a two thousand-year time-span. In 1997 Robbie the Pict proposed the rebuilding of a broch on Skye in order to provide a modern home. His suggestion did not meet with the approval of the archaeological authorities, but this does demonstrate the success of the broch as a physical statement that has retained a significance to the present day. The early medieval, Viking and Victorian evidence from other broch sites shows their significance throughout post-broch times. It is the contention of this speculative paper that brochs were built using an understanding of the past and that they were constructed in order to help to define and perpetuate a particular social order.

BIBLIOGRAPHY

Armit, I. (1997a) *Celtic Scotland*. London, Batsford.

Armit, I. (1997b) Cultural landscapes and identities: a case study in the Scottish Iron Age. In Gwilt, A. and Haselgrove, C. (eds) *Reconstructing Iron Age Societies*, 248-53. Oxford, Oxbow Books.

Armit, I. (1997c) Architecture and the household: a response to Sharples and Parker Pearson. In Gwilt, A. and Haselgrove, C. (eds) *Reconstructing Iron Age Societies*, 266-69. Oxford, Oxbow Books.

Ballin Smith, B (1994) *Howe: four millennia of Orkney prehistory*. Edinburgh, Society of Antiquaries of Scotland.

Brothwell, D. (1977) On a mycoform stone structure in Orkney. *Bulletin of the Institute of Archaeology, University of London*, 14, 179-90.

Bruck, J. (1995) A place for the dead. *Proceedings of the Prehistoric Society* 61, 245-78.

Bruck, J. (1999) Houses, lifecycles and deposition on Middle Bronze Age settlements in Southern England. *Proceedings of the Prehistoric Society* 65, 145-66.

Bruck, J. and Goodman, M. (1999) Introduction: themes for a critical archaeology of prehistoric settlement. In Bruck, J. and Goodman. M. (eds) *Making Places in the Prehistoric World: themes in settlement archaeology*, 1-19. London, UCL Press.

Cunliffe, B.W. (1971) *Iron Age Communities in Britain*. London, Routledge.

Cunliffe, B.W. (1991) *Iron Age Communities in Britain*. 3rd edition. London, Routledge.

Dalland, M. (1999) Sand Fiold: the excavation of an exceptional cist in Orkney. *Proceedings of the Prehistoric Society* 65, 373-415.

Davidson, J. and Henshall, A. (1989) *The Chambered Cairns of Orkney*. Edinburgh, Edinburgh University Press.

Fairhurst, H. (1984) *Excavations at Crosskirk Broch, Caithness*. Edinburgh, Society of Antiquaries of Scotland.

Fitzpatrick, A. (1997) Everyday life in Wessex. In Gwilt, A. and Haselgrove, C. (eds) *Reconstructing Iron Age Societies*, 73-86. Oxford, Oxbow Books.

Gosden, C. and Lock, G. (1998) Prehistoric histories. *World Archaeology* 30, 2-12.

Gwilt, A. and Haselgrove, C. (eds) (1997) *Reconstructing Iron Age Societies*. Oxbow Monographs 71. Oxford, Oxbow Books.

Hill, J. D. (1995) *Ritual and Rubbish in the Iron Age of Wessex*. British Archaeological Reports 242. Oxford : Tempus Reparatum.

Hingley, R. (1992) Society in Scotland from 700BC to AD 200. *Proceedings of the Society of Antiquaries of Scotland*, 1227-54.

Hingley, R. (1996) Ancestors and Identity in later prehistory of Atlantic Scotland. *World Archaeology* 28, 231-43.

Hingley, R. (1997) Iron, ironworking and regeneration. In Gwilt, A. and Haselgrove, C. (eds) (1997) *Reconstructing Iron Age Societies*, 9-18. Oxford, Oxbow Books.

Hingley, R. (1998) *Settlement and Sacrifice: the later prehistoric people of Scotland*. Edinburgh, Canongate.

Hingley, R. (1999) The creation of later prehistoric landscapes. In Bevan, B (ed) *Northern Exposure: interpretative devolution and the Iron Ages in Britain*, 233-52. Leicester, Leicester Archaeology Monograph.

Lindsay Scott, W. (1934-5) The chambered cairn at Clettraval, North Uist. *Proceedings of the Society of Antiquaries of Scotland* 69, 480-536.

Lindsay Scott, W. (1947-8) The chambered tomb of Unival, North Uist. *Proceedings of the Society of Antiquaries of Scotland* 82, 1-48.

Lynn, C. (1993) Navan Fort: new light on the Irish Epics, *Current Archaeology* 134, 44-9.

Oswald, A. (1997) A doorway to the past. In Gwilt, A. and Haselgrove, C. (eds) *Reconstructing Iron Age Societies*, 87-95. Oxford, Oxbow Books.

Parker Pearson, M. (1996) Food, fertility and front doors in the first millennium BC. In Champion, T.C. and Collis, J.R. (eds) *The Iron Age in Britain and Ireland: Recent Trends*, 1117-32. Sheffield, J.R. Collis Publications.

Parker Pearson, M. and Sharples, N. (1999) *Between Land and Sea: excavations at Dun Vulan, South Uist*. Sheffield, Sheffield Academic Press.

Raftery, B. (1994) *Pagan Celtic Ireland*. London, Thames and Hudson.

Ralston, I. (1996) Recent work on the Iron Age settlement record in Scotland. In Champion, T.C. and Collis, J.R. (eds) *The Iron Age in Britain and Ireland: Recent Trends*, 133-54. Sheffield, J.R. Collis Publications.

Rees, A. and Rees, B. (1961) *Celtic Heritage*. London, Thames and Hudson.

Renfrew, C. (1979) *Investigations in Orkney*. London, Society of Antiquaries.

Sharples, N. (1998) *Scalloway: a broch, late Iron Age settlement and medieval cemetery in Shetland*. Oxford, Oxbow Books.

Sharples, N. and Parker Pearson, M. (1997) 'Why Were Brochs Built? Recent Studies in the Iron Age of Atlantic Scotland'. In Gwilt, A. and Haselgrove, C. (eds.) *Reconstructing Iron Age Societies*, 254-65. Oxford, Oxbow Books.

Woodward, A. (1992) *Shrines and Sacrifice*. London, Batsford.

World Archaeology (1999) *The Cultural Biography of Objects*, Volume 31.

Life Histories and the Buildings of the Atlantic Iron Age

NIALL SHARPLES

INTRODUCTION

ECENT WORK in anthropology has emphasised that house shape and form not only provide shelter and comfort to the occupants (Carsten and Hugh-Jones 1995) but also a social framework through which individuals and groups can make sense of their lives. Structure is used to constrain and guide the body as it moves through space and in doing so mediates encounters between individuals. The process of architectural creation captures a particular event in time, and alteration and abandonment delimit a temporal sequence of considerable importance to the occupants.

Archaeological applications of these new approaches have been restricted in the British Isles. They have largely focused on the use of the house for mapping the inhabitants' cosmological understanding of their environment. The plan of the house appears as a template for the mental structures of the inhabitants. This type of approach has been particularly important in rethinking the Iron Age round houses both of southern England (Hingley 1990; Fitzpatrick 1994) and Atlantic Scotland (Pearson and Sharples 1999; Pearson and Giles 1999). The models suggested for these areas provide alternative views, (core/periphery and sunwise movement) of how this cosmology was envisaged. These may well respect a plurality of views in the past but they imply a general homogeneity of beliefs

throughout Britain which is otherwise difficult to perceive in the archaeological record.

In this paper I do not wish to examine these cosmological interpretations of the house; instead I wish to look at some other anthropological insights into how the house (or perhaps more appropriately a home) provides a framework for understanding the temporal sequence of prehistoric life. This is to conceptualise the house in terms of a life cycle. We can assume that a house undergoes the basic cycle of birth, life and death and that is analogous to that of an individual. Furthermore it is possible that the transitional points are significant events (liminal periods) which might form the focus for ritual or ceremonial activity. Archaeological applications of this form of interpretation are much rarer (Gerritsen 1999).

ATLANTIC SCOTLAND

I will place this discussion in the context of Atlantic Scotland as this is a region which should be at the forefront of understanding the social importance of domestic buildings. It has well preserved structures with associated floor levels which are of unrivalled quality in British prehistory. These houses provide an opportunity to explore attitudes to construction, use and abandonment which provide an alternative archaeological perspective on these new ideas.

The archaeological record for the Later Prehistory is dominated by the construction of brochs (see note 1) and these are found throughout, and indeed are used to define, the

Atlantic Province. I have argued, along with many others, that brochs are just one aspect of the settlement record of the region and that they can be understood as the apex of a relatively flattened hierarchy (Sharples 1999; Pearson, Mulville and Sharples 1996, Pearson and Sharples 1999) (see note 2). This implies the presence of other contemporary and related settlements whose inhabitants are in some way dependent on the inhabitants of the broch, though the precise nature of this relationship is open to debate.

In contrast to brochs there seems to be considerable variability in the domestic architecture of Atlantic Scotland with each geographical area having its own regionally distinctive form. The evidence from Shetland is at present minimal but wheelhouses occur around the broch at Jarlshof (Hamilton 1956) and at Old Scatness (Nicholson and Dockrill 1998), and circular radially divided structures have been noted in the recent excavations at Bayanne House, Yell (Wilson and Moore 1998). However, it is difficult to generalise on the basis of this limited information.

A distinctive feature of the Orkney evidence is the presence of village settlements around the brochs (Hedges 1987; Ballin Smith 1994). These are formed by irregular, polygonal houses sub-divided into two discrete spaces. Similar nucleated settlements are also known in Caithness (Fairhurst 1984) but the associated structures are often circular and there are also distinctive wag settlements in the southern part of the county which incorporate rectangular structures.

In the Western Isles the wheelhouse appears to be the established form of non-broch settlement and relatively large numbers of these structures have been excavated (Armit 1992). In contrast to the areas mentioned above these structures do not cluster around the broch towers but appear dispersed within the landscape in a physical environment quite different from the brochs (Sharples and Pearson 1997).

In this paper I wish to compare and contrast the life histories of the wheelhouses of the Western Isles and brochs (see note 3). I have chosen the former because large numbers have been competently excavated in recent years and they appear to have fairly consistent features which allow greater generalisation about life histories. In contrast, to generalise about brochs I will have to range more widely as there are very few recent excavations which provide full life histories. I want to present the evidence for use, abandonment and reuse, first for wheelhouses and then for brochs. This will highlight significant diffferences between wheelhouses and brochs which provide clear indications of the different roles they played in the mediation of social relations in the Middle and Late Iron Age of Atlantic Scotland.

WHEELHOUSE PRIMARY USE

The length of the primary occupation of any structure is very difficult to estimate as there are very few sites with chronological information from before and after the occupation. The clearest evidence for the life of a wheelhouse comes from excavation of the site at Cnip (Fig. 20) on the west coast of Lewis (Armit 1988). At this site large numbers of radiocarbon dates (Fig. 21) have been obtained from throughout the sequence of occupation.

The determinations from the phase 1 activity, which represents the construction and use of the original wheelhouse, are widely dispersed ranging from as early as the beginning of the first millenium BC up to the second century AD. Ian Armit who has kindly let me reference this material suggests (Armit forthcoming) that the early dates represent ancient material, deliberately incorporated during the construction of the wheelhouse and that the occupation is more accurately indicated by the later dates which are statistically indistinguishable from the phase 2 dates and would place the construction of the first phase, at the earliest, at the beginning of the first century BC.

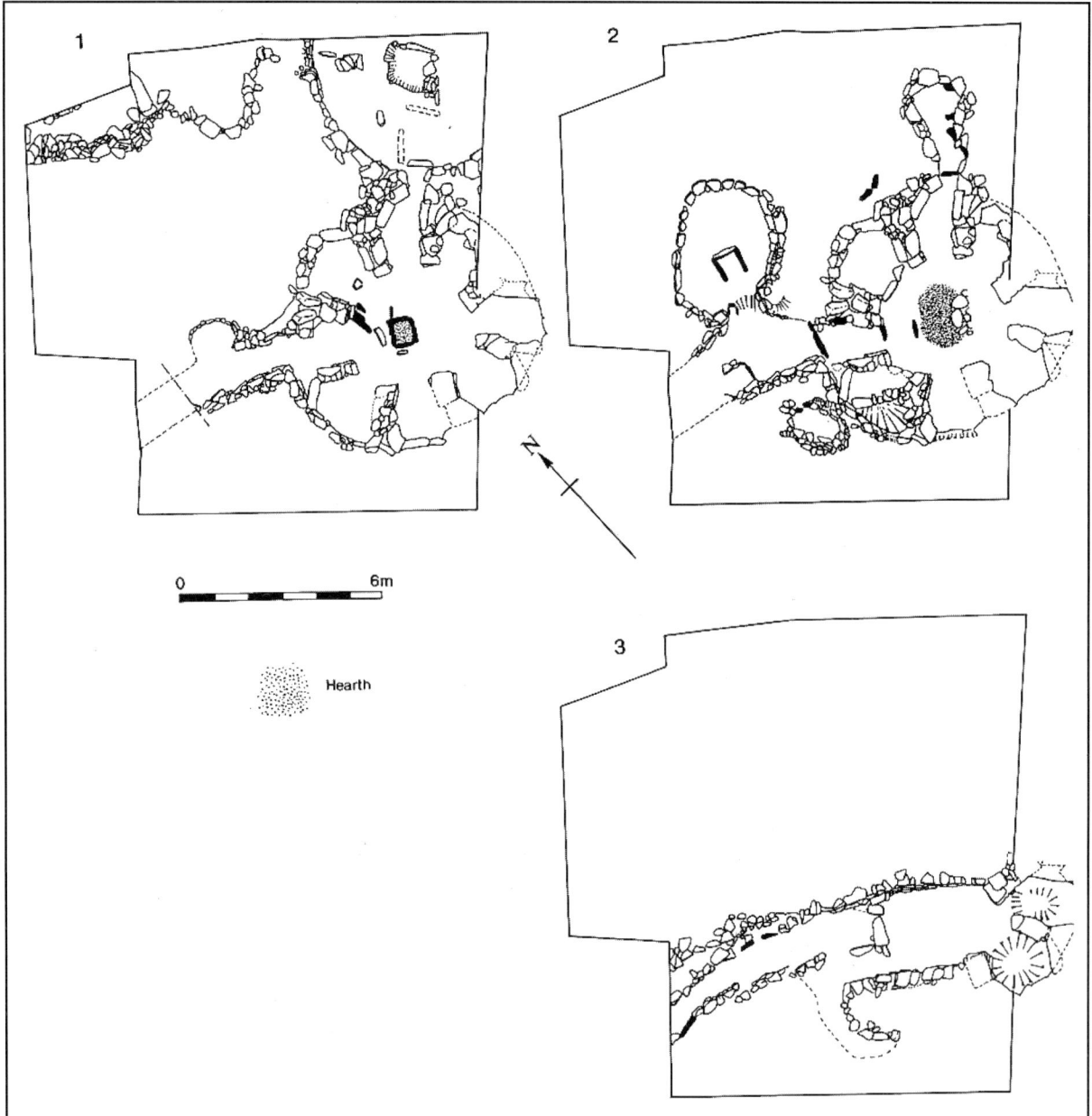

Fig.20 *A plan of the wheelhouse at Cnip showing the modifications that take place between Phase 1, 2 and 3 (Harding and Armit 1990.*

In contrast to the dating of phase 1, the dates for phase 2 and 3 are very consistent. Armit argues for the beginning of the second phase at the beginning of the first century AD and for the beginning of phase 3, and the end of phase 2, at the end of the first century AD. The end of the third and final phase of activity is placed, with caveats, in the middle of the third century BC.

These dates suggest we could have an occupation of little more than 150 years for the wheelhouse, up to the end of phase 2. During

these 150 years there were only minor alterations to the principal building, involving buttressing and blocking of some of the piers and aisles, and remodelling of the hearth. There were, however, substantial modifications to the subsidiary cells and the attached wheelhouse to the north. The evidence suggests we have residential activity spanning perhaps three to four generations.

The only other wheelhouse with a large number of radiocarbon dates is the example from Sollas in North Uist (Campbell 1991,

Atmospheric data from Stuiver et al. (1998); OxCal v3.5 Bronk Ramsey (2000); cub r:4 sd:12 prob usp(chron)

Cnip		
Phase 1		
GU-2756	2600±150BP	
GU-2754	2370±130BP	
GU-2758	2280±140BP	
GU-2755	1990±50BP	
GU-2757	1960±90BP	
Phase 2		
GU-2749	1920±60BP	
GU-2746	1930±90BP	
AA-29767	1910±45BP	
GU-2752	1900±50BP	
GU-2748	1890±50BP	
GU-2747	1890±50BP	
GU-2751	1850±50BP	
Phase 3		
GU-2742	1940±70BP	
GU-2743	1930±50BP	
GU-2745	1870±70BP	
GU-2741	1810±190BP	
GU-2744	1770±80BP	

2000CalBC 1000CalBC CalBC/CalAD 1000CalAD

Calibrated date

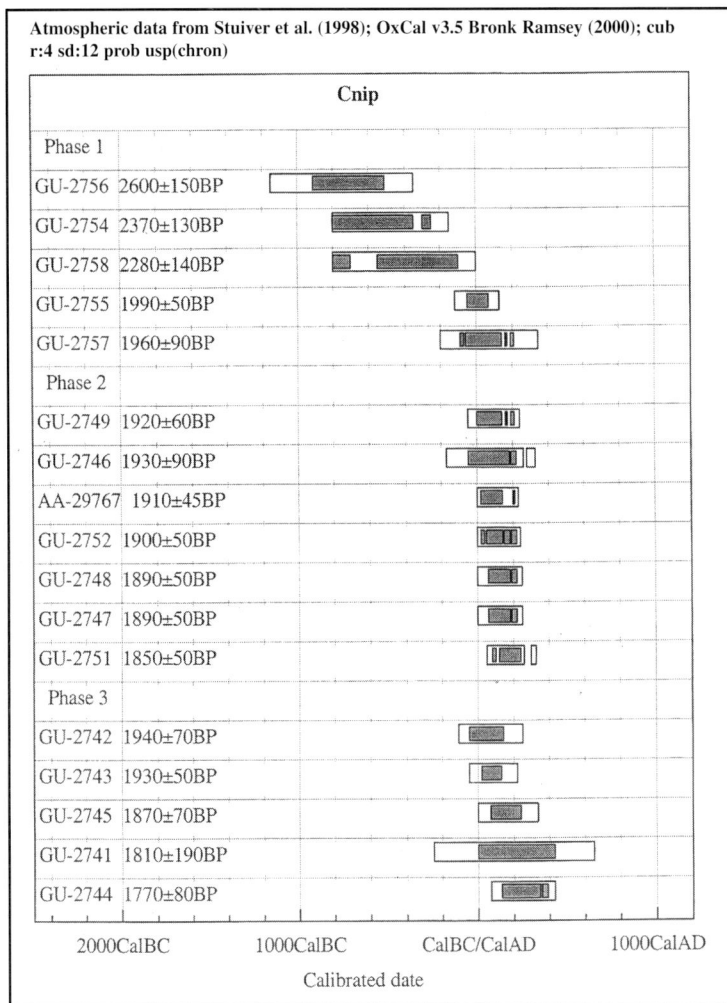

Fig. 21 *The radiocarbon dates from Cnip (Armit forth).*

140). Unfortunately most of the published dates come from the pits that precede the floor and so they do not provide an accurate indication of the life span of the house. However, there is no indication from these dates or from the material culture that the house was occupied for several hundred years.

The short length of occupation at Cnip and Sollas seems to be similar to that envisaged for other wheelhouses in the machair plain of South Uist. At none of these sites is there much evidence for significant modification of the principal structure during its occupation, nor do we have evidence for the accumulation of substantial deposits on the floor (see note 4) (though floor deposits may be regularly removed) and there is very little evidence for significant changes in the ceramic assemblage during the primary use of the wheelhouse. At

a number of sites including Sollas (Campbell 1991) and Kilphedir (Lethbridge 1952), thin sterile sand lenses have been noted within the floor layers and quite often these floors have been noted to be made up of a number of different layers. However, it is not clear what these variations represent as layers could accumulate as a result of activity and/or, the result of decay of organic material but they could also be deliberate make up layers. Sand could have been deliberately introduced to level floors or could be a natural wind blown accumulation if the roof was removed for any reason.

WHEELHOUSE 'ABANDONMENT'

The evidence for wheelhouse abandonment is best understood by a description of the site of A'Cheardach Mhor on the machair plain of South Uist (Young and Richardson 1960). The published section (Fig. 22) through this wheelhouse is very interesting. The fill of the wheelhouse is curiously devoid of stone and any evidence for the natural decay of the building. If one accepts the evidence from the well preserved wheelhouses of Cnip (Armit 1988) and Jarlshof (Hamilton 1956) then the walls of this structure should be several metres taller and the peripheral compartments corbelled. Not only do these structural features not survive but there is no evidence that they were ever present. It seems likely that the building was deliberately dismantled and then allowed to fill in with sand. The systematic nature of this stone removal suggests this was a specific event that marked the abandonment of the house and was not a long drawn out process of opportunistic robbing.

Evidence for the systematic dismantling in the Iron Age is present on many other wheelhouses and can range from almost total destruction to simply the removal of corbelling. Recent excavations at Bornish (Sharples 1999) have exposed a wheelhouse which has been almost completely destroyed; the only structural features to survive were a small portion of wall, the entrance threshold and the hearth. Sections through the site at A'Cheardach Bheag (Fig. 22; Fairhurst 1971) show a homogeneous brown sand infilling, containing stones which appear to be lying flat. This type of fill could not have occurred naturally. There is no evidence for the collapse of the superstructure and it seems likely that the wheelhouse was dismantled and deliberately infilled. At Sollas (Campbell 1991) the evidence suggests a sequence very similar to A'Chearach Mhor. The wheelhouse was systematically but only partially dismantled and infilled with sterile sand. One of the few sites which does not appear to have been systematically dismantled was the wheelhouse at Kilphedir (Fig. 22; Lethbridge 1952). The walls of this structure survived to over 2 m and show clear evidence of the lower levels of corbelling. The structure was infilled with blown sand and showed no signs of any secondary occupation. However, even at this site there was no evidence for the upper levels of corbelling in the fill and these stones must have been deliberately removed.

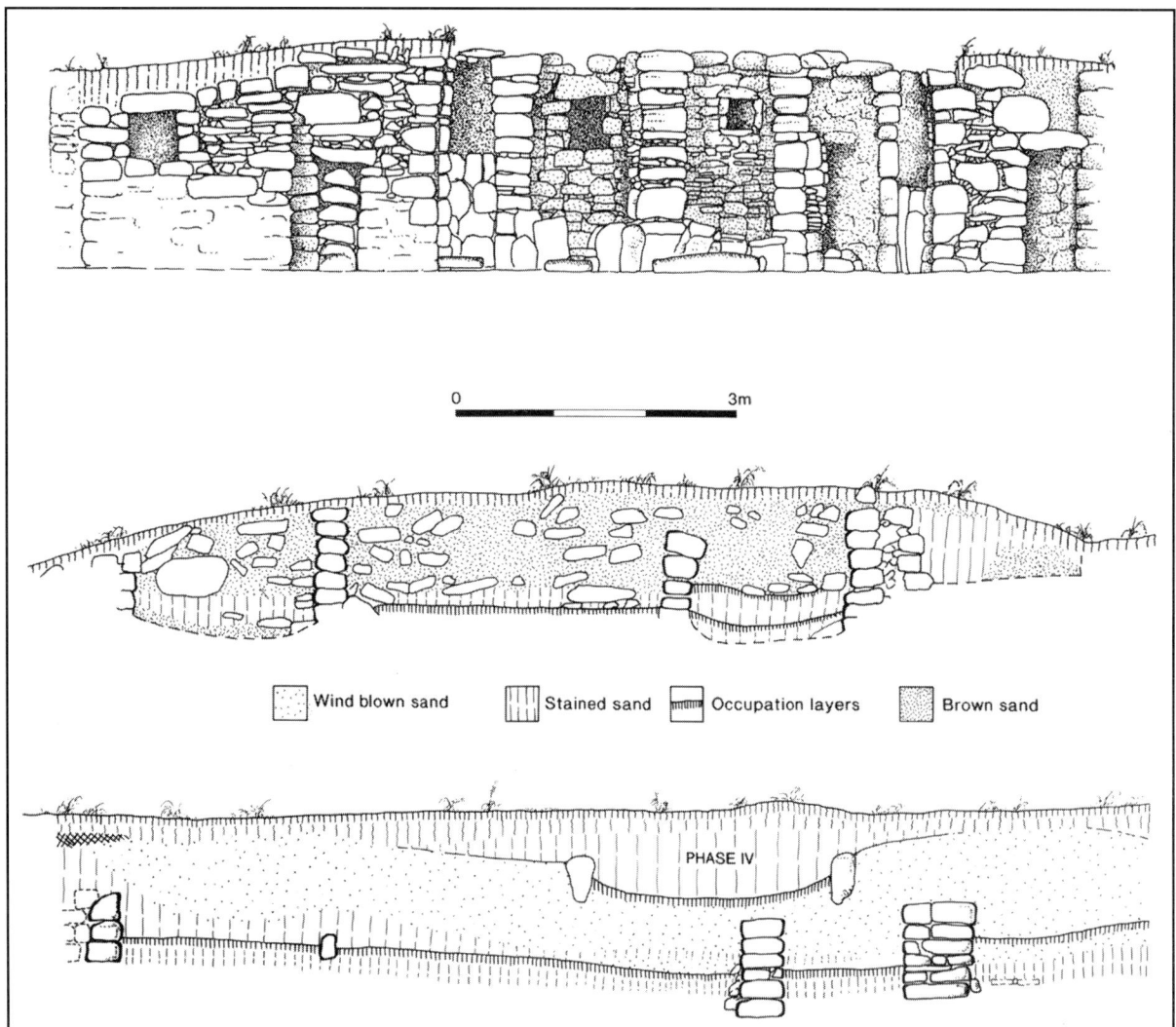

Fig. 22 *An elevation of the structure at Kilphedir and sections through the wheelhouses at A'Cheardach Bheag and A'Cheardach Mhor (After Lethbridge 1952, Fairhurst 1971 and Young and Richardson 1960).*

SECONDARY OCCUPATION

Despite the evidence for demolition, substantial modification or alteration of a wheelhouse, to create a new building, is not as common as one might expect. The most obvious example of this is the wheelhouse at Cnip and I have already referred to the phase 3 activity which marks the end of the wheelhouse. However, it may be significant that the reoccupation is not caused by the construction of a new wheelhouse. The structure built is a rectangular building with an internal area 3.5 m long and 2.2 m wide (Armit 1988, 29). The size of this structure suggests we are not dealing with a residential dwelling equivalent to, and replacing, the wheelhouse. This structure also had a relatively short life and when it was abandoned there is no evidence that the site was ever reoccupied.

After the abandonment of the wheelhouse of A'Cheardach Mhor, Young and Richardson (1960) suggest there were four significant periods of reoccupation (Fig. 23). The first reoccupation of the wheelhouse (phase II) is very ephemeral and was regarded as little more than temporary activity. The succeeding phase III activity was also very scrappy and was restricted to the area above the entrance. Both these occupations may represent ritual acts of remembrance rather than occupation. Only the phase IV occupation could be regarded as representing a significant domestic settlement and even this was not particularly well preserved. Finds from this occupation can be dated to the seventh or eight centuries AD and the occupation must be three to four

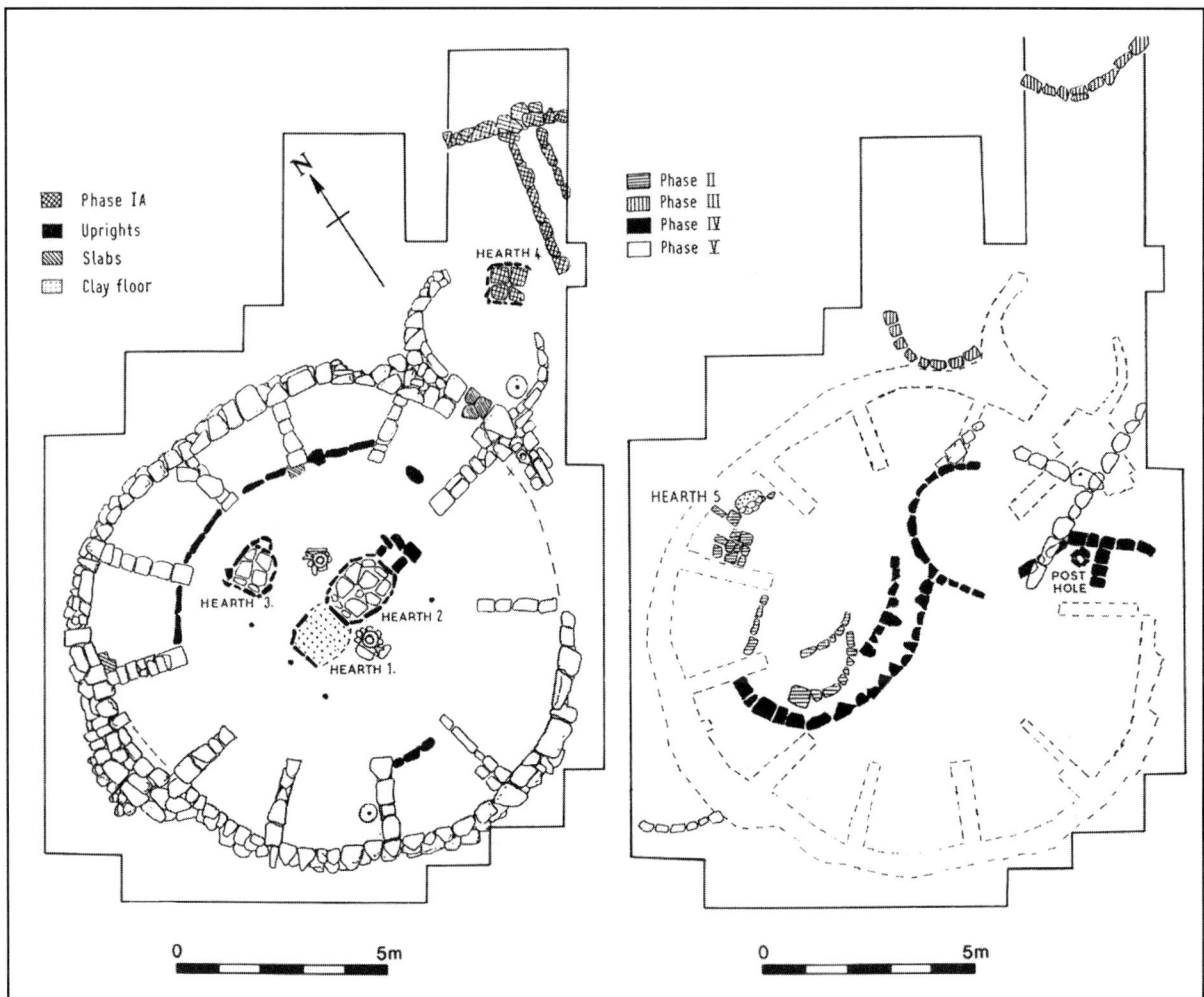

Fig.23 *A plan of the primary phase of the wheelhouse at A'Cheardach Mhor and the subsequent secondary occupations (after Young and Richardson 1960).*

hundred years after the original abandonment of the structure. The site was subsequently reoccupied in the Norse period (phase V).

A number of wheelhouses appear to be in locations that were left completely unused from their abandonment through to their discovery; these include Sollas, Kilphedir and probably A'Cheardach Bheag (Fairhurst 1971 does suggest a late reoccupation but this is not particularly convincing). At Bornish (Sharples 1999) the hole caused by the destruction of the wheelhouse is relatively quickly filled with layers of rubbish and the main settlement area moves some 100 metres to the north. A similar situation may exist at The Udal (Selkirk 1996) with the wheelhouse settlement on the south mound and the later 'jelly baby' settlement on the north mound.

THE LIFE CYCLE OF A WHEELHOUSE

I have tried to use the examples above to illustrate the life cycle of the wheelhouse and I would summarise this as:

A primary use which is fairly short. The dates at Cnip might suggest one generation but two or three generations is more likely. There is very little evidence for substantial modification of the central wheelhouse, though infilling of the aisled piers and replacement of the hearth is a common feature. Many of the subsidiary buildings attached to the main wheelhouse appear to undergo substantial modification which often involves complete abandonment or infilling.

Within one to two hundred years of their construction many of these wheelhouses have been systematically dismantled and abandoned. This can be clearly documented at a number of sites and contrasts with what we know about settlements belonging to other periods in the region (see note 5). The only occasion when this happens with a wheelhouse, at Cnip, it is clear that the secondary building has a considerably reduced function. The avoidance of the abandoned wheelhouse is also unexpected as it can be seen that, in

general, settlement on the Uist machair retains a focus on specific areas throughout the first millennia BC and AD (Sharples and Pearson 1999).

Clearly these decisions represent cultural choices that were of considerable importance to the inhabitants of the wheelhouses. It suggests that when the building was started it would only be expected to have a prescribed and relatively short life. Structural death occurred once the link between the original family and there descendants became tenuous and possibly diluted between several families. The stones used were then taken, probably to be incorporated into another building and perhaps providing an ancestral link between generations. Sufficient structural remains were left, however, to identify the original house and possibly to provide a focus for remembrance. The decaying house structure would be a visible and important feature of the later settlement landscape.

BROCHS

The amount of information available to discuss the occupation of brochs is not really comparable to that of wheelhouses. The size and complexity of the archaeology present on most brochs is daunting to all but the most extravagantly funded excavation. In recent years the complete excavation of a broch has been limited to The Howe in Orkney (Ballin Smith 1994), Upper Scalloway in Shetland (Sharples 1998) and Dun Mor Vaul in Tiree (MacKie 1974). However, there have been other important excavations at Dun Vulan in South Uist (Pearson and Sharples 1999), Berie in Lewis (Harding and Armit 1990) and Old Scatness in Shetland (Nicholson and Dockrill 1998).

PRIMARY OCCUPATION

The excavations at Scalloway give some indication as to the length of the primary occupation, though again the evidence is open to alternative interpretation. It was argued in

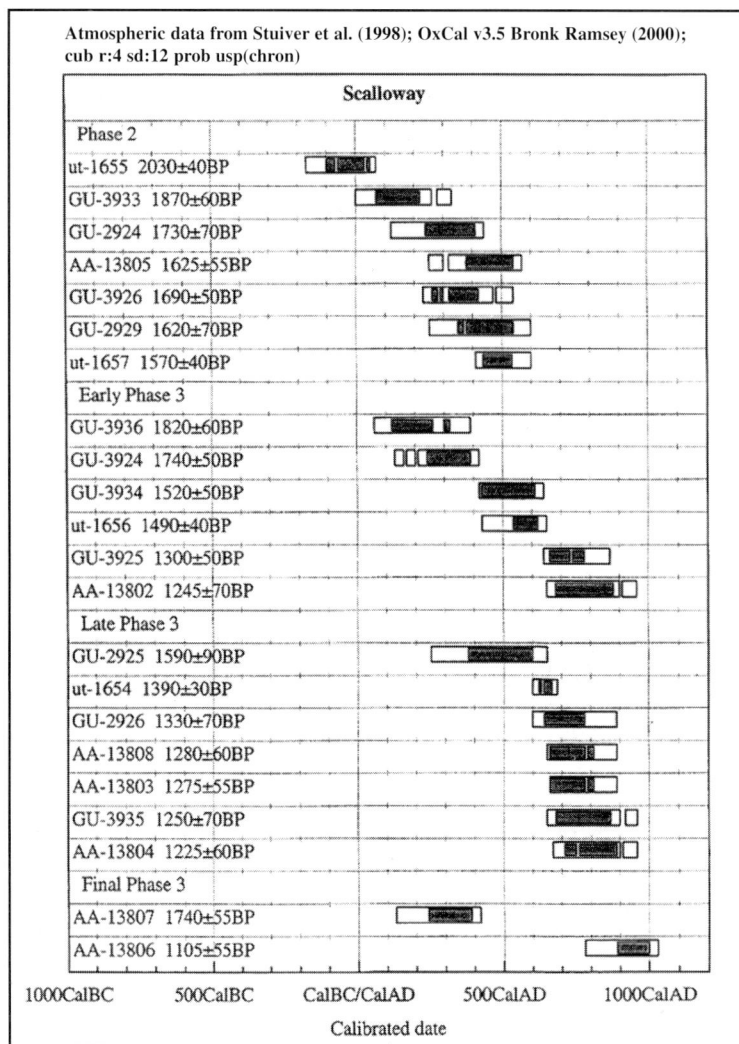

Fig.24 *The radiocarbon dates from Scalloway (after Sharples 1999).*

the original report that the primary occupation of the broch could last up to 600 years (Sharples 1999, 86-87). Radiocarbon dates (Fig. 24) for the initial occupation of the site suggests the broch was constructed sometime in the first century BC. The end of the occupation was well dated to around the fifth century AD when the interior of the building was subject to a massive conflagration. Unfortunately regular cleaning out of the broch meant the primary deposits were removed and it is only the activity immediately prior to the destruction of the broch that survives in the interior.

The only other well-documented broch excavation which might have provided an indication of the length of the primary occupation is The Howe (Ballin Smith 1994). However, this site is extremely complicated and the Orkney sites in general seem to have slightly different use lives. The principal observation to be made is that the site was continually occupied for over a millennium with the substantial roundhouse at its centre remodelled several times. The occupation of the phase 6 complex roundhouse and the phase 7 broch appears to have been only a hundred to two hundred years each (Carter in Ballin Smith 1994), but the stability of the much rebuilt structure could well be an issue on this site.

At Dun Mor Vaul, MacKie (1997, 148-9) has argued for an initial occupation divided into two significant phases prior to the dismantling of the broch tower. He argues that these phases spanned a period from about the first century BC to the second or third century AD (MacKie 1997, 178), but unfortunately the radiocarbon dates are too imprecise to corroborate this chronology. It is clear that during the use of the broch, in phase 2 and 3, there were significant changes to the nature of the occupation. Of some significance is the absence of a hearth in the early phases of activity; the central hearth does not appear until phase 3B. MacKie (1997, 154) suggests that this was because the broch was used as a refuge and not as a domestic settlement when initially constructed. However, it could be argued that this indicates the primary domestic space lay at the first floor level.

BROCH 'ABANDONMENT'

Evidence for the systematic abandonment and/or the demolition of brochs in the Middle Iron Age is a point of some controversy.

Gilmour argued at the conference for the systematic demolition of most broch sites but this is an extreme view. MacKie has suggested that Dun Mor Vaul was deliberately reduced in height at the end of phase 3 (1997, 149-150) and has also argued for the systematic demolition of Gurness and Midhowe (MacKie 1994, 138). The evidence is tentative and circumstantial (see note 6) but it is not an unreasonable interpretation. However, the evidence from Mousa indicates that the broch tower can survive a radical remodification of the interior, and at Upper Scalloway (Sharples 1999) and Old Scatness (Dockrill pers comm) the superstructure was only finally dismantled in the Norse period.

BROCH SECONDARY OCCUPATION

Most brochs that have undergone any form of competent excavation reveal traces of significant secondary occupations. For the purpose of this paper it will be sufficient to contrast the secondary occupation in Upper Scalloway with that present at Berie and at Dun Vulan in the Western Isles.

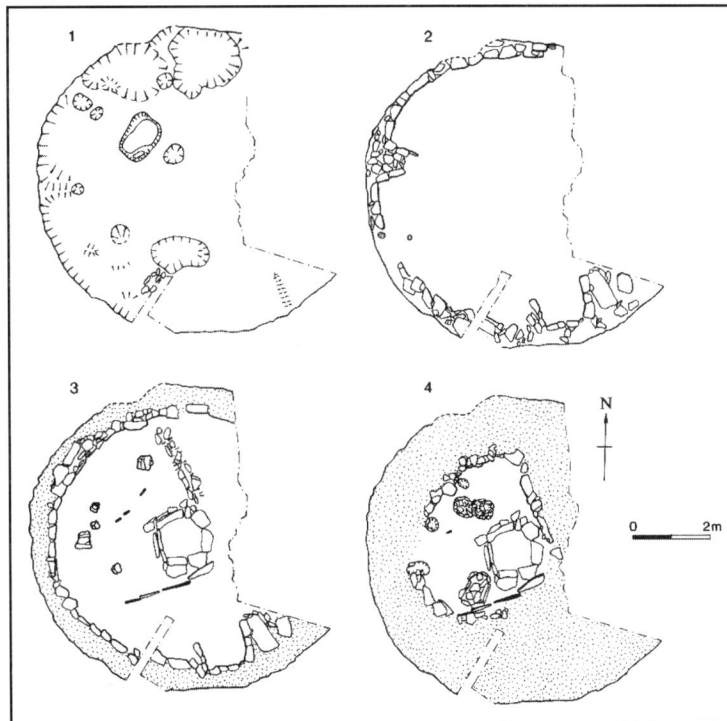

Fig.25 *A plan of the interior of the broch at Scalloway and subsequent structural modifications (after Sharples 1999).*

At Upper Scalloway the broch was reoccupied after the conflagration that marked the end of the primary occupation, and there were at least three structural modifications (Fig. 25) before the site was abandoned some four hundred years later in the eighth century (Sharples 1998, 78-79). Only in the Norse period was the structure substantially dismantled. The initial reconstruction inside the broch involved the construction of a casement wall with projecting piers, similar to those used in wheelhouse architecture. This pattern was also visible in the brochs of Levenwick (Goudie 1872) and Jarlshof (Hamilton 1956) on Shetland, and the former is the most complete example of a wheelhouse inside a broch. The second reconstruction consists of the construction of another circular casement wall, and although this incorporates some of the piers of the earlier rebuild, it does not involve the construction of new piers and clearly is not a wheelhouse. Only in the final rebuilding does the form of the internal structure deviate from the original circular shape. This final rebuilding is an irregular structure similar to that visible inside Mousa (RCAHMS 1946) where a sequence of modification similar to that at Scalloway appears to have occurred. Radiocarbon dates and artefactual material suggest the secondary activity at Scalloway was a continuous sequence spanning the period AD500-900 (Sharples 1998, 87).

The evidence from the Western Isles is in marked contrast to that from Shetland in that no secondary wheelhouses have so far been conclusively identified. MacKie has suggested that the phase 4 building at Dun Mor Vaul was a wheelhouse (1974, 49), but this assumes the complete removal of all drystone piers which is difficult to justify as the wall survives to a reasonable height. It is possible to argue that a number of the structures excavated by Beveridge in North Uist indicate wheelhouses built inside brochs, but the only recent attempt to prove this was only partially successful (Armit 1998); the excavations suggested a wheelhouse was secondary but did not clarify the nature of the primary structure.

Recent work at Dun Vulan in South Uist (Pearson and Sharples 1999) and Berie in Lewis (Harding 2000) have revealed quite different structures are present inside some brochs. Neither of these excavations have exposed primary deposits and the principal structures exposed are clearly built several hundred years after the construction of the broch, and at Berie at least they overlie a complex sequence of buildings which include an arc of walling similar to that found at Dun Mor Vaul. At both sites complex structures were present which subdivided the broch interior into a number of rooms connected and separated by passages and doorways (Fig. 26). The layout in both brochs is very similar. After passing through the original broch entrance, facing east, one enters a passage; on one side of the passage is the entrance to a small chamber, at Berie this lies to the right, at Dun Vulan to the left. One continues along the passage to enter a large roughly circular space, this is similar in size at both sites. Another small room is accessible from this space, again

at Berie this lies to the right at Dun Vulan to the left (see note 7). These cellular structures are similar to other Late Iron Age structures which are found in non broch sites and around brochs throughout the Atlantic province.

THE LIFE CYCLE OF A BROCH

The evidence is clearly rather poor even in comparison to the wheelhouse evidence discussed above. However, it is still clear that there are rather striking differences between the life history of a broch and a wheelhouse. There are suggestive indications that brochs were occupied for a considerable length of time before any significant structural modifications were required. At Scalloway six hundred years could be argued and at Dun Mor Vaul the occupation, though of indeterminate length, appears to have involved a significant reorganisation of the space inside the broch.

Secondary occupation is present in most brochs and appears to be long and complex. At many sites there is no obvious hiatus between the primary and secondary occupation and furthermore there is no obvious dismantling of the broch superstructure. This is best demonstrated by the broch of Mousa where there appear to be at least three remodellings of the interior, which all occur within the shell of the broch tower.

It would appear that brochs are normally continually occupied throughout the Iron Age. In the Middle Iron Age this reoccupation does not involve structural alterations but from about the fourth or fifth centuries AD reoccupation appears to require remodelling of the interior but not dismantling of the superstructure. This remodelling creates different spatial configurations of the interior. In the Western Isles these are significantly different but in Shetland there appears to be much greater continuity in the spatial configuration of the remodelling.

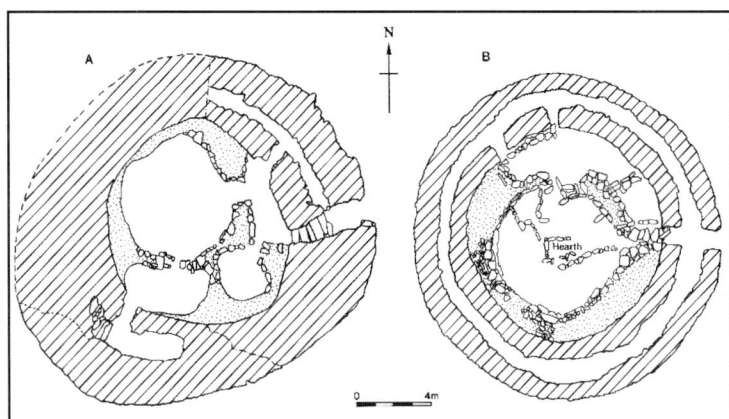

Fig.26 *A plan of the cellular structures inside the brochs of Dun Vulan and Berie (after Pearson and Sharples 1999 and Harding and Armit 1990).*

The desire to occupy brochs cannot simply be dismissed as a result of their architectural presence, but must reflect the importance of the structure and its association with the community. It is important to note that brochs are not occupied in the Norse period despite their importance in historical traditions. There is even some evidence, from Scalloway, that they were dismantled at this time and their locations were used for burial (ie Gurness, Graham-Campbell and Batey 1987, 127-129).

DISCUSSION

It may seem to many that what I am saying is not surprising or significant. Brochs are very substantial structures that were built to last and wheelhouses are comparatively fragile structures, built in an unstable landscape, which have to be regularly dismantled. Furthermore, being circular they are very difficult to integrate into later structures. It is all practical common-sense. However, I think there is more to it than this and to understand the full implications of the choices being made by these prehistoric communities we have to imagine the impact these decisions would have on the inhabitants of the buildings.

The creation of the broch would have seriously disrupted the natural patterns of inheritance that appeared to operate in relation to domestic buildings. On the one hand you have buildings which are routinely dismantled and destroyed after the direct descendants of the original inhabitant have all died. On the other, you have a building which is current throughout generations, whose construction is most likely to have occurred in a past beyond the memory of any living person and whose future reaches beyond the likely span of your life. Such a building is likely to be central to the community and it is hardly surprising that it provides a metaphor for a community and their relationship with the environment.

The different life histories of these structures also suggests that the relationship of ownership and occupancy may well be very different. In a wheelhouse I would envisage occupancy to be inherited within the family of the original owner. The construction of attached ancillary wheelhouses may reflect the requirement for extra space caused by a dependent but mature adult and spouse living in the house. This would explain why many of these ancillary structures frequently undergo much more radical changes than the principal structure. They would only be required at certain times and would go out of use when the transition was resolved either by movement out of the house or death.

In contrast the occupancy of the broch may not be an issue related to family inheritance. The occupants of the broch had a role within their local community which set them apart socially and geographically from other members of that community. This role gave them certain powers over other members of the community but it also gave them responsibilities which may have been onerous. For instance they may be required to guarantee the social and economic reproduction of the community. In the small scale societies envisaged in the Atlantic Province this role is very unlikely to be associated with an individual family and inherited through descent. This is not a clan system; that must have developed some time later. It is more likely that status was generated by action within the community and then acknowledged by the community through residence in the broch.

Status may fall to the oldest member of the community and be transferred at the death of the incumbent. Alternatively individuals could compete in a variety of ways for status. Routine mechanisms for competition would be through warfare (such as cattle raiding), trade and exchange (of which there is little evidence) and hunting (which does seem important) but we might also suggest other mechanisms such as agricultural prowess and the acquisition of ritual knowledge. In these circumstances residence within the broch might be much more regularly transferred.

If we return to our original analogy of the life cycle then we find that the broch never dies, it is constantly reborn by this form of occupancy, and provides a potent symbol of fertility and stability for the community.

An alternative way of viewing this symbolism is to envisage movement into the broch as akin to death. The brochs are closely associated with the ancestors by their use and location. Their very long life means that, unlike any other structures in use, these would have been occupied by individuals who were long dead and presumably known only through stories. Occupancy would be a very specific way of linking an individual and the communities' ancestors. Their location is also relevant, as Hingley (1999) has documented, brochs are sometimes constructed upon burial monuments, particularly in Orkney. In the Western Isles brochs are located outside the agricultural landscapes in the bog and moorland where Neolithic tombs still survive (Sharples and Pearson 1996). This would once have been the principal farmland prior to movement onto the machair in the Bronze Age.

BIBLIOGRAPHY

Armit, I. (1988) *Excavations at Cnip, West Lewis 1988*. Edinburgh, Dept Archaeology Project Paper 9.

Armit, I. (1992) *The later prehistory of the Western Isles of Scotland*. British Archaeological Reports British Series 221. Oxford, Tempus Reparatum.

Armit, I. (1998) Re-excavation of an Iron Age wheelhouse and earlier structure at Eilean Maleit, North Uist. *Proceedings of the Society of Antiquaries of Scotland* 128, 255-271.

Armit, I. (forthcoming) Anatomy of an Iron Age roundhouse: the Cnip wheelhouse excavations Lewis.

Ballin Smith, B. (1994) *Howe: four millenia of Orkney prehistory*. Society of Antiquaries of Scotland Monograph 9. Edinburgh.

Beveridge, E. (1931) Earth houses at Garry Iochdrach and Bac Mhic connain in North Uist. *Proceedings of the Society of Antiquaries of Scotland* 66, 32-67.

Campbell, E. (1991) Excavations of a wheelhouse and other structures at Sollas, North Uist, by R.J.C. Atkinson in 1956. *Proceedings of the Society of Antiquaries of Scotland* 121, 117-73.

Carsten, J. and Hugh-Jones, S. (1995) *About the house: Levi-Strauss and beyond*. Cambridge, Cambridge University Press.

Fairhurst, H. (1971) The wheelhouse site at A'Cheardach Bheag on Drimore Machair, South Uist. *Glasgow Archaeological Journal* 2, 72-106.

Fairhurst, H. (1984) *Excavations at Crosskirk Broch, Caithness*. Edinburgh, Society of Antiquaries of Scotland Monograph 3.

Fitzpatrick, A. P. (1994) Outside in: the structure of an Early Iron Age house at Dunstan Park, Thatcham, Berkshire. In Fitzpatrick, A. P. and Morris, E (eds) *The Iron Age in Wessex: recent work*, 68-73. Dorchester, Wessex Archaeology.

Gerritesen, F. (1999) To build and to abandon. *Archaeological Dialogues* 6.2, 78-97.

Goudie, G. (1872) Notice of excavations in a broch and adjacent tumuli near Levenwick in the parish of Dunrossness, Zetland. *Proceedings of the Society of Antiquaries of Scotland* 9 (1870-1872), 212-19.

Graham-Campbell, J. and Batey, C. E. (1998) *Vikings in Scotland: An archaeological survey.* Edinburgh, Edinburgh University Press.

Hamilton, J. R. C. (1956) *Excavations at Jarlshof, Shetland.* Edinburgh, Ministry of Public Works Archaeological Reports 1.

Harding, D. and Armit, I. (1990) Survey and excavation in West Lewis. In Armit, I. *Beyond the Brochs.* Edinburgh, Edinburgh University Press.

Harding, D. (2000) *The Iron Age settlement at Beirgh, Riof, Isle of Lewis: Excavations, 1985-95. Vol 1 The structures and stratigraphy.* Edinburgh, University of Edinburgh Department of Archaeology.

Hedges, J. W. (1987) *Bu, Gurness and the Brochs of Orkney Parts I, II and III.* Oxford, British Archaeological Reports British Series 164.

Hingley, R. (1990) Public and private space: Domestic organization and gender relations among Iron Age and Romano-British households. In Samson, R (ed) *The Social Archaeology of Houses,* 125-148. Edinburgh, Edinburgh University Press.

Hingley, R. (1999) The creation of Later Prehistoric landscapes and the context of the reuse of Neolithic and Earlier Bronze Age monuments in Britain and Ireland. In Bevan, B (ed) *Northern Exposure: interpretive devolution and the Iron Ages in Britain.* Leicester, Leicester Archaeological Monographs 4.

Lethbridge, T. C. (1952) Excavations at Kilphedir, South Uist, and the problems of brochs and wheelhouses. *Proceedings of the Prehistoric Society* 18, 176-193.

MacKie, E. (1974) *Dun Mor Vaul, an Iron Age Broch on Tiree.* Glasgow, Glasgow University Press.

MacKie, E. (1994) Gurness and Midhowe brochs in Orkney: some problems of misinterpretation. *Archaeological Journal* 151, 98-157.

MacKie, E. (1997) Dun Mor Vaul revisted: fact and theory in the reappraisal of the Scottish Iron Age. In Ritchie, G (ed) *The Archaeology of Argyll.* Edinburgh, Edinburgh University Press.

Nicholson, R. A. and Dockrill, S. J. (1998) *Old Scatness Broch, Shetland: Retrospect and Prospect.* Bradford: Dept Archaeol Sciences, NABO Monograph 2.

Giles, M. and Pearson, M. P. (1999) Learning to live in the Iron Age: dwelling and praxis. In Bevan, B (ed) *Northern Exposure: interpretive devolution and the Iron Ages in Britain.* Leicester, Leicester Archaeology Monograph 4.

Pearson, M. P., Mulville, J. and Sharples, N. M.(1996) Brochs and Iron Age Society: a reappraisal. *Antiquity* 70, 57-67.

Pearson, M. P. and Sharples, N. M. (1999) *Between Land and Sea: Excavations at Dun Vulan, South Uist.* Sheffield, Sheffield Academic Press.

RCAHMS (1946) *Orkney and Shetland.* Edinburgh, HMSO.

Selkirk, A. (1996) The Udal. *Current Archaeology* 13.3, 84-94.

Sharples, N. M. (1998) *Scalloway: A Broch and Late Iron Age Settlement and Medieval Cemetery in Shetland.* Oxford, Oxbow Monographs 82.

Sharples, N. M. (1999) *The Iron Age and Norse settlement at Bornish, South Uist: An interim report on the 1999 excavations.* Cardiff, Cardiff Studies in Archaeology Specialist Rep 16.

Sharples, N. M. and Pearson, M. P. (1997) Why were brochs built? Recent studies in the Iron Age of Atlantic Scotland. In Gwilt, A. and Haselgrove, C (eds) *Reconstructing Iron Age societies.* Oxford, Oxbow Monograph 71, 254-265.

Sharples, N. M. and Pearson, M. P. (1999) Norse Settlement in the Outer Hebrides. *Norwegian Archaeological Review* 32.1, 41-62.

Wilson, G. and Moore, H. (1998) Bayanne House. *Discovery and Excavation in Scotland 1997.* Edinburgh, Council for Scottish Archaeology, 71.

Young, A. and Richardson, K. M. (1960) A'Cheardach Mhor, Drimore, South Uist. *Proceedings of the Society of Antiquaries of Scotland* 93 (1959-60), 153-73.

NOTES

1 I am using the definition of a broch provided by MacKie (1965, 100) as I feel this is less confusing than the revised terminology promulgated by Armit.

2 Armit argued at the conference that brochs or complex Atlantic roundhouses are the principal form of settlement in many areas of the Atlantic province but this is based on a simplistic and misleading presentation of the evidence from Barra (see Sharples and Pearson 1996 for a detailed analysis of this argument).

3 I will be exploring wheelhouses in the context of the Outer Hebrides and not Shetland as it is clear from the excavations at Jarlshof (Hamilton 1956) that the life of a Shetland wheelhouse is different. A full understanding of the complexity of these will only be possible after the publication of the Old Scatness examples.

4 A possible exception is the wheelhouse at Bac Mhic Connain excavated by Beveridge. This appears to have had over a metre of deposits infilling the interior (Beveridge 1931) but the site had a complex history and it is not clear that the depth of deposits represents a single occupation.

5 In the Norse period houses are routinely rebuilt one on top of the other at sites such as Kilphedir and Bornish and often partially incorporate an old building into a new building (Sharples and Pearson 1999).

6 Smith pointed out in the conference that there was evidence for catastrophic collapse of the broch structure at The Howe and that the evidence from Midhowe and Gurness could be interpreted as attempts to shore up the broch rather than the result of its being dismantled.

7 It is interesting that the layout of these sites is very similar to phase 2 at Cnip (Armit 1988). One enters this complex, through a passage, from the west, and there is a subsidiary space to the left. Continuing along the passage you enter the main circular space. Another ancillary space is accessible from this room to the left.

The Decline of the Broch and New Beginnings(?) – Later Middle Iron Age Structures, an Orcadian Example

BEVERLEY BALLIN SMITH

INTRODUCTION

DUE TO the large scale excavations at Howe and Pool, Orkney and Old Scatness, Shetland, we are now in a position to better understand the pattern of post-broch structures and the multiplicity of their forms in the Northern Isles. Indeed, it must be said that the later Iron Age structures on Shetland have been better understood than those on Orkney because of the detailed excavations at Jarlshof and elsewhere undertaken by Hamilton and others from the 1930s to the 1950s (Hamilton 1956, 1968). However, there are problems that need to be addressed as part of a wider research agenda. Fojut summarised these into looking at *"the specific function and inter-relationship of broch and non-broch elements, both within sites and across the landscape"* (Fojut 1998, 12). This paper will look at some aspects of non-broch elements on sites from the end of the main broch use – the transition between the Middle and Later Iron Ages. From the work at Howe (Ballin Smith 1994), a date of sometime between the 2nd and 4th centuries AD is suggested, although this may well vary between different sites and different regions.

WHAT IS HAPPENING AT THE END OF THE MIDDLE IRON AGE, AND WHY IS THE BROCH IN DECLINE?

A brief summary of the early history of the settlement at Howe is given at the beginning of Ballin Smith (this volume). The origins of the settlement and its development encompasses eight major phases, but it is part of the later settlement in the early centuries AD which forms the object of discussion for this paper.

The evidence from Howe, at the transition of the broch period proper (early Phase 7) with the later broch period (later Phase 7), may be unique in the Iron Age of the Northern Isles in the events which took place. The evidence suggests that preserving the broch tower as a standing building was a constant problem for the Iron Age inhabitants of the site. The tower, erected without adequate foundations on the clay mound of a Neolithic chambered tomb without adequate foundations, was problematic from its inception. Slippage and collapse was evident from early in its construction. The repetitive nature of real and predictable structural collapse may indicate that the tower never attained the height, for example, of Mousa in Shetland. Even so, when it did collapse, rubble from its five metre thick walls was a serious problem for the inhabitants of the site. The danger of repeated broch wall slippage was such that the prone skeleton of a middle-aged man was placed in an abandoned cell at one end of a yard prior to a late, large collapse from the broch, instead of being more traditionally buried. This was also the case with three other skeletons of young children shallowly buried in the deposits and rubble of the same yard prior to eventual burial by masonry from the broch tower (Ballin Smith 1994, 262) (see below). After battling with the structural problems of the broch tower for possibly as much as two centuries, the inhabitants of Howe resorted to a new strategy.

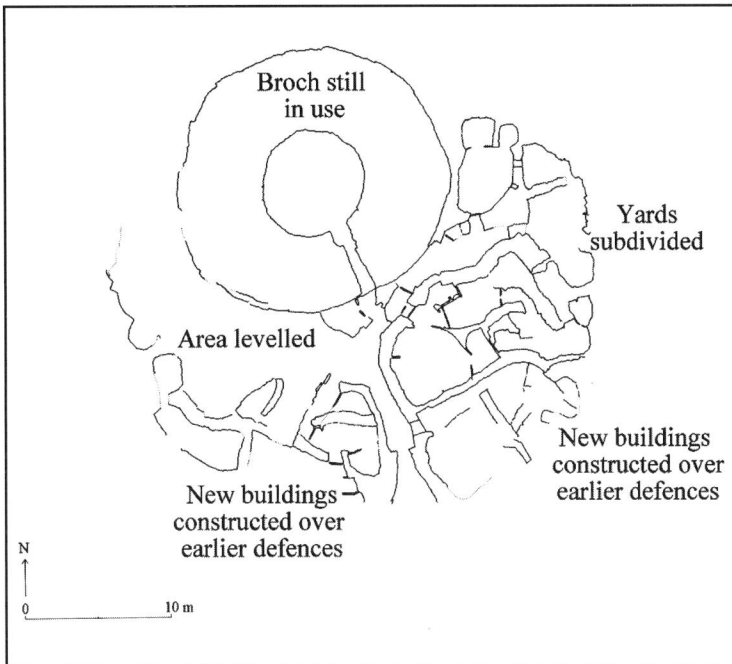

Fig.27 *Howe: plan of the broch settlement showing changes during the beginning of later Phase 7.*

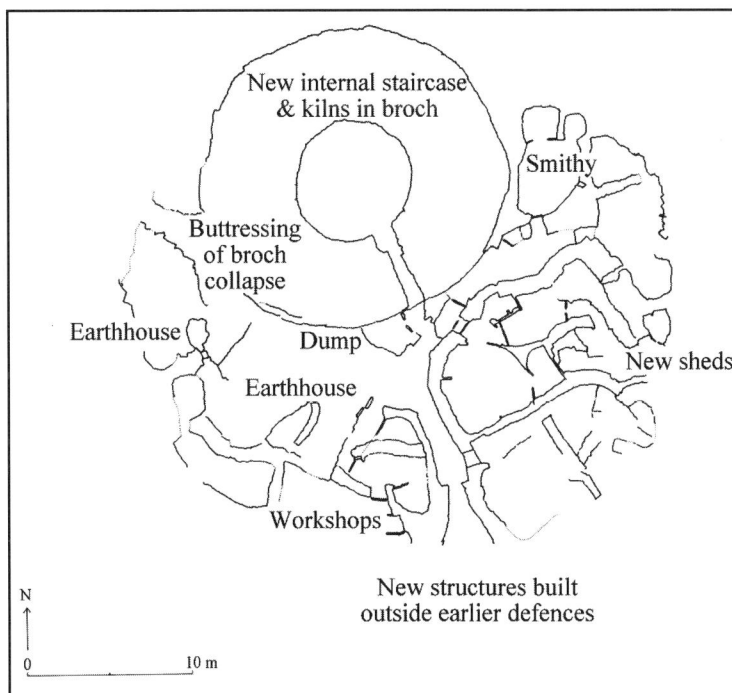

Fig.28 *Howe: alterations to the broch and settlement during later Phase 7.*

The southern forecourt area was perceived to be the area most under threat from collapse of the tower (Fig. 13). The three buildings to the south and west of the tower were deliberately levelled, and this was then followed by rebuilding away from the broch and over the already filled-in defences (filled in by the 1st century AD) (*ibid*, 89) (Fig. 27). Buildings to the east were slightly remodelled and the yards of two of them were subdivided, as if to make extra accommodation (Fig. 29). It is possible that other structures were built over the defences in the east at this time but this was not proven by excavation. While the structural alterations to the settlement were taking place, the tower collapsed to the south-west covering some of the new buildings across the forecourt area with stone to a depth of over two metres.

This spectacular event caused a final halt to any domestic occupation of the north-western area of the forecourt but not to the settlement in general. The collapsed rubble mass as well as the remaining wall face of the tower were subsequently buttressed. The rubble itself was put to use and an oval earthhouse was constructed within it. The buildings across the front of the broch were again remodelled, but instead of domestic dwellings, a second earthhouse and two workshops with industrial hearths were created (Fig. 28). At this time, buildings were noted south of the broch causeway, beyond the limit of the former defences. Although only partly excavated, both domestic and workshop activities were identified.

On the east side of the site, the yards of two of the houses were turned into what can only be described as domestic dwellings, and the former NE building changed from a domestic structure to an industrial smithy with the construction of a large iron-working hearth (Fig. 29). Construction of simple cellular structures or sheds against existing walls was attempted for extra accommodation or storage which may have had other purposes rather than for the simply domestic.

Occupation of the broch tower was still a major consideration for the inhabitants of the site in spite of the massive wall collapses, as the interior of the structure remained largely open. The western intra-mural staircase and landing, if they had not been severely damaged in a previous collapse, were now too dangerous to use and a replacement staircase was constructed inside the broch to link with the wall-head (Fig. 28). Gaining access to the top, or what remained of the top, of the wall was obviously still a necessity. The interior of the broch was cleared of rubble and reoccupied, but with some alteration which included the construction of two kilns. It is thought that a complete roof did not cover the broch interior at this time.

The beginning of the end of this later phase of activity within the broch came with the laying out of unthreshed barley in front of the kilns to dry. Unfortunately, the harvest caught fire causing damage to both the interior of the broch and the function to which it was put. To deal with this problem, some attempt was made to clear out the broch interior and dump the

Fig.29 *Howe: the NE building transformed into a smithy by the construction of a large industrial hearth.*

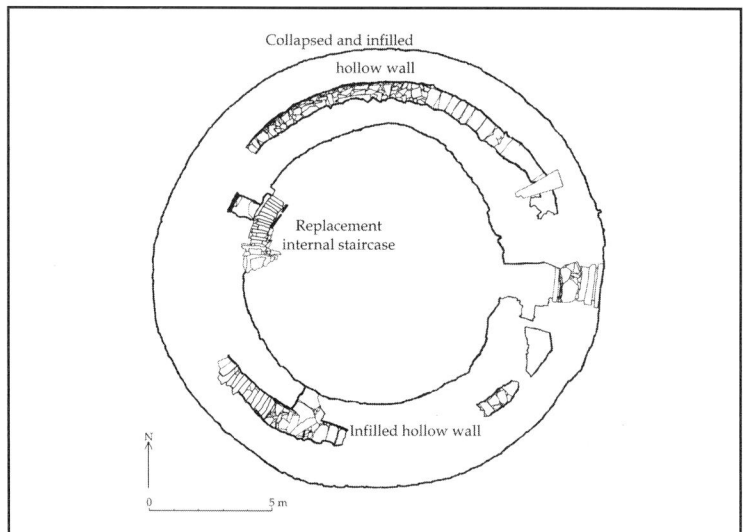

Fig.30 *Broch of Gurness: plan of the wall head of the broch identifying later changes and alterations to the structure.*

THE END OF THE BROCH

Some of the physical reasons why the broch at Howe was in decline have been addressed above and the stratigraphic evidence produced, but what of other brochs? The evidence for similar events can be seen in the surviving masonry at, for example, the brochs of Gurness and Midhowe. The former lost much external stonework to the west and the buildings close by are the least well preserved of those that surround the broch. A secondary stair was constructed inside the broch interior to attain the wall-head and evidence can be found that the hollow wall collapsed in on itself in the north-western part of the tower (Figs. 30 & 31). At Midhowe, an external ordered row of flagstones set on edge is prominent north of the entrance passage, where they can be interpreted as supporting the collapsed broch wall face (Fig. 32). The interior of the same stretch of wall was refaced and part of the adjoining hollow wall was filled in, possibly accidentally. The south side of the broch entrance also suffered collapse (Fig. 33). Sea

Fig.31 *Broch of Gurness: the collapsed and broken lintels of the hollow wall in northern arc of the broch. From the north-west.*

burnt debris on the southern forecourt just to one side of the broch entrance passage which still remained usable. Not long after this fire, the broch tower suffered its largest collapse, when its southern wall failed and its masonry fell to cover the southern forecourt.

Occupation carried on at the site, both on, and in, the rubble collapses from the broch and actually within the rubble which also began to fill the broch interior. Another two workshop floors were identified within the broch, but the end of the Middle Iron Age had been reached and the scene was set for the continuation of settlement in the Late Iron Age (or Pictish) period.

Fig.32 *Midhowe Broch: the buttressing against the collapsing broch wall north of the entrance. From the west.*

123

Fig.33 *Midhowe Broch: the collapsed broch wall south of the broch entrance. The filling within the hollow wall is visible, as are the broken lintels. From the west.*

erosion was considered by the excavators to be the main cause of the missing wall face at this point, but the intermittent blocking of the hollow wall at ground level suggests there may have been other factors involved such as the failure of the integrity of the structure.

From these examples it is interesting to analyse why Orcadian brochs suffered chronic instability and why others such as the Shetland brochs of Jarlshof and Mousa did not. Geological considerations and the quality of building construction may form only part of the story. As suggested elsewhere (Ballin Smith this volume), there may be underlying factors which could account for much of the failure of structures. The building history of the Old Scatness Broch will eventually be unravelled; preliminary results show that at least two later phases of building were inserted into the broch – a wheelhouse (structure 16) and a later double-clover leaf cellular structure (structure 7) (Bond and Dockrill 1999). But what of the broch itself? What does the evidence tell us about its constructional history and its viability as a structure?

The form of post-broch buildings on Orkney is quite different from that on Shetland where the insertion of wheelhouses into brochs seem to have been a common phenomenon, as

can be seen from the examples of Jarlshof, Mousa and Clickhimin. This evidence suggests that the Shetland broch interiors remained viable areas for redevelopment and reoccupation at the end of the middle Iron Age, or could easily be made so. But how long that redevelopment went on for, and what caused it in the first place, is something that might be elucidated by the Old Scatness Broch excavations. Instability and failure may not have been a major factor in broch remodelling on Shetland, but factors bringing about changes in style, and possibly function and status need to be addressed.

The human effort that went into preserving the broch, as a structure in its own right and as a viable building, is worth discussing a little further. It has been demonstrated that the inhabitants of the Howe were collectively employed in stabilising the dominant structure of their settlement. We cannot presume to glimpse the ideology which lay behind the concept of brochs; we can hazard guesses but they may not be halfway accurate. At Howe, the placing of the broch on a succession of earlier round structures on the top of a gutted Neolithic chambered tomb may well have held some special significance (see Richard Hingley this volume). The prominence and associations of the location due to the early history of the site were possibly important, but from a constructional point of view it would have been easier to have built on a green field site. The increasingly complex engineering feats needed to hold up the broch tower, and to keep holding it up in a semi-ruinous state, suggest a significance was given to the building which is obscured to our understanding. The technology of building ever more complex repairs, replacement staircases and buttresses at these Middle Iron Age sites indicate that the maintenance of the broch was important, as was access to the broch wall head. Was height, aspect or viewing for defence still important in the 2nd to 4th centuries AD? Did the broch still retain some *symbolic* meaning for its inhabitants that had to be maintained at all costs? Was the ideology of their beliefs or the status of their clan contained within this building? Collapsed, ruinous and rubble-filled brochs litter Atlantic Scotland, but few, if any, were dismantled by their inhabitants.

RELATIONSHIP OF LATER STRUCTURES TO THE BROCH

From the story at Howe, instability of the broch tower eventually caused problems for its surrounding village. Although they could be described as important buildings in their own right and survived in two cases over two metres in height (see Ballin Smith 1994), there did not seem to be an ideological, logistical or practical problem about levelling the village to make way for new buildings. The concepts and symbolism embodied within the broch did not appear to extend to the village. The attempt at rebuilding the surrounding structures, by implication, was a means of extending the life not only of the broch tower, and all it encompassed, but also that of the whole settlement. The relationship between broch and buildings was perhaps more complex than we have hitherto given thought to.

From the surviving evidence from the Northern Isles, only Howe appears to show the late redesigning of the village. Again, is this because of a unique set of circumstances or was the phenomenon unrecognised or too complex to contemplate at other sites such as Gurness, where during excavation, masonry which did not make a coherent pattern of building was simply cleared away? The excavations at Old Scatness may eventually indicate a similar, or a rather different story to that at Howe, but they give the best possible hope to finding out answers as to why brochs were remodelled and what the relationship of

other later structures was to them. Although arguably in different Iron Age regions, the Old Scatness Broch is the only directly comparable site to Howe because of its deep stratigraphy, complexity of buildings and the methodological approaches and excavation techniques employed.

THE PLACING AND FORMS OF LATER STRUCTURES

From the description (and illustrations), it is quite obvious that the original attempt to rebuild part of the Howe broch village was undertaken in order to perpetuate the nuclear form of settlement, although slightly distanced from the threat caused by the unstable broch. As has already been discussed, the defences that encircled the site had been filled in, and their function and their physical and conceptual restraints had long since disappeared. They were in fact available for constructional purposes. However, there seemed to be some initial reluctance to do away with the established pattern of the village altogether. The eastern side of the settlement remained largely intact and the entranceway was maintained along with the obstruction formed by the internal retaining walls to the former defensive clay rampart. Only one new structure, to the south, clearly made any attempt to change the prevailing pattern. It would almost seem that there was a cognisant rather than a physical problem in developing the settlement beyond its former limits.

The site evidence would suggest that the familiar was preferred, with the reuse of some orthostats and walls as foundations for the new buildings. Only one unit established a new pattern to challenge the age-old concepts enshrined in the broch, village and defences, by being constructed over the former clay rampart. A total remodelling of the east side of the broch village never took place. Alterations are recorded, with some consolidation of old walls and cells and the building of new walls and pavements in former eastern yards, but the Middle Iron Age settlement design largely survived. A complete gutting of the broch interior and its replacement with later structures comparable to the Shetland wheelhouse never occurred. It appears that old ways and patterns were important and were generally maintained. The relationship between broch and village survived although the actual details of that relationship may have altered.

The new buildings to the south of the broch were designed to be largely free-standing, although single-faced walls were used where they backed into rubble. Orthostats were reintroduced, along with new areas of paving, including that of the village entrance passage. Building forms were predominantly irregular, but more cellular than linear in shape. There did not appear to be a uniform plan to the remodelling, although that may be the result of poor structural preservation and of later plough damage. The cohesion of the earlier broch structures had been abandoned for ad-hoc buildings of a poorer quality and doubtful status. It is uncertain what proportion of the settlement was represented by these buildings given that the area outside the defences was not fully excavated. However, it would appear that no new stone was brought on to the site at this time, and no attempt was made to start building completely from new.

SOCIAL AND ECONOMIC CONSIDERATIONS

Within perhaps a few decades, what we perceive to have been a relatively high status settlement at Howe during early Phase 7 had been reduced in height, been partly cleared, subdivided and rebuilt, to resemble little more than a huge pile of stone in what could have been a builder's yard during later Phase 7; but what of the inhabitants?

There seems to have been a change in settlement organisation with the threatened collapse of the broch and the levelling of part of the forecourt. From what was a largely domestic settlement at the beginning of the Middle Iron Age, the site now exhibited evidence for a greater emphasis on sheds and workshops associated with iron-working and other activities. However, this interpretation may be inaccurate as workshops and sheds could have existed outside the ditch and rampart earlier in the Iron Age. During later Phase 7 the NE building was converted into a smithy, the new buildings on the forecourt were primarily associated with iron working activities, and the broch interior provided evidence for pottery manufacture, stone and bone working as well as for iron smelting.

Although the iron working activities at Howe were relatively small scale and the failure of iron smelting was high (see McDonnell in Ballin Smith 1994), the importance of iron and smiths to the community must be stressed (see Gerry McDonnell this volume). Iron may have been a rare and valuable metal on site in comparison with the numbers of ubiquitous stone tools. In general, the apparent tidiness implicit during the life of the main broch and settlement (early Phase 7) was missing from the later village reorganisation. Stone debris and discarded domestic refuse were never cleared away. At least one human body was not retrieved or was placed with others without ceremony in a disused part of the site (see below). As well as a change in the settlement pattern, there seemed to have been a decline in the social order.

This argument can be taken further to suggest that the reorganisation of the settlement also reflected a change and possible decline in the numbers of people living there. The poor quality construction, the numbers of industrial sheds, the apparent decline in domestic accommodation and the village's overall appearance, suggest a change of emphasis within the settlement and a population in decline and possibly in crisis. In spite of the physical effort required to maintain the broch tower (a perpetuation of the old), the input of energy into rebuilding the settlement was lacking in conviction, and the reoccupation of the broch and its external settlement was short lived. After the large southern collapse of the broch, many of the remaining buildings became uninhabitable and the broch was finally abandoned. With the demise of the broch came the abandonment of all it stood for and the inhabitants' identity may have perished in parallel. The status, concepts and ideology embodied in the broch disappeared into a pile of rubble which physically could not be resurrected.

Later evidence from the site suggests that the decline in settlement was real and not merely implied, and by the 4th century AD a single farmhouse was all that was left of the Middle Iron Age nucleated broch village. How much the decline of the broch mentally and physically affected its inhabitants is uncertain, but the hurried disposal of one adult, a *ca.* ten-year old girl, a ten-month old boy and a female foetus within debris in the remains of the NW building indicate some of the stresses on the local population. Traditional burial rites were overlooked and no formal graves were dug. The disposal of the four individuals seems to have taken place within a short space of time, indicating population and individual crises, an abandonment of social norms and a small, but visible, decline in the numbers of inhabitants at Howe. It is possible that a movement away from the site now occurred. The traditional Middle Iron Age society had broken down and the monumental architecture of the broch and its village were reduced to more vernacular proportions. More changes were to come in both social and settlement organisation, agricultural and hunting practices (see Smith and Dickson in Ballin Smith 1994, and Bond 1998) but these belong to the later Iron Age (Phase 8) and a separate story.

CONCLUSIONS

This story covers a short time span in the history of the Howe, but it is an important one when considering the decline of brochs in general. The physical aspects of that decline have been emphasised as the evidence survives for them and that decline can be seen, although with more limited evidence, at other Orcadian sites. External factors, such as outside contacts or lack of them, disease and environmental pressures of all kinds are still to be researched. It is hoped that the details of the story of Old Scatness will generally elaborate the decline of the broch and its settlement on Shetland as a symbol of the Middle Iron Age, and provide other, more exciting fragments of evidence to aid our understanding of this brief, but important period in time.

BIBLIOGRAPHY

Ballin Smith, B. (this volume) Brochs – complex settlements with complex origins.

Ballin Smith, B. (ed.) (1994) *Howe, four millennia of Orkney Prehistory*. Society of Antiquaries of Scotland Monograph Series 9. Edinburgh

Bond, J. M. (1998) Beyond the fringe? Recognising change and adaptation in Pictish and Norse Orkney. In Mills, C. M. and Coles, G. (eds.) *Life on the Edge: Human settlement and marginality*. Symposia of the Association for Environmental Archaeology No. 13. Oxbow Monograph 100. Oxford, Oxbow Books, 81-90

Bond, J. M. and Dockrill S. J. (1999) *Old Scatness Broch and Jarlshof Environs Project. Interim Report No. 4 1998-1999*. Shetland Amenity Trust and the University of Bradford.

Fojut, N. (1998) How did we end up here? Shetland Iron Age studies in 1995. In Nicholson, R. A. and Dockrill, S. J. (eds.) *Old Scatness Broch, Shetland: Retrospect and Prospect* Bradford, Bradford Archaeological Sciences Research 5 / North Atlantic Biocultural Organisation Monograph 2, 1-41.

Hamilton, J. R. C. (1956) *Excavations at Jarlshof, Shetland.* Edinburgh, HMSO.

Hamilton, J. R. C. (1968) *Excavation at Clickhimin, Shetland.* Edinburgh, HMSO.

Land-Holding and Inheritance in the Atlantic Scottish Iron Age

Ian Armit

INTRODUCTION

ATLANTIC Scotland contains two of the most striking, yet radically distinct, architectural traditions in Iron Age Europe: Atlantic roundhouses and wheelhouses. There has been a considerable amount of recent debate over the nature and social role of these building forms, for example, the ritual and cosmological role of wheelhouses (e.g. Armit 1996, Chap. 8; Parker Pearson and Sharples 1999) and the degree to which Atlantic roundhouses represent elite residences (e.g. Parker Pearson *et al.* 1996; 1999; Armit 1997, Gilmour and Cook 1998). Less attention has been paid to the transformations in the Atlantic Scottish settlement landscape at the end of the 1st millennium BC, in which both types of structure played a significant part. This paper reviews the relationships between the two types of building and makes some suggestions as to how these may reflect far-reaching changes in the settlement and land-holding patterns of Atlantic Scotland during the Iron Age. The emergent patterns for the Western Isles, where wheelhouses are most common, will be compared with the parallel but quite distinct situation in Orkney where wheelhouses remain stubbornly absent. Some mention will also be made of the evidence from Shetland where the settlement evidence suggests yet another variation on the theme.

The Atlantic roundhouse tradition encompasses the structures often known in the literature as brochs, duns, galleried duns etc (Armit 2003). In essence it comprises massive drystone-walled roundhouses of outwardly monumental appearance (Armit, this volume). The complex Atlantic roundhouses and broch towers, which form the most architecturally elaborate examples of this broad tradition, are

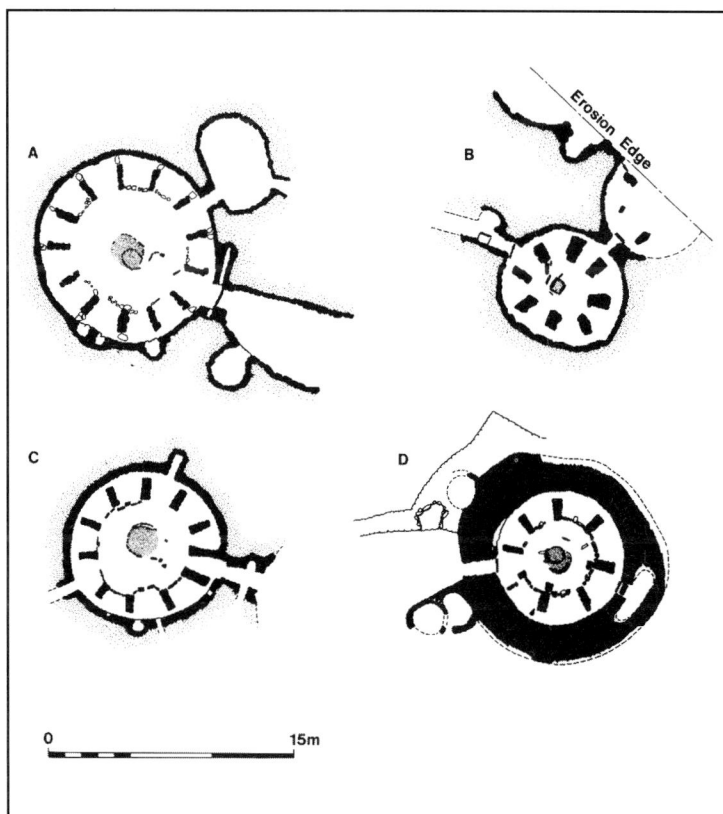

Fig.34 *Plans of wheelhouses in the Western isles: a. Sollas, North Uist; b. Cnip, Lewis; c. Kilpheder, South Uist; and d. Clettraval, North Uist.*

arguably the most overtly monumental domestic buildings of the British Iron Age. Their construction and general character have been discussed and described elsewhere (e.g. Armit 1996; 1997).

Wheelhouses, by contrast, are generally semi-subterranean circular buildings, often set into natural sand dunes or the ruins of older buildings (including former Atlantic roundhouses). They are characterised by their distinctive floorplan: a central area containing the hearth, surrounded by a series of radiating stone piers (see Armit 1996, Ch. 8 for a full discussion). The overall plan resembles the spokes of a wheel (Fig. 34). In many, if not most cases, only the upper elements of the wall and the central conical thatched roof would have been visible above ground-level. The contrast with Atlantic roundhouses, in terms of their relative imprint on the landscape, could hardly be more marked. Yet wheelhouses have, nonetheless, a quiet monumentality. The apex of the roof of even one of the smallest recorded wheelhouses, at Cnip in Lewis, would have risen some 6 m above the hearth, and the stone piers would have arched upwards around the central zone to create an intricate and imposing internal space (Armit 1996; forthcoming). Wheelhouses then, like Atlantic roundhouses, were monumental constructions, but their monumentality was entirely inwardly directed so that it could be appreciated only by the household and visitors. These were not buildings that acted in any way as statements of territoriality or control over land and resources.

While there are points of contact between the two traditions, e.g. in the approximate radial ordering of some Atlantic roundhouse interiors, e.g. Bu and Gurness (Hedges 1987), and rather more banal similarities such as basic circularity and the expert use of drystone masonry, the two traditions are quite distinct. This is particularly so given their geographical and temporal overlaps, the nature of which

will be discussed below. The small minority of free-standing wheelhouses in the Western Isles, e.g. Allasdale (Young 1952) and Clettraval (Scott 1948), may have looked superficially like the simple Atlantic roundhouses found many centuries earlier in the Early Iron Age of Orkney, e.g. Bu (Hedges 1987) and Pierowall (Sharples 1984) but it would be perverse to argue that this indicates a continuity or blurring of the two traditions.

ATLANTIC ROUNDHOUSES VS. WHEELHOUSES

As we have seen, wheelhouses are quite distinct from Atlantic roundhouses in a whole range of areas including their construction, layout, rigidity of design, and impact on the landscape. Some of the constructional distinctions can be summarised as follows:

Atlantic Roundhouses	Wheelhouses
Long roofing spans	Short roofing spans
Heavy use of timber	Minimal use of timber
Poorly insulated	Well-insulated
Exposed	Sheltered

Atlantic roundhouses were exceptionally extravagant buildings when viewed in terms of their environmental context. They seem to indicate conspicuous consumption of scarce structural timber and fuel, as well as a blatant disregard both for the conservation of heat and shelter of the roof from wind exposure. It may be that the environmental ill-adaptiveness of Atlantic roundhouses ultimately made their construction and maintenance unsustainable, encouraging the adoption of new architectural forms. This rather functionalist argument is in no way sufficient, however, to explain the appearance of the extraordinary architectural form of the wheelhouse which is far from being simply a scaled-down Atlantic roundhouse. It also begs the question of why such ill-adapted buildings as Atlantic roundhouses should have appeared in the first place and why they should have developed into increasingly extravagant forms over time. Another set of distinctions between the two architectural traditions may be more significant. These can be summarised as follows:

Atlantic Roundhouses	Wheelhouses
Prominent in landscape	Hidden in landscape
Outwardly monumental	Inwardly monumental
Limited defensive potential	No defensive potential

These distinctions suggest that Atlantic roundhouses and wheelhouses embody rather different relationships between the household and the landscape. They make quite different statements. It becomes crucial, therefore, to examine what we know of the relationship between these two architectural forms in order to explore how this distinction may have arisen.

DISTRIBUTION AND DATING

Wheelhouses have a famously peculiar distribution pattern. Large numbers are known from the Western Isles (i.e. the Outer Hebrides), a scatter in Shetland, and none has been found anywhere else. The absence of wheelhouses from Orkney must presumably be accepted as reflecting a prehistoric reality given the large amount of excavation there over many years. This distributional gap makes the virtually identical construction of Hebridean and Shetland wheelhouses all the more striking. Fully published excavations of Shetland wheelhouses are so far limited to those at Jarlshof (Hamilton 1956), which, like those in the Western Isles, appear to originate in the last centuries BC (Armit 1991), although with hints that the sequence stretches well into the 1st millennium AD. The dating picture for Shetland wheelhouses has been thrown into some confusion, however, by recent work at Old Scatness, where preliminary dating suggests that a wheelhouse of similar form to the 'classic' examples of Jarlshof and the

Western Isles, may still have been in use in the second half of the 1st millennium AD (Batt 2000). Given this potentially huge chronological disparity, and the small numbers of wheelhouses known in Shetland relative to the Western Isles, it is clearly not valid to generalise from one area to the other over such questions as the social meaning of wheelhouses and their relationships to Atlantic roundhouses. The main discussion here will, therefore, focus on the Western Isles, where the great majority of wheelhouses have been found. It is worth noting in passing, however, that the Shetland wheelhouses are, without exception, later than Atlantic roundhouses where the two forms occur together.

The relationship between Atlantic roundhouses and wheelhouses in the Western Isles is bedevilled by problems of chronology. Nonetheless, it is reasonably clear that, in broad terms, the pattern of settlement represented by wheelhouses is later than that represented by Atlantic roundhouses (Armit 1997), as one would expect by analogy with the Shetland evidence. That is not to say, however, that some Atlantic roundhouses, and particularly some of the most elaborate broch towers, may not have overlapped chronologically with wheelhouses.

The chronology of wheelhouses in the Western Isles seems to be clear in outline, although many more radiocarbon dates will be required to form a fully robust sequence (Armit 1996). The wheelhouse at Cnip was most probably constructed in the 1st or 2nd centuries BC and underwent a series of major alterations during the 1st century AD (Armit forthcoming). The latest dated wheelhouse in the Western Isles (so far) appears also to be the largest, at Sollas in North Uist, which appears to have been built in the 1st century AD (Campbell 1991; Armit 1996, 145-7 for a discussion of the radiocarbon dates). Other dating evidence relating to wheelhouses in the Western Isles is so far broadly consistent with the idea of a fairly narrow construction horizon somewhere in the 1st century BC/AD, although a saddle quern from the earliest of three wheelhouses at Foshigarry in North Uist (Beveridge 1930) may suggest a somewhat earlier date for the beginnings of the sequence there (Armit 1992). A Romano-British brooch from Kilpheder suggesting abandonment of that wheelhouse in the late 2nd century AD (Lethbridge 1952) or shortly thereafter, is probably the latest dateable find associated with a Hebridean wheelhouse in its original, unmodified structural form. Overall then, wheelhouse construction in the Western Isles may begin in the 1st or 2nd centuries BC, with many of the structures falling into disrepair by the end of the 1st century AD, although occupation of some sites continued long thereafter (Armit 1996). The striking homogeneity of design and construction of wheelhouses would certainly seem to support a relatively short period of construction (although the extremely late dates suggested for Old Scatness, above, suggest that this may not be the case for Shetland).

Independent evidence for the absolute date of Atlantic roundhouses in the Western Isles is extremely sparse, resting on a handful of radiocarbon dates, extrapolation from the rather better founded Orcadian sequence, and their few direct associations with wheelhouses. Several wheelhouses in the Western Isles, e.g. Garry Iochdrach and Cnoc a' Comhdhalach (Beveridge 1911; 1931), appear to occupy the ruins of Atlantic roundhouses. Re-excavation of another of these sites, at Eilean Maleit in North Uist, showed that the wheelhouse was indeed built into an earlier massive-walled structure, although it could not be proven beyond doubt that it was an Atlantic roundhouse (Armit 1998). Similar evidence from Allt Chrisal in Barra has suggested a similar and rather clearer sequence there (Pouncett 1999, 5-6). It would appear that, therefore, that as in Shetland, the Hebridean

wheelhouses as a group are later than at least some Atlantic roundhouses.

There are as yet no known simple Atlantic roundhouses known in the Western Isles of the type found to date to the Early Iron Age (around 700-400 BC) in Orkney. Excavated sites have all produced evidence for at least some element of architectural complexity, i.e. they are all complex roundhouses. Some of these, such as Dun Carloway and Loch na Beirgh, both in Lewis (Harding and Gilmour 2000), are also clearly broch towers. The lack of simple roundhouses would appear to suggest a relatively late appearance of Atlantic roundhouses in the Western Isles, perhaps some time around 400 BC. Such radiocarbon dates as do exist suggest that the complex roundhouse at Dun Bharabhat, Cnip was constructed prior to the 2nd century BC (secondary occupation, following major structural failure is dated to the 1st and 2nd centuries BC, see Harding and Armit 1990; Harding and Dixon 2000), and that Dun Vulan in South Uist seems to have required structural alterations at around the same time. The interpretation of this latter date is disputed, however (see Armit 2000; Parker Pearson and Sharples 1999). There is certainly, as yet, no evidence for any Atlantic roundhouse post-dating any wheelhouse, and the balance of evidence clearly suggests that Atlantic roundhouses as a group are earlier than wheelhouses. A suggested span of c. 400 – 100 BC for the construction of the majority of the Hebridean Atlantic roundhouses may not be too far wide of the mark (see also Gilmour, this volume), although it must be remembered that many Atlantic roundhouses continued to be occupied, some in highly modified form, for many centuries.

Although far more dates from secure contexts are clearly needed, particularly for Atlantic roundhouses, the relative sequence of the two structural types where they occur together, and the approximate dating spans suggested by the available dates, strongly implies that there was a chronological development in the Western Isles from one form of settlement to the other. Clearly this transformation of the settlement landscape did not occur overnight. There must presumably have been a period during which wheelhouse construction began within landscapes where Atlantic roundhouses were still the standard form of domestic settlement. To understand why the new architectural form developed it is useful to look briefly at the pre-existing pattern of Atlantic roundhouse settlement.

ATLANTIC ROUNDHOUSE SETTLEMENT PATTERNS

The social implications of Atlantic roundhouse distributions in the Western Isles have been reviewed elsewhere (Fig. 35; Armit 1992; Armit 2002) and will be only briefly summarised here. In essence studies focused on settlement in North Uist and Barra suggest that Atlantic roundhouses there formed the standard domestic settlement form for land-holding households. There were far too many of these structures for them solely to represent any stratum of society that could meaningfully be called an elite (Fig. 36). This point is reinforced by the presence of Atlantic roundhouses on small, resource-poor islands such as those south of Barra (ibid.). It is quite possible that there was some landless element of the population even if their existence cannot yet be documented archaeologically. In that very limited sense, then, Atlantic roundhouses may have signified status and relative material wealth: more importantly, however, they enabled individual households to make a clear imprint on the landscape, marking their local autonomy and control over land (ibid.).

The Atlantic roundhouse landscapes of the Western Isles, dating broadly from around 400-100 BC, thus appear to represent a society where individual households had considerable local autonomy, secure tenure of their land, and control over their own resources. A cautionary note is sounded, however, by recent work in South Uist which suggests that the much lower density of Atlantic roundhouses identified there may reflect the original prehistoric situation (Parker Pearson and Sharples 1999). Land-holding in South Uist, therefore, may have been rather differently

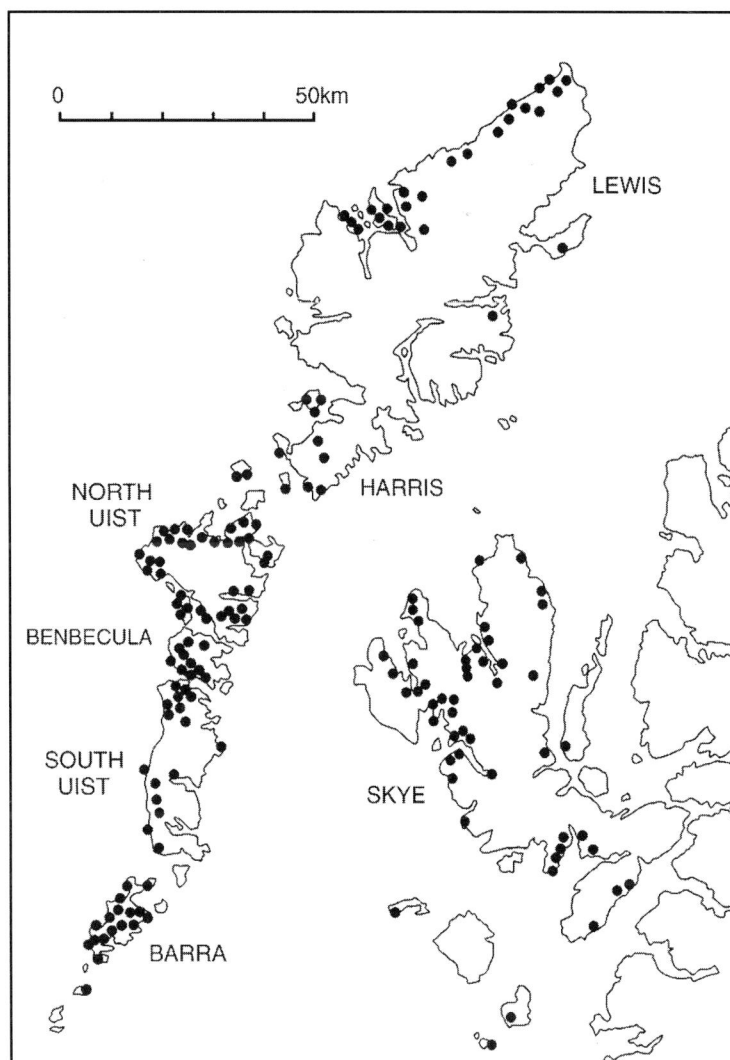

Fig.35 *The distribution of Atlantic roundhouses in the Western Isles and Skye. Note the high density and general regularity of distribution in North Uist and Barra in particular. Note also the far smaller numbers and lower density in South Uist and Lewis.*

133

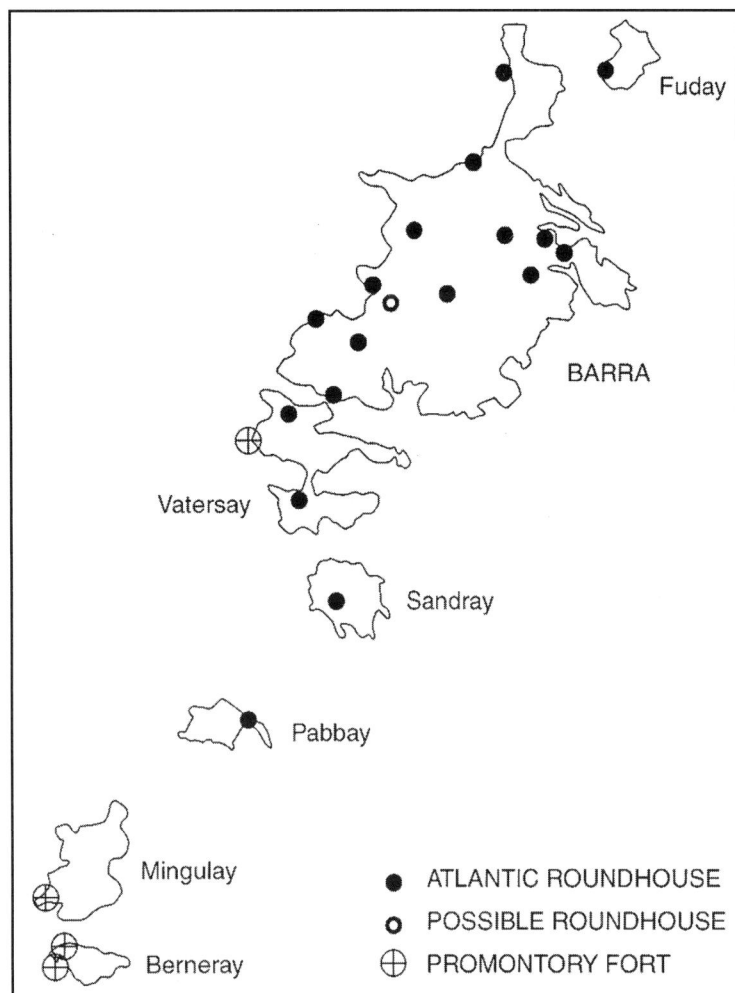

Fig.36 *The distribution of Atlantic roundhouses and related structures in Barra and nearby islands.*

roundhouses, and many, as we have seen, even occupy the shells of former Atlantic roundhouses. No significant change is discernible in the overall size of the population or its disposition within the landscape. The material culture associated with both types of site certainly does not suggest the arrival of new people or a new 'culture' associated with wheelhouses. What we seem to be witnessing is the adoption of a radically new form of architecture which, *inter alia*, seems to denote the emergence of a new type of relationship between certain households and the land they occupy. It also seems to signify, at least in the early stages of wheelhouse construction, a very marked embodiment of social distinctions between two groups of people: those who built and occupied wheelhouses, and those who continued to inhabit the remaining Atlantic roundhouses. So how did these distinctions emerge, and why?

SETTLEMENT TRANSFORMATIONS: SOME POSSIBILITIES

In the areas where their distribution has been most closely studied, such as Shetland (Fojut 1982) and parts of the Western Isles (Armit 1992), Atlantic roundhouses seem to fit into broadly coherent and surprisingly regular patterns across the landscape, generally falling rather neatly into identifiable blocks of land. Niall Sharples (this volume) stresses the continuity of individual Atlantic roundhouse settlements over many centuries, implying that these settlement patterns were stable and long-lived.

While it might seem unremarkable to those familiar with the study of Atlantic Scottish

organised, with lower status households being unable or unwilling to build and inhabit Atlantic roundhouses. This point will be discussed further below.

WHEELHOUSE SETTLEMENT PATTERNS

The distribution of wheelhouses in the Western Isles appears rather similar to that of Atlantic roundhouses, although it can only really be reconstructed with any semblance of confidence in North Uist, which had the benefit of Erskine Beveridge's extensive and largely indiscriminate archaeological investigations. Overall it seems that a broadly similar pattern of dispersed single-household farmsteads continued. Where estimates can be made (i.e. North Uist) wheelhouses seem to be no more or less dense than Atlantic

Iron Age, this manifest long-term stability of both settlement location and associated land-holding raises significant questions concerning the way in which these societies reproduced themselves over time. To appreciate the nature of the problem we must first look at the implications of some commonly-held but seldom-stated ideas of land tenure and inheritance. These all assume that farms were primarily held and worked by a single household, which might of course extend significantly beyond the nuclear family. The observed patterns of Atlantic roundhouse distribution do not suggest that land was worked communally by multiple households, although some communal activities, such as fishing, fowling, and aspects of the pastoral economy may well have been conducted as cooperative ventures.

Divisive Inheritance (Fig. 37)

It is often assumed that some form of partible inheritance was the norm for pre-Roman societies throughout much of northern and western Europe (cf. Charles-Edwards 1972). In a straight-forward system of partible inheritance the 'estate' of the parents is divided equally among all or some of the children, e.g. between surviving sons and/or daughters. While the original farmhouse might pass to the eldest sibling, it would generally do so with a significant reduction in associated land and resources as other siblings established their own farms within the original holding. Where a land-holder dies leaving no heir, the holding would be divided up between surviving kin. Thus archaeologically, over a number of generations, we should expect to see

several developments within the settlement landscape (Fig. 37):

1. A multiplicity of settlement units within any 'primary' land-holding
2. Periodic shifts in the location of the dominant settlement location within the holding, as individual households experience varying fortunes, including periods of decline, neglect and abandonment

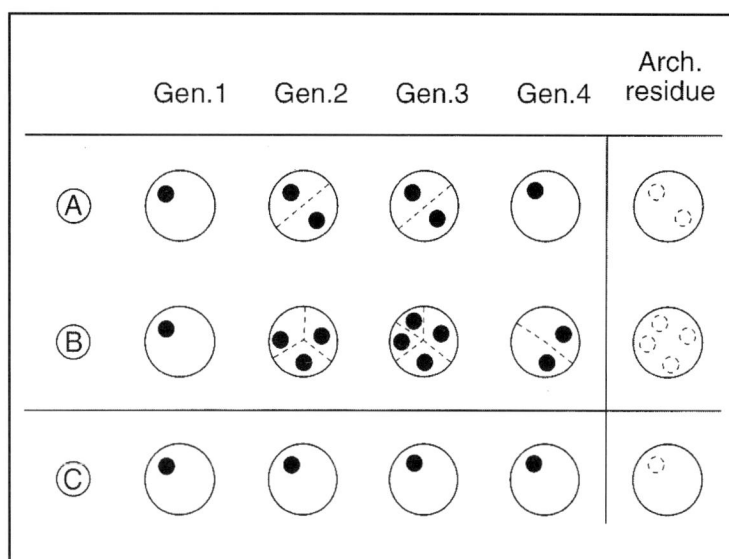

Fig.37 *The development of settlement in a hypothetical series of land-holdings over four generations (gen.1-4) under a system of divisive partible inheritance (examples A and B), contrasted with the archaeologically implied picture for Atlantic Scotland (example C).*

Example A shows relative stability: the land-holding is divided into two (in gen.2) but the second settlement fails after two generations so that the land-holding returns to its original size with its original focal settlement. The archaegological residue would be two settlement sites, one perhaps more substantial than the other.

Example B shows a messier and perhaps more likely pattern: at generation 2 the holding is divided into three parts. In generation 3 the part containing the original farm is further sub-divided so that there are four settlements in the original holding, of which the original farm is one of the smallest. By generation 4 the original settlement has failed and the holding has been divided among surviving settlements. The archaeological residue would be four settlement sites. There are of course endless permutations, but this scenario gives some flavour of what changes might occur even over a century or so.

Example C shows the pattern of stability implied by the surviving archaeological evidence from Atlantic Scotland, reflected in the archaeological residue of a single, continuously occupied settlement site.

3. The fragmentation and reallocation of certain 'vacant' holdings

All in all, the settlement pattern bequeathed to the archaeologist under such a system is likely to be complex and fragmented, and most unlikely to appear as coherent and well-fitted to the landscape as those represented by Atlantic roundhouses.

Other forms of partible inheritance can also be suggested, and some of these have significant differences in terms of their likely archaeological reflections, as I will discuss below. For present purposes, therefore, it is useful to describe this simple system of partible inheritance as 'divisive' inheritance, since one of its main outcomes is the fragmentation of land-holdings over a number of generations.

There are occasional hints that some system approximating to this model of divisive inheritance may have been in operation at certain times and places within Atlantic Scotland. The bipartite interiors of some Orcadian Atlantic roundhouses (e.g. Midhowe and Gurness) may indicate the division of previously unitary households. Similarly the rare pairing of Atlantic roundhouses, best exemplified by the remarkable proximity of Duns Troddan and Telve in Glenelg, hints at the splitting of a formerly unitary territory within the glen. Overall, however, given the time-span over which Atlantic roundhouses were occupied, the maintenance of specific buildings as continuous focal points within the landscape, and the lack of evidence for the fragmentation of holdings, seems incompatible with any long-lived tradition of divisive inheritance.

Unigeniture/Primogeniture

One implication of the apparent stability of Atlantic roundhouse settlement patterns is that Atlantic roundhouses and the land associated with them, were inherited by a single individual, e.g. eldest son or daughter (depending on whether a patrilocal or matrilocal system was practiced). Direct transmission of the intact land-holding and settlement from one generation to the next in this way seems far more in keeping with the surviving distributions of monuments in most areas. It is tempting, therefore, to suggest that some form of unigeniture may have been in operation. There are, however, some difficulties with this suggestion.

I will assume, for the sake of brevity, that the form of unigeniture most likely to have been practiced is primogeniture (eldest inherits), as this seems to have been the most common form in more recent periods, although ultimogeniture (youngest inherits) is also documented. It makes no difference to the argument which follows, which specific form is practiced, or whether inheritance passed through the male or female line.

In a broadly stable pre-industrial population, i.e. one which is simply replicating itself generation by generation, certain descent lines will naturally die out while others will increase. In theory then, some households will have no direct heir, while others should generate a surplus of siblings. In a system of straightforward primogeniture, these younger siblings would be effectively landless, while the eldest sibling would inherit not only the entire parent land-holding, but also potentially the vacant holdings of kin who have died without heir. Archaeologically, we might expect to see two distinct patterns:

1. The consolidation of ever-larger land-holdings
2. A steady increase in the number of landless families.

This again does not seem to accord with the pattern of settlement continuity seen in areas like Barra, North Uist and Shetland. Some social mechanism must presumably have existed to redistribute land-holdings within the community, to prevent both the growth of larger holdings and the emergence of a new landless class.

Redistributive Inheritance (Fig. 38)

Neither a simple application of primogeniture or the divisive form of partible

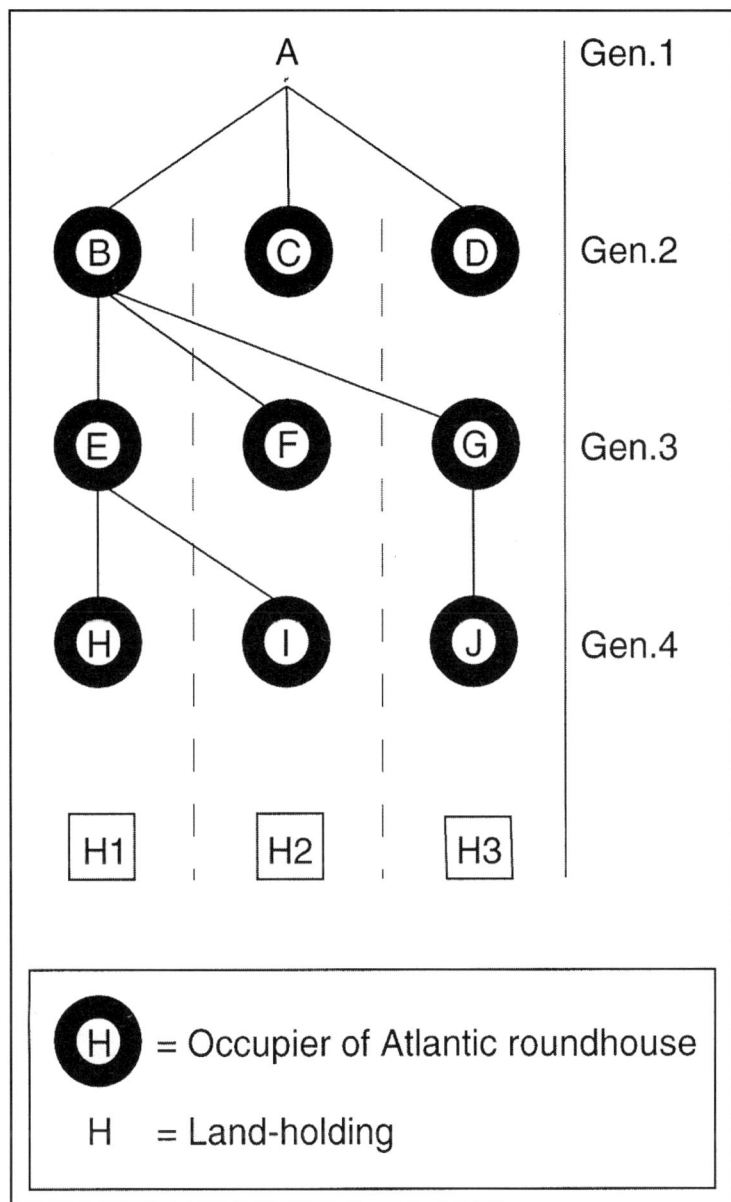

Fig.38 *The hypothetical redistribution of Atlantic roundhouses and associated land-holdings over four generations under a system of redistributive partible inheritance. In generation 2, three Atlantic roundhouses are established in three land-holdings. Two of these land-holders (C and D) die without heir, and the three holdings and Atlantic roundhouses are redistributed to the three inheriting heirs of B (E, F and G). The same principle applies in generation 4, with the redistribution of holdings among the heirs of E (H and I). In any given holding a continuity of settlement is maintained throughout.*

inheritance seems able to deliver the long-term stability of settlement apparent in Atlantic Scotland. There is, however, another form of partible inheritance that might account for such a pattern. This involves the redistribution of land-holdings within a kin-group, as appears to have been the case in Early Christian Ireland (cf. Charles-Edwards, 1972). Although previous authors have not tended to sub-divide the various possible forms of partible inheritance in any systematic way, it is useful to distinguish this particular form as 'redistributive' inheritance.

Under this system, areas of land encompassing multiple land-holdings are held or 'owned' by a kin group which may be defined in various ways. In Ireland in the 7th century AD, for example, the 4 generation *derbfine* was superseded by the 3 generation *gelfine* as the dominant unit by which 'kin' was defined (e.g. Edwards 1990, 53). Within the territory of the kin-group, individual households held and farmed individual land-holdings. Where land-holdings fell vacant they were allocated to younger kin who would simply take over the existing house and holding. Thus, assuming a broad stability in population numbers, the settlement pattern would remain more or less unchanged from generation to generation, and individual settlement locations (in our case the Atlantic roundhouses) would remain in continuous occupation (Fig. 38).

Redistributive inheritance clearly implies a fairly egalitarian social structure, at least within the kin-group with little or no sense of permanent individual 'ownership'

137

of land. We might expect such a system to reflect a fairly 'flat' social structure, with little variation in wealth or status between households. This would be consistent with the very limited evidence for concentration of wealth, craft specialisation and trade in the Atlantic Scottish Iron Age. This system further implies a strong sense of kin-group identity, and a powerful association between social identity and the land – a bond perhaps heightened and naturalised by the highly fragmented nature of the landscape which divides up easily into bounded blocks of cultivable land.

Transformations in inheritance patterns 1: The Western Isles

If we accept, for the time being, that some such system of land redistribution was probably in operation, then the settlement transformation that came with the adoption of wheelhouse architecture is all the more striking. From an earlier settlement pattern of broadly undifferentiated Atlantic roundhouse settlement, we see the appearance by the last century of a wholly distinct settlement form: the wheelhouse (Fig. 39). There were clearly now at least two types of household within the landscape, differentiated by the architectural form of their settlement. How then might such a picture have emerged from the system of redistributive inheritance described above?

There may be clues within the relationships between Atlantic roundhouses and wheelhouses described above. We have seen that there is nothing to suggest that the size and type of land-holdings associated with wheelhouses was different from that of Atlantic roundhouses. In some cases in fact, wheelhouses directly reoccupied the shells of disused Atlantic round-houses. The system of redistributive

inheritance may, therefore, have remained in operation to some degree, securing the survival of intact land-holdings, but some form of distinction must presumably have emerged between those who inherited and maintained Atlantic roundhouses, and those who established the new wheelhouse settlements.

The relationship between these two groups could take any one of a number of forms. It could be simply a question of relative wealth, as we have seen that Atlantic roundhouses would have been highly burdensome to construct and maintain. It may reflect some religious division, given the highly structured and ritualistic nature of deposition within wheelhouses. It is perhaps more likely on present evidence, however, that the division was a social one reflecting unequal control over resources.

It is difficult to maintain the traditional position, that there was some straightforward class division between broch lords and wheelhouse peasants (*cf.* Barber 1985). Wheelhouses were clearly monumental constructions, built presumably by people with a fair degree of social autonomy. Yet what they

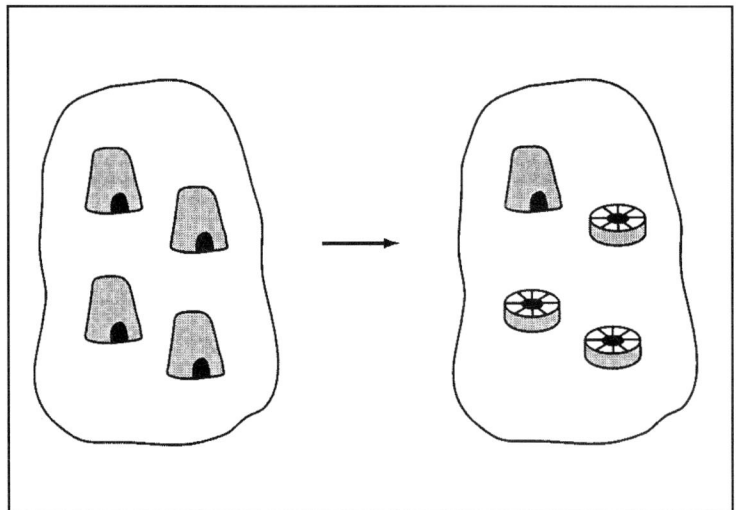

Fig.39 *A schematic view of the transition from a pattern of Atlantic roundhouse settlement to a pattern of wheelhouse settlement within a hypothetical island territory. An initial pattern of autonomous Atlantic roundhouse settlements transforms to a mixed pattern with a single Atlantic roundhouse and numerous wheelhouses, occupying broadly the same former land-holdings.*

quite obviously fail to do is to make any statement of control, authority or ownership within the landscape. It would appear, then, that although land-holdings may still have been redistributed in the same basic way, some

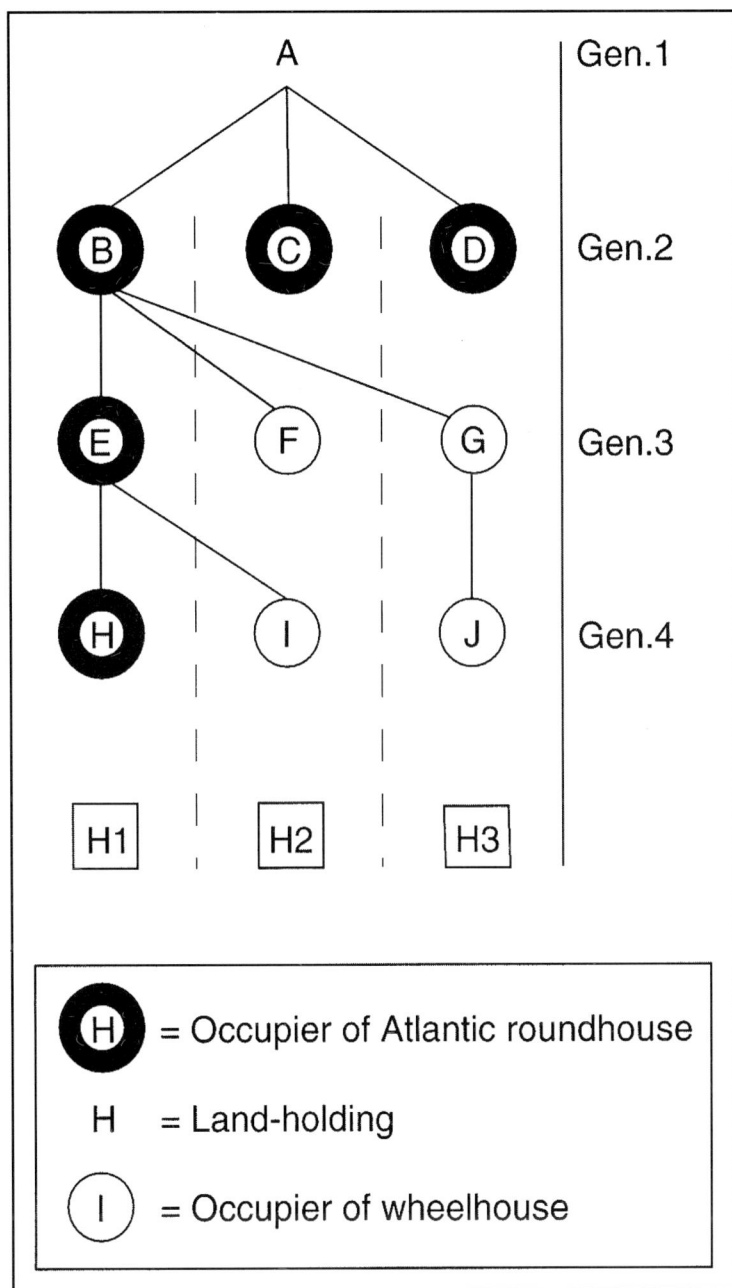

Fig.40 *The hypothetical redistribution of land-holdings over four generations, spanning the transition to the period of wheelhouse construction. As in Fig.38 Atlantic roundhouses are established in three autonomous land-holdings in generation 2. Two of these land-holders (C and D) die without heir. The senior inheritor of B inherits the Atlantic roundhouse in Holding 1, and the authority over Holdings 2 and 3 which now become dependent holdings farmed by the junior inheritors, F and G. The seniority of the main line of descent is confirmed in generation 4.*

element of differentiation had been introduced in the terms under which land could be held.

One possibility is that the senior heirs (perhaps the eldest siblings or cousins) within each kin-group may have become increasingly able to control the redistribution of land in such a way that they retained some authority over the reallocated holdings (Fig. 40). Thus, while younger siblings may have had inherited rights of residency in the holdings to which they moved, they may increasingly have owed their position to the eldest sibling who retained formal authority over the reallocated land. The construction or continued occupation of Atlantic roundhouses would presumably have been appropriate only to those who retained full land rights. Thus a two-tier system of autonomous and dependent holdings could have emerged from the earlier system, simply by a strengthening of the position of the eldest sibling. The origins of this evolved system may have been dormant within the older system, for example if the eldest son inherited their parent's house and land, and held some decision-making role over the dispersal of the younger siblings.

In summary then, the emergence of wheelhouses within a landscape formerly populated by Atlantic roundhouses may reflect the beginnings of explicit social ranking within previously egalitarian kin-groups. If so, this process was at a very preliminary stage, and it seems highly improbable that those living in wheelhouses were a subservient class, given their manifest ability to command significant resources in the design and

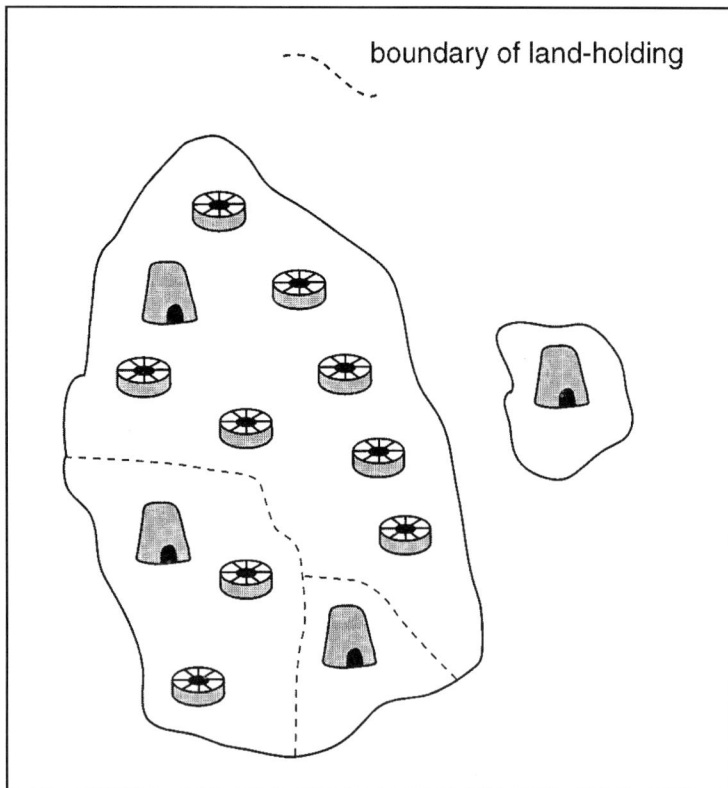

Fig.41 *A hypothetical island territory at the end of the 1st millennium BC indicating possible local differences in the development of settlement organisation. Some holdings remain isolated and autonomous, dominated by a single Atlantic roundhouse, while other groups of land-holdings have become consolidated with a surviving Atlantic roundhouse settlement dominating a variable number of dependent holdings farmed from wheelhouse settlements. The local variations will be governed by reproductive and economic success of individual families within the kin-group.*

construction of monumental houses (Fig. 41). Indeed the very complexity and intricacy of wheelhouses may be seen as an almost subversive architectural gesture by those who were now unable to display their wealth and status through the building of Atlantic roundhouses. We might speculate, however, that the two-tier system of inheritance might have carried with it obligations of labour or produce which may eventually have eroded the social autonomy of the wheelhouse-dwelling population, leading to entrenchment of social divisions. It is tempting to link such a development with the disappearance of widespread monumental construction which comes at the end of the wheelhouse period, perhaps in the 2nd century AD.

Transformations in inheritance patterns 2: Orkney and the North Mainland

A parallel but somewhat different development may be discerned in Orkney and Caithness. From as early as 700 BC we see in Orkney the appearance of isolated single farmsteads represented by a simple Atlantic roundhouse, as at Bu or Pierowall. This pattern, poorly-defined as it is, might suggest that a system of redistributive inheritance may also have been employed in these areas. By the 1st century BC, however, fully-fledged broch villages had appeared. The buildings that make up these villages seem wholly over-shadowed by the broch tower, and their architecture seems to embody their social and economic dependence. Atlantic roundhouses in Orkney were thus transformed from symbols of control over land, to symbols of control over people.

The nucleation of settlement around broch towers suggests that the dominant members of society in Orkney and Caithness may have been able to annex increasing amounts of land, which required more labour to work than was available in the traditional household. The nature of the architectural relationships between broch tower and village would suggest that the latter may have housed landless dependents. This in turn suggests that the emergent Orcadian elite had moved further and faster in establishing their social and economic dominance than had their counterparts in the west (Fig. 42).

One way in which this might have been achieved is by moving from redistributive inheritance to a system of primogeniture (as discussed above) in which vacant holdings were swallowed up and farmed centrally, rather than being assigned to junior siblings as

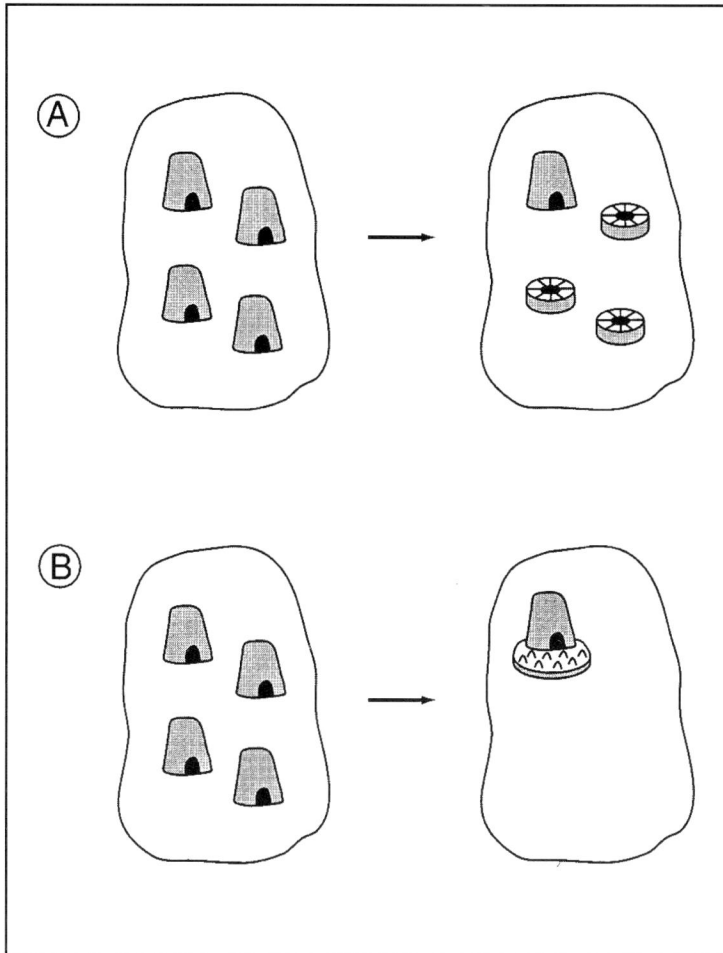

Fig.42 *A schematic view of changing settlement patterns and hypothetical territories during the last century BC: A = the Western Isles; B = Orkney.*

dependent but still identifiable land holdings. It would follow, therefore, that communities in Orkney and Caithness would have far more entrenched social differentiation by the end of the 1st millennium BC than their contemporaries in the Western Isles or Shetland. Such a scenario would be quite in keeping with the apparent evidence for Orcadian kingship and external links with south-east England (and ultimately the Roman Empire) which emerge in the 1st century AD.

ACKNOWLEDGEMENTS

I would like to thank Mark Gardiner and Simon Gilmour for their comments on a preliminary draft, and Libby Mulqueeny for preparing the illustrations.

BIBLIOGRAPHY

Armit, I. (1991) The Atlantic Scottish Iron Age: five levels of chronology. *Proceedings of the Society of Antiquaries of Scotland* 121, 181-214.

Armit, I. (1992) *The Later Prehistory of the Western Isles of Scotland.* Oxford, British Archaeological Reports, British Series No. 221.

Armit, I. (1996) *The Archaeology of Skye and the Western Isles.* Edinburgh, Edinburgh University Press.

Armit, I. (1997) Cultural landscapes and identities: a case study in the Scottish Iron Age. In Haselgrove, C. and Gwilt, A. (eds) *Reconstructing Iron Age Societies*, 248-53. Oxford, Oxbow Books.

Armit, I. (1998) Re-excavation of an Iron Age wheelhouse and earlier structure at Eilean Maleit, North Uist. *Proceedings of the Society of Antiquaries of Scotland* 128, (1998), 255-72.

Armit, I. (2000) Review of *Between Land and Sea*, by Mike Parker Pearson and Niall Sharples, *Antiquity* 74, 283, 244-5.

Armit, I. (2002) Land and freedom: implications of Atlantic Scottish settlement patterns for Iron Age land-holding and social organisation. In Ballin-Smith B. and Banks, I. (eds.), *In the Shadow of the Brochs*, pp. 15-26. Stroud, Tempus.

Armit, I. 2003. *Towers in the north: the brochs of Scotland.* Stroud, Tempus.

Armit, I. (in prep.) *Anatomy of an Iron Age roundhouse: the Cnip wheelhouse excavations, Lewis.*

Barber, J. (1985) *Innsegall.* Edinburgh, John Donald.

Batt, C. (2000) Carbon, coins and calibration: constructing a chronology for Old Scatness, unpublished paper presented to the Old Scatness Day Seminar, 6th May 2000, Edinburgh.

Beveridge, E. (1911) *North Uist.* Edinburgh, Brown.

Beveridge, E. (1930) Excavation of an earth house at Foshigarry and a fort, Dun Thomaidh, in North Uist. *Proceedings of the Society of Antiquaries of Scotland* 65, 299-357.

Beveridge, E. (1931) Earth houses at Garry Iochdrach and Bac Mhic Connain in North Uist, *Proceedings of the Society of Antiquaries of Scotland* 66, 32-67.

Campbell, E. (1991) Excavation of a wheelhouse and other Iron Age structures at Sollas, North Uist, by R. J. C. Atkinson in 1957. *Proceedings of the Society of Antiquaries of Scotland* 121, 117-173.

Charles-Edwards, T. M. (1972) Kinship, status and the origins of the hide. *Past and Present,* 56, 3-33.

Edwards, N. (1990) *The Archaeology of Early Medieval Ireland.* London, Routledge.

Fojut, N. (1982) Is Mousa a broch? *Proceedings of the Society of Antiquaries of Scotland* 111 (1980-1).

Gilmour, S. and Cook, M. (1998) Excavations at Dun Vulan: a reinterpretation of the reappraised Iron Age. *Antiquity* 72: 327-37.

Hamilton, J. R. C. (1956) *Excavations at Jarlshof.* Edinburgh: HMSO.

Harding, D. W. and Armit, I. (1990) Survey and excavation in west Lewis. In Armit, I. (ed) *Beyond the Brochs.* Edinburgh, Edinburgh University Press, 71-107.

Harding, D. W. and Dixon, T. N. (2000) *Dun Bharabhat, Cnip: an Iron Age settlement in west Lewis – Volume 1: the structures and material culture,* Calanais Research Series No. 2, Dept. of Archaeology, University of Edinburgh.

Harding, D. W. and Gilmour, S. (2000) *The Iron Age settlement at Beirgh, Riof, Isle of Lewis, Excavations 1985-95, Volume 1,* Calanais Research Series No. 1, Dept. of Archaeology, University of Edinburgh.

Hedges, J. W. (1987) *Bu, Gurness and the brochs of Orkney Vol. 1-3,* 163-5. Oxford, British Archaeological Reports, British Series 165.

Lethbridge, T. C. (1952) Excavations at Kilpheder, South Uist, and the problem of brochs and wheelhouses. *Proceedings of the Prehistoric Society* 18, 176-93.

Parker Pearson, M. and Sharples, N. M. (1999) *Between land and sea: Excavations at Dun Vulan, South Uist,* (Sheffield Environmental and Archaeological Research Campaign in the Hebrides, 3). Sheffield, Sheffield Academic Press.

Parker Pearson, M., Sharples, N. and Mulville, J. (1996) Brochs and Iron Age Society: a reappraisal. *Antiquity* 70, 57-67.

Parker Pearson, M., Sharples, N. and Mulville, J. (1999) Excavations at Dun Vulan: a correction. *Antiquity* 73, 149-152.

Pouncett, J. (1999) *Allt Chrisal, T17: a preliminary report on the excavation of Iron Age and later structures*, 1996-1999, unpublished report, Dept of Archaeology, University of Sheffield.

Scott, L. (1948) Gallo-British colonies; the aisled roundhouse culture in the north. *Proceedings of the Prehistoric Society* 14, 46-125.

Sharples, N. M. (1984) Excavations at Pierowall Quarry, Westray, Orkney. *Proceedings of the Society of Antiquaries of Scotland* 114, 75-126.

Young, A. (1952) An aisled farmhouse at the Allasdale, Isle of Barra. *Proceedings of the Society of Antiquaries of Scotland* 87, 80-106.

Towards a Geography of Shetland Brochs

(reproduced from Glasgow Archaeological Journal, Vol. 9, 1983, by kind permission)

Noel Fojut

Summary

A VARIETY of simple techniques based upon the distribution, location and siting of Shetland's brochs, when used in conjunction with data from excavated sites, allows a partial reconstruction of the forces behind the observed patterns of broch-period settlement. The various spatial influences are examined at a number of scales, and the results used to construct a model of settlement location in relation to the physical environment. The process of model-formation demonstrates the potential of fieldwork as a source of illumination where excavation evidence is scanty.

Introduction

Geography and Iron Age Shetland

In recent years archaeologists have become increasingly aware of a wide range of techniques, all based upon relatively simple analytical and predictive statistics, which permit a more rational and quantified approach to the interpretation of patterns in field observations. In most instances, new techniques have been presented in isolation and somewhat baldly, using single examples to demonstrate the validity of a given method but seldom examining more general applications (Hodder and Orton 1976). The present study represents an attempt to build techniques together towards an overall picture, a 'geography' of the period under consideration.

Conventional geographies set out to organise known facts into a logical sequence. For past periods, where some or many of the 'facts' are missing, such an approach is unsatisfactory, and much of the effort is required simply to establish the facts to be described. The most promising approach is to study the field observations at a series of gradually more local scales, integrating whatever excavations can add, and to extract general patterns that contribute towards the desired 'geography' of the period. Since so much of the original society is not amenable to this type of study, the final results are partial, based upon factors which can be measured in the field and which have a spatial expression. Any conclusions are at best concerned with the economic-environmental sphere of human activities although strictly limited inferences may be possible in the socio-political sphere. The end product is a model based upon materialistic considerations, and it is presented for modification by the less tangible aspects which must for the present be ignored for lack of good data.

In theory, a 'geography' can be constructed for the past of almost any area at any period. Clearly, such geographies will be more or less reliable, and at this early stage of research it is as well to limit the study by certain criteria. A well-defined region is required, and it is no coincidence that studies to date have been almost exclusively concerned with islands or island groups. There is, apart from their inherent attraction for many workers, a great deal in favour of islands as objects of study.

144

They are self-defining, tend to have simple social organisation and are little affected by pressure from neighbouring areas. To consider the later Iron Age: a geography of Orkney may be of less general interest than a geography of Manau, but it is much easier to achieve. Just as archaeology has tended to concentrate upon marginal situations, because it is here that evidence survives best, so geography has tended to develop in situations where study can be concentrated by means of natural or accidental limits to areas of human activity. So past geographies may be expected to be worked out in marginal self-defining regions, as here, for Shetland.

The second limiting criterion is the problem of site recognition, and in particular the need to be able to identify a sizeable majority of a particular site-type and to be moderately sure that sites were in use simultaneously: this can be resolved either by selecting types where considerable dating evidence is available (as here, brochs) or by choosing monuments which are believed to have had prolonged usage, such as chambered tombs (Renfrew 1979). In addition, it is necessary to have a reasonable possibility of reconstructing the appropriate environment. In Scotland, these considerations automatically lead the student to the bulkier and more numerous site-types, cairns, forts and brochs, and to the more marginal areas, often islands or remote portions of the mainland. The present study, of Shetland brochs, is no exception.

Like all island groups Shetland is satisfactorily defined by the sea, and this is of value in reconstructing the organisation of land-holdings and inter-regional contacts. Further, the Shetland landscape can be shown to have changed relatively little in the two millennia since the Middle Iron Age. Even sea-level change has been limited to a slight rise, resulting in little loss of land except in the southern extremity of the Mainland. The principal changes have been as a result of human activity, and include widespread stripping of workable peat, creation of new arable land and changes in the extent of settlement nucleation. The most striking changes in land-use and organisation have been relatively recent, and there is ample evidence to suggest that rural life, up to the end of the nineteenth century, had changed but little since Iron Age times (Smith 1977).

The brochs of Shetland

Although broch-like structures are no longer so restricted in time as was once believed (Hedges and Bell 1980), those of Shetland do seem, in general, to be quite similar in architectural terms; they may have been built over a relatively short space of time and have been in use contenporaneously (Fojut 1982). Further, it does seem that Shetland brochs have both survived well and been well recorded; in fact recent fieldwork has tended to reduce the numbers of brochs rather than to add new examples. The principal complications are the presence of a number of other Iron Age defensive sites, some of which may be contemporary with brochs, and a few domestic sites which have produced 'broch' pottery (Fojut 1985). These sites, being few in number and generally in the more marginal parts of the islands, can be integrated with the broch distribution with little effect upon the latter.

Apart from published excavation reports, the information used in this study derives mainly from an extensive fieldwalking programme that covered the entire coastline plus the inland valleys and basins. Only areas of deep peat and barren, boggy moorland were ignored. Further information was gathered from maps published by the Macaulay Research Institute (soils and land-use), and the Institute for Terrestrial Ecology, and use was made of air photographic survey material held by the University of Aberdeen.

All reputed broch sites, and many other monuments, were visited and assessed in terms of structure and setting. This work produced a large body of data concerning both architecture and location, and it is the latter material that forms the basis of the following discussions.

DISTRIBUTIONS

Analysis of broch distribution

Cursory examination of the distribution map (Fig. 43) reveals that Shetland's seventy-five most convincing brochs are neither regularly spaced over the islands, nor evenly spread along the fifteen hundred kilometre coastline. Rather, brochs occur in clusters in certain areas, such as the south Mainland, and sparsely in others. This pattern was examined using the standard test for clustering in distributions, the Nearest Neighbour Index (Clark and Evans 1954). The test statistic, R, is defined as the ratio of (a) the observed average distance between sites and their nearest neighbour sites to (b) the average distance which would be expected if sites were located at random. It varies from zero (sites all clustered together, or in very tight local clusters) through unity (sites spaced at random) to 2.1941 (sites - spaced as far apart as possible). The formula is

$$R = \frac{do}{2\sqrt{(N/A)}}$$

Where: do = average distance of sites to nearest neighbours
  N = number of sites
  A = area of study region

With the Shetland brochs, a value of 1.272 is obtained for the test statistic from an average distance to nearest neighbour of 2.787km. This suggests that the distribution is slightly more regular than random, a result clearly at variance with the visual assessment of distribution. The complicating factor is the so-called 'edge effect', a statistical weakness to which the method is prone when used on an area which has a high degree of fragmentation, or where sites lie closer to the boundaries of the area than to their nearest neighbour. In fact, most Shetland brochs lie closer to the coast than to the next broch, and the islands have a high degree of fragmentation, with one kilometre of coast for each hundred hectares of land. Thus the edge effect is strong and distorts the Nearest

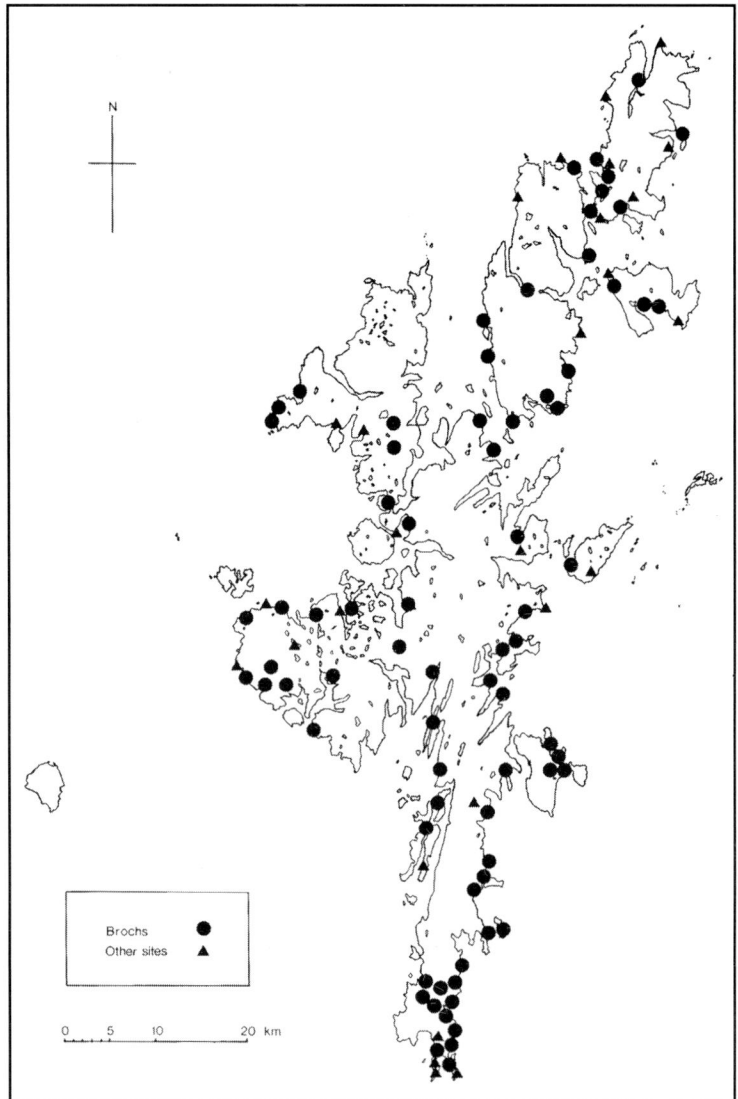

Fig.43 *Iron Age sites in Shetland.*

Neighbour Index. To overcome this, the land area was split into eight units on the basis of natural divisions, and test statistics calculated for each as follows:

South and Central Mainland 0.789
West Mainland 1.432
North Mainland 0.913
Bressay 0.908
Whalsay ....insufficient
Yell 1.387
Unst 1.086
Fetlar...0.895

These values, with much reduced edge effect, reflect the observed pattern with clustered sites in South Mainland, sites evenly spread along the coast in Yell and West Mainland, and a more or less haphazard scatter elsewhere.

Reasons for distribution

Having shown that there is a distribution with pronounced local variations, it remains to attempt an explanation. There are two general possibilities:

1. Brochs were located with regard to the siting of their neighbours (i.e., a socio-political constraint).
2. Brochs were located with regard to the physical environment (i.e., an economic-physical constraint).

It has been remarked at various times (e.g. Stout 1911) that brochs form inter-visible chains across the landscape, presumably to allow rapid visual communication, for example in case of surprise attack. This concept arose when brochs were still thought of as Celtic watchtowers against Viking invasion. In fact, it is simple to show that such chains of communication do not exist in Shetland, even when fog is absent. Fig. 44 demonstrates this, showing lines of intervisibility based upon a

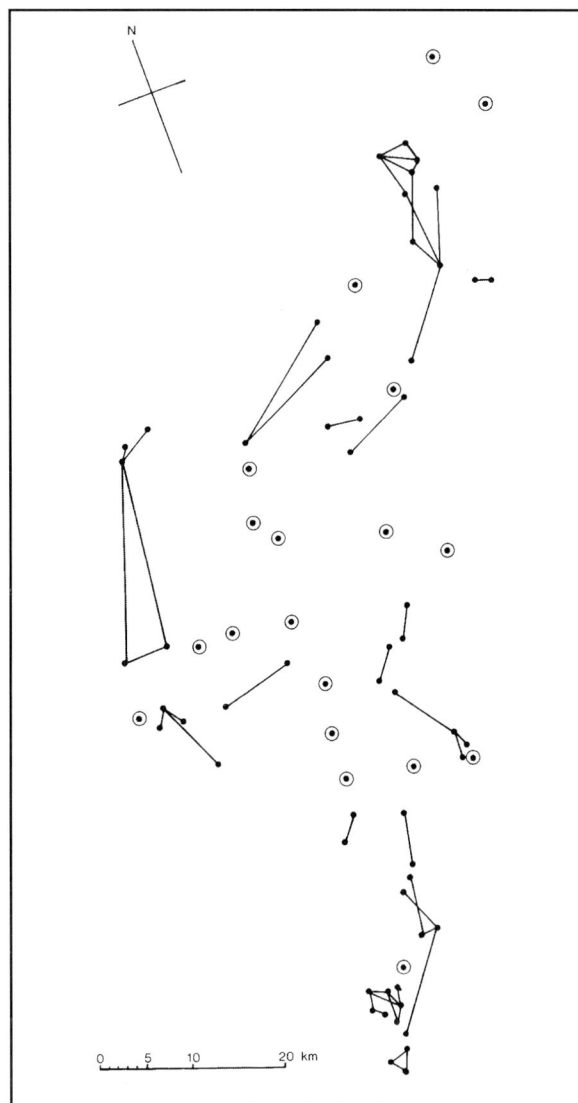

Fig.44 *Lines of broch inter-visibility.*

(probably excessive) broch height of ten metres. Some brochs actually seem to have been built in places which are particularly devoid of vantage-ground, and the general pattern is that brochs seem to be sited so that they have a good view of the immediate surroundings, with less regard paid to more distant prospects.

It is of interest to note that brochs occur in pairs or small groups; such a pattern might result either from mutual hostility or from mutual co-operation. In the case of a confrontation it is advantageous to live as close as possible to the common territorial boundary with the potential aggressor, so that defence may be rapidly mobilised. It is also of advantage to live near to the common boundary if mutual co-operation is practised at certain phases of the agricultural cycle, or in hunting or fishing. On the other hand a distribution where brochs are evenly separated suggests rather more self-sufficiency, with a desire to centralise the location of the community relative to economic activities. This would only have been favoured when there was not felt to be any advantage in living closer to a neighbouring community for either of the above reasons.

Relationship with environment

The foregoing considerations are concerned solely with the role of contacts among communities. However, the single factor most affecting site location was presumably the quality of the local environment: it is plain that brochs will not be found in areas which could not have supported broch-size populations, such as the deep peat of central Yell. Environmental quality is a compound of a number of factors such as soil quality, aspect, exposure, water supply, climate and availability of building materials. Proximity to the coast has also been important throughout Shetland's history and presumably earlier. Looking at the generalised pattern of each factor in turn, it is possible to assess the importance of each in selection of areas for settlement; however it must be borne in mind that such selection may have taken place many generations before the communities began to construct brochs, and that the concept developed by Hamilton (1957) of a mass immigration from the Scapa Flow area of Orkney becomes less likely as more sites are excavated in Orkney, notably Howe of Howe (pers. comm. B Smith, NoSAS).

(i) The chi-squared test is the technique used to compare the distribution of brochs and of generalised environmental factors. This well known test is not rigorously defined here, as it

is easily accessible, but can be summarised as follows. The area under study is divided into classes for each variable, for example well-drained, average, poorly drained, waterlogged. The percentage of land area falling into each category is measured and then the total number of sites is allocated to each class according to the measured proportions. This forms an 'expected figure', describing how the archaeological sites would most likely be distributed if they had been located without reference to the factor under consideration. The actual location of the sites is then examined, to produce an 'observed' distribution. The difference between the expected and observed patterns can be expressed as a statistic, and standard tables exist which allow the researcher to state the probability with which an observed pattern might be expected to occur. If that probability is low (the value used here is 1%) it means that the distribution of sites is so unlike the background pattern of the environmental factor that the difference requires to be explained by reasoned argument.

Examining each factor in turn, a number of situations were noted in which it appeared statistically unlikely that brochs were located regardless of the variable concerned. Arable land, solid geology, bioclimate and landscape unit all seem to have affected the selection of broch areas while, surprisingly, availability of water supply does not seem to have been important. Each of these can be examined in detail.

(ii) *Soils* in Shetland are generally so poor that it is hardly an exaggeration to say that the present pattern of land-use and soil quality is to a great extent man-made. Wherever settlement has been longest established, there the soil will be best due to long manuring and mixing - peat with sand, sand with peat and clay, and seaweed with all. But where settlement, even long lasting, has been deserted, soils rapidly become waterlogged and revert to a state of low fertility. For the present study a map was compiled, by field observation and air-photograph comparison, of all land which is now or was once under arable crops. For the Iron Age this is an over-estimate of what land would have been used, but rates of peat growth since the Iron Age suggest that no large areas of potentially fertile land would have been covered since the broch-building period. The statistical analysis showed that broch sites are far more frequently than not on or beside land of arable potential (47 on, 28 not) although such land only makes up 13.5% of Shetland's land area. When it is realised that the values used for land of arable potential cannot fail to have overestimated the Iron Age land resource, it seems clear that the presence of land which could be cultivated was a major factor in the choice of territory made by the ancestors of the broch-building communities. However, this is over simplistic. It is far more probable that the forerunners of these communities settled more widely over the land, but that the natural potential of certain areas was too low; thus in these areas settlement either failed, or it survived but the communities remained too small, poor or unimportant to become involved in broch construction. This is borne out strongly by the fact that brochs are generally in areas which offer sizeable units of good land, suggesting that there was a threshold below which communities either did not build brochs or else moved to join a nearby community when defence became necessary. In recent years, a few possible communities of this type have been located, most notably at Underhoull and Mula, both in Unst, where open settlement seems to have continued throughout the broch period (Small 1966; P Moar, pers comm; and fieldwork).

(iii) *Solid geology* also shows an interesting relationship to broch areas; most brochs stand on areas which furnish good building stone even though such stone forms less than half of Shetland's foundation. Unlike land quality it is fair to assume that solid geology has not changed since the Iron Age, although there have certainly been major changes in drift deposits through peat cutting, sand blow and coastal erosion. However, looking solely at the nearest available solid rock outcrop, the pattern still remains that brochs are rarely found on areas of poor building stone. A first explanation might be that brochs were only built where stone was suitable, or that brochs were built everywhere, but only survived when good stone allowed them to be well-built. In the former case we might expect to find a few brochs on poor areas, but built of 'imported' stone. In fact only one broch was identified as standing on different bedrock to that of its construction, and this (Burgan in North Mainland) is made of an intractable granite while it stands on a fissile gneiss. It appears that available rock was of more importance than rock quality, since at Burgan a hillside scree some distance away provides granite blocks, while the gneiss would require quarrying nearby. In fact, as Plate 7 shows, broch builders could use almost any stone to good effect, so it seems unlikely that all brochs did fall down when built of less promising materials.

A more subtle influence is probably at work. It has been shown by Chapelhow (1965) that the basic materials for soils in Shetland are usually determined closely by the underlying geology, despite the effects of the several glaciations that Shetland has undergone. It so happens that the better building stones tend to break down into more satisfactory parent material for soil - sandstones, grits, limestones and the more fragmented gneisses as opposed to granites, greenstones or the acid lavas of Eshaness. Thus more population concentration, and hence more brochs, might be expected on these rock-types. In fact, since stone-robbing is usually most severe in areas of high population, it is likely that brochs will have disappeared in some areas of better land,

149

and that the original distribution was even more heavily biased towards areas providing good stone and good land.

(iv) *The effect of climate and natural vegetation* involves consideration of many factors. Maximum and minimum temperatures, accumulated temperatures, average rainfall, ratio of rainfall to evaporation, maximum windspeeds, mean windspeeds, exposure, altitude, distance from coast all affect the potential natural vegetation complexes, which are also influenced by past history and chance events. The factors are so closely inter-linked that it is convenient to follow the approach of Birse, Dry and Robertson (1971) in forming categories based upon combinations of the above variables. Under this system of bioclimatic zonation, Shetland may be divided into areas displaying eight types of bioclimate, all hyperoceanic (and incidentally with high percentages of airborne salt, even for this type of bioclimate). The types range from humid southern boreal (for example the area around Jarlshof) with damp conditions and moderate temperatures in sheltered locations, to extremely humid lower orohemiarctic (on the hilltops of Unst and North Mainland) with very wet conditions, low annual temperature accumulation and exposed conditions.

A simple division of the types into favourable and unfavourable, with regard to agriculture, shows as expected that the majority of Shetland brochs lie in areas which have one of the two bioclimatic classes which could be called 'mild'. It is of interest that, while the overall distribution clearly shows a link with the bioclimate, this overall result conceals an important internal variation.

Table 8 shows clearly that, while nearly all brochs which have a good extent of potential arable land lie within areas of mild bioclimate, those brochs without much good land are more or less evenly split between mild and severe zones. This suggests that there may have been broch economies which were not particularly

Bioclimatic type	Much potential arable	Little potential arable
Mild	45	15
Severe	2	13

Table 8 *Comparison between climatic type and land quality for each broch.*

dependent upon crop-raising, an idea pursued further below.

On a purely local scale, few brochs are sited in sheltered positions, as such positions are generally overlooked by steep slopes and thus less suitable for defence. Also, sheltered sites are not normally well placed for outward vantage. Although we may assume that the broch walls were sufficient proof against even Shetland gales, it is of more than passing interest that the thicker walled brochs do tend to stand in the most exposed locations. It is true that these locations are the headlands and open coasts which might have met the first onslaught of any attackers, so there may be strategic as well as climatic considerations operating here.

(v) *Broch localities,* or the position of brochs in the general landscape, are of further interest, particularly in the way in which the arable core of each territory relates to the surrounding landscape. Six categories of landscape unit are of general occurrence in Shetland:

1. Bay head or coastal valley
2. Open coastlines
3. Isthmuses
4. Promontories
5. Inland valleys or loch basins
6. Open moorland.

Table 9 shows that brochs are preferentially associated with open coastlines and inland valleys and basins, and that they appear to avoid open moorland, isthmuses and bayhead/coastal valley situations even though

	Non-broch arable units	Broch arable units	Total
Bayhead/valley	77	27	104
Open coastlines	11	24	35
Isthmuses	15	4	15
Promontories	6	3	9
Inland valley/basin	5	12	17
Open moorland	29	5	34
	143	75	218

Table 9 *Arable or potential arable areas (as large as the smallest one associated with any broch) compared with the distribution or such areas associated with brochs. Where a broch does not stand on an arable area, the figures for broch arable areas includes the nearest arable area to that broch.*

the last still comprises the largest single type of arable area associated with brochs.

The preference for inland basins suggests that shelter from salt-laden winds might have been a consideration, as does the avoidance of isthmuses. Hardest to explain is the relative avoidance of bayhead areas, and here it may be that defence is the controlling factor; many of Shetland's small bays, enclosed between steep headlands, would allow a sea-borne attacker to approach quite close before being observed. This is not the case on the more open coasts, where brochs seem to be preferentially sited. Also, the more open coasts tend to be better drained than the bayheads which are often marshy, even with modern drainage techniques.

(vi) W*ater supply,* when surveyed for each broch, produced an interesting result in that it, traditionally regarded as of the utmost importance in defensive location, does not seem to have had much influence on broch locations; the pattern of broch to water-supply distances is almost identical to the pattern of distances from randomly selected locations to water supplies. Allowing for the fact that even a shallow well would not fail to strike water in most of Shetland, and that the immediate surroundings of most brochs are obscured by debris, it is most realistic to conclude that the presence of an ample supply of water was not a controlling factor in broch location. This was the case not because water was not important,

but because it is so nearly ubiquitous in the Shetland landscape as not to require any special effort in choosing a site. Only the sandy areas of Dunrossness have water supply problems and the excavated broch here, Jarlshof, was provided with an adequate well.

(vii) *Coastline* is the last, and perhaps the most important, factor to be considered at the overall scale. It is frequently remarked that brochs are coastally distributed in most areas where they occur, and this can be seen from the location map (Fig. 43) to be the case even in Shetland, where it is almost impossible to be far from the shore. A convenient method for the absolute measurement of 'coastalness' has been unavailable in the past, but is in fact simply achieved. Using a random sample of points in Shetland, such as the intersections of lines on the National Grid map reference system, it is tedious but straightforward to calculate distance to the coast. A graph of the numbers of random points at different distances from the sea is drawn, and then a similar graph for the distances of the sites under study to the sea is superimposed, as in Fig. 45.

The ratio of the gradients of the two curves gives an absolute measure of the coastal preference, or otherwise, of the sites investigated and, as an incidental bonus, the slope of the background curve gives a useful measure of the fragmentation of any area of land: the steeper the slope, the more the area is

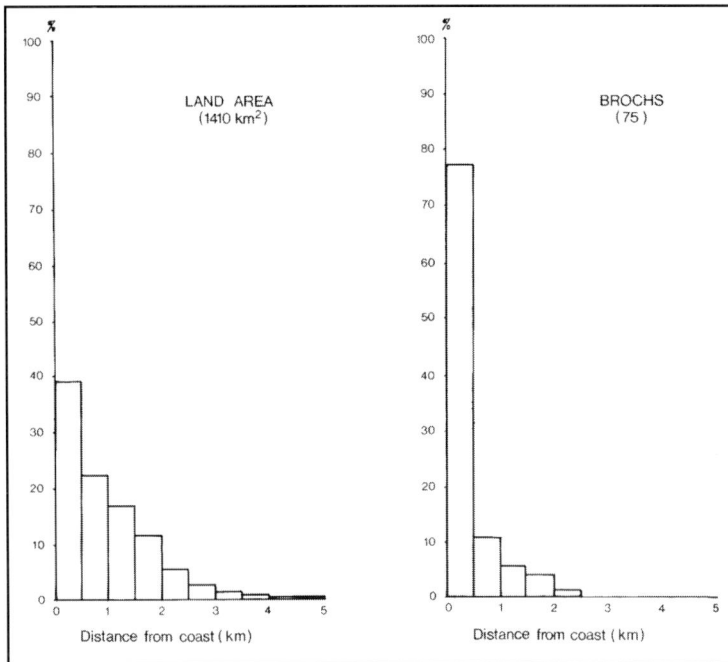

Fig.45 *Comparative distribution of land area and brochs with respect to the coast.*

interpenetrated by the sea. In the present example, Shetland's brochs are almost exactly three times more likely to lie on the coast than would be the case if they were sited at random.

However, this high degree of preference for the coast is somewhat misleading; it was often noted that brochs mapped as being on the coast are not, in practical terms, coastal as they may be sited on cliffs which render the shore inaccessible (Fig. 45). This trait is most noticeable in that group of brochs classed above as standing on open coasts. Here the brochs are mostly some distance away from the nearest landing-place, while bayhead brochs tend to be sited on or beside their landing beaches. This would support the view advanced above, as it suggests that bayhead communities would require a defence ready to hand, as they could have received little warning of a raid, while dwellers on the open coast, who could see attackers approaching while some distance away, could afford to site their brochs in more defensive, less convenient, positions.

Also to be considered is the role of coastal change in influencing the distance of brochs from the coast. Most parts of the Shetland coast are reasonably steep, and here the overall slight falling of land relative to the sea will have had little effect. Since this change is estimated at a maximum of two metres since the Middle Iron Age, it is only on the relatively few areas of low coast that land loss has been great, in particular around Pool of Virkie, where the brochs at Eastshore and Jarlshof have been halved by the sea (Plate 8). It is also in these low shore areas that sand accumulation has been greatest, producing the settlement-burying mounds such as those at Jarlshof, Sumburgh Airport and Lunabister. In a few other cases brochs have been eroded by cliff attrition, as at Balta and Mossbank, but in general losses of land in this way have not been great. Most Shetland cliffs are not actively under marine attack and seem to be gradually stabilising themselves to present conditions after the last main phase of erosion, which can be tentatively ascribed to a raised sea-level in early post-glacial times. This same sea-level may be responsible for the only trace of a raised shoreline visible in Shetland, under the flat area now occupied by Sumburgh airport (Lamb, pers comm). One final, and not insignificant, effect of the slight rise in sea-level since the Iron Age is that a number of brochs sited originally upon promontories are now upon tidal islets, and a few upon tidal islets are now cut off at all times. On the other hand, deposition of sediment by the rising sea has united island brochs such as Noonsbrough (Plate 9) to the shore. The effects of sea-level change are never constant, nor easily predictable.

Summary of environmental relationships

To summarise this survey of the relationship of broch distributions to general environmental factors, it is sufficient to remark that the most influential factors seem to be those which determine the capacity of the local land for agriculture, and that these factors are very closely related. Thus brochs are found to be associated with good land, good building stone and mild climate, but in fact these three resources tend to occur together in any case. The second main influence is clearly the presence of the sea, which has always played a vital although variable role in Shetland's economy, and which dominates the landscape. On the other hand there seems to be little evidence to show that brochs were located with reference to the position of other brochs, suggesting that the broch communities were either not the only units in Shetland, or else did not exploit all the land to its full potential.

TERRITORIES AND ECONOMY

It has already been remarked that the contemporaneity or otherwise of brochs, or any other class of site, is a vital consideration when undertaking any analysis of location or distribution. It is worth noting that Shetland brochs do not occur in close proximity to each other (as, for example, the three Orkney brochs at Midhowe, Rousay) and that each broch seems to be associated with an intuitively defined 'territory' unique to itself. Both observations suggest that Shetland brochs, if not built at identical dates, may nevertheless all have been in use at the same time. Before any further analysis of territorial division or economic organisation is possible, it is first necessary to test this suggestion.

Defining broch territories

To test the likelihood of broch contemporaneity in Shetland, a limited area was selected as a case study. This was the most southerly part of the mainland, which not only has the closest grouping of broch sites but in which it also seems most likely that agricultural resources, as opposed to marine, were of prime importance. In this area there is a fair chance that all former broch sites have been located, although the discovery in 1974 of a broch beside the access road to Sumburgh airport points to the inadvisability of being dogmatic about this. There are twelve known brochs and the test is based upon the arable potential of the territories assigned to each broch. The actual method of assigning territorial boundaries is of interest in itself.

Fig. 46 shows the two stages in delimiting broch territories. In the first map the land has been split by the Thiessen polygon method, in which the perpendicular bisectors of lines joining each broch with every other are extended to form polygons, within which every point is nearer to the central broch than to any other. This method will be familiar to students of Orkney chambered tombs (Renfrew 1979, Fraser 1980). However, these polygons seem a little unrealistic as they cut across natural features which might serve to unite or divide farmland. A little modification on the basis of the present day landscape helps to produce more plausible territories, while adhering broadly to the formal divisions. It is perhaps no

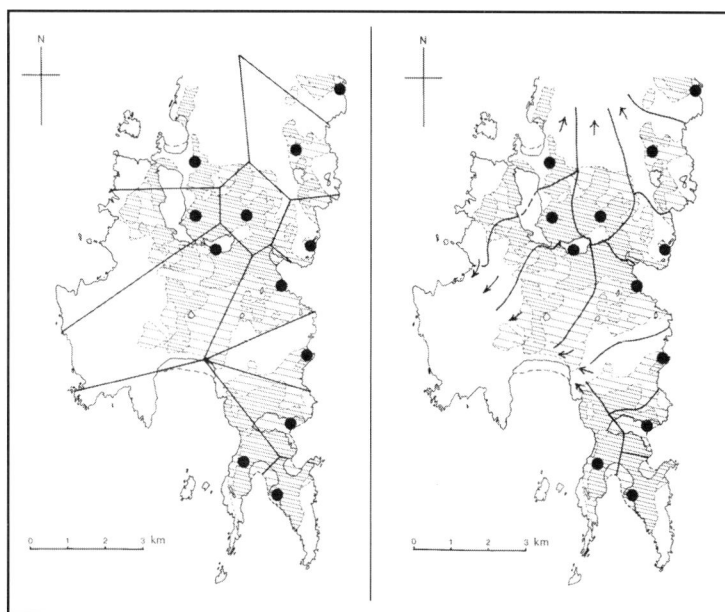

Fig.46 *Thiessen polygon method (left) and modified polygon method (right) of territorial divisions in Dunrossness.*

coincidence that the polygons, when thus rationalised, tend to have an arable core with a pastoral surround and access to the sea, as in the second map.

Iron Age crop yields

From the map the extent of modern and former arable land can be measured. While it would be rash to assume that all of this was in use at any one time in the past, the concern here is with potential crop production. Given the estimated acreage it is relatively easy to calculate the population which could have been supported in an average year. The key assumptions are the crop and the efficiency of the agricultural system, and data for both is based upon pre-Improvement Orkney bere cultivation (Fenton 1978, 336). It seems highly likely that bere, or barley, has always been Shetland's principal crop and it may be assumed that, in the absence of new methods of tillage or traction and with seed grain being saved unselectively from the previous year's local harvest, changes in cultivation technique between the early years of the first millennium and the late eighteenth century were not particularly marked. Fenton quotes yields of around 1250 kilograms per hectare which, allowing a generous amount for seed, leaves

approximately 1000 kg/ha for human consumption. There is no reason to assume that the yield of Iron Age varieties was in any way inferior to these recent ones, and in fact it may well have been superior. The arable land appears to have been arranged in small fields so the banks, pathways and ditches between plots may have taken up about 5% of the acreage. Assuming also that about one third of the total was left fallow, it is possible to construct a table showing the minimum (as at present) and maximum (if all possible land used) yield from each area and, using the approximate value of 210 kg/person/annum as the minimum basis for a cereal-dominant diet as calculated by Clark and Haswell (1967), this allows an estimate of the range of population size, as in Table 10.

Thus, even allowing a low estimate of production, each broch area could, in an average year, have produced enough grain to feed a population well in excess of one hundred. It is doubtful whether, at least in Shetland, the population associated with most brochs was greater than this, In reality, of course, much land would have been used as better quality grazing, thus lowering the optimum productivity per hectare in absolute terms, but diversifying the economic basis to

Site	Present Arable	Maximum Arable	Effective Area	Population
Clumlie	57.5 ha	130.0 ha	34.5 to 78.0	164 to 372
Scousbrough	155.0 ha	180.0 ha	93.0 to 108.0	443 to 515
Lunabister	130.0 ha	170.0 ha	78.0 to 102.0	372 to 487
Skelberry	140.0 ha	175.0 ha	84.0 to 105.0	401 to 500
Dalsetter	47.5 ha	105.0 ha	28.5 to 63.0	135 to 299
Loch of Brow	167.5 ha	320.0 ha	100.5 to 192.0	479 to 917
Southvoe	107.5 ha	230.0 ha	64.5 to 138.0	307 to 659
Clevigarth	52.5 ha	110.0 ha	31.5 to 66.0	149 to 315
Eastshore	45.0 ha	120.0 ha	27.0 to 72.0	128 to 343
Virkie	152.5 ha	180.0 ha	91.5 to 108.0	433 to 515
Jarlshof	125.5 ha	140.0 ha	75.3 to 84.0	359 to 401
Mean value	**107.3ha**	**169.1ha**	**64.4 to 101.5**	**305 to 483**

Table 10 *Estimates of arable land and population size for South Mainland brochs.*

provide for that not infrequent event, a total or near-total failure of the crops due to adverse weather. Adding to this the marine food resources, there can be little doubt that even the most crowded part of Iron Age Shetland could have supported, adequately and often comfortably, communities at each broch simultaneously. But the potential is all that can be demonstrated, Even excavation of every broch would be unlikely to prove conclusively that all were used at one and the same time. For the sake of convenience it will be assumed below that all broch communities were using their brochs as centres of daily life contemporaneously. The converse would not invalidate any of the discussions, but would merely allow the inhabitants of each area to extend their sphere of operations a little wider.

Total resource exploitation

Even in the relatively well-favoured southern Mainland there is a considerable variation in the ease with which the three basic types of resource – arable, pastoral and marine – could have been exploited. This leads on to a consideration of the possible variety within the overall economy of the Shetland Iron Age. The division into territorial units may be extended, using the same methods as above, to cover the whole islands (Fig. 47). Each territory can be characterised by its resource potential, and even a simple classification into good or poor for each of the three resource categories results in eight different combinations, and presumably also in eight contrasted potential economies. The permutations are set out in Table 11.

It would appear that, while some arable land is usually required, the existence of a sizeable area of good land is in fact less important than either good grazing land or good access to the sea. Arable land is, in fact, the most dispensable of the three types of resource. In general the rule is 'a little cropland, plenty of grazing, and access to the shore', but the variations within this are very wide. It remains to be seen whether the sea was a strong attraction in itself, in resource terms, or whether the strongly coastal distribution of brochs reflects a similar coastal bias to good quality land, but there can be little doubt that, once by the shore, broch inhabitants would

Fig.47 *Suggested extent of each broch's main area of economic activity.*

Area type	Arable	Pastoral	Marine	No. of areas
A	good	good	good	21
B	good	good	poor	10
C	good	poor	good	9
D	good	poor	poor	1
E	poor	good	good	18
F	poor	good	poor	8
G	poor	poor	good	6
H	poor	poor	poor	2

Re-organised, the data reads:

Good arable potential	41
Good pastoral potential	57
Good marine potential	55
Average 'score' out of 3	2.04

Table 11 *Classification of broch territories in Shetland according to natural resource potential.*

have used a wide variety of marine products to supplement and extend their economic base.

By roughly calculating stock-carrying and crop-raising capacities, it can be shown that most types of territory would have had little difficulty in supplying food for upwards of one hundred people, even in poor years. The wider the spread of the resources, the more resilient would have been the local economy. Thus types A, B and E could best have survived lean years, while types C and D might have had problems in particularly poor harvest years. Areas type F and G would presumably have led more of a bare subsistence mode of existence, while inhabitants of the two type H areas, in their desolate, rock-grit and infertile patches, must have found life consistently grim.

This simplistic view must be modified in a number of ways. First, there are other resources not considered, notably the valuable asset of nesting seabirds which tend to make their home in the more remote parts of the islands, such as on the cliffs fringing type H Loch of Houlland. Of the fifteen areas rated poor on two or three main resource types, six are near large present-day nesting sites. The

second main modification is to introduce the concept of trade, or exchange. The diet in the area around type D area, Skelberry, would have benefited from exchange with that of type C Dalsetter, and so by extension over the whole islands. Even the more marginal areas would have been able to enter into exchange by reason of their stocks of the less basic but perhaps more valued resources. In particular, there are many useful products of the sea which today vary markedly in their availability around the Shetland coast. Some areas are rich in driftwood, others in seals, and yet others were once favoured by large schools of ca'ing whales; the annual variability of the appearance of various species of fish is still observed. Thus while each area could, sometimes by the utmost care and economy, have functioned independently, it is more rational to suppose that exchange operated, mainly on a local scale, in such a fashion that the diet of each community was not strictly controlled by the resources within its territory. Whether or not this degree of inequality and interchange led to the establishment of specialisms in other than primary production has yet to be established, but it would be logical for at least some processing to have been carried out before exchange: dried fish travels better than fresh, and seal oil more conveniently than dead seals. As yet nothing is known about metal production, but as most iron and bronze appears to have been imported, this would suggest that metallurgy could have been restricted to a few sites with access to fuel and good trade contacts.

In summary, then, the broch period economy of Shetland would have witnessed a way of life little different from that which obtained into the eighteenth century, with small communities, often in isolated areas, making the most of their local resources and occasionally indulging in trade for luxuries or scarce goods. Finally, it might be remarked that the presence of a large number of defensive structures cannot fail to suggest that there were those groups whose ideas of trade differed radically from modern norms.

Population estimation

Cunliffe (1978, 7-9) has suggested that methods of quantifying the carrying capacity of regions should rank high among research priorities, illustrating this assertion with the example of Shetland in the Iron Age. Coincidentally, work on this problem was in progress at that date. There are two general approaches to the question of estimating the carrying capacity of a given area from fieldwork evidence.

Alternative approaches

The *overall* approach, exemplified by the work of Heisler (1978), takes data relating to a whole region, calculates total food-producing capacity, and then allocates this according to the number of known sites of the period under study. Working on Iron Age Caithness, this approach used total acreages of different land qualities, an estimate of the food-producing value of each under the assumed agricultural system of the period, and an allowance for marine inputs, The total calorific production was then divided by the average human requirement and by the number of brochs to produce an average population per broch of 213 individuals (Heisler, *op cit).*

The alternative approach, which has not yet been widely used, could be termed the *synthetic* method, operating as it does by combining the detailed assessments for the capacity of each site's territory to produce a figure for total carrying capacity. This technique involves rather more calculation and

fieldwork, but can be advanced as preferable for three main reasons:

1. Variability in the economic landscape can be built into the estimate from the beginning, rather than introduced at the end of the calculations as a likely source of error.
2. Flaws in the basic reasoning are probably easier to identify when small, known areas are under study. Such errors may be missed in handling masses of generalised data.
3. The basic data for overall estimates tends to be gathered for purposes other than archaeology, and may not be suitably classified. Likewise, verification of the precise nature of the archaeological sites may be neglected less obviously in the overall approach.

But perhaps the most important criticism of the whole concept of carrying capacity is that it is an abstract notion. What most studies of past situations require is a population figure, not a population capacity figure. The former is inherently lower than the latter, simply because human groups do not use all resources to full capacity. The main cause of this inefficiency in resource use is that human beings operate as communities rather than as individuals. The overall carrying capacity model is based upon the distribution of the maximum number of human units in accordance with the distribution of resources, and assumes that these resources were used to the full. A synthetic carrying capacity model assumes that resource exploitation is efficient but restricted to specified territories within the study area. This is halfway to reality, in which communities of individuals operate in a fashion which is not only restricted in scope but also of variable efficiency.

Because human effort is habitually organised through groups who reside in close proximity, it follows that there is spatial variation in the use of resources. Land nearer to the residence of the community is used more intensively than land of similar quality at a greater distance. The emphasis is on the efficient use of the most restricted of all human resources - time. For every economic purpose, there is a given distance from home at which the activity ceases to be considered worthwhile. Modern studies of peasant communities suggest a limit of 5km as the critical distance for arable farming. For pastoral farming the critical distance would be greater - for the collection of building stone (in a Shetland environment), much less. The centre of settlement in each territory sits at the centre of a series of patterns of resource utilisation, each of which is characterised by a fall in efficiency with distance from home. It is extremely difficult to calculate allowances for this inefficiency which will convert overall estimates of carrying capacity into realistic estimates of population, but with the synthetic approach such allowances can be built into the calculations from the start, based on the character of each site's territory.

Population of Shetland in the Iron Age

In the case of Shetland we can estimate that there may have been at most 100 broch communities, the sites of 75 of which survive. The population range of each territory can be assessed by the simple techniques used above, with varying allowances for the extra inputs of marine resources. The minimum population which could have constructed a broch, and carried on the daily work of subsistence agriculture, is probably around 40 individuals (25 able-bodied adults), while there is obviously a maximum set by the size of the territory, the quality of the land and other resources, and the amount of living space provided by a broch and any contemporary outbuildings. Extreme examples of population maxima in Shetland may range from 50 at more remote sites to 200

at sites such as Eastshore. The mean figure is just over 80. Given 100 brochs, this gives a broch-period population of about 4000-8000, plus a small figure for isolated groups not participating in broch-building and use. Certainly, the likely maximum Iron Age population would not be above 10,000. The overall carrying capacity technique suggests an Iron Age potential of over 30,000. To set these figures in perspective, the population of the islands is at present in the order of 24,000, having risen sharply from a pre-oil figure of 17,000. The peak population during the intensely commercialised fishing boom of the mid-nineteenth century was 33,000.

Comparison of the two estimates suggests that, unless a vast number of broch sites have disappeared (and the nature of the reconstructed territories argues against this), the Iron Age population was using resources to about one quarter of their full capacity. This is an interesting result, especially when added to the circumstantial evidence which suggests that all potential broch territories did not have brochs. There would seem to have been more than a little 'slack' in the Shetland economy at that time.

SITES AND MOTIVES

Rationale of site selection

Fieldwork data can usefully be used at a scale more local than that above, with examination of the siting of each broch within its own territory. There is, by definition, one centre of human activity within any territory. The location of this centre in relation to the physical and economic landscape is determined by a combination of human decisions, weighing up the advantages of different sites, and of historical accident and inertia. Given a clear area and new settlers, it is logical to suppose that careful choice would select the settlement site most suitable for conducting the prevailing way of life. In the sole recorded instance of settlement of a new island, that of Iceland by the Norse, the sagas record that the incoming settlers threw their seat-pillars into the sea and built where these reached the shore. It is a strange coincidence that the seat-pillars invariably seem to have found the best land! Once a site is established, inertia becomes important, for as the way of life, or the environment, gradually changes, it is normal for settlement to lag behind in the old site rather than moving with the changing needs of the time. This constitutes the 'historical accident' element of settlement studies. Unless a major new element enters into consideration, the siting pattern of any series of communities is normally anachronistic, relating to an earlier date. This can clearly be seen at a number of Shetland brochs, such as Jarlshof and Clickhimin, which are not on prime defensive sites but instead occupy the sites of former dwellings.

The example of Shetland brochs provides an interesting combination of two sets of constraints in selecting broch sites within territories. On the one hand is the need to have a site which is as convenient as possible for the activities of daily subsistence. On the other is the need to select a site that will contribute towards the defensibility of the broch itself. In Shetland, the system of life seems to have changed little in prehistoric times, or indeed until the eighteenth century (Fojut 1981) so the dictates of convenience would tend to keep settlement on, or close to, old sites. The need for defence seems to have originated with the construction of brochs. Convenience finds the ideal site at such brochs as Footabrough, West Mainland, where a broch occupies a dry site at the head of shingle beach, where a stream runs through good land to the sea. Defence reaches its ideal in such sites as Burland, on a cliffed promontory and only approached across a bare neck of land, or Balta on its small island. In general terms, a convenient site for Iron Age settlement in Shetland would be dry but near to fresh water, beside or in the arable land,

with access to the sea and to the grazing land. A defensive structure needs a water supply, although this is an effective ubiquity in Shetland, and must have a site which would prevent a concerted rush on the wall-foot, particularly at the entrance. Burland (Plate 10) typifies such a site.

By examining the extent to which these two sets of requirements are in conflict, it is possible to suggest which was more important to the broch builders. In fact it is possible to go further and to assess the extent to which the needs of defence distorted the siting pattern required by normal life.

Defensive qualities

The defensive advantage of sites can readily be classified by very simple experimental archaeology: starting from a given distance, the researcher attempts to reach the broch as fast as possible. The longer this takes, and the more exhausted the experimenter is on arrival, the better the site is for defence. Similar assessment of the potential of other likely sites within each territory allows the establishment of three categories:

1. Brochs on the best defensive site in the territory
2. Brochs on a site which is as good as any other in the territory
3. Brochs not on good defensive sites.

It should be noted that, while there can only be one site for class 1, and several for class 2, there will be a multiplicity of potential class 5 sites in any territory. This reduces the chance of a broch being sited on a highly defensive site for other reasons. It also makes simple methods of analysis, such as the chi-squared test, impossible. For the 75 Shetland brochs, the distribution is as follows:

Class 1   47
Class 2   24
Class 3   4

Qualities of convenience

Convenience of siting is a little harder to categorise, chiefly because there are several activities to be considered. Using the general rule that the most labour-intensive activities will have the strongest effect upon site choice, it would be logical to expect Shetland brochs to lie within the arable land, near to the head of the landing beach. Four types of site can be recognised, and are displayed schematically in Fig. 48:

1. Central
2. Eccentric
3. Peripheral
4. External

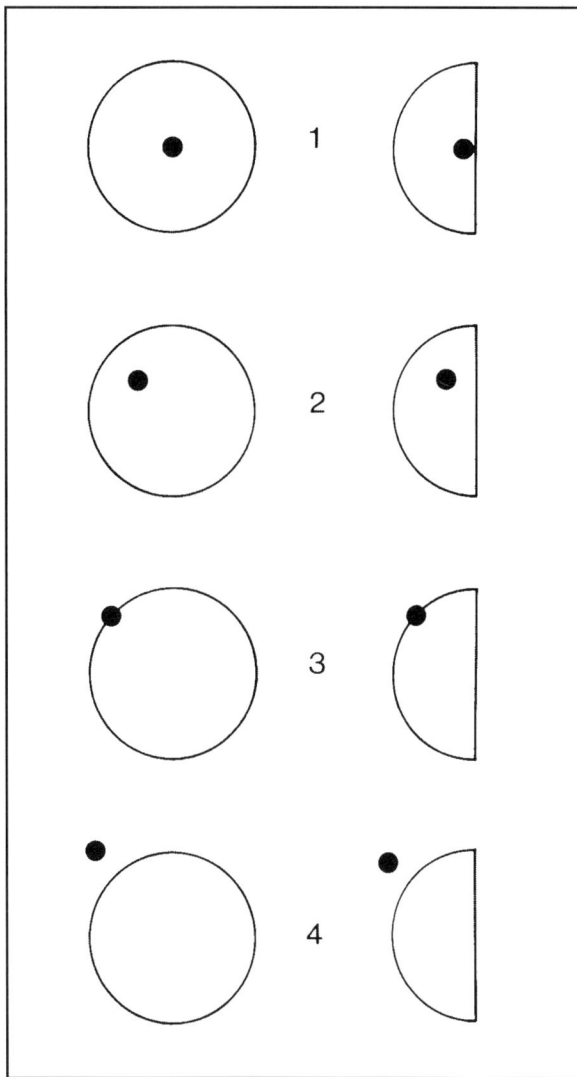

Fig.48 *Scematic relationships of brochs to arable land.*

This categorisation is not adequate, for it is quite possible for a site to be central yet inconvenient. Clickhimin on its loch islet, or Burrian on a rocky knoll, are examples. A modified classification disposes of these problems (Table 12):

Class	Composition
A	Central and eccentric, unless difficult of access
B	Peripheral, plus A where difficult of access
C	External, plus peripheral where difficult of access

The Shetland sites fall thus:

Class A   26
Class B   21
Class C   28

Table 12 *Convenience qualities of Shetland broch sites.*

This fairly even distribution must, once again, be seen against a perspective in which there are more poor sites and fewer good sites present within the natural landscape.

Conclusions on Siting

Correlating the two considerations, defence and convenience, a contingency table can be constructed (Table 13).

Defensive considerations clearly outweigh convenience, at least on the basis of these somewhat subjective figures. There are only 12 brochs which have sites more convenient than defensive: Brough (Bressay), Brough Lodge,

		Defensive Status			
		A	**B**	**C**	
Convenience	**1**	15	8	3	26
status	**2**	8	12	1	21
	3	23	5	0	28
		46	25	4	75

Table 13 *Correlation of defence and convenience.*

Clumlie, Cullingsburgh, Gord, Gossabrough, Hamnavoe, Housabister, Jarlshof, Levenwick, Southvoe and Virkie. With the exception of Gord all are near to, or coincident with, later settlements, and six show clear signs of pre-broch settlement. These might be cited as examples where the inertia of an established site has overcome the need to choose a new site in response to new requirements.

More interesting still are the four brochs within this group which are on sites with no defensive potential whatsoever: Clumlie, Gord, Housabister and Southvoe. All are more than 500 metres from. the nearest defensive site. Closer examination of those brochs on defensive sites which were not the best in their territory shows an analogous result: if the siting of the broch on the best defensive site would have taken it more than five minutes hard walking further from the centre of daily life, then a less than ideal defensive site was used. The builders of Shetland brochs seem to have had a clear mental evaluation of the usefulness of a defensive site: it was worth about five minutes extra walk from the scene of their daily toil. This presumably implies that the broch itself was seen as sufficient defence, with a good defensive site being merely a useful bonus if it could be achieved. This impression is supported by the distribution of broch outer ramparts in Shetland; these do not bear any relation to the defensive nature of the broch sites themselves, occurring with impartiality on almost impregnable sites and also on those with little natural defence (Fojut 1985). Either the broch builders had great confidence in the broch itself, or else they did not expect it to be tested.

From this brief examination of broch siting, several points can be gleaned. The chief is that brochs are sited defensively where this does not cause undue inconvenience in the business of subsistence. Also of interest is the observation that, in a number of instances, brochs were built on flat sites without additional outworks, suggesting both confidence and a problem: why do some brochs have outer defences, when others in weaker natural situations do not? This question is outside the scope of the present study, and is considered elsewhere (Fojut 1985).

A SETTLEMENT MODEL

Interpretation of evidence

Having studied the nature of the evidence that can be gained, at a number of scales, for the construction of a geography of Shetland brochs, it is now necessary to structure these results in a meaningful fashion. A number of options are open: a traditional 'regional' geography, a detailed exposition of selected examples of broch/ territory relationships, or a quasi historical narrative. All have both advantages and disadvantages. Regional description of the well-established, orderly form, such as that found in encyclopediae, requires a great deal of background information about climate, natural environment and society. This information, in so far as it is available, relates to a few specific sites rather than the general Shetland situation, so a geography of this type would require quite unacceptable levels of extrapolation. This is unfortunate as a standard form of this type would allow ready appreciation of the overall picture of broch-period environment and society. The data is simply inadequate.

Selection of and expansion upon a few of the 75 broch sites and territories would allow an in depth insight into the functioning of the broch period economy, but would almost certainly tend to under-emphasise the very wide range of site and environment which has been identified. Having details of the setting of 75 brochs, it would be a waste of data to select only a handful of 'typical' cases for description. A historical narrative tends also to remove the precise details, through generalisation rather than through exemplification. This approach allows the construction of a geographical model that is based upon all the evidence which is available, and structured through the scales, or levels of detail, at which fieldwork data can be gathered.

This third approach - the construction of a theoretical history of the way in which a given community comes to be living in a broch at a given point in the landscape - is attempted here. The basis of the approach is that decisions affecting the location and siting of brochs, which represent the centres of activity of small communities, tend to be structured in time. The wider the scope of the decision, the earlier in time it must be made. There are three levels of decision-making in almost all prehistoric (and later) location processes:

1. Establishment in region
2. Selection of territory
3. Choice of settlement site

That settlers reached Shetland we know. Provided we can understand their way of life, their origin is not particularly important, unless it can be shown that their approach to the environment is biased by the nature of their background. This was the case with the Scandinavian settlers, who seem to have brought with them an essentially Norse way of life not always in keeping with the Shetland environment, at least in its early days. In the case of the broch-building communities, on the other hand, it seems that the majority were of long-established local stock, and had been so thoroughly adapted to local conditions that, by the time broch-building began, their ultimate origin was an irrelevancy in understanding their actions.

The mechanism of regional choice can therefore be viewed in very simple terms. A group of people, displaced from their last area of residence, arrives in Shetland. If there is a suitable land-unit unoccupied, they move in. If not, they must either displace an existing group, amalgamate with such a pre-established

group, or move on in their search. In the first instance they will presumably seek the best area they can find. In the second and third, they will be taking over an existing territory. In the last case, they will not become involved at all.

In the case or a group arriving in an area where there is a choice or land for settlement, it may be assumed that they will look for what is, to their perception, the best available combination and concentration or desirable attributes. The ranking or these various attributes has been established above by empirical methods. It remains to ascertain the date at which this territorial selection took place. In the case of the Shetland brochs there is good evidence to suggest that the territories were established before the brochs were built, probably some considerable time previously. It has been shown elsewhere (Fojut 1985) that there are a number or Iron Age settlements with foci whose size indicates communities smaller than those associated with brochs. These tend to occupy interstices in the broch distribution, and to occur in areas which would be considered marginal for the establishment or a broch-sized group. Since the general material culture or these sites parallels that of the brochs, it may be asserted that the communities of Iron Age Shetland were already in place when the broch idea was introduced, and that there was a critical size or group below which brochs could not be, or were not, constructed. This, of course, runs against Hamilton's arguments in favour or massive immigration immediately prior to Shetland broch-building (Hamilton 1957, 46; 1968, 45). The artefactual sequences emerging from Orkney brochs in the Scapa Flow area, whence Hamilton derived Shetland's broch building incomers (pers. comm., B Smith, NoSAS), support the impression given by critical re-examination of the sequences from Jarlshof and Clickhimin: the main period or Orkney-to-Shetland influence is post-broch rather than pre-broch. It may be assumed that Shetland brochs were built by established communities.

Therefore, although a sequential pattern of regional and territorial selection can he reconstructed, it is only at the most local of levels, with the choice of site, that the broch itself makes an appearance in the synthesis. At higher levels, the consideration is of the location of a population group; at the site level on the other hand the nature of the broch structure is of significance, for brochs are highly specialised constructions with certain requirements, such as solidity of foundations, which are not necessarily shared by all contemporary dwellings. The defensive nature of brochs is the new element in the siting equation.

Constructing a 'model'

The whole of this complex process of selection can be structured into a 'model', or generalised framework, using the data obtained from the various analyses described in this paper. The model is of flow-diagram form and attempts a description of the portion of the prehistoric decision making process which was founded upon economic, and therefore environmental, considerations, where such considerations had a spatial dimension. The model must remain partial, for it cannot deal with those factors affecting decisions which did not have a direct spatial expression. Superstition, religious belief, historical accident, tradition, social structure and prehistoric politics must all be largely excluded. These, perhaps the most fascinating aspects of the society under study, remain largely inaccessible. The location model, presented as Fig. 48, depends upon four vital assumptions, all of which might well have been open to disturbance from the 'non-spatial' factors cited above.

1. The settlement process functioned through the action of groups and not individuals.

2. Groups were able, initially, to select the best available areas for settlement within Shetland.

3. Groups were capable of rationally assessing, and responding to, the environment, changes in it, and changes in their own needs.

4. Settlement sites were chosen according to the dictates of the subsistence mode of life to minimise wasted time and maximise use of resources, except where outside consideration necessitated divergence from this 'least effort for greatest return' ideal.

Testing the model

The structure of the relationships portrayed in the flow diagram (Fig. 48) is, in effect, a summary of the various individual hypotheses developed to account for regularities in the observed data. The model can be checked at a number of levels. At the most basic, the individual data-elements can be re-checked in the field or from maps.

Secondly, the analyses of data can be examined to verify the numerical correctness of the results. At a slightly higher level, consideration may be afforded to the suitability of the methods chosen for these analyses, and tests run with other available techniques to ascertain whether or not observed regularities are a false result due to the use of particular techniques rather than to real patterns in the data. But these are all tests of the building blocks which compose the structure of the model.

The linkages of the model are not so amenable to ready verification. Since they are hypotheses which involve all of the results of the analysis, they are more likely to be proved wrong by identification of radical errors in the primary data or analyses than they are to be shown to be false in their own right. This is because it is extraordinarily difficult to disprove any reasonably rational hypothesis. The best test for the model is to examine its

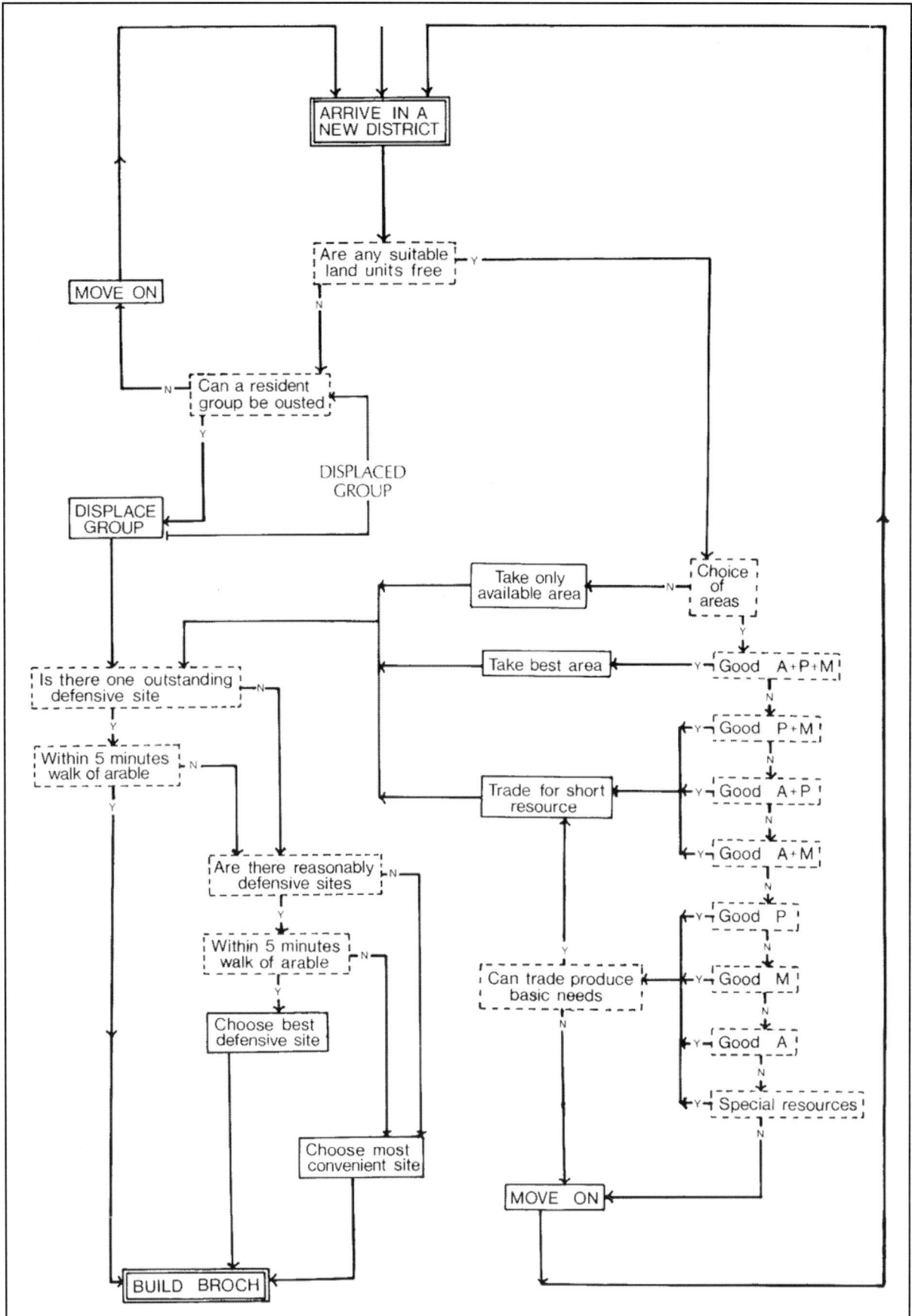

Fig.49 *Partial model of settlement location. Direction of linkages shows sequence of decision-making. Solid-edged elements represent <u>actions</u>, those with broken line edges represent <u>appraisals</u> (Y=yes, N=no).*

general applicability to other situations. If the model cannot be adapted to other areas and/or periods, then it may not be wrong, but will none the less lack utility, which is for all practical purposes equivalent.

Nevertheless, some aspects of the model can be tested in a general fashion. If, for example, more brochs were to be discovered in Shetland it would be fair to expect their environmental and siting parameters to accord with the overall model. More important, if a number or brochs were selected for total excavation (admittedly a most unlikely proposition at present) it might be possible to test the assumptions advanced regarding the relationships between natural endowment or territories and diet or inhabitants. Such excavations might also succeed in identifying activities or specialised types at certain brochs: the processing of seal or seabird oil, for example, should leave fairly easily recognisable traces.

But most aspects of the background assumptions are not amenable to definitive proof. The extent of territories must always be a matter for informed guesswork, as must the precise nature of the threat against which brochs were built. In some cases more definition could be afforded to certain areas, but only at tremendous cost of time and effort. It is conceptually possible to establish the extent or Iron Age arable land in detail, but the scale of the project would be immense, involving more than the total effort so far devoted to palaeobotany in the whole of Scotland.

Therefore, as suggested above, it seems that the only good test for the model is to attempt to establish its powers of general explanation. If the type of model presented here does not prove adaptable to other past situations, there may indeed be good reason to question the rationale assumed for the Iron Age location process itself.

CONCLUSION AND PROSPECT

The model presented here is a first stage. There should be two sequels, first a study of comparative situations to ascertain the general applicability of the approach, and second, study of the non-spatial factors to allow a complete settlement model to be attempted. The main result of this study, and indeed its purpose, has been the delineation of the variation and regularity in the geography of Shetland's brochs. The classification of broch territories and site types has made possible the extension, on a sound methodological basis, of our picture of the organisation of life in the Iron Age of the area. The general approach, with its power for identifying patterns and classes among unexcavated sites, might be advanced as a possible tool for rationalising the selection of sites for excavation, a process which is at present more than a little haphazard. And even if this is a vain hope, the techniques outlined should allow sites excavated for other reasons to be set into a firmer geographical context.

ACKNOWLEDGEMENTS

This article is a condensation of part of a research thesis sponsored by Scottish Education Department and completed at Glasgow University under the supervision of Professor L Alcock and Dr E W MacKie. Both have given valued advice on archaeological matters, as has Mr P Winham. Fieldwork was facilitated by Mr A Williamson of Lerwick Museum. Ms P Love has assisted throughout with informed criticism and painstaking proof-reading.

Glasgow, January 1982

This paper is published with the help of a grant from the Carnegie Trust for the Universities of Scotland.

Any Closer Towards a Geography of Shetland Brochs?

Noel Fojut

"TOWARDS a Geography of Shetland Brochs", reproduced here, was written in 1982 and published in the Glasgow Archaeological Journal, volume 9 (1983) pages 38-59 and microfiche. It was based on fieldwork and research undertaken between 1976 and 1979. The Tall Stories Conference provides an opportunity to introduce this paper to a wider, and younger, audience. The Glasgow Archaeological Society has kindly consented to its re-publication, and it is presented here as published, with the exception of some minor updating of references and silent correction of a few typographic errors. Note that in it the site now known as Old Scatness is referred to as Virkie.

BRIDGING THE GAP BETWEEN FIELD SURVEY AND EXCAVATION?

If we accept current chronologies, the period of time since the active research published in the 1983 paper represents 1 percent of the time that has passed since the *floruit* of brochs. Work by others over two decades has provided considerable detail about brochs and their communities, and has moved us closer towards an understanding of their detailed cultural affinities and economics. It was the task of the many other contributors to the Conference to describe their own research. The present note simply introduces the reprint and briefly considers how far the paper's conclusions, factual and theoretical, have stood the test of time.

Despite the positive reaction to the paper when published, exemplified by the kind words of MacKie (1987), no other researchers have stepped into the breach and extended the approaches advocated in this paper to other parts of Scotland, or to other types of monument. Such action was suggested as on of two ideal sequels to the publication.

This lack of follow-through can be attributed to several factors: not least the tendency of research students to avoid each other's footprints. There has been, in the 1980s and 1990s, an increasing attention in university departments to project-linked research. There is no doubt that the funding injected into excavation in the last two decades has produced a rapidly increasing body of excavation data that is a fertile source for theses. Also, there has been a tendency for research that is not excavation-based to focus on cultural resource management. These trends are all very understandable: in the late 1970s, the prospect of any more large-scale broch excavations looked slight, but since then circumstances have changed and there have been extensive excavations at several sites.

The evidence from these excavations appears not to contradict the general theories advanced in 1983, but these were so general and so pragmatic that perhaps this was never to be expected. There still remains a substantial gap between the detailed but limited findings from excavations and the

Plate 9. *Noonsbrough: the broch, now reduced to a grassy mound flanked by later masonry, was connected to the shore by a causeway (right). Since the Iron Age a shingle beach has grown up between broch and shore (left), illustrating the effect human activity can have upon natural processes. (page 155)*

Plate 10. *Burland: the damaged entrance passage emerges close to the top of cliffs, necessitating an awkward turn for anyone approaching the broch from the landward side. (page 162)*

Plate 11. *Caisteal Grugaig, showing the scarcement approaching close to the level of the rock outcrop. (page 190)*

Plate 12. *Dun Troddan, a rare broch with excavated evidence for a ring of stout posts set into the floor. (page 191)*

"grand picture" painted here. With the benefit of hindsight, and 20 years working for Scotland's national heritage agency, it was perhaps a naïve expectation to expect that the two approaches might ever meet, with a large enough number of excavations to provide a real test for the geographical theories.

OUTSTANDING QUESTIONS?

That said, the author remains convinced that the framework advanced provided, and continues to provide a convincing outline for the locational economics of middle Iron Age Shetland. But this is a paradigm only for the materialistic aspects of society. What progress has been made on the second sequel identified in 1983: research into the non-material aspects of broch life?

Here we may cite evolving ideas of ritual significance in the orientation and division of internal space within Iron Age domestic and monumental architecture, perhaps first clearly drawn together by Fitzpatrick (1994) and since elaborated with respect to the broch province by Parker Pearson and collaborators (Parker Pearson 1996, Parker Pearson, Sharples and Mulville 1996). Such concepts might help to explain the orientation of broch entrances, although it must be borne in mind that if brochs did, indeed, contain raised floors, then the point of access to the upper floor is unlikely to have been in line with the entrance through the stone outer structure. This would present a problem of choice for the dwellers. It is much to be regretted that no broch upper floor has survived, nor is ever likely to be found in any recognisable form. In the absence of an entrance to the daylit world outside, such a raised floor might settle the current disagreement over how far ritual, and how far need for daylight, dictates the layout of functional areas relative to doorways within Iron Age round houses.

There are many other areas of general archaeology to be addressed in which results

are more likely to be forthcoming, and not just about brochs. The role of non-broch settlement of similar period in the overall structure of society remains obscure (Fojut 1985). So does the sequence and absolute date of settlement on broch sites: were they all pre-existing settlements or were some founded *ab initio*? Many detailed aspects of brochs and their kindred remain to be considered: for example the question of timber supply, considered separately at the Conference (Fojut, this volume). Given a free choice and ample funds, it would be illuminating to excavate a broch located in an area of apparently poor environmental potential – a type H setting to use the 1983 terminology – to investigate the idea of specialised economic niches such as exploitation of seabird colonies. Excavating an inherently "poor" site would also be a splendid complement and contrast to the work at fertile Old Scatness, as near to a tropical location as Shetland offers.

NEW DISCOVERIES

The question of whether or not broch territories could be suggested, whether such territories continues to provide enough food for "broch-sized" communities, and whether all brochs in Shetland could have been occupied at the same time was a central part of the paper. It focused on southern Dunrossness, where brochs are most closely spaced, and concluded that hypothetical territories could relatively easily have supported sizeable communities at each broch site contemporaneously.

Such arguments would have been undermined by the existence of many more brochs in this area. In fact, since the 1970s, there has only been one discovery of what may be a new broch in southern Dunrossness, at Toab (HU 388116 approximately). Allowing for sea-level rise and loss of flat land around Pool of Virkie, the interpolation of this broch site into the 1983 patterns does not demolish the thesis. More to the point, there has been very extensive survey in this area, and the discovery of only one possible additional site might serve to underline the basic point made in 1983: that most locatable brochs have probably been located.

That said, an unpublished part of the research thesis looked at predicting gaps in the broch distribution: areas that appeared to have the attributes of "broch territories" but lacked brochs (Fojut 1980). This was not published at the time for fear it would bias subsequent field search, leading to circular arguments about environment and broch location. Had it been published, would the author subsequently have been proved prescient?

In addition to the possible site at Toab, there have been definite brochs identified since at Cloddie Knowe and Upper Scalloway, and convincing field evidence of brochs noted at Lunna and Voe, with less definite evidence on Papa Stour. These are shown here (Fig. 50), overlaid on the earlier unpublished map of gaps. Readers may draw their own conclusion.

CONCLUSION

Overall, and despite many gaps, no-one can contest the statement that we know much more about Shetlands brochs than we did 20 years ago. If the old paper republished here has made some contribution to those advances, even if only by stimulating disagreement, the author rests content.

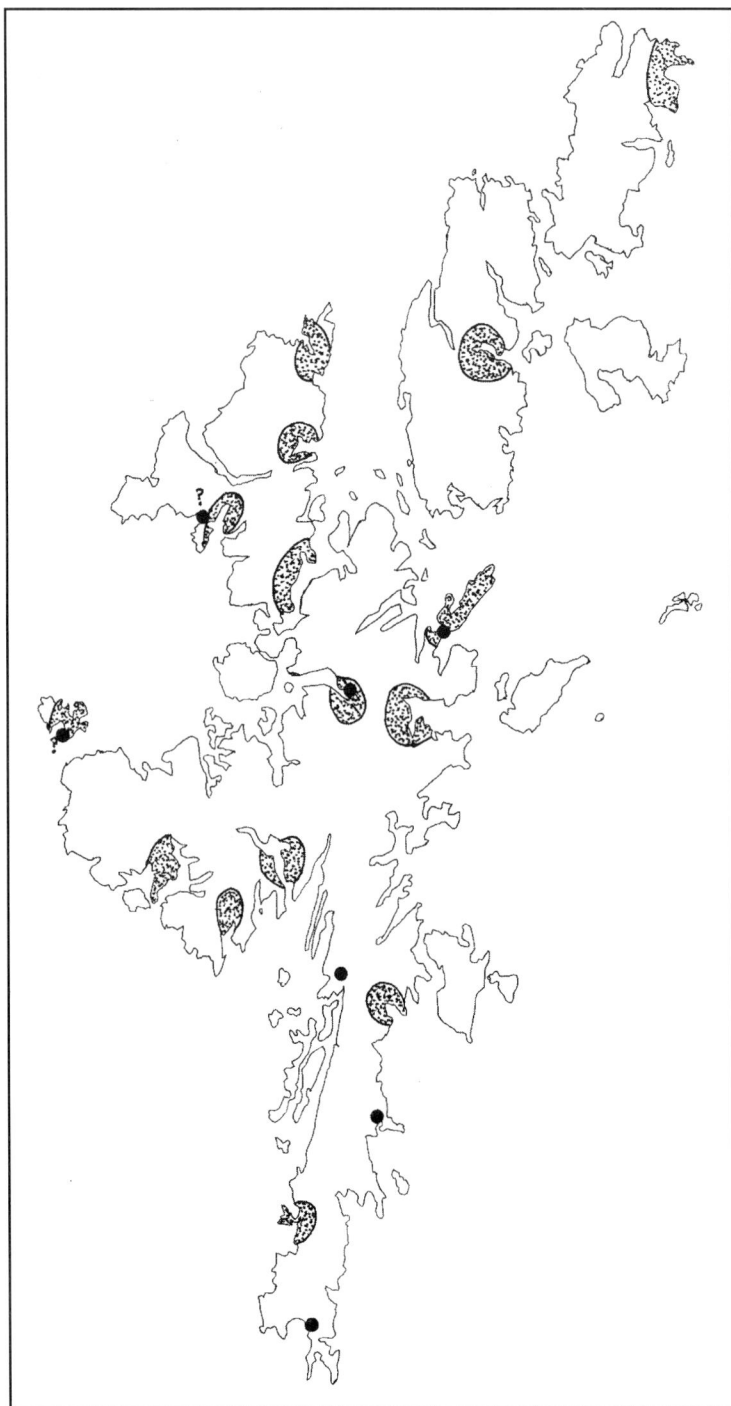

Fig. 50 *Broch sites discovered in the last 20 years and the locations where brochs might yet be expected to be found.*

BIBLIOGRAPHY

Birse, E. L., Dry, F. T. and Robertson, L. (1971) *Assessment of Climatic Conditions in Scotland.* Aberdeen, Macaulay Institute of Soil Research.

Chapelhow, R. (1965) On glaciation in North Roe, Shetland. *Geographical Journal 131, 60.*

Clark, C. and Haswell, M. R. (1967) *The Economics of Subsistence Agriculture* (3rd edition). London, Macmillan.

Clark, P. J. and Evans, F. C. (1954) Distance to nearest neighbour as a measure of spatial relationships in populations. *Ecology* 35, 445.

Cunliffe, B. and Rowley, T. (ed.) (1978) *Lowland Iron Age Communities in Europe* (British Archaeological Reports, International Series, 548). Oxford, BAR.

Fenton, A. (1978) *The Northern Isles: Orkney and Shetland*. Edinburgh, John Donald.

Fitzpatrick A. P. (1994) Outside in: the structure of an Early Iron Age house at Dunston Park, Thatcham, Berkshire. In Fitzpatrick, A. P. and Morris E. (eds) *The Iron Age in Wessex: Recent Work*, 68-73. Dorchester: Wessex Archaeology.

Fojut, N. (1980) *The Archaeology & Geography of Shetland Brochs*. Unpublished PhD thesis, University of Glasgow.

Fojut, N. (1981) *A Guide to Prehistoric Shetland*. Lerwick, Shetland Times.

Fojut, N. (1982) Is Mousa a broch? *Proceedings of the Society of Antiquaries of Scotland* 111 (1980-1).

Fojut, N. (1983) Towards a geography of Shetland brochs. *Glasgow Archaeological Journal* 9, 38-59.

Fojut, N. (1985) Some thoughts on the Shetland Iron Age. In Smith, B. (ed.) *Shetland Archaeology*. Lerwick, Shetland Times.

Fraser, D. (1980) Investigations in Neolithic Orkney. *Glasgow Archaeological Journal* 7, 1.

Hamilton, J. R. C. (1957) *Excavations at Jarlshof, Shetland*. Edinburgh, H.M.S.O.

Hamilton, J. R. C. (1968) *Excavations at Clickhimin, Shetland*. Edinburgh, H.M.S.O.

Hedges, J. W. and Bell, B. (1980) That tower of Scottish prehistory - the broch. *Antiquity* 54, 87

Heisler, D. M. (1976) Man-land relationships in Iron Age Caithness, Scotland. Paper presented at 75th Annual Meeting of the American Anthropological Association, Washington.

Hodder, I. R. and Orton, C. R. (1976) *Spatial Analysis in Archaeology*. Cambridge, Cambridge University Press.

MacKie, E.W. (1987) Impact on the Scottish Iron Age of the discoveries at Leckie broch. *Glasgow Archaeological Journal* 14, 1-18.

Parker Pearson, M., Sharples, N. and Mulville, J. (1996) Brochs and Iron Age society: a reappraisal. *Antiquity*, 70 (1996) 57-67.

Parker Pearson, M. (1996) Food, fertility and front doors in the first millennium BC. In Champion, T. C. and Collis, J. R. (eds) *The Iron Age in Britain and Ireland: Recent Trends*, 117-32. Sheffield, Sheffield University Press.

Renfrew C. (1979) *Investigations in Orkney*. (Report of the Research Committee of the Society of Antiquaries of London, 38.) London, Society of Antiquaries of London.

Small, A. (1966) Excavations at Underhoul, Unst, Shetland. *Proceedings of the Society of Antiquaries of Scotland* 97 (1965-6), 225

Smith, H. D. (1977) *The Making of Modern Shetland*. Lerwick, Shetland Times.

Stout, E. (1911) Some Shetland Brochs *.Proceedings of the Society of Antiquaries of Scotland* 46 (1910-1), 94.

Continuity or Change: Exploring the Potential

VAL E. TURNER & STEPHEN J. DOCKRILL

INTRODUCTION

THIS PAPER seeks to explore the potential for studying the location of broch sites in relation to other archaeological elements of the landscape. Did the presence or absence of earlier settlement influence the location of broch sites, and did, in turn, the location of broch sites determine subsequent landuse? This paper is very much an interim account of work in progress and the original conference paper set the research agenda for Phase 3 of the survey section of the Old Scatness and Jarlshof Environs project as well as our own personal research agendas.

At the same time as Dockrill has been excavating at Old Scatness, Turner initiated a programme of intensive field survey as an integral part of the project. The survey is filling out some of the details of human activity in the landscape spanning a period of 5000 years and is helping to overcome problems of archaeological visibility. It has long been assumed by archaeological visitors to Shetland that all the major archaeological sites in Shetland are known, either because they have long been observed or because the knowledge of sites exists in the folk memory (Fojut pers. comm.). The accidental discovery of the broch of Upper Scalloway, the confirmation of the broch site at Aith's Voe, Cunningsburgh and, in 1997 as a result of this survey, the discovery of the Broch of Toab, has demonstrated the potential for significant new discoveries by systematic field work. Now,

alongside the spectacular sites, a wide spectrum of new information is beginning to emerge.

Field survey is, of necessity, a broad brush approach. Identifying sites from the topographical remains has inherent dangers, as was apparent when the supposedly Viking site of Kebister was excavated (1985 – 87). The site was found to extend from the Iron Age into the 16th century, but the Norse period was the one era which was totally absent from the archaeological record. Now however, in the South Mainland, limited geophysical survey and trial excavation are beginning flesh out the story of the area. By contrast, the excavation at Old Scatness is providing us with the opportunity to examine a relatively small area in meticulous detail. We believe that the integration of the two archaeological approaches provide us with the best chance of understanding Iron Age Shetland and establishing the degree to which there was either continuity or change in the way the landscape was managed.

One of the major factors which may have influenced broch situation was the pre-existence of established infields and adjacent economic resources. Childe (1935, 204) observed that brochs were always on good agricultural land. In his pioneering work of the late 1970s, Fojut agreed with Childe's total of 75 Shetland broch sites (Fojut 1983, 40). Of these he identified 41 broch sites as having good arable potential, 57 as having good pastoral potential and 55 as having good marine potential. Clearly broch dwellers would have to feed and keep themselves and the control of the economic resource would have provided the wealth to construct these status sites. But the question, also addressed by Cowley (this volume) remains: to what extent did this determine where brochs were built and to what extent did the pre-broch economy influence the decision?

The survey, which began in 1995, incorporates the hinterland of the four most southerly brochs in Shetland: Jarlshof, Old Scatness, Eastshore and Toab (Fig. 51). Excavations and survey at all of these sites apart from Toab, have revealed settled foci which span several millennia. The Broch of Toab is an unknown quantity because it is

enclosed by modern development on three sides. The extent of the remains on the east side is not obvious by field observation and has yet to be tested by geophysics.

Some of the most promising topographical survey results from the study area to date have come from the area to the north and west of Eastshore. Here the quality of archaeological survival is equal to some of the spectacular, and more widely known, archaeological landscapes in Shetland, such as those the West Side of Shetland Mainland. Not only this, but the remains appear to extend, relatively uninterrupted, northwards to the next broch along the coast: the Broch of the Cletts (or Clevigarth). Clevigarth appears to be very different in character to Old Scatness, Eastshore and Jarlshof, having no extensive broch village around it. The broch is on less fertile land and is situated on a cliff top. Nevertheless it is adjacent to a field system, whether Bronze Age or later prehistoric, situated immediately to the south. Soil sampling has been undertaken here by Turner, the results of which are eagerly awaited.

EASTSHORE AND ITS ENVIRONS

In the area surveyed around Eastshore, the potentially pre-historic monuments, excluding the broch, include a series of substantial dykes aligned predominantly roughly north-south. They have been classified as being prehistoric because of the meandering course which they take and the orthostats and smaller stones which protrude from them. (The authors are aware that fealie dykes from the crofting period also meander, but these are generally devoid of protruding stone. Nevertheless, a degree of

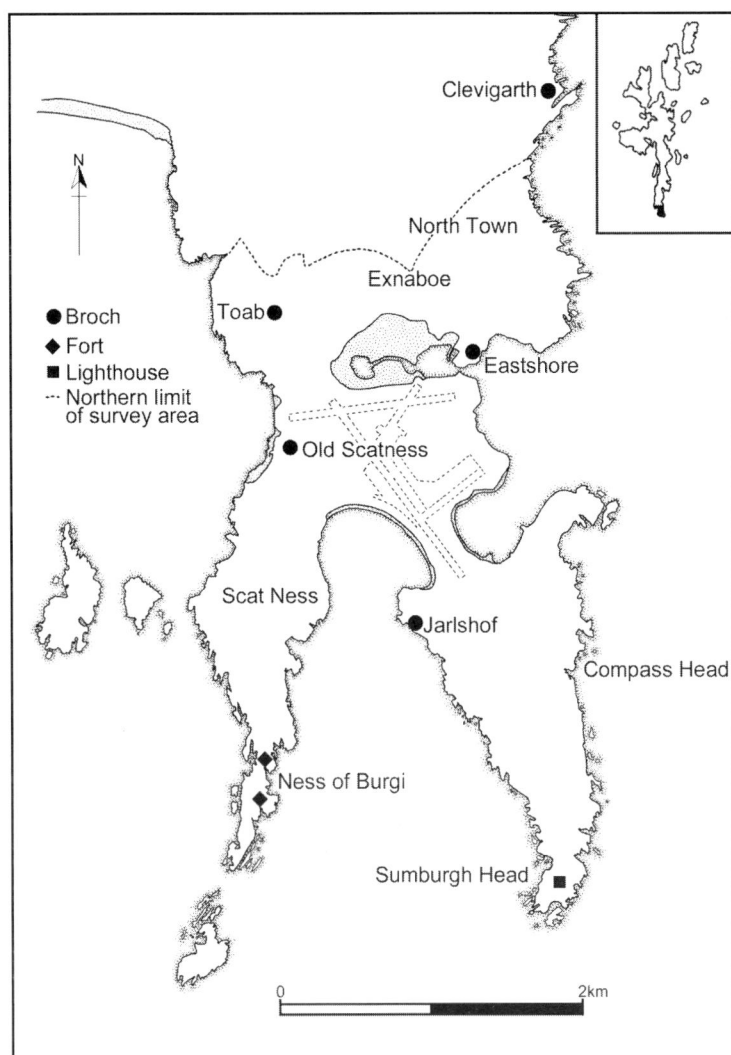

Fig.51 *Dunrossness, South Shetland. Map showing broch sites, including Old Scatness and the area of field survey carried out between 1995-2003. (Dan Bashford)*

173

caution must always be exercised when identifying sites by morphology alone.) Burnt mounds have been identified in two locations and probable chambered cairns in three. There are two of what appear to be prehistoric house sites, one of which is a classic "homestead" site, (a house situated within an enclosure) and with a distinctively separate field system adjacent which may not be contemporary. There is also a group of three houses on lower lying ground, one of which remains as a single mound, another which appears to be figure-of-eight-shaped and a third which has indications of a heel-shaped forecourt. However, depending on which angle they are viewed from, either of the two latter could also be interpreted as being more rectangular and so could equally be classified as potential Norse long houses.

The location of these remains are, to a degree, influenced by environmental factors: the burnt mounds occur next to fresh water supplies; the chambered cairns are located in prominent situations, having good visibility. The dykes and house sites, however, have no obvious environmentally determined relationship. One group of houses occurs on what is now enclosed, coastal land, where the presence and density of rigs testify to an intensive crofting use in more recent times. A single house and the homestead both occur on much higher land which was in use as common grazing until about 20 years ago, when it was taken in and reseeded. The field system which lies adjacent to the homestead, and has only one clearance cairn discernible, is on land which today would seem very unpromising for agriculture. The character of these fields are, however, very reminiscent of the field systems at the Scord of Brouster and Pinhoulland recorded by Whittle (Whittle 1986).

Remains from the Norse period have been only tentatively identified. There are three potentially Norse groups of buildings amongst the crofting remains immediately to the NW of the broch. These underlie later crofting remains. The kale yard of these remains incorporates a meandering stone dyke along its southern edge, and this appears to be prehistoric in character. Further to the NE, there are the two possible Norse buildings, although as observed above either, or both, of which could be of prehistoric date. Both groups of houses are situated in areas which were in heavy usage during the crofting period and the Norse remains around the broch represent a re-use of the broch area itself.

A little to the north a second complex of later buildings include a dwelling house, outhouses, a kale yard and a corn-drying byre and kiln. A second corn-drying byre and kiln has been restored in the modern village of North Exnaboe, situated on the edge of the survey area. The total number of crofting families and their relationship to the three horizontal mills, where an entire mill pond and dam system was created, needs to be established together with the historical framework for the area. Indeed, there are aspects of Eastshore's past for which the evidence is essentially documentary, such as the Hanseatic and Scottish trade based here (Melton 2002). A fish drying beach to the east of the broch, together with a stone-built boiler for producing fish oil or cootch kettle, are among the few tangible remains of the 19th century fishing station, an activity which was also of enormous economic importance to the area.

The western most side of the survey area was affected by 20th century military activities. It was a good strategic position for monitoring the movements of shipping along the south-east coast of Shetland. This area is also pock marked with quarry holes which follow outcropping ridges of sandstone.

JARLSHOF AND ITS ENVIRONS

Immediately around the guardianship site of which the broch at Jarlshof forms a part, cultivation has continued into the present day and the remains of the past are less visible. Geophysical survey in the front garden of the Sumburgh Hotel, together with associated test excavation, have demonstrated that there are several buildings concealed below the ground which, like Jarlshof, has been subject to intermittent inundations of blown sand. (Hunter *et al.* 1993).

Not only has the land along the west coast of the Sumburgh Head peninsula been subject to intermittent sand blow which will have potentially concealed any low lying sites, but, at the same time coastal erosion has removed quantities of land. Half the broch has been lost to the sea and Ian Morrision, who has dived off shore at Jarlshof, has identified a 30m coastal shelf extending out from the present shore line (pers. comm.) This loss of as much as 30m of land may have extended for much of the length of the west coast of the Sumburgh Head – Compass Head peninsula. A similar loss of land, and therefore sites, may have taken place at Eastshore. Although situated on the east coast, there too the broch is cut in half as a result of coastal erosion.

The remains of a prehistoric complex are aligned along the hill between Sumburgh Head and Compass Head. This includes a house site, an adjacent field system, a cairn (which interestingly resembles an Orcadian Bookan style stalled cairn rather than the typical Shetland chambered cairn) and quarrying along a seam of siltstone. This complex is situated occur at approx. 40m above sea level. It would appear from excavations at the Scord of Brouster (Whittle 1986) and from observation elsewhere in Shetland, that cultivation at 40m was viable at some periods of Shetland's past. The remains at this height appear date from the Bronze Age in some areas of Shetland, and elsewhere to the period of secondary Norse settlement. Whether it was climatic deterioration, soil exhaustion, peat growth, or other factors which led to their abandonment, the remains

of these upland sites have been protected from destruction by their location on land which is now only used for grazing.

There are other Iron Age sites in the area, most notably the two blockhouse forts on the Scat Ness peninsula to the west, and Low (1774) recorded what may have been another such building under the lighthouse at Sumburgh Head.

Jarlshof has a number of well known Viking and Norse buildings situated within the Guardianship area. To date no further Norse remains have been positively identified outside it. There are a number of possible explanations for that which include coastal erosion, the use of timber and other perishable materials, and the reuse of sites for present occupation. Some of the remains which have been identified by geophysical survey in the Sumburgh Hotel gardens may prove to be Norse in date (Hunter, 1993). The presence of Norse inhabitants, both of lowly and of elevated status, in the area is well attested in the Orkneyinga Saga.

OLD SCATNESS AND ITS ENVIRONS

The land surrounding the Old Scatness broch has experienced mixed fortunes. The land to the east is still under cultivation, although trial pits have established that the plaggen soil continues in that direction. The land to the south contains a mound which has all the characteristics of a second settlement mound, which is extremely intriguing. To the north the use of the airport during the war has left its distinctive mark of concrete platforms, Nissan huts and the like. The subsequent expansion of the airport in the 1970s was destructive, but has had its compensations with the discovery and excavation of what was, until 2003, Shetland's earliest dated site, a cist found under the control tower (Hedges and Parry 1980) and the excavation of the house sites under the runway (Downes and Lamb 2000). Indeed, it was the construction of the road to the Control Tower that first revealed the previously unknown broch site itself.

The area around the Broch of Toab is heavily built up. Its location, opposite the shop, in the heart of the modern village, is almost the ultimate indication of continuity of settlement. The detail of the heavily crofted landscape around Toab has yet to be established.

BROCH TERRITORIES

At the moment each "broch territory" remains loosely defined. In 1951 Childe wrote "As to government without inscribed documents we can form no idea at all of the extent of the political units, save very tentatively… The extent of its territory can hardly ever be inferred directly." (Childe 1951, reprinted 1963, 58). Can intensive field survey begin to push back the limitations? Will it be possible to take Fojut's Thesian polygons and relate them to real territories and impose archaeological data to identify a continuity in the way the resources were used? This investigation has yet to amalgamate the field survey results with Fojut's definition of broch territories and to look for correlations with physical boundaries, both geographical and human in origin, which may define territorial limits. Will we be able to trace these boundaries backwards in time and did they continue forwards?

The number of people who could have been supported by each area at any given time is almost impossible to establish. Fojut (1983, 48) estimated a population of between 128 – 343 for a territory based on Eastshore broch. Renfrew calculated that a living population of 20 was the minimum required to build an average Orcadian chambered cairn in a five year period (Renfrew, 1979). Shetland chambered cairns appear to be much simpler affairs, and even the Orcadian figure only presupposes a maximum population of 60 in the area. (Any population estimate derived from that figure would have to be based on the, almost certainly incorrect, supposition that the cairns were contemporary). The extant houses at Eastshore, which are equally unlikely to be contemporary, are scattered throughout the landscape. The use of the land above 30-50m has been taken as being indicative of a high population (Fojut 1983), and the patterns of longhouse distribution, which we are observing in Unst, would seem to bear this out. If this was true in the earlier prehistoric period, then it is only patchily observable in the visible record. By contrast, Whittle suggests that suitable land may not have been the sole factor determining settlement. He cites independence, equal access to various resources and an emphasis on spacing between settlements as potential influences on settlement location (Whittle 1986, 145). Clearly social organisation is not static: it could be inferred that the presence of three chambered cairns represents a minimum of three Neolithic territories within what is apparently one broch territory. The earlier house sites are diffuse; broch society is apparently more centralised. The difficulty of identifying frameworks for societies in the absence of documentary evidence is enormous: but is it insurmountable? What we do have is evidence of the available resource base and how it was used.

As Dockrill has demonstrated (this volume), occupation on the site at Old Scatness has resulted in construction, re-use, demolition and dumping of domestic midden material, with high levels of fuel ash, which have gradually accumulated to form a "settlement mound" over the generations. He has shown that there is continuity on the site itself from the Early Iron Age (ca. 300BC) to the Norse period (ca. 1100AD), and the indications are that the site was more or less continuously in use up until the twentieth century.

Simpson's investigation of the early soil sequence indicates the potential to take the occupation sequence back to the Late

Neolithic/Early Bronze Age (Simpson *et al.*, 1998). It is the presence of these cultivated soils, indicative of barley production (Bond *et al.* this volume) which makes these settlements sustainable over long periods of time. The intensive cultivation of the infield over generations results in the infield becoming an important resource in its own right. As cultivation was so intensive by the broch period, it is possible that the arable area given over to barley may have been significantly less than that originally proposed by Fojut (1983, 48).

Whilst the soil evidence indicates a continuity of infield cultivation, management practices changed and developed. By the time Old Scatness Broch was built, the infield was an inherited, valuable, economic resource, and this must have exerted an influence over the location of the broch settlement (Dockrill 1998, 77). The same phenomenon might have been equally true at Jarlshof and at Eastshore, (also see Cowley this volume) as well as more widely. All three sites combine an attractive economic location in terms of access to the marine and intertidal resource with an arable infield inherited from earlier generations.

McDonnell (this volume) believes that the evidence of metal working found in the Pictish phases of the sites at Upper Scalloway, Howe of Howe, Mid Howe and Old Scatness, indicate that these sites all continue to be high status into the Pictish period. If the Pictish estate was then taken over by the Vikings, at what point would the established territorial organisation collapse? Could the pattern of land holding continue into the Viking period? And how did it become modified subsequently by political and economic events?

In 1984 Brian Smith remarked on the fact that the "spheres of influence" (or broch territories) identified by Fojut (1983, 49) in Iron Age Dunrossness are almost identical to the seventeenth century scattald (tax unit) map (Smith 1984, 106). Smith has since retracted this statement (Smith 2000) making the point that continuity of settlement is very different from continuity of administration. However, the RCAHMS Historic Landuse Assessment (2004) shows a remarkable correlation between 19th – 20th century croft land and broch location (first observed by Piers Dixon, RCAHMS). When Shetland fell first under Scandinavian rule, and subsequently under Scottish authority, the changes were reflected architecturally at Jarlshof. Would combining the archaeological evidence with the historical evidence clarify the picture particularly given that each generation had to work within the same geographical constraints as their predecessors?

Did broch territory boundaries still exist when the Vikings arrived and, if so, had the territiorial divisions of the broch period defined significant divisions in the Late Iron Age? Would a new regime entirely ignore pre-existing boundaries? Would such boundaries be easier to maintain than to obliterate or were there compelling reasons to obliterate them? If potential broch territory boundaries can be identified, the next task will be to see if they can be observed in documented patterns of subsequent land use.

To return to the 75 broch sites considered by Fojut, he determined that 47 of them were situated on the most defensive site in an area, and a further 24 were situated on one of a number of potentially good, defensive sites (Fojut 1983, 50). He also identified the coastline and the relationship of brochs to one another as being key factors in determining location and this must undisputedly be the case (*ibid.*, 44).

Some Shetland broch settlements such as Burland, attached to the shore by a precipitous cliff, or West Burrafirth or Copister, both of which now stand on offshore islands, seem to be primarily defensive; their location makes no sense in any other terms. Pairs of brochs, such as Mousa and Burraland, or the five Orcadian brochs situated along the southern shore of Rousay, facing the brochs of Gurness, the Knowe of Stenso and Burgar, dominate the seaboard. Furthermore, the Tingwall Valley, which boasts what is perhaps the best agricultural land in Shetland, is broch-free.

Perhaps inevitably, given the logistics of and reasons for, the excavation of broch sites, there has been a presumption in favour of excavating those which are accessible today and have multi-period settlement around them. The excavation of a broch which appears to be in an isolated situation with no obvious evidence of apparent continuity and a similarly detailed examination of the evidence for its economy would repay investigation.

Perhaps the closest that we have come to this to date, has been the work carried out by John Hunter at Landberg in Fair Isle. Landberg is a promontary with precipitous cliffs on either side, excavated because it was threatened by puffin burrows. Expecting to find an Iron Age blockhouse fort, Hunter discovered that the story was rather more complex, the site having had a more extensive use (Hunter 1997). In addition to what may have been part of a blockhouse, there were later Iron Age buildings and a sequence of hearths that both pre and post-dated them. On the basis of the bronze working moulds which were recovered, Hunter speculated about possible continuity into the Viking period. This was followed by a break in the record prior to the building of a chapel in the 14th or 15th century.

Landberg appears to be the only defended Iron Age site in Fair Isle and so the entire island may have been considered its hinterland. In an unpublished statement written during the course of the excavation for the commendable purposes of keeping the people of Fair Isle informed of developments (1997), Hunter has suggested that this may have been an example of the Church being given land by wealthy individuals, which were often former forts or enclosures, where the area of land granted was easily definable. He suggested that this may have even happened in the pre-Viking period.

The results of Moore and Wilson's recent excavation of the undefended Iron Age site at Bayanne will inevitably also shape our thinking. Why was this site not developed as a broch site, when both its location and its rich pre-broch culture would appear to make it a good candidate?

Further south in Britain, unrest was giving rise to the building of hillforts. A feeling of unrest may well have transmitted itself up the country, and even if the feeling was imagined rather than real by the time it got to the north of Scotland, was broch building a response to this unease? Was it a way of allowing people to keep a weather eye on the sea; to control the approaches and to be able to communicate potential danger from one broch to the next? Does the similarity of proportions and scale of the majority of brochs in Shetland presuppose an organised Shetland-wide plan for broch building (Fojut 1982)? How were these people supported economically? And if we do envisage a society which was internally co-operative, we have to question whether there were ever any such things as formal broch territories at all? Although we are only at the start of our investigations, reading the landscape through field survey presents us with a tool to move forward and maybe, just maybe, we have an opportunity to establish some answers.

ACKNOWLEDGEMENTS

The authors would like to thank Brian Smith and Jimmy Moncrieff for comments on an earlier draft of this paper.

BIBLIOGRAPHY

Childe, V. G. (1935) *The Prehistory of Scotland*. London, Kegan Paul, Trench, Trubner and co.

Childe, V. G. (1951) *Social Evolution*. London and Glasgow, Fontana

Dockrill, S. J. (1998) Northern Exposure: Phase 1 of the Old Scatness Excavations 1995-8. In Nicholson, R. A. and Dockrill, S. J. (eds.) *Old Scatness Broch, Shetland: Retrospect and Prospect*, 59-80. Bradford, Bradford Archaeological Sciences Research 5 / North Atlantic Biocultural Organisation Monograph 2.

Downes, J. and Lamb, R. (2000) Prehistoric Houses at Sumburgh in Shetland: Excavations at Sumburgh Airport 1967 – 74. Oxford, Oxbow Books.

Fojut, N. (1982) Is Mousa a broch? *Proceedings of the Society of Antiquaries of Scotland* 111 (1980-1), 220-228.

Fojut, N. (1983) Towards a geography of Shetland brochs. *Glasgow Archaeological Journal* 9, 38-59.

Hedges, J. W. and Parry, G. W. (1980) A Neolithic multiple burial at Sumburgh Airport, Shetland. *Glasgow Archaeological Journal* 7, 15-26

Hunter, J. R. (1993) An Archaeological Assessment of the Jarshof: Sumburgh Hotel Site. Unpublished report for Shetland Amenity Trust.

Hunter, J. R. (1997) The Landberg Promontary Fort. Unpublished, circulated in Fair Isle.

Low, G. (1774) *A Tour through Orkney and Schetland 1774*. Kirkwall, William Peace and Son.

Renfrew, C. (1979) *Investigations in Orkney*. London, Society of Antiquaries.

Simpson, I. A. Dockrill, S. J. and Lancaster, S. J. (1998) Making arable soils: anthropogenic soil formation in a multi-period landscape. In Nicholson, R.A. and Dockrill, S. J. (eds.) *Old Scatness Broch, Shetland: Retrospect and Prospect*, 111-126. Bradford Archaeological Sciences Research 5 / North Atlantic Biocultural Organisation Monograph 2.

Smith, B. (1984) What is a scattald? Rural communities in Shetland 1400 – 1900. In Crawford, B. (ed.) *Essays in Shetland History*, 99 – 124. Lerwick, Shetland Times.

Smith, B. (2000) *Toons and Toonships.* Lerwick, The Shetland Times.

RCAHMS (2004) Historic Landuse Assessment, Shetland.

Whittle, A. (1986) *The Scord of Brouster: an early agricultural settlement on Shetland*. Oxford, Oxford University Committee for Archaeology Monograph No. 9.

Architecture, Landscape and the Political Geography of Iron Age Caithness and Sutherland

D. C. COWLEY

INTRODUCTION

SETTLEMENT in Northern Scotland underwent radical change between about 500 BC and AD 500. This paper examines the evidence for settlement during this period in two contrasting areas (Fig. 52), one of lowland, the other upland, and discusses some of the implications of this evidence for the political geography of the area in the Iron Age. The lowlands are predominately in Caithness, forming the north-east corner of the mainland and extending down the east coast in an increasingly narrow coastal plain into Sutherland. In Caithness this area is bounded by the Flow Country and a fringe of hills in the west of the county, merging with the upland area, which takes in the greater part of Sutherland. Most evidence for settlement in northern Scotland is in the east. To the west, where the ground becomes increasingly mountainous, the potential locations for settlement are not only more limited, but have been less intensively surveyed. The patterns discussed below may be less relevant to these areas on the rugged north-west coast of mainland Scotland.

Hut-circles, which had dominated the settlement record since at least the early second millennium BC, show an increased tendency for elaboration in form during this period

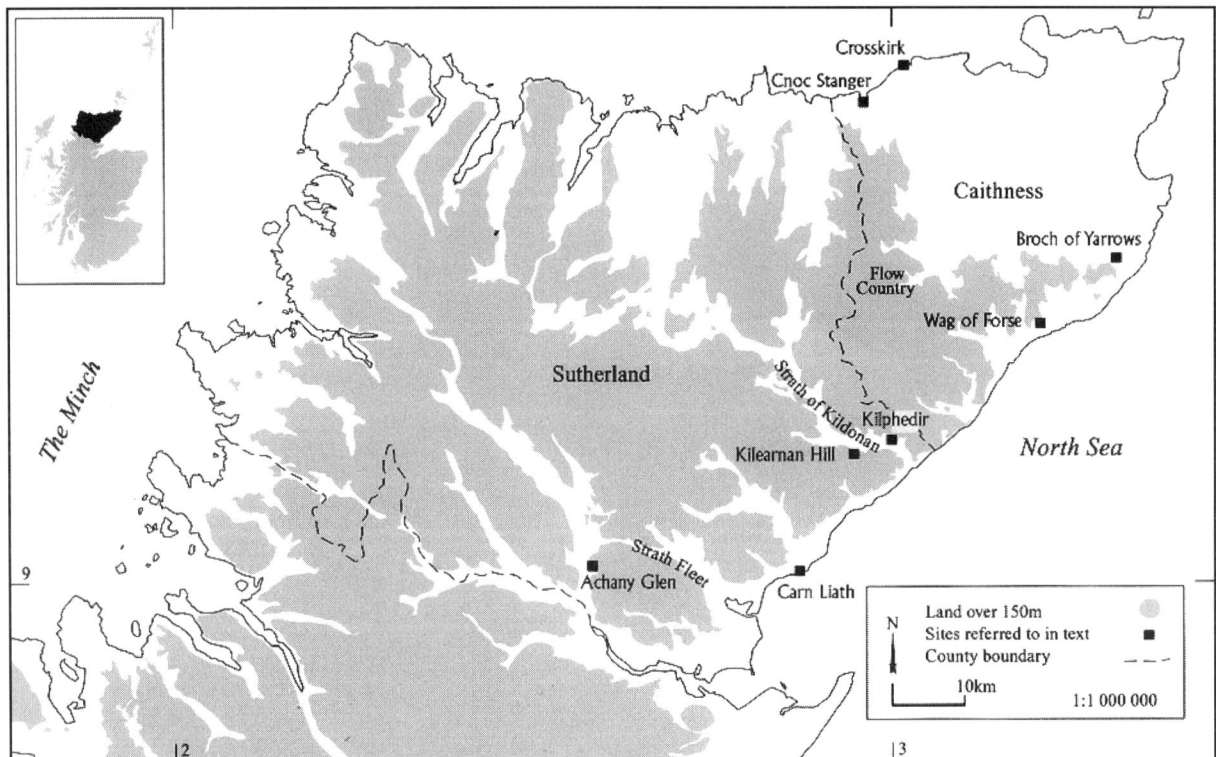

Fig.52 *Location of study area and sites referred to in the text.*

180

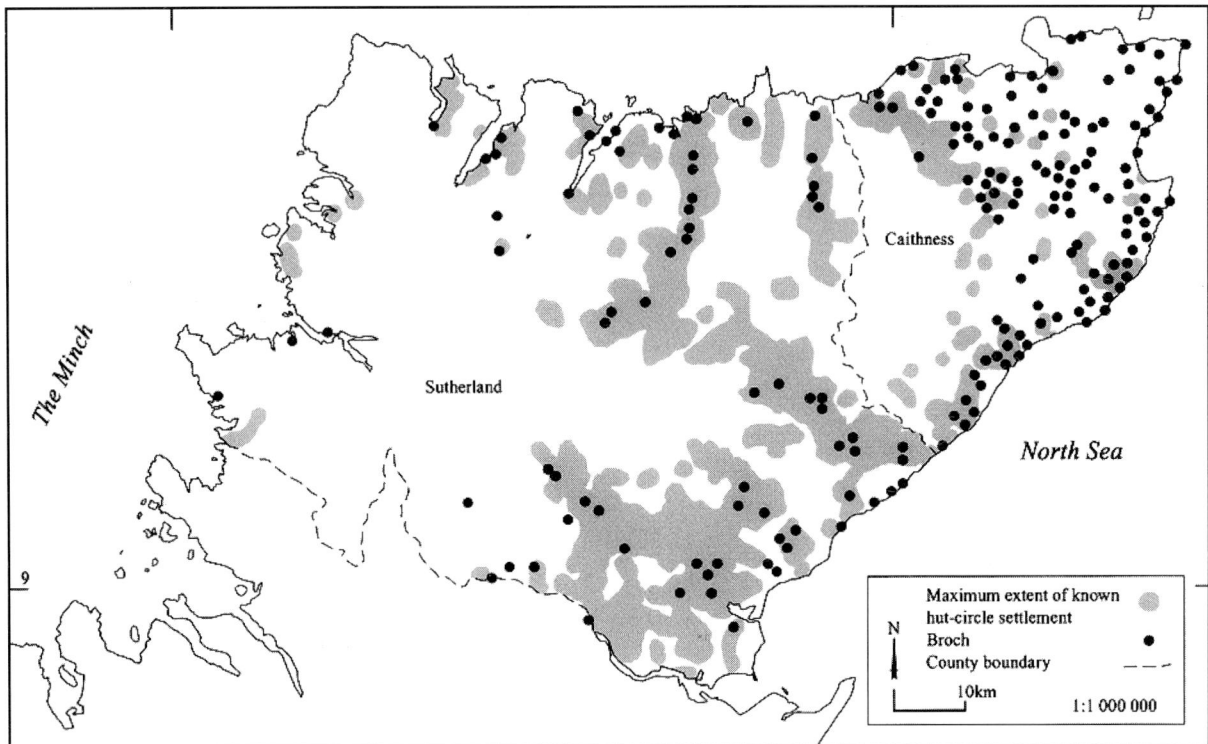

Fig.53 *The distribution of brochs in Caithness and Sutherland shown against the extent of known hut-circle settlement.*

(Cowley 1999, 69). This process culminates in the construction of brochs in the final centuries BC and early centuries AD. In comparison with even some of the largest diameter hut-circles that had gone before, the brochs were monumental stone buildings (the term is used here to include Broch Towers and 'Complex Atlantic Round-houses' (c.f. Armit this volume), with a clear emphasis on monumentality). Regional variations become evident in the early centuries AD as settlement in lowland Caithness becomes increasingly nucleated around brochs, and by at least the early first millennium AD subrectangular buildings replace round-houses. In upland Sutherland by contrast hut-circles appear to continue in use into the early, and perhaps even middle, centuries AD and there is no trend towards the nucleation of settlement around brochs.

LOWLAND SETTLEMENT PATTERNS

The rolling lowlands of Caithness are now largely improved grassland, and relatively intensive landuse over the last two millennia has skewed the survival of structures towards large monuments, such as brochs (Fig. 53). Ephemeral structures stand little chance of survival outside small pockets of unimproved ground and this is reflected in the discrete patches of known hut-circle settlement lying in rough pasture and moorland on the western fringe of the major concentration of brochs. Only one modern excavation has been undertaken on the site of a hut-circle in Caithness, at Cnoc Stanger, Reay, and this retrieved a stack of successive houses probably dating to around 1000 BC (Mercer 1996). While the dating of other hut-circles is unknown, none have the features that might suggest a date in the later first millennium BC, such as associated souterrains (see below). The majority may date to the second millennium BC and the first half of the first millennium BC.

The distribution of brochs in the lowlands of Caithness and down the eastern coastal strip of Sutherland is in complete contrast to that of

181

the hut-circles. The brochs spread across the greater part of the area and provide a focus for contemporary and later extra-mural settlements; they may also occupy sites of earlier settlements. In contrast, the hut-circles are disposed around the fringes of the distribution of brochs, and this may reflect a contraction in the extent of settlement during the first millennium BC as hut-circle settlements on higher ground were abandoned. Towards the end of the later first millennium BC other building types may have replaced hut-circles and by the early centuries AD sub-rectangular and oval building forms emerge (Cowley 1999, 71-3). These are often clustered around brochs, such as at Carn Liath (Love 1989), Crosskirk (Fairhurst 1984), Yarrows (Fig. 54a) and the Wag of Forse (Curle 1948; Baines 1999), forming small nucleated settlements also found in Orkney (Armit and Ralston 1997, 185; Ballin Smith 1994; Hedges 1987, 14). By the beginning of the first millennium AD, therefore, settlement in lowland Caithness appears to have been largely concentrated into nucleated settlements incorporating oval and sub-rectangular buildings, frequently centred on a broch, and replacing the hut-circle settlements.

UPLAND SETTLEMENT PATTERNS

The upland portion of the study area extends across from western Caithness, into the east- and north-draining straths of Sutherland (Fig. 52). A distinct lacuna in the distributions of various types of settlement to the east of the Caithness/Sutherland boundary represents the extensive deep peat deposits of the Flow Country. The brochs in the uplands have a dispersed distribution along the straths and do not occur in the density seen in the lowlands (Fig. 53). The spacing of brochs tends to be regular, disposed at intervals along the sides of valleys in commanding locations, emphasising their monumental construction which may extend beyond stout walls to the provision of spectacular outworks (Figs 54b and 55; RCAHMS 1993).

The physical isolation of these upland brochs from other structures is marked; there are no signs of any earlier or extra-mural settlement remains in their immediate vicinity. Though the brochs are physically isolated from other structures, they generally lie within, or at the fringes of areas of hut-circle settlement. These factors contribute to a strong impression

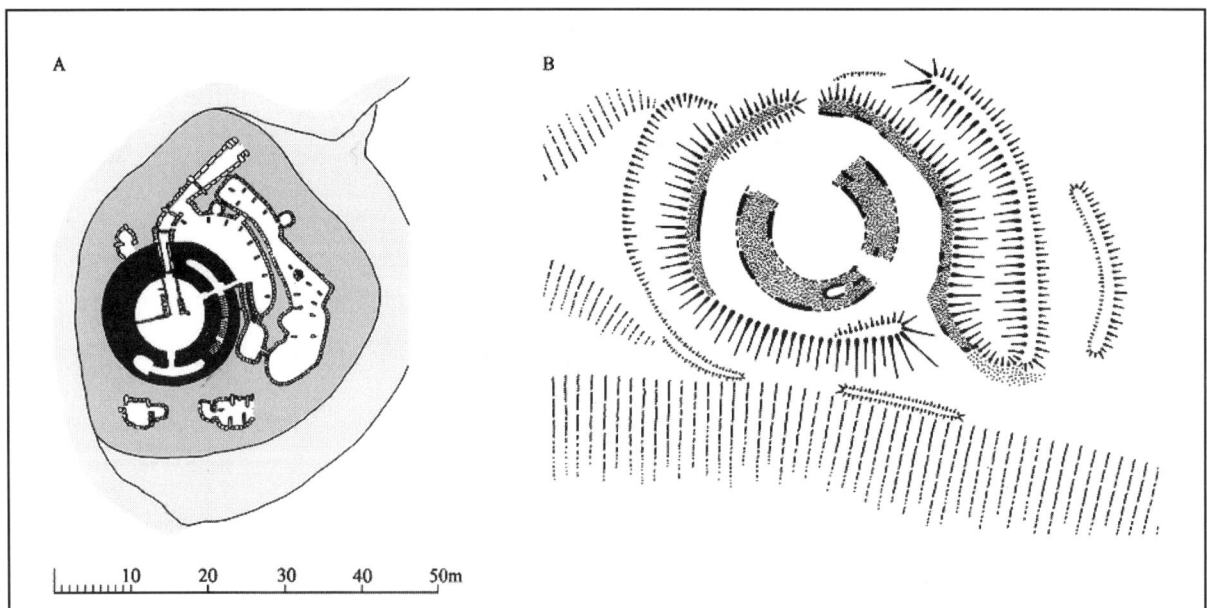

Fig.54 (a) Plan of Broch of Yarrows after Anderson (1873), showing the disposition of aisled buildings around the broch entrance and nearby cellular structures, in a form of nucleated settlement typical of lowland areas. (b) Suisgill, a broch with outworks in the Strath of Kildonan.

Fig.55 *Kilphedir, Strath of Kildonan, Sutherland (NC 91 NE 27, neg. no. A 22612) – an impressive broch with outworks dominating the middle reaches of the Strath.*

that the brochs have been planted into the landscape and are not the result of local evolution in the settlement pattern. The low numbers of brochs, and lack of attendant extra-mural buildings, also suggest that they cannot have housed the totality of the population.

Excavation and survey in Sutherland however, has produced evidence for settlement contemporary with the broad date range for the brochs. Across the higher ground in these northern uplands there is a phase of abandonment of some areas at around 1000 BC, demonstrated, for example, at Achany Glen, Lairg (McCullagh and Tipping 1998). However, in slightly lower lying areas there are large numbers of settlements which may post-date 500 BC. These include some of the larger settlements incorporating hut-circles with associated souterrains or other subsidiary spaces and developed field-systems. Furthermore excavations of hut-circles at Kilphedir (Fairhurst and Taylor 1971) and Kilearnan Hill (McIntyre 1998) in the Strath of Kildonan have also produced radiocarbon dates in the early to mid-first millennium AD. Clearly hut-circle settlements continued to be occupied well into the early centuries AD and throughout the date range for the construction

of brochs. The contraction in the overall extent of settlement in upland areas may be widespread, but it is not consistent with a complete abandonment of all hut-circle settlements.

If, as has been suggested, brochs and settlements of hut-circles coexisted in upland areas during the final centuries BC and early centuries AD, the differences in scale of these buildings is likely to have reflected a distinct hierarchy of settlement, with some of the more simple hut-circle forms at the bottom and the monumental brochs at the top. The range of hut-circle forms, from simple ring-banks to complex structures incorporating souterrains, indicates that the settlement hierarchy was probably more complex than the baldly stated extremes. However, the pre-eminence of brochs in such a hierarchy is reinforced by their dominant locations in the landscape. Brochs were also perhaps the first buildings to be built with permanence in mind (Baines 1999, 82), though longevity of occupation requires to be demonstrated archaeologically, rather than assumed (Cowley 2003, 77-81).

Subrectangular buildings, such as those found clustered round brochs in lowland Caithness, occur in relatively small numbers in the uplands, forming a dispersed distribution of isolated structures (Baines 1999, 77-9; Cowley 1999, 71-2). Their distribution is also concentrated on the periphery of lowland Caithness, and in areas such as Glen Loth to the south of the Strath of Kildonan, where the flag-stones that are so fundamental to their construction occurs.

REGIONAL SETTLEMENT VARIABILITY

By the end of the first millennium BC the trajectories of settlement in these two adjacent areas had clearly separated to some extent and although the date of divergence is not known it may lie in the final centuries BC. The proliferation of brochs providing foci for nucleated settlements of subrectangular and oval buildings in lowland areas is a feature of the settlement pattern that Caithness clearly shares with Orkney to the north. It is equally clearly at marked variance to upland Sutherland to the south and west. Other changes in settlement patterns during the mid first millennium BC may have included a trend from an earlier pattern of more mobile settlement to increased sedentism, and the consequential creation of relatively formal field-systems (Halliday 1999). The development of new building forms and settlement layouts in lowland Caithness may carry with it the implication of an evolving social structure, while the maintenance of hut-circles in upland Sutherland may be an indication of conservatism. The pattern of broch distributions also suggest that they developed initially as part of a general change in settlement in Caithness, while they were introduced to upland Sutherland, in a fully fledged form, contrasting starkly in form and distribution with the 'indigenous' hut-circle settlements.

SETTLEMENT STRUCTURE AND POLITICAL GEOGRAPHY

What are the reasons for this clear difference in the patterns and forms of settlement at this time? Caithness and Orkney have a relatively wide economic base (Fairhurst 1984, 173); at the very least they are fertile and have ready access to the sea. These advantages may have stimulated the developments of elites at an early date, providing the preconditions for the development of more complex political organisations. In the first instance, upland areas may have been more conservative and become relatively marginalised by contrast, though in the competitive environment that is implied by the evidence for emerging elites it is unlikely that the significant resources such

areas represented, in grazing and timber for example, would be ignored for long.

In this context the role of brochs as symbols of authority is fundamental. Most recent interpretations of brochs have followed Barrett (1982) in stressing their role as expressions of local authority, serving to emphasise and legitimise control over people and other resources, the need for which would be most acutely felt during times of instability and competition. In Caithness and Orkney, where a greater part of the population may have lived in and around brochs this emphasis on local authority may be appropriate. However, it is also likely to have carried with it some implications for a wider authority, though this authority need not have been expressed through architecture in such a straightforward manner (for contrasting views on brochs as expressions of hierarchy see Armit 1990, 1997; Sharples and Parker Pearson 1997; Sharples 1998).

In upland areas the symbolism of brochs may have been more complex. It has already been suggested that the upland brochs are unlikely to be a local architectural development, and Caithness and Orkney, where brochs form a part of a settlement continuum, seem likely candidates for their immediate origins (Fairhurst 1984, 181). The pattern of upland brochs, most clearly seen in the Strath of Kildonan, where they are disposed in a regular pattern, strongly suggests that they were the centres for landholdings or estates (in a loosely defined sense), controlling a territorial unit still dotted with hut-circle settlements. These estates may, in the context of an established power base to the north, represent an aspect of authority imposed from outside the area. The brochs, deliberately placed for maximum visibility in the landscape and often supplemented by impressive outworks (Figures 54b, 55), would have been a powerful, if rather crass, symbol of this authority. As such they would have functioned

Plate 13. *Driftwood on an Unst beach. Could a broch be roofed and floored with material such as this? (page 195)*

Plate 14. *Shallow voes characterise much of the Shetland coastline, often partially infilled with sediment, as at Burrafirth in Unst. Do they contain evidence for Iron Age maritime capabilities? (page 197)*

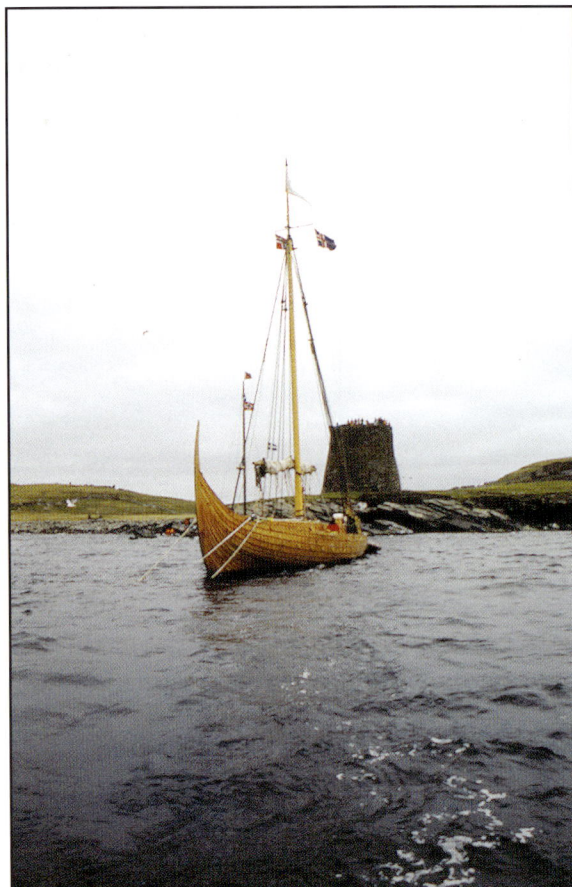

Plate 15. *The first photograph of a broch: Harald Maddadarson's ship lies off Moseyarborg in 1153. (page 251)*

Plate 16. *In 1790 the new Nesting parish church was built between Housabister and Brettabister because of the convenient quarry, alias broch, nearby. (page 253)*

Plate 17. *Area west of Culswick, Sandsting. The imposing broch and ramparts dominate a hilltop, and down-slope is seen the late 18th century 'outset' farm of Brough, built from pillaged rubble. (page 258)*

both in maintaining the local relations required for running an estate, and would also have legitimised the external authority.

This pattern of influence on upland areas from lowland Caithness may have continued into the mid first millennium AD and finds further expression in the distribution of wags. In Caithness these oval and subrectangular buildings are a recurrent feature of nucleated broch and post-broch settlements in the first half of the first millennium AD. Their distribution in upland areas is very different, disposed as isolated structures around the tops of valleys and into niches of the landscape that suggest a process of colonisation and infilling, rather than a development from a local building tradition. However, with their low visibility in the landscape the wags cannot have served as symbols of authority in the same way as the brochs. Indeed the need to reinforce authority through symbols such as brochs may have passed, though the distinctive wag architecture would have been a powerful way of stating an affiliation which would be all the more marked in the context of colonisation and a changing social order.

SUMMARY AND CONCLUSION

Across Scotland as a whole there are marked regional variations in the trajectory of settlement evolution between about 500 BC and AD 500. In Caithness and Sutherland these may have manifested themselves in the increasing political marginalisation of upland areas as the more fertile lowlands saw the development of elites and wide-ranging power structures. The development of these political structures may have prompted competition over valuable resources in the upland areas, such as grazing, timber and people. The establishment of estates based around brochs in Sutherland may be one response to this competition, which saw the increasing formalisation of wide-ranging authority emanating from lowland areas across increasingly large tracts of the uplands. As this

political organisation became more securely established, the role of brochs in legitimising authority would have passed, though the timing of such redundancy may have varied from area to area. Indeed the roles and local chronological, political and social contexts of brochs across the north demonstrate a considerable regional diversity, clearly illustrated in Caithness and eastern Sutherland (Fairhurst 1984, 180-2; Armit 1997). In the exploration of these aspects of Iron Age regional political geography in the north there is the potential to identify the origins of the more complex power structures that developed later in the first millennium AD.

ACKNOWLEDGEMENTS

My thanks to colleagues, in particular Strat Halliday, for comments on various drafts of this paper; also to Georgina Brown for preparing Figures 52-54, which together with Figure 55 are Crown Copyright: RCAHMS.

BIBLIOGRAPHY

Anderson, J. (1873) Notice of the Excavation of the Brochs of Yarhouse, Brounaben, Bowermadden, Old Stirkoke, and Dunbeath, in Caithness, with Remarks on the Period of the Brochs; and an appendix, containing a Collected List of the Brochs of Scotland, and Early Notices of many of them. *Archaeologica Scotica* 5, (1873), 131-98.

Armit, I. (1990) Epilogue: The Atlantic Scottish Iron Age. In Armit, I. (ed.) *Beyond the Brochs*, 194-210. Edinburgh, Edinburgh University Press.

Armit, I. (1997) Architecture and the household: a response to Sharples and Parker Pearson. In Gwilt, A. and Haselgrove, C. (eds.) *Reconstructing Iron Age Societies: New approaches to the British Iron Age*, 266-9. Oxbow Monograph British Series 71. Oxford, Oxbow Books.

Armit, I. and Ralston, I. B. M. (1997) The Iron Age. In Edwards, K. J. and Ralston, I. B. M. (eds.), *Scotland: Environment and Archaeology, 8000 BC-AD 1000*, 169-93. Chichester, John Wiley and Sons.

Baines, A. (1999) Breaking the Circle: Archaeology and Architecture in the Later Iron Age of Northern Scotland. In Frodsham, P., Topping, P. and Cowley, D. (eds.) *We Were Always Chasing Time. Papers presented to Keith Blood*, 77-85. Northern Archaeology, Volume 17/18 (Special edition).

Ballin Smith, B. (ed.) (1994) *Howe; Four Millennia of Orkney Prehistory, Excavation 1978-1982*. Edinburgh, Society of Antiquaries of Scotland Monograph 9.

Barrett, J. C. (1982) Aspects of the Iron Age in Atlantic Scotland. A case study in the problems of archaeological interpretation. *Proceedings of the Society of Antiquaries of Scotland* 111 (1981), 205-19.

Cowley, D. C. (1999) Squaring the Circle: Domestic Architecture in Later Prehistoric Sutherland and Caithness. In Frodsham, P., Topping, P. and Cowley, D. (eds.) *We Were Always Chasing Time. Papers presented to Keith Blood*, 67-75. Northern Archaeology, Volume 17/18 (Special edition).

Cowley, D. C. (2003) Changing places – building lifespans and settlement continuity in northern Scotland. In Downes, J. and Ritchie, A. (eds.) *Sea Change: Orkney and Northern Europe in the later Iron Age AD 300-800*, 75-81. Balgavies, Angus, the Pinkfoot Press.

Curle, A. O. (1948) The Excavation of the "Wag" or Prehistoric Cattle-fold at Forse, Caithness, and the Relation of "Wags" to Brochs, and implications arising therefrom. *Proceedings of the Society of Antiquaries of Scotland* 80 (1945-6), 11-25.

Fairhurst, H. (1984) *Excavations at Crosskirk Broch Caithness*. Society of Antiquaries Monograph Series No. 3.

Fairhurst, H. and Taylor, D. B. (1971) A hut-circle settlement at Kilphedir, Sutherland. *Proceedings of the Society of Antiquaries of Scotland* 103 (1970-1), 65-99.

Halliday, S. P. (1999) Hut-circle Settlements in the Scottish Landscape. In Frodsham, P., Topping, P. and Cowley, D. (eds.) *We Were Always Chasing Time. Papers presented to Keith Blood*, 49-65. Northern Archaeology, Volume 17/18 (Special edition).

Hedges, J. W. (1987) *Bu, Gurness and the Brochs of Orkney, Part III: The Brochs of Orkney*. British Archaeological Reports British Series 165. Oxford, BAR.

Love, P. (1989) Recent excavations at Carn Liath broch, Golspie, Sutherland. *Glasgow Archaeological Journal* 15, 157-69.

McCullagh, R. P. J. and Tipping, R. (eds.) (1998) *The Lairg Project 1998-1996 - The Evolution of an Archaeological Landscape in Northern Scotland*. Edinburgh, Star Monograph 3.

McIntyre, A. (1998) Survey and excavation at Kilearnan Hill, Sutherland, 1982-3. *Proceedings of the Society of Antiquaries of Scotland* 128 (1998), 167-201.

Mercer, R. J. (1996) The excavation of a succession of prehistoric round-houses at Cnoc Stanger, Reay, Caithness, Highland, 1981-2. *Proceedings of the Society of Antiquaries of Scotland* 126 (1996), 157-89.RCAHMS (1993) *Strath of Kildonan: An Archaeological Survey*. Edinburgh, The Royal Commission on the Ancient and Historical Monuments for Scotland.

Sharples, N. (1998) *Scalloway: A Broch, Late Iron Age Settlement and Medieval Cemetery in Shetland*. Cardiff Studies in Archaeology, Oxbow Monograph 82. Oxford, Oxbow Books.

Sharples, N. and Parker Pearson, M. (1997) Why were brochs built? Recent studies in the Iron Age of Atlantic Scotland. In Gwilt, A. and Haselgrove, C. (eds.) *Reconstructing Iron Age Societies: New approaches to the British Iron Age*, 254-65. Oxbow Monograph 71. Oxford, Oxbow Books.

Brochs and Timber Supply - A Necessity Born of Invention?

NOEL FOJUT

INTRODUCTION

MANY STUDIES of brochs in the Northern and Western Isles of Scotland have concentrated upon architectural details, typological theories, artefactual associations or environmental setting. With the exception of stone, where the evidence points to use of the nearest local sources (Fojut 1983, 43), the question of how construction materials were acquired and gathered together on site has not been subjected to much critical scrutiny.

This paper examines the case of timber supply. It is now accepted doctrine that the stone structure of every broch housed, or was intended to house a roofed wooden structure of considerable complexity. Pre Iron Age precedents for timber building in the Isles are reviewed, as are precedents for brochs' internal fittings throughout Scotland. Needs and possible sources of construction timber and its transport are considered, and conclusions drawn about the social and technological capacities implied by the presence of such structures in what would have been largely treeless environments. A series of important implications and questions arise, relating on the one hand to archaeological assumptions and architectural possibilities and

on the other to maritime technology and regional economic and political relationships. It is hoped to shed a little light upon the accuracy of the accepted architectural and functional views of brochs themselves.

Finally, it must be noted that this paper has its origins in a more general note on the potential importance of non-stone building in the Shetland archaeological record (Fojut 1996) and was initially conceived as a contribution towards a major conference on

Fig.56 *Reconstruction drawing of Dun Carloway broch, Lewis, showing timber uprights and modified A-frame roof construcition (reproduced by permission of Museum nan Eilean, Stornoway).*

Fig.57 *Conjectural intior of upper floor at Midhowe broch, Orkney (reproduced by permission of Historic Scotland).*

Midhowe, Orkney, under the guidance of the present author (Fig. 57). Turning to text rather than illustration, we can cite various authorities:

Excavation evidence suggests that each broch may have had an inner structure of stone and wood. The surviving stone tower is to some extent a shell, within which once sat the real dwelling place, possibly with one or more raised timber floors and covered with a thatched timber roof (Fojut 1993, 2).

And:

..a ledge built into the wallface. On this seems to have rested a platform upheld by a ring of posts, in effect an upper wooden floor around a central circular space. Holes for the posts for this raised floor have been found in several brochs and in two, upper ledges or scarcements which supported a roof above it. (MacKie 1975, 76).

As a final example:

..brochs ...would have made heavy demands on the fragile woodlands of the islands for their great conical roofs and timber floors, perhaps necessitating importation of timber from the mainland. (Armit and Fojut 1998, 16).

maritime archaeology, to be written jointly with Ian Armit. Its final form will perhaps demonstrate why the original version was not completed or delivered in that forum.

TIMBER STRUCTURAL ELEMENTS IN BROCHS – THE CONCEPT

The most recently published reconstruction drawings of a broch interior are those based on Dun Carloway, Lewis, prepared by Alan Braby for Ian Armit and Museum nan Eilean, Stornoway, and reproduced here with permission (Fig. 56). Also relevant is the more intimate interior depiction prepared recently for Historic Scotland information boards at

TIMBER STRUCTURAL ELEMENTS IN BROCHS – THE EVIDENCE

Perhaps we should look again at the evidence. It is stated and accepted that a typical broch has one or two scarcements, raised ledges on the interior wallface on which the outer edges of floors or roofs sat, and a ring of post holes at the primary floor level in which posts would have sat to support these upper floor levels and roofs. The usual absence of hearths from primary broch floor levels has been read by most recent commentators as implying the presence of hearths at a raised level on the hypothetical upper floor, although MacKie (1975, 79) has pointed to the other possibility, the absence of any formal hearth from the primary broch design. This argument, somewhat revised more recently (MacKie 1987, 16) was because the brochs were believed to originate as communal defences for occasional use, not permanent dwellings. Equally, the removal of cooking to a place apart would be a sensible fire precaution, given the potential blast-furnace effect so evident to anyone who has stood inside Mousa on a windy day.

The first point to be addressed is: how widespread is the evidence for the structural features, the scarcements and post-rings, which support (literally and metaphorically) these assumptions?

Scarcements are, indeed, almost ubiquitous, wherever interior wallfaces survive above 1.7m. So widespread, in fact, that Fairhurst, in his account of Crosskirk, Caithness, is at pains to explain why that broch lacked one, placing the site early in the development of brochs and therefore before sophisticated roofing techniques had evolved (Fairhurst 1984, 68) – an argument that sits oddly with the known presence of large diameter timber roundhouses elsewhere in Scotland fully as early.

The case of Caisteal Grugaig, Lochalsh (Plate 11) where the scarcement is little more than 1m above a sloping floor level, has been advanced to argue for such low-set scarcements being for raised floors, not roofs (Graham 1949, 17-18) although in practice it would be perfectly possible to construct a conical roof with reasonable floor clearance at this site (see Fig. 58). Indeed, there are good precedents for timber roundhouses elsewhere in Scotland where all or part of the roof structure appears to have rested directly on the ground, for example at the Dunion, Roxburghshire (Rideout 1992, 113).

Graham may been considering only a pent-roof, inward-sloping arrangement, although he

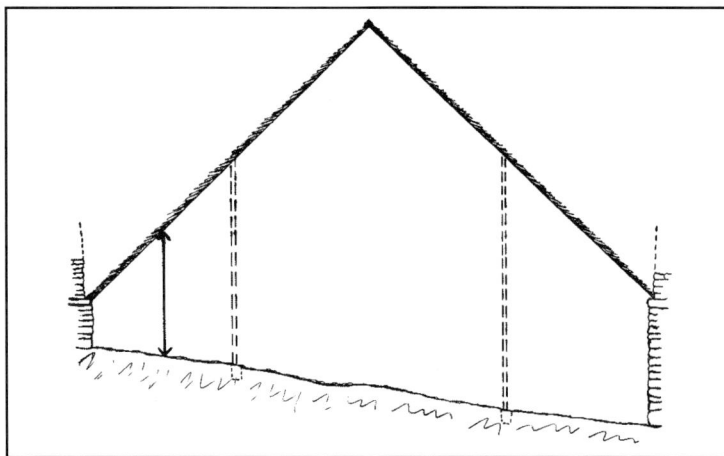

Fig.58 *Schematic cross-section of Caisteal Grugaig, Lochalsh, showing the effect of placing a conical roof on the scarcement. The arrow represents a length of 1.8m – a reasonably tall adult.*

had earlier rejected such an idea for Dun Troddan, where the scarcement is about 1.9m from ground level (Graham 1947, 69). There are few brochs with double scarcements. At Mousa, where both scarcements are set low down in the broch, with no upper scarcement, this might suggest a two-storey roundhouse set low in the tower. At Dun Telve the upper scarcement is some 9m above ground level and it is hard to see explain how this could have functioned unless as the roof support for a multi-storey construction which was braced against the inner wallface with no surviving architectural evidence except for a standard lower scarcement.

Rings of floor-set postholes or even post pads are much more elusive. There is a small but respectable number of brochs where apparently primary floor levels have been reached. Within this select sample, post-rings appear to be present only at four: Dun Troddan in Glenelg, Leckie and Buchlyvie, both in Stirlingshire and, probably, Carn Liath in East Sutherland. Additionally, the semi-broch at Rhiroy (Ruigh Ruaidh), Wester Ross, produced a circuit of postholes. At Clickhimin and Scalloway, both in Shetland, short arcs have been used to imply complete rings despite the lack of convincing evidence

The excavation evidence from Buchlyvie and, almost certainly, Carn Liath is for settings of posts which pre-date the brochs (Main 1998, 296-298; Love 1989, 159-160). At Buchlyvie only "a suggestion" of a post ring 1.4m to 1.7m from the inner wallface could be adduced for the period of the broch itself (Main 1998, 300). Only at Leckie and at Dun Troddan, and at Rhiroy, is there a complete ring nearly concentric with the broch (MacKie 1983, 62; Curle 1921, 90-1; MacKie 1980, 43). Partial arcs were found at Scalloway and at Clickhimin (Sharples 1998, 26; Hamilton 1968, 111). Scalloway's arc of 3 post-holes is described as "concentric to the inner face of the broch wall", an assertion not supported by the published plan. At several other sites, the absence of post-holes was seen as a feature to be explained away, by later disturbance or by incomplete excavation. More than one report speaks of posts "being removed" prior to later reconstruction, although without post-holes to demonstrate their putative existence in the first place. In fact, of the 20 or so brochs where sufficient apparently primary floor was exposed to make a judgement, under excavation standards which might have been expected to notice such things, only the six cited show anything like a ring or partial ring of post holes.

Turning to the dimensions of these posts, information is scantier than one might hope. Scalloway displayed one actual post-pipe of about 20cm diameter (Sharples 1998, 26). Dun Troddan's post-holes were 30-35cm across (Curle 1921, 91) and Leckie's of similar or slightly larger dimension (MacKie 1983, figure 5). The Clickhimin report illustrates but does not give dimensions for an arc of posts which appear to be no larger in diameter to that at Scalloway (Hamilton 1968, 111 and figures 8 and 11). Of all the brochs excavated to floor level, only two, Dun Troddan (Plate 12) and Leckie, definitely held rings of posts consistent with the massive timbers suggested in our favourite reconstructions. It may be more than coincidence that both are in areas where large

trees are present today and would have been present in the Iron Age.

A further aspect worth examination is the spacing of these post rings from the inner wallface. All the examples except Dun Troddan and Leckie have their posts 1.4 to 1.7m from the inner wallface, rather than nearer to the centre. It would appear that only at the two proven examples of brochs with massive post rings are the posts set, as might be expected, about halfway from the inner wallface to the centre. The semi-broch at Rhiroy might also be admitted to this select group in view of its similarity to a broch in all respects except full circularity.

All the other broch interior posts are more consistent in scale and placing with internal subdivisions of the ground level than with support for upper levels, be it floors or roofs. In Hamilton's view, the scale and arrangement of postholes at Clickhimin suggested a relatively flimsy lean-to gallery against the inner wall face, with an open court. This form of internal layout (which would have allowed light into the interior, as well as much rain) has been rejected by most recent commentators, who draw parallels with the acceptance of almost no natural light inside structures as recent as the island blackhouses built into the early years of last century (Hamilton 1968, Armit and Fojut 1998). However, it serves to indicate the slight nature of the posts suggested by the posthole evidence.

In short, either a substantial number of excavators of moderate to good standard have missed massive post rings, or these are the exception rather than the rule. This particularly worrying, given that the post-ring is now routinely cited as a standard broch feature by eminent authorities, as noted above.

A circle of eight massive post-holes was found... and they confirm that Leckie was indeed a broch (MacKie 1983, 62).

Fortunately, all may not be lost, since there are still many brochs left with their central floor deposits not fully examined – Mousa to name but one. So this gloomy summary may be capable of substantial revision in future. But for the present, we need to reconstruct on the evidence we have, or rather do not have.

NO VISIBLE MEANS OF SUPPORT?

Despite the lack of posthole evidence, and despite the fact that only Scalloway has produced anything like convincing excavated evidence for traces of roofing materials (Sharples 1998, 30-1) few would now advocate roofless

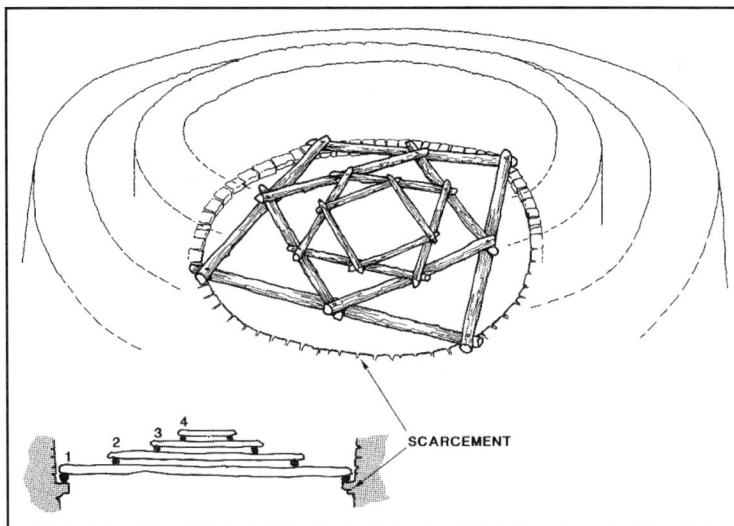

Fig.59 *Schematic drawing of main members for reducing polygon roof frame.*

brochs, whether or not the raised floors so beloved of reconstruction artists and their expert guides were universally present. So is roofing and/or constructing a raised platform impossible without a post-ring at ground level?

Much debate has been conducted on this, especially in the early twentieth century, including careful consideration of a stone dome (usefully summarised in Graham 1947, 72-75). There seem to be two possible constructional systems which would provide a basis for either floor or roof: the reducing polygon or the stressed ring-beam, both made possible in brochs by the massive counterweight provided by the stonework of the walls. Both techniques require the stability of an outer stone structure that will not prevent outward displacement of the load-bearing members of the roof/floor it contains. This implies a mass of wall material rising higher than the lower edge of the roof. Only the floor-set post ring, where the posts take the main weight, would allow a roof to sit on top of the wallhead.

Graham (1947, 70) describes, with some scepticism, the reducing polygon approach, based on a square of timbers anchored at 4 points on the inner wallface, overlain with a lesser square and so forth (Fig. 59). In

geometrical terms, a triangle is the simplest approach and gives the fastest closure, while any other polygon would do. The more sides to the polygon, the slower the closure but the shorter the structural timbers required – a factor which may be relevant when considering timber sources. This mode of construction seems most suited to roofing rather than flooring, although it could easily enough be levelled up if required by building up the outer edges. It might be particularly apt below a turf thatch roof, giving very good support for a relatively low pitch.

The principal arguments against this method of roofing are three. That identified by MacKie (1975, 76) is that one might expect projecting blocks rather than continuous scarcement ledges, or at least reinforced points along those ledges where the principal members abut the broch wallface. However, at Mousa there are, indeed, several protruding masonry blocks high up in the inner wallface, a fact which MacKie appears not to have recalled when elaborating, and then rejecting, Graham's square-on-square flat roof construction (MacKie 1975, 76). In the fragmentary upper levels of the few surviving tall broch towers, a set of large protruding blocks would be less likely to attract attention than a continuous ledge, so careful re-examination might be worthwhile, although one fears that broch stonework may by now have become homogenised during several generations of careful conservation. Among unconsolidated brochs, such protruding blocks are only recorded at Culswick in Shetland. Secondly, there would be a great strain on the points at which each upper square rests on that below – at the lowest level, there would be one quarter of the roof weight borne vertically on each of 4 points halfway along an unsupported timber about 7m long, requiring that timber to be of considerable girth. Thirdly, the downward pressure on the anchorage corbels would be very great, and might cause them to rotate outwards and downwards or simply to shear. But, given sufficiently stout construction, the technique is feasible, and perhaps not worth the gentle scorn of Fairhurst (1984, 68).

A more sophisticated approach to roofing, which could be adapted to flooring only at some considerable effort and waste of space, would be a conical construction set into a ring-beam (Fig. 60). A collar of solid timbers, pre-checked for joints, would be fitted around the inner wall-face, resting on the scarcement. From this, diagonal members would spring inwards, rising to meet either at an apex or at a smaller dimension ring-beam. For efficient construction and weight transmission, an angle of around 45 degrees would be best. Less would impose too great a stress through the upper wall, tending towards shear failure in the upper courses, while greater would impose too great a downward force on the scarcement, tending to dislodge its constituent slabs through rotation. A 45-degree roof-slope might be a little high for turf thatching, but would support reed, straw or heather thatch comfortably. To use this construction to support a complete or annular wooden floor might be possible, especially as a floor would be lower in the wall so that a greater overlying mass of masonry would allow the springing angle to be less that for a roof.

Finally, an A-frame construction (as shown in Fig. 56, above) would, by absorbing the stresses and strains within its cross-members, allow a conical roof to be constructed which was strong enough simply to sit on top of the broch. However, the practical difficulties of constructing and lifting into position the principal frame seem to be excessive, given that within the confines of a broch it would be next to impossible to raise the main diagonal timbers and then insert the bracing cross-piece. Perhaps this would be a suitable area for experimental archaeology?

Nonetheless, there are at least 3 feasible approaches to roofing and flooring which do not require floor-set timber post-rings. It must also be borne in mind that many northern brochs, especially in Orkney and Caithness, contain slab-built ground-level subdivisions which could easily have been carried high enough to support a floor at, say, 2m above the ground level. One would still expect such a floor to have been supported on wood, if not entirely wooden, simply because of the dangers and problems of creating a large raised level surface with stone slabs alone.

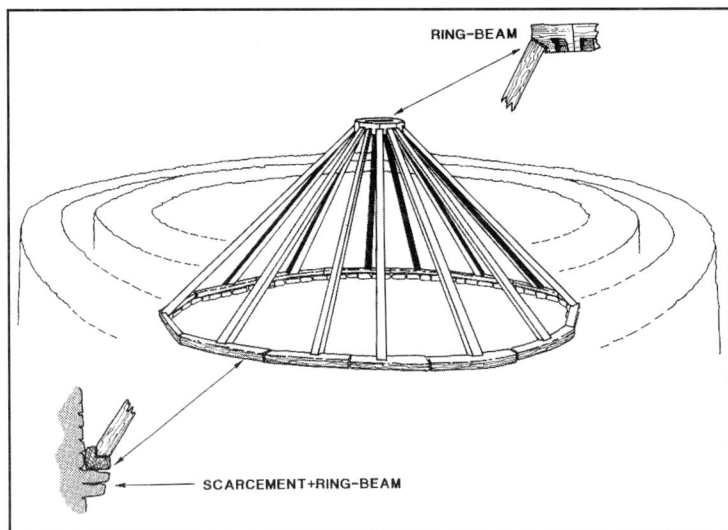

Fig.60 *Schematic drawing of main members for ring-beam and conical roof frame.*

THE BROCH BUILDER'S TIMBER NEEDS

This study has its genesis in the reflection that all of Shetland's brochs were some distance from any reliable timber supply, at least for larger structural members, although doubtless infilling material could have been obtained from driftwood or from sparse clumps of shrubby woodland which might still have survived there into the Iron Age. In other parts of Scotland, there might have been more timber, but not necessarily on site. Given the need to acquire timber for each broch is it possible to quantify the size and number of principal timbers needed in each of the roofing and flooring systems described, to cast light upon the possible mechanics of acquisition?

There are four cases to consider: the heavy post-ring brochs such as Troddan and Leckie, brochs using the reducing-polygon approach, brochs using ring-beam technology and A-frames. We have to make many assumptions, the chief of which is how much risk of collapse was acceptable to the builders – a calculation not unknown to the modern construction industry. Although more sophisticated quantity-estimating techniques might be applied, for the sake of comparison the use of a sketch construction and estimates of cross-sectional size based on the views of experienced Historic Scotland works staff has been used here. The relativities between the three constructions remain much the same, although using a stronger or slighter construction obviously affects the volumes/weights, but not the lengths, of timbers required.

For the sake of illustration, a hypothetical broch of 10m height to wallhead and 10m inner diameter has been used, with the roof conical and sitting within the inner wallface or on the inner wallhead.

"Classic" post-ring and conical
- 8 upright posts, each c. 10m long, minimum diameter 25cm.

- 12 diagonal beams, each c. 7.5m long, minimum diameter 10cm.
- smaller timbers to complete.

Reducing polygon "dome"
- 4 primary beams, each c. 7m long, minimum diameter 25cm.
- 4 secondary beams, each c. 5m long, minimum diameter 20cm.
- 4 tertiary beams, each c. 3.5m long, minimum diameter 15cm.
- 4 quaternary beams, each c. 2.5m long, minimum diameter 10cm.
- smaller timbers to complete.

Ring-beam and conical
- 12 diagonal or more beams, each c. 10m long, minimum diameter 15cm.
- 12 ring-beam sections, each c. 2.8m long, minimum diameter 15cm.
- smaller timbers to complete.

A-frame
- 12 diagonal beams, each c. 7.5m long, minimum diameter 15cm.
- 6 tie-beams, each c. 10m long, minimum diameter 10cm.
- smaller timbers to complete.

It will be seen that the least demand on timber volume for main structural members is that of the most sophisticated techniques, the ring-beam and the A-frame, while the classic post-ring form requires the greatest mass. The technique requiring least skill but with greatest risk of collapse occupies a middle position.

It is worth noting that the main roof members below the thatch roofing would have been linked with interwoven small wood, to resemble a wattle hurdle. This, plus the slight binding effect of the thatch itself, would have tended to make the roof more of a single slightly flexible unit and less of a series of separate elements. This would have helped spread stresses around the roof structure, evening out the load on the scarcement ledge.

SOURCES OF TIMBER FOR SHETLAND'S BROCHS

Although it should not be forgotten that wood was required for more than just roofs and floors – furnishings, space dividers, doors, and so forth, it is clear that no Iron Age Shetlander would have built a broch without being assured of a supply of the main structural members. Having set out the shopping list above, where did this come from?

Shetland had many roofed structures before brochs, of course, but perhaps the only earlier structure on a similar scale was Stanydale, and here the two post-holes each contained pair timbers, each formed of two pieces of spruce, *Picea sp.* (presumably strapped together). The largest of these timbers was only 25cm across (Calder 1950, 190-1). Although Calder considered importation not impossible, he preferred driftwood as a source. There was evidence, in the form of exotic timber species, for the use of non-local sources of wood at Stanydale (Calder 1950, 190-1) and at Clickhimin (Hamilton 1968 167-8). Clickhimin's timbers, in addition, showed clear evidence of boring by marine organisms.

One problem with driftwood is that it is notoriously hard to work, tending to be heavy (even when dried), laden with salt and fibrous in texture. We know relatively little about Iron Age woodworking tools, but can perhaps suggest that sophisticated carpentry in driftwood was beyond the available technology. Driftwood might have been used as the "smaller timbers to complete" referred to above, but it seems less than likely that such operations as splicing to obtain longer load-bearing members. If driftwood was used for building, much of what came ashore would have been useless for roofing, even allowing for the fact that a degree of non-straightness could be accommodated within roof structures (Plate 13). Even less of the available driftwood would have been suitable for creating the sort of level flooring beloved of reconstruction artists: plank flooring requires long, straight, timbers of relatively even grain.

If the builders of Stanydale, which so far as we know appears to be of a uniquely large scale, had to improvise and join timbers to obtain the size they wanted, this may suggest that even in the late Neolithic the driftwood supply was not considerable. By the Iron Age driftwood was still in evidence, and was assumed to be the source at Clickhimin, where chips attributed to re-working or structural timbers were of "pine, willow and spruce, the latter predominating". Spruce at this date did not grow in Britain, the nearest source being Scandinavia or North America. If driftwood was the source, marine currents would support a North American origin for this, and there is a single reference in the literature to what may have been Quebec Pine, *Pinus strobus* (Hamilton 1968, 168).

There are known to be ruins of at least 50, and perhaps as many as 75, brochs or broch-like structures in Shetland, and we may hypothesise the total loss of evidence for at least another 25, perhaps more. Bearing in mind all the necessary *caveats* about the length of the period over which brochs were built there, it must be the case that in Shetland a broch was built or rebuilt, on average, some time between once every year and once every 3 years. Each would have required re-roofing at regular intervals. Was Shetland receiving enough driftwood in the middle Iron Age? And, perhaps more to the point, was there a sufficiently strong social mechanism to organise the collection, stockpiling and preferential use for broch-building of all substantial timbers? And, finally in this list of imponderables, was driftwood gathered from all of Shetland for each broch, or were local beaches only accessed within each of 75 or more "broch territories"?

How might driftwood collection have operated in Iron Age Shetland? Did one collect the driftwood first and then construct the

197

broch, or start on the broch sure in the knowledge that winter storms would deliver the necessary timber? Surely there was never quite such abundance as this?

The usual view on driftwood is that the forests of Eastern North America at this date were essentially virgin woodland, with large numbers of trees falling into rivers and being undermined by coastal erosion, to be swept out to sea and deposited on European shores at the other end of the North Atlantic Drift. Leaving aside the fact that we do not know the Drift was operating then as now, was this enough to bring the necessary supplies to Shetland? It may be that we can never know, but it seems rather unlikely. At the present day, timber cover in the supposed source area is greatly reduced, and rivers and the sea are combated by erosion protection measures. Almost all of Shetland's driftwood today is cut timber, washed from deck-cargo on ships plying the North Sea and North Atlantic. Telephone poles washed away from distant shorelines are more frequent than trees with attached roots.

The alternative is that broch building was supported by organised timber importation. The obvious source would be the northern Scottish mainland. Evidence for contemporary vegetation might suggest potential sources of supply in the firths of eastern Sutherland and Easter Ross, or else the sea lochs of Wester Ross. But there are two objections. One is the dominance of spruce in the wood samples from Shetland brochs. Admittedly the examples are few in number, and all of the spruce chips at Clickhimin could have come from one very modest timber. The other is the existence in these very areas of established populations, building brochs on their own account.

Setting aside the spruce factor, does our present knowledge and understanding of Iron Age northern Scotland suggest that such a trade could have taken place? This question is more complex than it at first appears, if the

means of transportation is considered. Not only are technical matters concerned, but also the social and political structures of the time. It is not tenable to argue that the people of Wester Ross or East Sutherland could have been indifferent to the question of the defensive capabilities of Shetland because they were remote one from the other. If timber could be imported, then vessels existed sufficiently developed to enable hostilities at this range also. Therefore, this hypothetical timber trade would only be feasible if there was a sufficiently stable political climate to make mutual defence a desirable option. In short, if trade in timber did take place, this must surely imply that the inhabitants of the supplying region had no urgent territorial ambitions in the locations being supplied or vice versa. Otherwise, they would be supplying defence material to their potential target.

An alternative view is that such large geographical areas as these did not function as co-ordinated units in the middle Iron Age. Instead, it might be argued, long-distance ties of family, trade or obligation were dominant. So individual Shetland broch-builders might have obtained timber from their specific contacts in the south, while they, and their contacts, maintained attitudes of mutual hostility or defiance to their immediate neighbours. It has been argued by several writers (O'Neill 1954; Fojut 1994, 53) that brochs make most sense in a social climate of small-scale sporadic raiding in which slavery is a likely consequence of defensive failure – assuming brochs are required to make practical, as opposed to symbolic, sense. This would accord well with a society moderated through dispersed kin-groups rather than by extensive geographical hegemonies.

Was there an alternative to north Scotland as a timber source? Western Norway is a longer sail although simple enough to navigate. The waters are more exposed for the Shetland crossing and the winds are contrary for much of the year. On the other hand, spruce is native to Norway, and spruce appears most frequently of all wood in broch construction contexts, limited as these are. On balance, the Scottish option is preferable, given prevailing wind patterns to move laden ships north and east towards Shetland and the absence of any demonstrably Scandinavian parallels in the artefactual record for the Shetland Iron Age. The spruce found on sites would thus continue to be interpreted as driftwood.

If importation took place, technologically it implies vessels of sea-going capacity by the middle Iron Age, capable of towing or carrying large baulks of timber. It is generally accepted that the Picts had marine competency by the time Burghead was built, perhaps in the 5th century AD. In the absence of literary or material evidence this has not been considered for earlier periods. But an effective navy does not arise out of a few coracles overnight.

Is it completely impossible that the evidence for Iron Age navigation may yet appear? The gentle drowning of Shetland's coastline and the low shores of the sheltered inner voes make it eminently possible that, somewhere, the remains of an Iron Age hulk survive to be discovered by chance or some future search technology. In fact the potential for all kinds of maritime survival in the voes is high, and would repay systematic consideration as predictive approaches and geophysical technology develop (Plate 14)

CONCLUSION

To summarise, in note form:

1. The evidence for massive timber flooring and roofing structures within brochs is, in general, more scanty than is generally acknowledged.
2. There are roofing and flooring techniques which are technically feasible for brochs and which would leave no structural trace on their ground floor.
3. If brochs were roofed in any way at all, timber was required in quantity.
4. Shetland's vegetation precludes local sources for this timber, leaving driftwood or importation as options.
5. Driftwood appears to be an unreliable and possibly inadequate source.
6. Importation requires certain inter-linked socio-political and technical assumptions, but these are not unthinkable.
7. Systematic search for evidence of maritime capabilities in broch-period Shetland presents an exciting and potentially rewarding area for future development.

NOTE

In the discussion following delivery of this paper at the Conference, the idea of roofing with similar techniques to those used to construct timber-framed skin boats was advanced. This has a number of attractions for Shetland, not least cutting out most, if not all, of the need for non-local materials. The load imposed on the wall-head or scarcement would be much lower, and there would be no need for additional supporting posts. However, fitting such a roof into place and ensuring it was waterproof might be difficult, although by no means impossible. It would have very poor heat insulation properties and would require regular maintenance, but perhaps not much more than thatch. The author is aware of no evidence for such roofing strategies on permanent structures at an appropriate date in the NW European archaeological record. However, given the sceptical comments expressed in this paper on received wisdom regarding traditional roofing theories, it would be inadvisable to dismiss the idea of "a giant inverted coracle" out of hand.

ACKNOWLEDGEMENTS

This paper drives many of its ideas from discussions over the years with almost every active excavator and student of brochs. Particular debts are due to Ian Armit, with whom it was first sketched out, and Bob McIlwraith who provided advice on timber dimensions and the problems of working driftwood. Alan Braby drew Figs 59 and 60 especially for this paper.

REFERENCES

Armit, I. and Fojut, N. (1998) Dùn Chàrlabhaigh and the Hebridean Iron Age. Stornoway: Urras nan Tursachan

Calder, C. S. T. (1950) Report on the excavation of a Neolithic Temple in the parish of Sandsting, Shetland. *Proceedings of the Society of Antiquaries of Scotland* 84 (1949-50), 185-205.

Curle, A. O. (1921) The broch of Dun Troddan, Gleann Beag, Glenelg, Inverness-shire. *Proceedings of the Society of Antiquaries of Scotland* 55 (1920-21), 83-94.

Fairhurst, H. (1984) Excavations at Crosskirk Broch, Caithness. Edinburgh: Society of Antiquaries of Scotland Monograph 3.

Fojut, N. (1983) Towards a geography of Shetland brochs. *Glasgow Archaeological Journal* 9, 38-59. [*Reproduced in this volume, 147-168*].

Fojut, N. (1993) The Brochs of Gurness and Midhowe, Orkney. Edinburgh: Historic Scotland.

Fojut, N. (1994) A Guide to Prehistoric and Viking Shetland. Lerwick: The Shetland Times.

Fojut, N. (1996) Not seeing the wood: an armchair archaeology of Shetland. In Waugh, D. (ed) *Shetland's Northern Links: Language and History*, 105-118. Lerwick: The Shetland Times.

Graham, A. (1947) Some observations on the brochs. *Proceedings of the Society of Antiquaries of Scotland* 81 (1946-7), 48-99.

Graham, A. (1949) Notes on some brochs and forts visited in 1949. *Proceedings of the Society of Antiquaries of Scotland* 83 1948-9, 12-24.

Hamilton, J. R. C. (1968) *Excavations at Clickhimin, Shetland*. Edinburgh: Ministry of Public Works Archaeological Report 6.

Love, P. (1989) Recent Excavations at Carn Liath, Golspie, Sutherland. *Glasgow Archaeological Journal* 15, 157-169.

MacKie, E. W. (1975) The brochs of Scotland. In Fowler P. J. (ed) *Recent Work in Rural Archaeology*. Bradford-on-Avon: Moonraker.

MacKie, E. W. (1980) Dun an Ruigh Ruaidh, Loch Broom, Ross & Cromarty: Excavations in 1968 and 1978. *Glasgow Archaeological Journal* 7, 32-79.

MacKie, E. W. (1983) The Leckie broch, Stirlingshire: an interim report. *Glasgow Archaeological Journal* 9, 60-72.

MacKie, E. W. (1987) Impact on the Scottish Iron Age of the discoveries at Leckie broch. *Glasgow Archaeological Journal* 14, 1-18.

Main, L. (1998) Excavation of a timber round-house and broch at the Fairy Knowe, Buchlyvie, Stirlingshire 1975-8. *Proceedings of the Society of Antiquaries of Scotland* 128 (1998) 293-417.

O'Neill, B. H. St. J. (1954) The date and purpose of the brochs. In Simpson W. D. (ed) *The Viking Congress*, 46-52. Lerwick, Shetland Times.

Rideout, J. S. (1992) The Dunion. In Rideout, J. S., Owen, O. A. and Halpin, E. *Hillforts of Southern Scotland*. Edinburgh: AOC Scotland Ltd Monograph 1.

Sharples, N. (1998) *Scalloway: A Broch, Late Iron Age Settlement and Medieval Cemetery in Shetland*. Oxbow Monograph 82. Oxford, Oxbow.

Cutting Edge - The Search for the Iron Age Metals' Economy

J. Gerry McDonnell & Stephen J. Dockrill

INTRODUCTION

BROCHS, through their archaeological visibility have been a focus for investigation, study and debate in the later part of the 19th and throughout the 20th century. Interpretations have ranged from defensive refuges, watch towers/signal stations, forts and farms. Even today their definition, origin, and function are still able to arouse fierce debate.

The brochs have been studied in relation to environmental data, in particular their place in arable agriculture. Dockrill strongly argues for the importance of barley production and postulates the role of the broch as a central storage and processing structure (Dockrill 1998, 77). Equally he does not disregard other important agricultural resources notably pasture and wild animals as being particularly significant for island communities the sea. Yet, as Dockrill underlined (*ibid.*), the role of metallurgy within all these crafts and industries is significant yet rarely considered. Hingley (1992) also noted the importance of metallurgy but noted it required further work and did not consider it further.

The aim of this paper is briefly to review the evidence for the use and manufacture of metal artefacts at Jarlshof, Clickhimin and Old Scatness, and to place this evidence within the wider context of the metallurgical resource in Shetland.

THE METALLURGICAL AND RELATED RESOURCES OF SHETLAND

Mykura (1976, 117-118) summarised the evidence for viable mineral resources and Campbell discussed some of them in relation to the finds at Scalloway (Campbell 1998). The complex geology of Shetland offers the potential for the presence of a number of ore deposits. Both copper and iron have been mined in the recent past, and there are small veins of lead and zinc. The major copper deposits occurs as a vein deposit at Sandwick (HU438248) predominantly in the form of malachite ($CuCO_3$) in the upper parts of the vein, at depth it was a sulphide, chalcopyrite ($CuFeS_2$). The malachite would be easily smelted, whereas chalcopyrite is more difficult to extract clean metal from due to the presence of sulphur and iron. Historical records show that this was mined between 1789 and the early 1920s and an estimated 12,000 tonnes have been removed (Mykura 1976, 117). Pure chalcopyrite was mined in the 1880s at Setter (HU435256). Smaller deposits occur in east Mainland, e.g. at Levenwick, the Bight of Vatsland and on the east coast of Bressay. At Quendale (HU368127), Wick of Shunni (HU350150) and Garths Ness (HU 364113), places within sight of Scatness, small veins of complex iron and copper sulphides occur. In the nine thousand years between the last glaciation and the Bronze Age, the exposed deposits would have become oxidised, and no doubt quantities, possibly 100kgs, of easily smeltable carbonate or oxide ore would have been available. Significant amounts of copper ore were exposed on Fair Isle, for example at Copper Geo (HU 203728). Eight different mineral types have been identified within this deposit.

The deposits of lead and zinc are much smaller, and galena has been recorded at a number of vein deposits, e.g. Vidlin Voe (HU481666), and in southern Yell (HU500799). The zinc occurs as sphalerite (zinc blende, i.e. zinc carbonate).

There are two main deposits of iron, a hematite vein associated with the copper at Sandwick, and a major lenticular magnetite deposit in north mainland at Clothister Hill, Sullom (HU342729). Across the sound from Scatness, at Garths Ness (HU364113) pyrite (iron sulphide) is associated with the chalcopyrite/pyrrhotite vein. Again, the weathering of the deposits since the last Ice Age would have oxidised and altered the exposed and upper parts of the vein to an oxide/carbonate or hydroxide form more suitable to smelting. Iron ore extracted from this vein, as well as charges of the magnetite ore, have been smelted in the experimental furnaces at Old Scatness. In other parts of Britain probably the most important iron deposit in the Iron Age was bog ore. The ore recovered from the excavations at Howe in Orkney was bog ore (McDonnell 1994). Such deposits would have been available in Shetland.

Mykura (1976) does not mention any deposits of gold or silver in Shetland and even though granite occurs in Shetland there are no tin deposits.

The evidence of the mineral deposits show that South Shetland is not only agriculturally rich, but also had easily available copper and iron ores, with lead and zinc also available further to the north. In the direct locality of the broch sites at Jarlshof, Old Scatness and Toab copper and iron deposits would have been readily available. The richer ores of Sandwick could have been accessed by the five

other brochs between Toab and Moussa, Burrland being the closest to the veins.

The other requirements for metalworking were clay to build furnaces and to make crucibles and moulds. There are abundant small deposits of clay in the area. Metallurgical processes require assured fuel supplies. Although peat charcoal can be made, there are questions as to whether it would be strong enough for use in smelting furnaces. During smelting it is essential that there is space between the fuel (and ore) to enable the gasses to pass through; in Iron Age Yorkshire the size of charcoal is in the order of 2cm square and about 4cm long. The charcoal impressions in the smelting slag from Howe (McDonnell 1994) were slightly smaller. A weak fuel would crush and dampen the furnace, causing the smelt to fail. Peat charcoal may be prone to this, which would exclude it as a smelting fuel. Local history records (Shetland Museum pers. com.) that peat was used for iron smithing, but it not clear whether it was charcoaled. Peat (or peat charcoal) could have been used for secondary copper alloy working (melting and casting).

THE EVIDENCE FOR METAL WORKING AND METAL USE

Re-considering the evidence for metalworking associated with broch sites is severely constrained because the majority of broch excavations failed to recover the data, in particular the ironworking slags. Any subsequent discussion and interpretation is flawed by poor understanding of metalworking processes, e.g. distinguishing smelting, the extraction of metals from their ores, and smithing – the secondary working of metals and alloys to make artefacts. More recent excavations, e.g. Howe (Ballin Smith 1994) and Scalloway (Sharples 1998) have demonstrated the range of metalworking activities occurring at these sites. However, the rescue nature of both excavations constrained the recovery techniques used and therefore only a partial picture of metalworking activity was revealed. The Old Scatness project has a programme of magnetic susceptibility characterisation of contexts and bulk sampling of all significant contexts. The latter has demonstrated a major enhancement in recovery of metalworking evidence, in particular the recovery of hammerscale.

1. Jarlshof

The excavations at Jarlshof recovered an exceptional quantity and quality of evidence for secondary copper alloy working in the Late Bronze Age (Curle 1933, 1935; Hamilton 1956, 28-29 32-33, 38-39) in Building I. Numerous pieces of clay mould for artefacts ranging from pins and gouges to knives, axes and swords were recovered (Hamilton 1956, Fig 14, 28). These exhibit complex casting technology, lugged, i.e. interlocking bivalve moulds, as well as moulds interpreted as deriving from the lost wax process. Copper alloy working continues into the Iron Age, evidenced by more clay mould runner/riser fragments (Hamilton 1956, 64), but the artefact type cannot be identified. Hamilton (1956, 39) notes that copper was locally available and that tin would need to have been imported. However he expresses the view that these crafts could be considered to either be of low status, dirty or risky by stating that: "The smith set up his workshop in one of the abandoned dwellings". Curle (1933, 123-124) noted that no crucible fragments were found, and identified one pit as a casting pit (Curle 1933, 91-92). The only evidence for ironworking is the recording of a single piece of iron slag, interpreted by Hamilton "as slag from a bloomery" (Hamilton 1956, 33, Building IVc); presumably by that he meant smelting slag. The Viking period at Jarlshof shows a dramatic increase in the evidence for iron working (Hamilton 1956, 116).

In contrast to the substantial evidence for copper alloy working, only three metal artefacts were recovered from late Bronze Age contexts, a ring and two pieces of plate. It is probable that the pieces of plate would be either of copper or leaded copper and not tin bronze (see 4.2 and 4.4 below for comparative analyses). No metal finds were recovered from the Iron Age Phase. The Viking Phase reflects the evidence of the metalworking activity with a significant increase in the number and range of both ferrous and non-ferrous metal artefacts recovered.

2. Clickhimin

In contrast to Jarlshof there was no evidence recovered for metalworking in the Late Bronze Age or Early Iron Age (the Iron Age Farmstead) phases of the site. In the Fort Phase, Hamilton claims evidence for the manufacture of iron artefacts (Hamilton 1968, 78), but does not specify the nature of the evidence to support this. A "pipe bowl" crucible was found "indicating that (bronze) smelting was carried out on the islet" (Hamilton 1968, 80). Similarly in the Broch Phase a single fragment of crucible was recovered. In the Wheelhouse Phase two "pipe bowl" crucibles were recovered as well as "iron clinkers in association with an oval setting of upright stones" (Hamilton 1968, 133). Clickhimin lacks any substantial reported evidence for metallurgical activity in any period.

Again in contrast to Jarlshof, there was no evidence recovered for metal artefacts from the Late Bronze Age or early Iron Age (the Iron Age Farmstead) phases of the site. In the Fort Phase two small copper alloy artefacts were recovered. The Broch Phase revealed an increased number of copper alloy artefacts. In the Wheelhouse Phase numerous copper alloy artefacts as well as a single silver ring were recovered. Although no iron artefacts survive Hamilton argues the evidence of hones is indicative of the use of (edged) iron tools (Hamilton 1968, 133). In contrast to Jarlshof, the survival or recovery of evidence for the use of metal is very poor. However, non-destructive XRF analyses (Table 14) of some of the Clickhimin artefacts argues for high levels of metallurgical technology. The analyses show that four of the seven artefacts are tin bronzes, all of which have a low percentage of other alloying elements. There are three major effects of alloying, firstly the melting temperature of the alloy is significantly lowered compared to pure copper. The melting point of pure copper is 1086oC, but a slightly leaded tin bronze containing 10% tin, would probably be fully liquid at *c.* 950-1000°C. Secondly, the addition of alloying elements increases the hardness of the alloy, thus a tin-bronze is significantly harder and tougher than either pure copper or pure tin. Thirdly, and highly importantly, the addition of alloying elements will alter the colour of the alloy. Thus increasing the tin content will change the colour of tin bronze from red through orange to grey/white. The colours of alloys can also be altered by surface coatings e.g. gilding, or by patination processes.

The Fort Phase "nail" (CLN7088) was manufactured from a tin bronze containing low zinc and lead levels (Table 14). A similar composition is shown by the pin shaft of the same date (CLN7954). Of particular interest are the three fish gorges. The earliest fish gorge (CLN7958 Broch Period) was manufactured from copper with a trace of lead. This gorge would have been extremely soft and ductile. The two later examples (Wheelhouse) (CLN75130 and CLN75131) were manufactured from tin bronze containing a low percentage of zinc, lead, and silver. Since the analytical technique is surface sensitive it indicates that at least the surfaces of these two gorges were enriched in silver to give a 'silvery' appearance, a clear indication of sophisticated metallurgical control. The two rings (CLN7089) are made from similar alloys, i.e. copper with additions of tin, zinc and lead, a so-called low alloy 'gunmetal'.

The presence of trace levels of zinc and lead is of particular interest, since Iron Age copper alloy artefacts from England have very low zinc contents (Dungworth 1996). The zinc is correlated with lead and may indicate exploitation of one of the local lead/zinc veins.

CLICKHIMIN	phase	ARTEFACTS									
Ref Num		Description	Cu	Sn	Zn	Pb	Sb	As	Ag	Ni	interpretation
CLN7088	IA Fort Phase 2	Cu alloy nail	MA	MA	MI	MI					tin bronze, with low zinc and lead
CLN7954	Broch	Pin shaft	MA	MA	MI	MI					Tin bronze with low percentage of zinc and lead
CLN7958	Broch	Fish Gorge	MA			TR					Copper with trace of Pb
CLN75130	wheelhouse	Fish Gourge	MA	MA	MI	MI			MI		Tin bronze with low percentage of zinc, lead and silver
CLN75131	wheelhouse	Fish Gorge	MA	MA	MI	MI			MI		Tin bronze with low percentage of zinc, lead and silver
CLN7089		Ring 1	MA	MI	MI	MI					
CLN7089		Ring 2	MA	MI	MI	MI					Low alloy gunmetal
										MA - Major element; MI – Minor Element; Tr – Trace Element	

Table 14 *X-ray Fluorescence Analyses of Clickhimin Copper Alloy Artefacts (by kind permissions of the Shetland Museum). (Notes Accelerating Voltage = 50kV, Current 150 mA) Rhodium target, Count Time – 300 seconds (live).*

3. Other sites

The more recent excavations, e.g. Howe (Ballin Smith 1994) and Scalloway (Sharples 1998) have revealed more evidence for metalworking. At Scalloway, a small number (about 12) of crucibles and mould fragments confirm secondary copper alloy (tin bronze) and precious metal (gold and silver) working (Campbell 1998). The majority (8) of the fragments derived from Phase 3, the external broch settlement dates to 500-1000AD. Both iron smelting and smithing were identified; Salter (1998) argued for smithing within the broch and smelting outside. However, the quantities recovered are very small compared to Howe, Orkney, which revealed evidence of both smelting and smithing (McDonnell 1994) associated with the later occupation of the broch. In Phase 7 (1-4th centuries AD) 14kg of ore, 36kg of smelting slag and 31kg of smithing slag were recovered. Three furnaces were identified and one building was identified as a smithy. In Phase 8 (4th-8th centuries AD), 14kg of ore, 34kg of smelting slag and 15kg of smithing slag were recovered and an ironworking area was identified, but no furnaces survived.

4. Old Scatness

There is as yet, not unexpectedly, no firm evidence for iron smelting on the site, although several pieces of ironworking slag could derive from this process. One certain piece of iron tap smelting slag has been recovered, but this dates from contexts that are pre-17th century, and may be Viking. The majority of the typical ironworking fayalitic slag derives from iron smithing; examples have been recovered from contexts dating from the 1st century BC onwards. It is certain that no smithy, or forge building has yet been revealed.

The intense sampling strategies employed at Scatness have ensured that the recovery of hammerscale, the microscopical residues of smithing (ranging in size, but less than 10mm) have been checked for and recovered. Two forms of hammerscale occur: flake, derived from hammering iron artefacts at the anvil, and spheroidal hammer scale, derived from slag expelled during fire welding.

Fragments or complete examples of steatite, stone, and clay moulds have been recovered. Three of the stone moulds have been identified as 'ingot' moulds, yet their presence on occupation sites has never been satisfactorily explained. This type of mould is found on many types of settlement site from many periods in Britain. However their presence raises questions as to their true function; ingots are usually cast on primary production sites, i.e. where the smelted metal was produced for trade. Why should ingot moulds appear to be so prevalent in the archaeological record, when primary production sites are so rare? One of the moulds would result in a square sectioned narrow casting (6mm wide and 6mm thick) but each end thins, so that each end is a thin wedge shape. One purpose of such a shape may facilitate the thinning of the cast rod, e.g. for drawing down the rod for wire production. Thus they may not be ingot moulds, e.g. for trade metal, but a stage in the production process of specific artefacts or parts of artefacts. The 2000 excavation recovered a large number (c. 60) of clay mould fragments for the production of ring headed pins and penannular brooches. These are currently being studied (Milne et al. 2003), however one point to note is that, as in the Bronze Age mould dump at Jarlshof, no crucibles were found in association with these moulds. Two possible interpretations may be put forward, firstly that the workshop is in another, as yet unexcavated building, or that alloys were melted and cast without the use of crucibles, e.g. directly from a small furnace structure. Except for a few pieces of pottery no other hand-recovered material culture was recovered in association with the moulds, i.e. they were not part of a domestic midden dump. Several

| | ARTEFACTS | | | | | | | | | |
Ref Num	Description	Cu	Sn	Zn	Pb	Sb	As	Ag	Ni	interpretation
17285	Cu alloy Ring	MA	MA							tin bronze
15817	Cu alloy Pin	MA			Tr					Copper with trace of lead
7151	worked sheet	MA								Copper
17217	rolled sheet	MA			Tr					Copper with trace of lead
12251/1	crucible frag	MA	MA	Tr	Tr			MA		
12251/2	crucible frag	MA	MA							
12251/3	crucible frag	MA	MA							
12251/4	crucible frag	MA	MA							
12251/5	crucible frag	MA	MA					MA		
11757	crucible frag	MA	MA							
						MA - Major element; MI – Minor Element; Tr – Trace Element				

Table 15 *X-ray Fluorescence Analyses of Metalworking Finds From Late Iron Age Buildings/Contexts at Old Scatness (Notes Accelerating Voltage = 50kV, Current 150 mA) Rhodium target, Count Time – 300 seconds (live).*

crucible fragments as well as droplets of metal (casting spills) reveal evidence of copper alloy working at Old Scatness. Non-destructive XRF of a sample (n=6) of these show that all were used to melt tin bronze, and in two instances silver was also melted in the crucibles (Table 14).

Study of the material from the Late Iron Age and Pictish middens has revealed better evidence of blacksmithing, in particular fragments of stock iron and most interestingly a number of small (*c.* 30x20mm) thin iron plates, some with rivet holes. A number are so corroded that there is no metal left, and some may be natural concretions of iron formed in the soil. These are being interpreted as boat nails and rivets. Their deposition in middens indicates the burning of ships timbers, probably in domestic hearths. This would suggest that there was a sufficient/plentiful supply of iron and that there was no need to recycle these nails.

So far, over 20 copper alloy artefacts or fragments of Viking date or earlier have been recovered, a sample of which have been analysed by non-destructive x-ray fluorescence. Examples include sheet (pure copper, one with a trace of lead, see Table 15). A pin was also manufactured from copper with a trace of lead. A (finger?) ring was made from

a tin bronze. Comparison between the XRF data from Clickhimin and Scatness artefacts show that the Clickhimin tin bronzes contain traces of lead and zinc whereas the Scatness ring contains no such traces, nor do five of the six crucible fragments analysed. The other crucible fragment contained all four elements (Cu, Sn, traces of Pb and Zn), but also had been used for silver. Therefore it could have been used to melt tin bronze (containing no trace lead or zinc) then lead, then silver.

DISCUSSION

The combination of artefactual and metalworking evidence recovered from pre-Viking levels at the Shetland broch sites demonstrates that there was a low level of precious metalworking using silver. Evidence derives from the Clickhimin fish gorges and the crucible fragment from Scatness. The presence of crucibles testifies to the working of copper alloys. These are consistently tin bronzes, with (at Clickhimin) a low level of lead and/or zinc present. The latter may be indicative of the exploitation of local lead/zinc ores. It is noted that at Jarlshof the phenomenal evidence for copper alloy working in the Late Bronze Age is not matched by the recovery of these tools, nor with the recovery of crucible fragments. The absence of tin bronze swords and axes from the excavations at Jarlshof demonstrates that copper alloy usage at these sites was far more extensive than either the crucible/mould or artefactual evidence suggests. This pattern would appear to be starting to emerge at Old Scatness with the pin and brooch moulds recovered in the 2000 excavation season.

The levels of tin in the Iron Age material, as indicated by the qualitative XRF analyses would suggest that there is no 'debasement' i.e. lower levels of tin, of these artefacts compared with those in Southern Britain. This observation requires testing by quantitative analyses, because if proved correct, then the implication is that either tin bronze was being traded into Shetland, or that high tin bronzes were traded in and diluted with local copper, or tin ingots were traded in and mixed with locally produced copper. All three scenarios could apply. There is one small cassiterite deposit in Scotland (Stephenson and Gould 1995, 207, 213) but the most important source is Southwest Britain. There is a significant deposit in Islay and neighbouring Argyle (Callender and Macaulay 1984). A superficial examination of the data suggests that the Sandwick deposit in Shetland is by far the largest in northern Scotland and the Northern Isles, and notably in nearby Scadinavia. Otherwise the nearest other major sources in Britain are Ireland and northern England. Therefore the metalliferous deposits of southern Shetland must be considered a potential major source for prehistoric northern Scotland. Irrespective of whether Shetland was 'self-sufficient' in copper, lead/zinc and iron, there would have still been a need to import tin. The indications at both Jarlshof and Scatness of possibly some of the largest assemblages of mould fragments in British prehistory must indicate the importance of this technology in the economic base of these sites. In order to import tin (or high tin bronze) some other commodity must have been exported. The export could have been "added value"

finished artefacts such as swords and axes in the Bronze Age, brooches and pins in the Iron Age, or some other commodity, such as fish, barley or slaves.

The interpretation of evidence of ironworking is more complex. In the past slags were rarely recovered, identified, recorded or quantified, and when recovered the interpretation was questionable, e.g. a tendency to interpret all iron slags as smelting slags. Data was not available to appreciate the complexity of the ironworking process which generates a range of slags. More recent excavations have begun to redress the problem. The evidence from Howe (McDonnell 1994) is still the most compelling for iron smelting and smithing at Broch sites. It demonstrates that iron was used on the sites and at times was smelted and smithed at the Broch (Ballin-Smith 1994, 228-234). The importance of iron cannot be underestimated. There is clear evidence for smithing at Old Scatness in the Late Iron Age in the form of slags, hammer scale and rods and bars of iron. These are currently being studied. Iron is vastly superior to the other metals used in antiquity in two ways: firstly its ores are ubiquitous, secondly its properties, especially if enhanced as steel, are far superior to tin bronzes.

A craftsperson using iron or preferably steel-edged tools has a tremendous advantage over those using other technologies. Thus the butcher, boat builder, woodworker, farmer have far more efficient tools than their non-iron using predecessors or counterparts, and the ability for increased production is manifest. In the case of agriculture, the tool assemblage of the Bronze Age farmer was similar to that of their Neolithic counterpart. The adoption of iron provides the basis for another agricultural revolution, growth in production, the production of surpluses etc.

Thus, we would argue that the control of iron technology, its production and use, enhances the power of those that control it. In epic poetry the swordsmith is of the highest status. So it is no surprise to see at Howe high levels of iron smelting, a large group of stock iron and extensive smithing evidence. Furthermore, the evidence from Howe would suggest that contra Hamilton's assertion that smiths occupied "abandoned buildings," the smith was at the very heart of the settlement. The evidence of micro-slags, specifically hammerscale at Old Scatness suggests that similar levels of activity are being recovered.

The Iron Age metals economy of Old Scatness, and possibly that of all of the southern Shetland brochs, focuses on the production and use of iron in addition to the trade of goods to enable the non-ferrous, copper alloy metallurgy (in particular the importation of tin or tin rich alloys) to be maintained. The metals economy is indivisible from other economic bases and models of broch society. Metal production and manipulation requires guaranteed fuel supplies which in Shetland, with the exception of peat, are in short supply.

CONCLUSIONS

There is strong evidence for metal production, metalworking and metal use associated with some broch sites. In particular the evidence from both Bronze and Iron Age contexts would suggest a sophisticated metals economy. It is possible that the mineral resources of Shetland, in particular the copper ore deposit at Sandwick was of major significance in the prehistoric metallurgy of northern Britain. The production of tin bronze artefacts would require the importation of either tin bronze or raw tin. In either case a significant export commodity must have been available to support the levels of industry indicated by the tin bronze casting evidence. Both copper alloy and iron technology would appear to play a vital role in broch economies, whether this applies to all broch sites or only some remains yet to be resolved. The Scatness

assemblage, with the potential for more evidence to emerge, will make a substantial contribution to our understanding of prehistoric metal economies as well as the wider economic bases of broch and non-broch sites.

ACKNOWLEDGEMENTS

The authors wish to acknowledge the kind help of Shetland Museum for permitting the Clickhimin artefacts to taken to Bradford for analysis. Thanks to Val Turner for transporting them safely.

BIBLIOGRAPHY

Ballin Smith, B. (1994) *Howe: Four Millennia of Orkney Prehistory.* Edinburgh, Society of Antiquaries of Scotland Monograph Series Number 9.

Callender, R. and Macaulay, J. (1984) The Ancient Metal Mines of the Isle of Islay, Argyll. *British Mining 24.* Northern mine research society: Sheffield.

Campbell, E. (1998) Metals. In Sharples, N. *Scalloway, a Broch, Late Iron Age Settlement and Medieval Cemetery in Shetland,* 95-96. Oxford, Oxbow Books

Curle, A. O. (1933) Account of further excavation in 1932 of the prehistoric township at Jarlshof in Shetland on behalf of H.M. Office of Works. *Proceedings of the Society of Antiquaries of Scotland* LXVII (1932-3), 83-136.

Curle, A. O. (1935) An account of the excavations on behalf of H.M. Office of Works of another prehistoric dwelling (No V) at Jarlshof, Sumburgh, Shetland in the summer of 1934 *Proceedings of the Society of Antiquaries of Scotland* LXIX (1934-5), 85-107.

Dockrill, S. J. (1998) Northern Exposure: Phase 1 of the Old Scatness excavations 1995-8. In Nicholson R. A. and Dockrill, S. J. (eds) *Old Scatness Broch, Shetland: Retrospect and Prospect*, 59-80. Bradford, Bradford Archaeological Sciences Research 5 / North Atlantic Biocultural Organisation Monograph 2.

Dungworth, D. B. (1996) The production of copper alloys in Iron Age Britain. *Proceedings of the Prehistoric Society* 62, 399-422.

Hamilton, J. R. (1956) *Excavations at Jarlshof, Shetland*. Ministry of Public Buildings and Works Archaeological reports No 1. Edinburgh, HMSO.

Hamilton, J. R. (1968) *Excavations at Clickhimin, Shetland*. Ministry of Public Buildings and Works Archaeological reports No 6. Edinburgh, HMSO.

Hingley, R. (1992) Society in Scotland from 700BC to AD 1200. *Proceedings of the Society of Antiquaries of Scotland* 122, 7-53.

McDonnell, J. G. (1994) Slag Report. In Ballin Smith, B. (ed.) *Howe: Four Millennia of Orkney Prehistory*. 228-234. Edinburgh, Society of Antiquaries of Scotland Monograph Series Number 9.

McDonnell, J. G. (1998) Irons in the fire- evidence of ironworking on broch sites. Nicholson, R. A. and Dockrill, S. J (eds) *Old Scatness Broch, Shetland: Retrospect and Prospect*, 59-80. Bradford, Bradford Archaeological Sciences Research 5 / North Atlantic Biocultural Organisation Monograph 2.

Milne, J., Dockrill, S. J. D. and McDonnell, J. G. (2003) *Metalworking at Old Scatness, Shetland*. Poster presented at the Archaeometry Conference, Oxford.

Mykura, W. (1976) *Orkney and Shetland. British Regional Geology*. NERC Institute of Geological Sciences, HMSO.

Salter, C. (1998) The ferrous evidence. In Sharples, N. (1998) *Scalloway, a Broch, Late Iron Age Settlement and Medieval Cemetery in Shetland*, 124-5. Oxford, Oxbow Monograph 82.

Sharples, N. (1998) *Scalloway, a Broch, Late Iron Age Settlement and Medieval Cemetery in Shetland*. Oxford, Oxbow Monograph 82.

Stephenson, D. and Gould, D. (1995) *The Grampian Highlands. British Regional Geology*. London, HMSO.

Living Off The Land:
Farming and Fishing at Old Scatness

Julie M. Bond, Rebecca A. Nicholson & Ian Simpson

INTRODUCTION

THIS PAPER discusses the economic and environmental evidence from the excavations at Old Scatness Broch, Dunrossness, Shetland; specifically, the animal and plant remains recovered and the study of the soils surrounding the site. The excavation and post-excavation study of Old Scatness is ongoing, but the importance of the settlement and the parallels with other Northern Isles sites are such that preliminary conclusions can be usefully drawn. As well as the very good archaeological reasons for investigating a site such as Old Scatness, there are good environmental reasons for its study. Some of these are to do with the situation of Shetland itself, some with specific factors at Old Scatness.

The far northerly situation of Shetland makes it an interesting area in which to study the development of early agriculture and fishing. The climate is marginal compared to most of Britain and this, combined with a short growing season, ensured that at times early agricultural practices would have been tested to the limit (Johnston 1999, 5-10; Coppock 1976). Island habitats impose their own constraints and the risk management strategies of people in a marginal area may be different from those of communities in 'safer' environments. Small island populations, of plants, animals and humans, are more vulnerable to extinction and may adopt quite broad subsistence strategies to cope with

possible catastrophic changes in their resource base (Bond 1994; Keegan and Diamond 1987).

Models based on the principles of island biogeography may be of use in understanding interactions between people and their environment in island archipelagos (see MacArthur and Wilson 1967). The introduction of new types of plants and animals from a parent land mass may be restricted or slowed down by the barrier of the sea. The flora and fauna of islands are generally more restricted in range than those of large land-masses, and may change to adapt to the particular circumstances of island life. For example, it has long been noted that island races of large mammals seem to be smaller than their mainland counterparts (perhaps because of food restrictions) whilst small animals may be larger, possibly because of a lack of predators. Shetland house mice are amongst the largest recorded in the world (Johnston 1999, 108).

The insertion of humans into the equation may turn the tables completely. Introductions may no longer be dependant on chance, but on boat technology, trading relationships and other cultural factors; the sea may no longer be a barrier but a highway. These considerations mean that changes in the palaeoeconomic record – the introduction of crops and animals, the utilisation and sometimes extinction, of resources such as peat as well as of plants and animals – takes on a new significance.

One of the things which makes Old Scatness important in terms of environmental archaeology is that there is as yet so little palaeoeconomic evidence from Shetland. Soil conditions in Shetland are often wrong for the survival of bone, being acidic and poorly drained and many important excavations took place in the days before sampling for economic data became commonplace. There is, for example, no meaningful economic data from the site of Jarlshof, one of the most important sites in Northern Isles archaeology which is in many respects very similar to Old Scatness and which is less than one mile south of the newer site (Hamilton 1956). As well as adding to contemporary debate in archaeology, the data from Old Scatness adds another layer to our understanding and interpretation of older sites.

Like Jarlshof and like many sites in the Northern Isles, the settlement at Old Scatness seems to have a long stratigraphic sequence; it occupied the same space for a very long time. This is especially valuable as it provides an opportunity to study the 'time depth' of the economic evidence, rather than deal in 'time slices', as environmental archaeologists often have to do. A long sequence of occupation deposits allows investigation of very interesting questions, such as how agriculture and subsistence patterns develop over time and the relationship between these changes and the society which produces them.

We are conditioned to the idea of economic change in prehistory in the south of Britain, for example with the advent of Roman occupation (e.g. Van der Veen 1992) but agriculture in the Northern Isles has always suffered from the perception that it is 'traditional' and therefore unchanging. Ironically, this may have been fostered by the excellent ethnographic accounts available for Orkney and Shetland (Fenton 1978). Through research such as that at Old Scatness it is becoming apparent that there are real and important changes in agricultural practice during the first millennium AD in the

Northern Isles and that the economic evidence has a vital part to play in understanding the nature of the Atlantic Iron age.

THE EVIDENCE FROM OLD SCATNESS

The Old Scatness settlement site is situated in the southernmost part of Mainland Shetland in southern Dunrossness, next to the Links of Sumburgh, where Sumburgh airport is now situated (see Dockrill and Batt, this volume).

One of the principle objectives of the Old Scatness Broch research programme is to integrate the evidence from excavation with an extensive sampling programme for biological remains and dating (C14, OSL and archaeomagnetic), with on-site measurements for soil pH and magnetic susceptibility, off-site soil sampling for dating and micromorphological analysis of the buried agricultural soils and with lipid analysis of both soils and pottery (Nicholson and Dockrill 1998). At the time of writing, the broch-period levels of this deep and extremely complex site are still to be investigated, and this paper concentrates on the post-broch Iron Age. As the radiocarbon, OSL and archaeomagnetic dates now available demonstrate, the oldest part of this sequence is considerably earlier than expected (Dockrill and Batt, this volume). This section reviews the current data for the site and though in places the data presented are necessarily preliminary findings, there are useful observations and comparisons thatwhich can be made as the basis for future discussion and research.

Domestic mammals

The work on the mammal bone from the prehistoric contexts at Old Scatness is still at an early stage. Work on the assemblage from the Iron Age middens which fill Structure 12 (Dockrill and Batt, this volume) suggests a higher percentage of sheep on this Shetland site when compared to many Orkney sites such as, for example, the environmentally similar site of Pool, Sanday, Orkney (Bond 1998 and forthcoming). The proportions of pigs present is also lower than at Pool, where they commonly form 15-25% of the assemblage. The proportion of pigs kept seems to have varied greatly in the Northern Isles in the historical period. There is no mention of them in the Crofter's Commission enquiries on south Mainland Shetland (Napier Commission 1883, 1207-18) and on Sanday, Orkney in the late eighteenth century, there were 135 pigs against a human population of 1772 (Stat. Acc. 45), yet in the 1790s some areas of Shetland were said to have many swine (Fenton 1978, 497).

The percentage of neonate cattle (that is, calves which have died in the first few weeks of life) is as high in some contexts at Old Scatness as on many Orkney sites, including Pool (Bond 1994; 1998). Given the fragility of the bone from these Iron Age contexts, the original percentage of neonates may have been even higher. The presence of a substantial percentage of neonate cattle bone in an assemblage is often interpreted as indicating a dairying economy, the young calves being killed to increase the quantity of milk available to humans (e.g. Legge 1981). The meaning of large numbers of neonate cattle in an assemblage is still hotly debated among archaeozooloogists and this is not the place to rehearse the arguments (see for example McCormick 1992; Halstead 1998; Parker Pearson *et al.* 1996; Hunter *et al.* forthcoming; Gilmour and Cook 1998) but an interpretation as a form of dairying practice is tentatively suggested for these Iron Age assemblages from Old Scatness.

High numbers of cattle neonates are generally found in sites in the Northern and Western Isles, from a wide range of periods (Bond 1998; Noddle 1977; Rowley-Conwy 1983). Halstead (1998) suggests this may be because opportunities for crop production were limited by a short or poor growing season

or by poor soils. As we aim to demonstrate below, crop production at Old Scatness does not seem to have been limited by poor soils in the Iron Age. Nevertheless, Halstead's idea that it may be the marginality of these sites which leads to the early adoption of dairying is an interesting one.

Fishing

The fish bone assemblages from Old Scatness are of great importance in allowing the study of fishing strategies and techniques from the prehistoric period through to the nineteenth century, and have only been obtained by the assiduous sieving of large quantities of earth from the site. Viking and Norse fish assemblages from the Northern Isles have been quite well-studied and much data has been assembled, but the earlier and later material is not so well-known (Barrett *et al.* 1999). This is a very brief and interim summary of the material at Old Scatness; some further details can be found in Nicholson (1998).

Preliminary inspection indicates that the earliest material recovered from the site so far, from the fill of the roundhouse, Structure 12 (and dated to 1st century BC- 1st century AD, Dockrill and Batt, this volume) comprises almost exclusively bones from first and second year saithe (*Pollachius virens*) – known locally as sillocks and piltocks. From the first summer after hatching, until two or three years old, these fish are found in dense shoals close to the Shetland coastline and have traditionally formed a staple food, particularly valuable in years of agricultural failure. The scarcity of larger fish in these early deposits indicates conservatism on the part of the fishers, possibly borne out of a lack of fishing gear suitable for offshore fishing, but more probably due to the absence of necessity: it was not necessary to take greater risks or use more sophisticated equipment to provide sufficient fish for a basically agricultural economy.

Sillocks and piltocks could provide a dietary supplement in good years and a famine food when the harvest failed. Similar evidence from Scalloway demonstrates that in both the broch-period and in the later Iron Age, fishing was small-scale and shore-based and/or coastal, although the range of taxa exploited was greater than that indicated at Old Scatness (Cerón-Carrasco 1998).

Saithe, of varying sizes, formed the main catch at Old Scatness throughout the site's occupation. Since saithe are particularly widespread in fast tidal races around Sumburgh Head their dominance in the fish assemblages of all periods indicates only that the fisheries were mainly prosecuted in local waters. By the Viking/Norse period at least, larger fish represent a significant offshore fishing strategy, and at this period cod (*Gadus morhua*) also begin to be fished, representing some 20-25% of the catch. While large fish can even now be occasionally caught in shallow, coastal waters (and would probably have been more common in these waters in the past), the ratio of large:small fish seems to have significantly increased with, or by, the Viking occupation. Was this because the Vikings brought in new technology, or perhaps because the well-known trade in stockfish provided additional stimulus to catch more fish? There is no evidence to suggest that the inhabitants of Old Scatness were involved in the stockfish trade, but it is likely that new boat technology became available at this time. Offshore fishing also required long fishing lines for hand-line fishing, and the fibre for these lines would have been a constant requirement. Flax may possibly have been used for this purpose, though its introduction to many sites in the Norse period is unlikely to be due to this single factor (see below; Bond and Hunter 1987; Bond forthcoming, for more detailed discussion). Finds from block 7.1 at Scalloway indicate that here, too, larger cod-family fish (Gadidae) were increasingly targeted in the

Norse or early medieval period (Cerón-Carrasco 1998).

In contrast to the earlier material, the post-medieval fish bone assemblages from Old Scatness were overwhelmingly dominated by large (over 0.7m) and very large (over 1m) saithe. These fish constituted over 75% of the assemblage, with cod comprising a further 11% and ling (*Molva cf. molva*) 6%. Significantly, while documentary evidence points to the importance of sillocks and piltocks as both famine food and for liver oil (a major export from Dunrossness), we find little archaeological evidence for them at this date.

Fowling

Bird bones were never particularly frequent at Old Scatness, and it would seem that fowling, like fishing, was primarily conducted as part of a mixed, but basically agricultural economy. It is instructive, however, to contrast the evidence for bird exploitation from the bone assemblage recovered from Structure 12 (the early roundhouse, see above) with that from Structure 6 (a Late Iron Age wheelhouse, containing fills dating from the mid-seventh to the late ninth centuries AD; see Dockrill and Batt, this volume). Although the findings are preliminary, it would seem that the midden fills of Structure 12 contained greater proportions of ducks (mainly the eider duck *Somateria mollissima*), geese (*Anser* sp(p.)) and auks (particularly the guillemot *Uria aalge* and the Great auk *Pinguinus impennis*) than did the fills within Structure 6, which were dominated by bones from large gulls (greater black-backed *Larus marinus* and herring/lesser black-backed *Larus argentatus/fuscus*, some butchered) and shag (*Phalacrocorax aristotelis*). Other Shetland sites have produced few well-dated bird bones, so there is little locally with which to compare the Old Scatness material; however Orkney sites do not, as a whole, indicate a similar increase in the exploitation of seabirds and gulls over time in proportion to wildfowl and auks (Mead 1999), and we may be seeing only the influence of small sample size at Old Scatness.

Changes in crop production over time

The earliest assemblage of charred plant remains yet examined from Old Scatness is from the midden infill of the early roundhouse, Structure 12, and probably dates to the 1st century BC – 1st century AD (Dockrill and Batt, this volume). The only crop present in the sample is six-row barley, mostly hulled with a small proportion of naked barley (*Hordeum vulgare* and *H. vulgare* var *nudum*). The assemblage also contains culm bases – the bottom of the cereal stem. There is a wide range of weeds present which include both nitrogen-loving plants such as Chickweed (*Stellaria media*) and plants of damper ground such as Blinks (*Montia fontana*). The assemblage is almost identical to that seen at Tofts Ness, Sanday, Orkney; an Early Iron Age site in a very similar environment (Dockrill *et al.* 1994; Bond in Dockrill *et al.* forthcoming) The assemblage suggests intensively manured and cultivated barley fields, where the cereal stems are perhaps being pulled whole from the soil rather than being cut with a sickle.

Charred plant assemblages from later contexts at Old Scatness seem very different to the earliest yet examined. A sample from Structure 7, the Late Iron Age structure within the broch tower (Dockrill and Batt, this volume) differed from earlier material at Old Scatness in an important respect: cultivated oats, *Avena sativa/strigosa*, were present. It is now becoming apparent that cultivated oats were an important 1st millennium AD introduction to many Northern Isles sites. Cultivated oats were found in Late Iron Age deposits at Scalloway Broch in Shetland and Howe in Orkney and were introduced at much the same time at Pool in Orkney (Holden and Boardman 1998, 99; Dickson 1994, 125; Bond 1994, 180; Bond 2002). Its presence in Structure 7 at Old Scatness, but not in the earlier Structure 12 middens, suggests that the Old Scatness settlement fits into this same pattern.

Oats will grow successfully on much poorer land than barley. The oat identified at Pool in Orkney was the black oat (*Avena strigosa*), which can be grown on very sandy soil. By growing oats, land unsuited to barley could be brought into cultivation, thereby increasing overall grain production. The weed assemblages from Pool bear this out, with the introduction and increase of weeds of poorer land such as *Spergula arvensis*, the corn spurrey (Bond 1994, 193-5). The same weed species appear at Old Scatness along with the cultivated oats in the Structure 7 assemblage, suggesting that here too, the poorer or less well-manured land was being utilised for oat cultivation.

As well as being an important human food, oats can be used to feed animals. A crop which not only extends the amount of cultivable land but which also provides storable winter fodder for cattle, pigs and horses would have been an extremely important innovation and one which has perhaps been underestimated in its significance.

One sample from Structure 7, the late cellular structure, produced a large number of charred grains of hulled barley at an estimated density of almost 100 cereal grains per litre of sample. The grain seemed to have been cleaned, as there were few weed seeds but some straw fragments in the sample, suggesting a crop which had caught fire either late in processing or in storage within the multi-cellular building. The Pictish-style multi-cellular building, Structure 5, also produced high concentrations of hulled barley in its (later) fill. Recent excavations at Old Scatness have revealed what appears to be a very early corn-drying structure built into a late phase of Structure 21 and apparently dating to the early centuries AD. The fill of this feature has not yet been examined in detail, but it contains a large quantity of cleaned barley.

215

Large concentrations of cleaned grain were found at the brochs of Howe in Orkney and Scalloway in Shetland (Dickson 1994, 134; Holden 1998, 126). At the non-broch site of Pool in Orkney, the Late Iron Age buildings contained several large dumps of charred grain with densities of up to 64 charred grains per litre of sample, a phenomenon not seen in any of the earlier contexts at the site, though Pool has deposits dating from the Neolithic to the Late Norse (Bond 1994, 246). Present evidence suggests that large concentrations of charred grain are not routinely found on Northern Isles sites until the broch period or later. If this is true, what may be happening is a change from the small-scale, day-to-day processing of grain to a larger scale processing and storage operation.

Flax (*Linum usitatissimum*) is a crop which appears to be a late introduction to many Northern Isles sites. So far, it has been found in only two contexts at Old Scatness, both apparently Viking in date. At Howe broch in Orkney and Scalloway broch in Shetland, flax seems to be a Late Iron Age introduction, but at Old Scatness it has so far only been found in the Viking-period midden which fills a Pictish-style multicellular building (Structure 5). At Pool on Sanday, flax was also a Viking-period introduction. Flax can produce both linseed oil and fibre, both extremely useful commodities, but its growth and preparation are time-consuming and it takes land otherwise available for barley production. These factors may explain why its introduction throughout the Northern Isles was not immediate, though its presence on many Northern Isles sites suggests there was more incentive to grow the crop by the Norse period.

THE OLD SCATNESS SOILS:
CHANGES IN MANAGEMENT PRACTICES OVER TIME

An extensive sampling and analytical programme, focussed on the buried anthropogenic soils which surround Old Scatness, is integral to the research design of the Old Scatness and Jarlshof Environs Project. Conventional soil analytical procedures and thin section micromorphology have been used to characterise the soils. A brief summary of the research is given here; further details can be found in Simpson *et al.* (1998).

Surveying along transects from the site, using hand auger and EDM, has established the extent of the anthropogenic soils. Soil profiles obtained from an east-west transect incorporate the edges of the settlement mound and allow the profiles to be related to site stratigraphy. Stratigraphic and dating evidence indicates that Late Neolithic/Early Bronze Age, Iron Age, Norse and post-Norse phases can be distinguished (Fig. 61).

The Neolithic and Bronze Age soils were predominantly based on the quartz sands which can still be seen below the early soils on the western edge of the site. The nature of these soils would have made them liable to wind erosion and summer droughtiness. Features such as bone fragments in the soil suggest the addition of domestic waste to the soil to increase the organic content. Later in the Bronze Age sequence the soils are redder in colour and examination shows the presence of ash; fine charcoal, fragments of heated stone, fragments of animal bone (some burnt) and fractured diatoms, all indicating substantial application of ash derived from a peaty fuel, along with other domestic waste.

The Iron Age soils around Old Scatness are very different in character. They are intensively cultivated soils, with evidence of very different land-management practices involved in their maintenance. Domestic wastes and ash continued to be added to the soil, but animal manure was also incorporated. Micromorphological features indicate that this manure was possibly in the form of turves from podsolic soils which had been used as animal bedding and had absorbed their waste.

The collection of animal waste for manuring in this way involves some form of

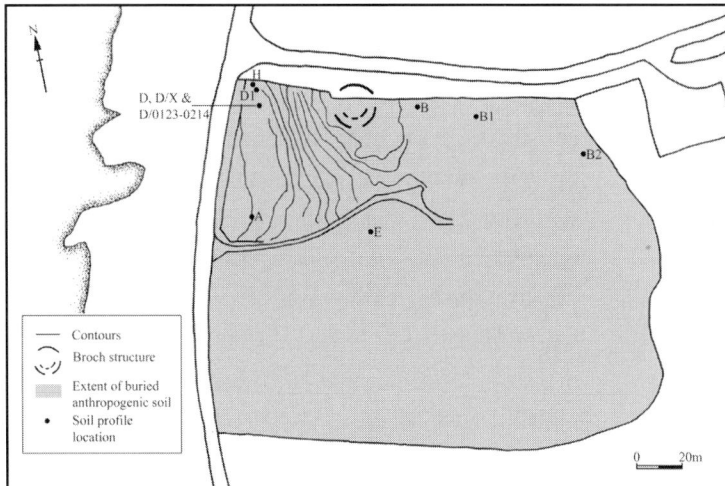

Fig.61 *Old Scatness broch, showing the extent of the buried soil located by auger and the location of sample profiles. More recent excavation indicates anthropogenic soils continue further east.*

coralling or stalling, and indicates an intensity of stock management which might not otherwise be suspected. The possibility of dairying at Iron Age Old Scatness, mentioned above, would also require a higher degree of control over the cattle, perhaps with the stalling of animals, and might indicate the source of this manure. The intensification of agriculture suggested by the quantities of charred barley and the introduction of cultivated oats is paralleled in these changes in soil management.

The Norse and post-Norse soils are characterised by the presence of calcareous windblown sand; sand movement across this lowest part of the Ness is still observable today. The Norse soils have been amended with animal manures and turf, but the post-Medieval and later soils, containing increasing amounts of windblown sand, have only a limited amendment from domestic waste. Some of the reasons for this apparent decline in agricultural activity around a site which was occupied and used until modern times, may perhaps be related to social factors. The scale of agriculture at this later period may also have affected the material available for manuring and the form of agriculture practiced. For example, evidence given to the Members of the Crofters Commission who visited Shetland

in 1883 clearly indicates that the size of the crofts around South Cunningsburgh (reportedly five to ten acres) meant that livestock carrying capacity was limited to perhaps a cow and a horse, with only the better crofts having any sheep and some having only a single cow. Laurence Jarmson, fisherman and crofter, complained to the Commissioners that the crofters had been prevented from taking turf from the hill to add to the soil, and now had to make do with what seaweed they could collect, since they could make very little farmyard manure with one cow; 'We used to go to the hill, and take off the soil and mix it with cow-dung to make manure, but we are greatly prevented from doing this now, and the most we use is sea-weed'. The Commissioners asked Jarmson if it was the experience of the older people that the land had deteriorated in quality and Jarmson answered 'Materially, since we were prevented from taking the soil out of the hills to make manure' (Napier Commission, 1883, 1218). The evidence of the crofters is a salutary lesson in how strongly agricultural intensification and decline is bound up with cultural and economic factors. This would have been as true in the Iron Age as it was in the nineteenth century.

CHANGE AND INNOVATION IN SHETLAND'S PREHISTORIC AND EARLY HISTORIC ECONOMY

The modern excavation and sampling methods used at sites such as Howe, Pool, Scalloway and Old Scatness mean that it is now possible to distinguish broch and post-broch occupation phases, and to begin to build up a picture of the development of subsistence patterns in the Northern Isles. Although many of the findings presented here are preliminary, some extremely interesting patterns are beginning to emerge.

The evidence suggests increasing agricultural intensification in Iron Age Orkney and Shetland. In the earliest assemblages yet investigated at Old Scatness (dating to the first century BC or the early part of the first century AD) there is only one cereal, barley. By the Late Iron Age a new crop, oats, had been introduced, and there may have been the taking-in of new but poorer agricultural land by settlements such as Old Scatness to make room for the new crop. There is also evidence for intensification of manuring practices with the use of animal manures, perhaps linked to dairying and the consequent stalling of stock.

The concentration of crop processing and bulk storage of the processed grain appears to have been a Late Iron Age development at Old Scatness, as at other Northern Isles sites.

There are high numbers of neonate calves in some of the Old Scatness assemblages, perhaps the by-product of a dairy system. Old Scatness shows broadly similar trends to other Northern Isles sites, but there are also intriguing differences from Orcadian settlements such as Pool, for example in the lower numbers of pigs and higher proportion of sheep.

It is highly likely that many of these agricultural changes are interlinked. The growing of oats may have allowed more stock to be kept, and would perhaps facilitate the development of dairying. Stock which were stalled through the winter (quite possibly a necessity with pregnant or lactating cows) and fed on oats as well as other materials, would have made possible the collection of animal manure, perhaps on hill turves used as bedding. The use of animal manures would have increased the yield of barley from the good land and, if used on the poorer sandy land, would have helped to stabilise its structure.

With so much effort being put into the land, there may have been little energy or will to improve the catches from the fishing which would nevertheless have supplied a useful food supplement and a necessary lifeline if crops failed or animals died (which are always possibilities in such a marginal situation). In later Norse and post medieval phases at Old Scatness the fishing seems to have taken on a greater prominence. In the post medieval phases the farming seems to have been less successful, with less effort being made to maintain the fertility of land which had been worked from at least the Bronze Age.

It is not yet possible to say whether this change in emphasis in the Late Norse and post medieval periods was due to improvements in fishing technology, changes in the social structure or in trading patterns, a deterioration in the environment due to increasing amounts of windblown sand, the lack of sufficient manure due to size of smallholdings or landlord's orders, or a combination of these and other factors. It is nevertheless clear that, within the constraints of a broad-based economy necessitated by risk-management in a marginal environment, it is still possible to see change and innovation in agricultural practice throughout the occupation of the Old Scatness settlement. That many of the most important changes on sites like Old Scatness took place in the Iron Age rather than later periods is unexpected, and demands further study.

ACKNOWLEDGEMENTS

The Old Scatness/Jarlshof Environs Project is sponsored by BP Operating Company Limited, EC Objective 1, Historic Scotland, Robert Kiln Trust, Scottish Hydro Electric plc, Scottish Natural Heritage, Shetland Amenity Trust, Shetland Enterprise Company, Shetland Islands Council and the University of Bradford

BIBLIOGRAPHY

Ballin Smith B. (1994). *Howe – Four Millennia of Orkney Prehistory*. Edinburgh, Society of Antiquaries Monograph 9.

Barrett, J. H., Nicholson, R. A. and Ceron-Carrasco, R. (1999) Archaeo-ichthyological evidence for long-term socio-economic trends in Northern Scotland: 3500 BC to AD 1500. *Journal of Archaeological Science* 26: 353-388.

Bond, J. M. (1994) *Change and continuity in an island system; the palaeoeconomy of Sanday, Orkney.* Unpublished Ph.D. thesis, University of Bradford.

Bond, J. M. (1998) Beyond the fringe? Recognising change and adaptation in Pictish and Norse Orkney. In Mills, C. M. and Coles, G. M. (eds.) *Life on the Edge; Human Settlement and Marginality,* 81-90. Symposia of the Association for Environmental Archaeology 13, Oxbow Monograph 100. Oxford, Oxbow Books.

Bond, J. M. (2002) Pictish pigs and Celtic cowboys; food and farming in the Atlantic Iron Age. In Ballin Smith B and Banks I (eds.) *In the Shadow of the Brochs; the Iron Age in Scotland,* 177-184. Stroud, Tempus Publishing Ltd., 177-184.

Bond, J. M. (forthcoming) The environmental evidence. In Hunter J. R., Bond J. M. and Smith, A. N. (eds.). *Archaeological Iinvestigations at Pool, Sanday, Orkney.* Society of Antiquaries of Scotland, Monograph

Bond J. M. and Hunter, J. R. (1987) Flax growing in Orkney from the Norse period to the 18th century. *Proceedings of the Society of Antiquaries of Scotland* 117, 175-181.

Cerón-Carrasco R. (1998) Fish. In Sharples, N. M. *Scalloway: A Broch and Late Iron Age Settlement and Medieval Cemetery in Shetland,* 112-116 and 118-119. Oxbow Monographs 82. Oxford, Oxbow Books.

Coppock, J. T. (1976) *An Agricultural Atlas of Scotland.* Edinburgh, John Donald.

Dickson, C. (1994) Plant remains. In Ballin Smith, B. (1994), 125-139 and Fiche.

Dockrill, S. J., Bond, J. M., Milles, A., Simpson, I. and Ambers, J. (1994) Tofts Ness, Sanday, Orkney. An integrated study of a buried Orcadian landscape. In Rowley-Conwy P. and Luff R. (Eds.) *Whither Environmental Archaeology?* 115-132. Association for Environmental Archaeology/Oxbow Monograph 38, Oxford, Oxbow Books.

Dockrill, S. J, Bond, J. M., Smith, A. N. and Nicholson, R. A. (forthcoming). *Excavations at Tofts Ness, Sanday, Orkney.* Society of Antiquaries of Scotland Monograph.

Fenton, A. (1978) *The Northern Isles: Orkney and Shetland.* Edinburgh, John Donald.

Gilmour, S. and Cook, M. (1998) Excavations at Dun Vulan: a reinterpretation of the reappraised Iron Age. *Antiquity* 72, 327-337.

Halstead, P. (1998) Mortality models and milking: problems of uniformitarianism, optimality and equifinality reconsidered. *Anthropozoologica* 27, 3-20.

Hamilton, J. R. (1956) *Excavations at Jarlshof, Shetland.* Ministry of Works Archaeological Reports No.1. Edinburgh, HMSO.

Holden, T. (1998) Agricultural practice. In Sharples, N. M. (1998) 125-7.

Holden, T. and Boardman, S. (1998) Crops. In Sharples, N. M. (1998) 99-106.

Hunter, J. R., Bond, J. M. and Smith, A. N. (forthcoming). *Investigations at Pool, Sanday, Orkney.* Society of Antiquaries of Scotland, Monograph.

Johnston, J. Laughton (1999). *A Naturalist's Shetland*. London, T. and A. D. Poyser.

Keegan, W. F. and Diamond, J. M. (1987) Colonisation of islands by humans; a biogeographical perspective. In Schiffer, M. (Ed.) *Advances in Archaeological Method and Theory* 10, 49-92. New York & London, Academic Press.

Legge, A. J. (1981) Aspects of cattle husbandry. In Mercer, R. (Ed.) *Farming Practice in British Prehistory*, 169-181. Edinburgh, Edinburgh University Press.

MacArthur, R. and Wilson, E. O. (1967) *The Theory of Island Biogeography*. Princeton New Jersey , Princeton University Press,.

McCormick, F. (1992) Early faunal evidence for dairying. *Oxford Journal of Archaeology* 112, 201-9.

Mead, P. (1999) Exploitation of the wild bird resource in the Northern Isles over three prehistoric time periods. Unpublished undergraduate dissertation, University of Bradford.

Napier Commission (1884) E*vidence taken by Her Majesty's Commissioners of Inquiry into the Condition of the Crofters and Cottars, vol 2*. British Parliamentary Papers, Agriculture vol 23. HMSO (Reprinted, Irish University Press).

Nicholson, R. A. and Dockrill, S. J. (1998) *Old Scatness Broch, Shetland; retrospect and prospect*. Bradford Archaeological Sciences Research 5, NABO Monograph 2. Bradford, University of Bradford/Shetland Amenity Trust/North Atlantic Biocultural Organisation.

Nicholson, R. A. (1998) Fishing for facts: a preliminary view of the fish remains from Old Scatness Broch. In Nicholson, R. A. and Dockrill, S. J. (1998), 97-110.

Noddle, B. A. (1977) The animal bones from Buckquoy, Orkney. In Ritchie, A. Excavation of Pictish and Viking-age farmsteads at Buckquoy, Orkney. *Proceedings of the Society of Antiquaries of Scotland* 108, 174-227.

O'Sullivan, T. (1998). The mammal bone. In Sharples, N. (1998), 106-110 and 127-130.

Parker Pearson, M., Sharples, N. and Mulville, J. (1996). Brochs and Iron Age society; a reappraisal. *Antiquity* 70, 57-67.

Rowley-Conwy, P. (1983) The animal and bird bones. In Hedges, J. W. Trial excavations on Pictish and Viking settlements at Saevar Howe, Birsay, Orkney. *Glasgow Archaeological Journal* 10, 73-124.

Sharples, N. (1998). *Scalloway: a Broch, Late Iron Age Settlement and Medieval Cemetery in Shetland*. Cardiff Studies in Archaeology, Oxford, Oxbow Books.

Simpson, I. A., Dockrill, S. J. and Lancaster, S. J. (1998) Making arable soils: anthropogenic soil formation in a multi-period landscape. In Nicholson, R. A. and Dockrill, S. J. (1998), 111-126.

Stat. Acc. Sir John Sinclair (ed.) *The Statistical Account of Scotland 1791-1799*, vol. 19, *Orkney and Shetland*. (Facsimile edition, Thomson W P L and Graham J J (eds) Wakefield 1978).

Veen, M. van der (1992) *Crop Husbandry Regimes. An archaeobotanical study of farming in Northern England 1000BC-AD500*. Sheffield, J R Collis Publications.

Towards an Economic Landscape of the Bhaltos Peninsula, Lewis, During the Mid to Late Iron Age

RUBY CERÓN-CARRASCO, MIKE CHURCH & JENNIFER THOMS

INTRODUCTION

THIS PAPER presents a provisional model of an economic landscape using archaeological evidence. The model uses a holistic approach to interpret palaeoeconomic data recovered from three sites on the Bhaltos Peninsula on Lewis (Fig. 62), an area of considerable environmental diversity with a rich and well-preserved archaeological record (Armit 1994). The sites, from which the palaeoeconomic data was retrieved, date from the Middle to Late Iron Age and were excavated between 1985 and 1995 as part of the University of Edinburgh's Calanais Archaeological Research Project (Harding 2000). This project has involved excavation and post-excavation analysis by a number of researchers, with the palaeoeconomic data principally analysed by the authors.

At the time of excavation the three sites were of particular interest because they were regarded as representing the main Iron Age settlement forms common throughout the Western Isles (Harding and Armit 1990): an "island dun" at Dun Bharabhat (Harding and Dixon 2000), a "broch" at Loch na Beirgh (Harding and Gilmour 2000) and a wheelhouse and cellular complex at Traigh Cnip (Armit forthcoming). Further Iron Age monuments have been located across the peninsula (Armit 1994; Armit and Dunwell

1992). The contexts from which the evidence derives are predominantly related to post-broch occupation. Also, two of these sites have structures that can be classed as complex Atlantic roundhouses towards the base of their structural sequences, therefore suggesting sustained management of the environmental resources of the area.

This preliminary study is based on three categories of palaeoeconomic evidence:
- the botanical evidence, from pollen and macrobotanical remains,
- the aquatic faunal evidence from fish, cetacean bones and molluscan shells,
- the faunal evidence from terrestrial mammal and bird bones.

A model is proposed whereby these different strands of evidence may be considered holistically to build up an economic landscape of the Bhaltos Peninsula in the mid to late Iron Age.

THE STUDY AREA

The Bhaltos Peninsula (Fig. 62) is situated on the west coast of Lewis and contains most of the characteristic landscapes seen across Lewis and the Western Isles (Armit 1994). Traigh Clibhe and Traigh Cnip are typical of the small beaches that are found along the west coast of Lewis. Conversely, the wider machair of Traigh na Beirgh resembles the more continuous machair plain of the Uists, though

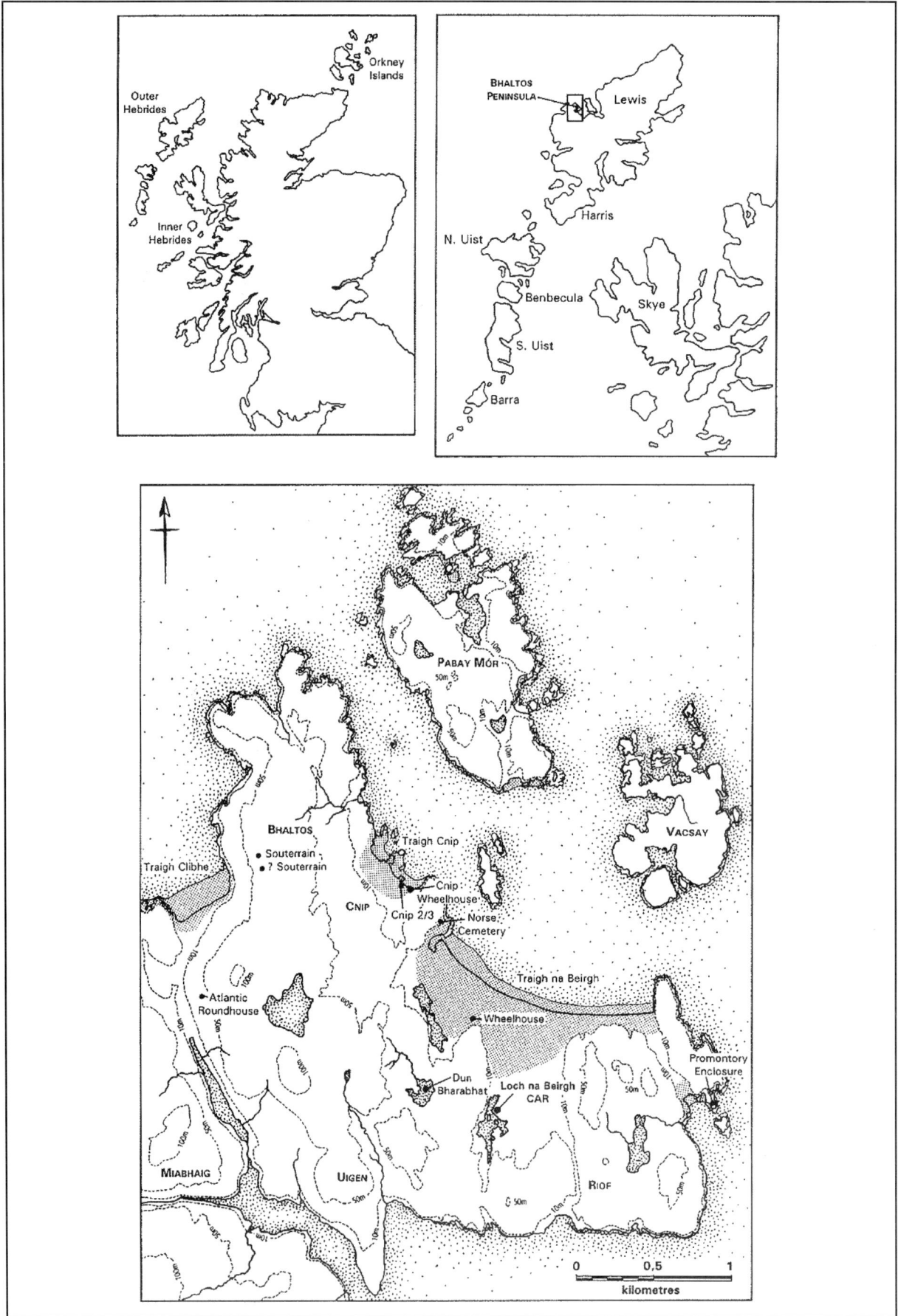

Fig.62 *Location map of study area. Source: Harding and Gilmour (2000).*

on a much smaller scale. The coast rises and falls to form a varied coastline of sandy beaches, machair, cliffs and low rock platform. Much of the rest of the peninsula is made up of hills interspersed with small lochs. This topography prevents the formation of the widespread blanket bog that is prevalent across most of the interior of Lewis including the nearby Uig Peninsula. However, patches of well-humified deep peat are found within certain areas, such as small troughs and hollows.

While the landscape may have altered since the Iron Age, the elements from which it was comprised will have already been present. For example, the form and extent of the beach and machair of Traigh Cnip and Traigh na Beirgh will have varied, due to rising sea levels and the dynamic nature of the machair system. Geomorphic and bathymetric survey by researchers at the University of Edinburgh (Skinner 1995; Dixon, pers. comm.) have shown that during the first half of the first millennium AD Loch na Beirgh would have been more extensive, with the site presumably surrounded by water. Also, the machair could have extended further seaward, with a eustatic sea level rise since the time of reconstruction in the order of 0.5 to 1 metre (Ritchie 1985). In general however, we can assume that the landscape units were in broadly similar positions in the mid to late Iron Age to those of today.

The general Holocene vegetation history of the peninsula can be reconstructed through three pollen records from Loch na Beirgh (Lomax 1997) and Loch Bharabhat (Lomax and Edwards 2000). The Late glacial and Holocene profile from Loch Bharabhat was taken from the sediments and detrital mud of the loch. At approximately 3700 cal. BP, a major loss of relatively mixed woodland occurred, with a rapid spread of heathland taxa and evidence of arable and pastoral activity within the catchment. Erosional

disturbance of the catchment increases through the Late Bronze Age and Iron Age, presumably as a direct result of the islet occupation and associated settlement. A small rise in arboreal taxa, including Scots Pine (*Pinus sylvestris* L.), oak (*Quercus* sp.) and alder (*Alnus* sp.) occurs during the mid to late Iron Age. This tree pollen may be secondarily derived from erosion of the surrounding soil (Lomax and Edwards 2000, 111), or may represent a localised copse or small extent of woodland within the catchment. The two profiles from Loch na Beirgh were taken from the infilled loch deposits adjacent to the islet on which the site is situated. No radiocarbon dates have been taken for the profiles but the chronological coverage is assumed to be contemporary with the site's occupation during the accumulation of the loch deposits of the first millenniums BC and AD (Lomax, pers. comm.) The catchment reflects the extra-local vegetation of the loch and encroaching machair, with the profile dominated by aquatic taxa and herbs of dry, light soils. Interestingly, there is also a significant proportion of barley (*Hordeum* type) pollen, with a marked correlation with pollen of the cabbage family (Brassicaceae). The importance of these records in reconstructing the actual Iron Age landscape can be seen below when used in conjunction with the on-site evidence from the three sites that comprise this study.

THE ARCHAEOLOGICAL SITES

Dun Bharabhat is located in a small loch within the hilly interior of the peninsula (see Fig.62). The structural sequence begins with ephemeral Early Iron Age activity underlying the construction of the complex Atlantic roundhouse. This, in turn, was modified to form a simple cellular unit, which used the interior of the roundhouse and a remodelled gallery. Radiocarbon dating indicates the roundhouse was occupied within the second half of the first millennium BC, with the occupation bracketed by a date from the primary or pre-roundhouse levels of 2550±50BP (GU-2436) and two dates from the secondary occupation destruction layer of 2100±50BP (GU-2435) and 2010±50BP (GU-2434). Excavation concentrated on the roundhouse and an adjacent structure that had slumped into the loch and therefore required underwater investigation (Harding and Dixon 2000).

The wheelhouse and cellular complex at Traigh Cnip was also multi-phase (Harding and Armit 1990; Armit forthcoming). The structural sequence started with two adjoining wheelhouses, one incomplete, which had been subsequently modified to create a sequence of cellular units and a substantial rectilinear structure. Extensive radiocarbon dating suggests the entire sequence was relatively short lived from the 2nd century cal. BC to the 2nd century cal. AD (Armit 1996; forthcoming).

The final site examined is the complex Atlantic roundhouse at Loch na Beirgh. It is situated towards the rear of Traigh na Beirgh, in a loch that has progressively silted up with windblown sand and organic deposits. During the Iron Age, this accumulation raised the level of the loch and resulted in successive superimposed phases of occupation within the structure, presumably in an attempt to maintain dry foundations. A sequence of deposits of over 2.5 metres has already been uncovered, with the primary levels of occupation of the secondary roundhouse and complex Atlantic roundhouse still to be excavated. The known structural sequence starts with the complex Atlantic roundhouse, followed by the construction of a substantial secondary roundhouse within the structure's interior, the upper levels dated by radiocarbon to the 2nd to 4th centuries cal. AD. There then appears a complex sequence of smaller cellular units, radiocarbon dated to the 3rd to 6th centuries cal. AD. These are replaced in due course by 'figure-of-eight' buildings dating to

the second half of the first millennium cal. AD from artefact association. Only the upper stratigraphic levels of the secondary roundhouse have been excavated and at this point and below, the deposits display signs of almost permanent waterlogging and the concomitant preservation of organic material (Harding and Gilmour 2000).

SAMPLING AND ECOFACT PRESERVATION

The sites were excavated by different researchers from the University of Edinburgh between 1985 and 1995. Consequently, diverse sampling and recovery strategies were employed. In general all mammal bone was hand retrieved and the plant macrofossils, fish bone and shell recovered from bulk samples taken when the excavator deemed the context interesting (*judgement* sampling; Jones 1991). At Loch na Beirgh, only the levels excavated in 1995 were sampled on a statistically representative basis, with samples taken from 20% of the contexts (*random* sampling; Jones 1991) as well as *judgement* samples (Church 1996).

The preservation of different classes of ecofact and artefact varied depending on the sedimentological characteristics of the site. This variability is demonstrated scientifically through the analysis of the routine soil tests undertaken for each of the bulk samples (Church 1996; Church and Peters 2000; Church forthcoming a). For example, bone was best preserved in the alkali machair conditions at Cnip and the seasonally waterlogged levels at Beirgh. At Dun Bharabhat, the underwater excavations recovered well preserved bone as well as abundant organic materials, such as wooden artefacts and other uncarbonised plant macrofossils. However, the bone and uncarbonised organic preservation on the land based excavations at Dun Bharabhat was extremely poor, due to the acidic nature of the soil (see Fig. 63). Finally, in the upper levels of the secondary roundhouse stratigraphy at

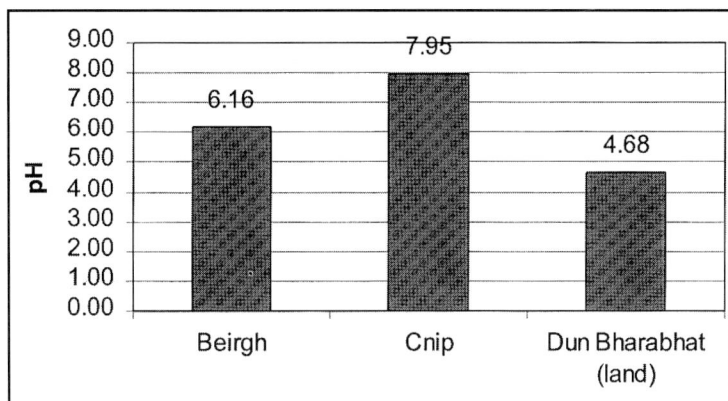

Fig. 63 *Mean pH values for each site.*

Beirgh the deposits displayed signs of near permanent waterlogging with the resulting good preservation of organic material.

THE ON-SITE EVIDENCE

The evidence presented here summarises the key findings from the three palaeo-economic categories outlined above. Each section outlines a number of recurring themes of resource exploitation and management apparent across the three sites.

1. *The macrobotanical evidence*

The wood charcoal routinely recovered from bulk samples from the three sites comprised two main groups; the first consisting of small native roundwood and the second consisting of very small fragments of timber, mainly of coniferous species (Church 1996; 2000; forthcoming b). Fig. 64 outlines the species recovered, the wider diversity of species present at Beirgh probably reflecting the much greater volume of samples recovered from the site. Evidence for structural material came from burnt timbers within a destruction level of the secondary occupation at Dun Bharabhat and from *in situ* timber furnishings within the waterlogged deposits at Loch na Beirgh. The Dun Bharabhat material consists of Scots Pine (*Pinus sylvestris* L.), perhaps from the small coverage of local woodland suggested by the pollen record, and spruce (*Picea* sp.) driftwood (Church 2000). The wood from Loch na Beirgh consists of *in situ* uncarbonised posts and wattle-work of coppiced hazel (*Corylus* sp.), which could have come from a local, managed, source. Some of the hazel roundwood still retained the coppice heel, indicating tearing from the stool of the tree.

Tree cover throughout the Western Isles was greatly reduced by the Iron Age (Fossit 1990; Birks 1994; Brayshay and Edwards 1996; Lomax 1997; Lomax and Edwards 2000), so timber would have been a very valued resource. The small fragments of native roundwood are presumably locally derived, with some timber, such as the Scot's Pine and driftwood, also available from the island and shoreline. However, the evidence for the structural material outlined above derives from internal furnishings and insubstantial fragments of a wider structural organic form. Therefore, it is possible that a regional trade in timber would have been needed to sustain the level of material required for the major super-structures of the Atlantic round-houses (Fojut, this volume; but see Church 2002).

The assemblages also contain widespread evidence of moorland exploitation. The evidence derived

	Cnip	Dun Bharabhat	Loch na Beirgh
Number of bulk samples	44	25	70
Locally derived			
Birch	*	*	*
Hazel	*	*	*
Juniper			*
Ling heather	*	*	*
Scots Pine	*	*	*
Willow	*		*
Locally/mainland derived			
Oak	*		*
Pomoideae undiff.	*		*
Ex British Isles driftwood			
Douglas Fir			*
Fir			*
Pine	*	*	*
Spruce		*	*

Fig. 64 *Wood charcoal recovered from the three sites.*

from sedimentary analysis of ash and heathland carbonised plant macrofossils. Detailed mineral magnetic analysis was undertaken to source the fuel types that produced the ash spreads and hearth material across the sites (Peters *et al.* 2004). This analysis involved comparison of archaeological deposits with samples from experimental burning of different fuel sources at Calanais Farm (Peters *et al.* 2001). Fig. 65 compares the archaeological samples to the discriminant analysis of the experimental results. This illustrates that well-humified peat was the main fuel type, with a consistent magnetic signal from some of the samples plotting just to the right of the experimental data. This pattern has been interpreted in the light of further analysis on other sites across Lewis as representing a specific regional source for the three sites (Peters *et al.* 2004). Other plant material was also gathered from the heathland. Heather (*Calluna/Erica* spp.) was the most common form of charcoal across all of the sites, demonstrating its importance as an economic resource. Other heathland plants recovered include bracken (*Pteridium* sp.), sedges (*Carex* sp.) and various berried plants, such as the bearberry (*Arctostaphylos uva-ursi* (L.) Sprengel) and the crowberry (*Empetrum nigrum* L.). This demonstrates that the heathland, in

particular the large tracts of inland blanket bog, were an important economic hinterland for the Bhaltos Peninsula. The evidence indicates selective management of the various plant resources including possible co-operation between the sites in terms of resource procurement, perhaps involving communal effort in the peat and heather gathering. It also implies a long-term stability in the division and tenure of the peatlands, as occupation of the three sites spans over half a millennium.

The remains from the three sites relating to cereal agriculture also show a remarkable conformity. The most important species is six-row hulled barley (*Hordeum vulgare* var. *vulgare* L.), though the two row species (*Hordeum distichum* L.) of both the hulled and naked variety are also present. The weed flora associated with the crop generally indicates light and well-drained soils. There is also a strong association with wild turnip (*Brassica rapa* L.), a plant which commonly grows with barley and oat cultivation in the machair (Pankhurst and Mullin 1994). Its presence, in association with the crop and other weed flora, indicates that the likely area for cereal cultivation was the machair and this is confirmed by the local pollen spectrum from Loch na Beirgh (Lomax 1997). The ubiquity of common chickweed (*Stellaria media* (L.) Vill.) within the weed assemblages suggests the input of dung into the machair soil, as the species is an indicator of a nitrogen rich soil environment. This may represent field rotation between pastoral and arable agriculture, on a seasonal or spatial basis, or the deliberate incorporation of dung into the soil as a fertiliser and stabiliser.

The presence of cereal sized culm bases across all three sites indicates that the crop was gathered by up-rooting, presumably for ease of harvesting as well as maximising the straw return. This method

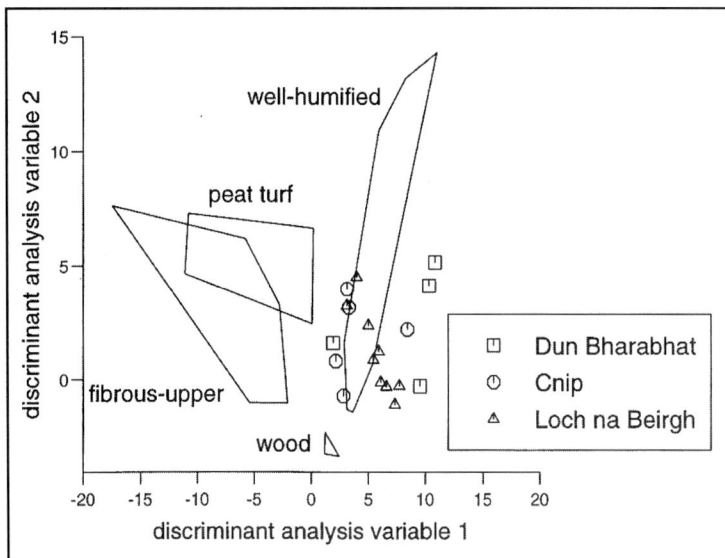

Fig.65 *Discriminant analysis biplot of ash samples.*

would have been very damaging to the fragile surface of the machair, presumably leading to erosion, principally by wind. This may explain the accelerated rate of machair encroachment and infilling of Loch na Beirgh throughout the Iron Age. It also explains the need for the reactive strategies of fertilising the soil by animal dung, through direct middening or field rotation, which would have increased both the fertility and stability of the soil. The crop appears to have been processed off-site before the cleaned grain was taken on to the site. This is confirmed by the high proportions of grain compared to the other parts of the crop plant and other weed seeds, though differential carbonisation may account for absence of certain crop parts (Boardman and Jones 1990). Drying the barley, to remove the hulled material, occasionally led to unintentional carbonisation, as did cooking accidents.

2. *The aquatic faunal evidence*

The fish remains recovered at Cnip and Beirgh, show that both marine and freshwater habitats were exploited (Fig. 66). At Beirgh, the Primary Cellular Phase produced sufficient fish remains to allow a comprehensive analysis (Cerón-Carrasco 2002) while at Cnip, the Cellular Phase produced most of the fish remains from the site. The analysis suggests that fishing was primarily for small-scale subsistence. The main species exploited was saithe (*Pollachius virens* L.) and both first and second year fish were taken. These would have been easily caught from rocky locations from the safety of the shore, with many of the other marine species accidentally taken (Fig. 66). Young saithe are found close inshore particularly during their first two years. Their growth averages 15 cm annually for the first three years. Size analysis of the bones demonstrates that they were caught throughout the year rather than in a single short season. The saithe present in these assemblages were specimens measuring 15-30 cm in length.

The rocky shore environment appears to have been exploited at both sites, though freshwater species were more common at Beirgh than at Cnip. Salmon (*Salmo salar* L.) and trout (*Salmo trutta* L.) may have been caught by hook or by using traps or nets in the streams and lochs. Salmon and sea trout may also have been caught at sea from the shore. Human groups in the Outer Hebrides, as elsewhere in Scotland, have exploited salmon and trout. These species however have not played a greater role in the economy of the islands in the past probably due to the variety, abundance and availability of marine species (Campbell and Williamson 1979).

Another important indicator of marine exploitation derives from the molluscan remains. The most common species represented at Cnip was the common limpet *(Patella vulgata* L.) and the edible periwinkle (*Littorina littorea* L.). Limpets are widely found on all rocky shores throughout the Scottish coast, and have been traditionally used as bait and as food. The edible periwinkle is found in rockpools along the shoreline and was probably gathered by hand. At Beirgh edible mussels (*Mytilus edulis* L.), were the most common species present. It is worthy of note that mussels have not only been used as food but also as bait for sea fishing, in particular for trout and eel (*Anguilla anguilla* L.), both of which

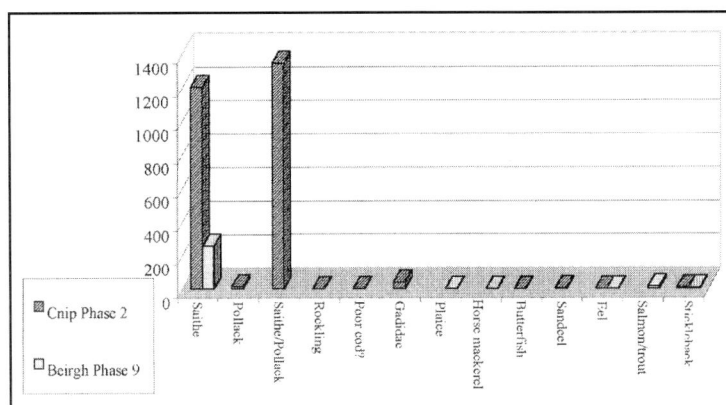

Fig.66 *The fish remains recovered from Cnip and Beirgh.*

were present at Beirgh. Other edible molluscs recovered were the common oyster (*Ostrea edulis* L.) and the razor shell (*Sollen marginatus* L.).

By examining the marine molluscs recovered at these sites a range of uses can be identified such as food and fishing bait. Furthermore the presence of other marine organisms such as the sea urchin, a food rich in iron, may indicate that this also served as a useful addition to the diet.

There are also non-edible species present in the assemblages, such as the flat periwinkle (*Littorina littoralis* L.). This species is usually found on rocks as well as seaweed, such as the wracks. A number of other seashell species recovered, *Cingula cingulus* (Montagu), *Rissoa parva* (da Costa) and a tube-dwelling polychaete, *Spinorbis borealis* (Daudin), indicate that these may have arrived at the sites as a by-product of seaweed. Their presence on site, especially in their burnt form at Cnip, has been interpreted as evidence of the burning of seaweed (Cerón-Carrasco forthcoming). The ash of seaweed has a number of uses, including fertiliser; in Martin's accounts (1716) it is also mentioned that the ashes of seaweed served to preserve the meat of seal that was also salted.

3. *The terrestrial fauna and bird evidence*

The four main species retrieved from the excavations were sheep (*Ovis aries* L.), cattle (*Bos taurus* L.), red deer (*Cervus elaphus* L.) and pig (*Sus domesticus* Erxleben 1777). Their relative abundance is shown in Figure 67. The data comes from the final cellular phase at Beirgh (Thoms 2005), the wheelhouse and secondary phases at Cnip (McCormick forthcoming) and a small assemblage retrieved from the underwater contexts at Dun Bharabhat (Gilmour and Cook 1998).

The faunal assemblages from the peninsula are unusual in Late Iron Age Atlantic Scotland because of the high proportions of red deer present within them. McCormick (forthcoming) draws attention to the high number of red deer bones retrieved at Cnip and observes that the exploitation of these animals would allow a greater use of the upland landscape, deer being able to survive on rougher, more exposed ground than the other herbivore species. He further suggests that the red deer may have been managed in some way in the Western Isles in the Late Iron Age.

The term "managed" is deliberately vague but is used in the context of this paper to imply some form of control of the herd. This may be only at the level of restricting its movement (keeping off agricultural land), but conceivably may include controlling population structure by selective culling. The range of ages of red deer present at Cnip and Beirgh argues against a hunting model, where one would expect a selection of one age group. This could either

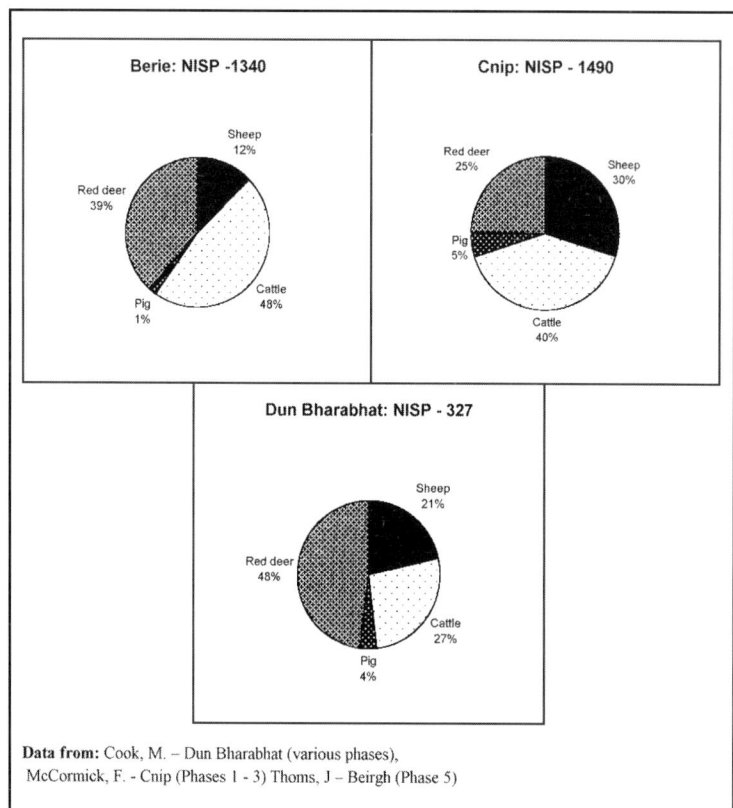

Data from: Cook, M. – Dun Bharabhat (various phases), McCormick, F. - Cnip (Phases 1 - 3) Thoms, J – Beirgh (Phase 5)

Fig.67 *Bhaltos sites: Proportions of species – number of identifiable specimens (NISP).*

be the older, larger, stronger animals, representing an efficient hunting strategy, or symbolic trophy; or, the age group selected could be or the more easily captured younger, smaller, weaker individuals.

Sheep and cattle of all ages, including neonates, were present on both sites indicating they were breeding on or near the sites. As shown above the archaeobotanical evidence suggests that the arable land was predominantly on the machair, therefore the question arises of how the animals were prevented from destroying the crops. This topic has been neglected in faunal studies of Atlantic Scotland, probably because of the difficulties of recognising evidence of animal control in the archaeological record. A number of options exist for animal management, including herding, tethering, or enclosing within walls or fences. Alternatively, the system of transhumance, moving animals and people to temporary summer pasture, may have been in use. These strategies are difficult to spot in the archaeological record. Apart from the danger of animals destroying crops, fragile machair soils are likely to be destabilised by trampling in winter. Due to the unsuitability of the machair land for livestock it seems likely that the upland wet grassland was used for livestock grazing during the summer months. However, the availability of wild plants, including seaweed, along the shoreline and dunes would have provided valuable winter grazing for all herbivores so this may have encouraged, or necessitated, the use of this land despite any erosion damage caused.

The presence of pig is problematic here also, as their foraging behaviour would have been similarly damaging to the sandy soils of the machair. The small quantity of pig in the Bhaltos assemblages suggests that perhaps one or two pigs were kept at a time. These could have been easily restrained by tethering or enclosing.

Animals that can be regarded as non-domesticates, such as cetaceans (whales and dolphins), seals and seabirds are also present in the assemblages of the Bhaltos sites. This indicates opportunistic use of resources such as beached whales, breeding seals and nesting seabirds.

The mixed economies suggested by the range of species present on all sites indicate sustainable use of the surrounding landscape. The exploitation of red deer may be a reflection of this, suggesting the optimum use of higher, poorer quality land, which deer are better able to convert to meat than are cattle and sheep (McCormick forthcoming)

DISCUSSION

The nature of resource exploitation changed slightly from phase to phase and site to site. However, there was a marked similarity between the site assemblages that suggested continuity of economic practice in the study area, over a period of half a millennium. Therefore, the findings from the three sites are integrated to present the general themes of resource exploitation and management for each of the lines of evidence. The first stage in this process involves the formation of a provisional model.

Figure 68 outlines the key economic practices in the area, to form a model of the economic landscape. Exploitation of some resources are indicated by more than one category of evidence, for example seaweed use can be inferred from charred botanical remains as well as by association with small molluscan fauna as described above. This provisional model does not represent landscape reconstruction in the physical and spatial sense, but rather highlights an economic landscape that can be reconstructed to a greater or lesser extent for most sites that produce ecofactual and artefactual assemblages. A reconstruction of the physical economic landscape is only possible through the integration of the off-site palaeoenvironmental proxy records, such as

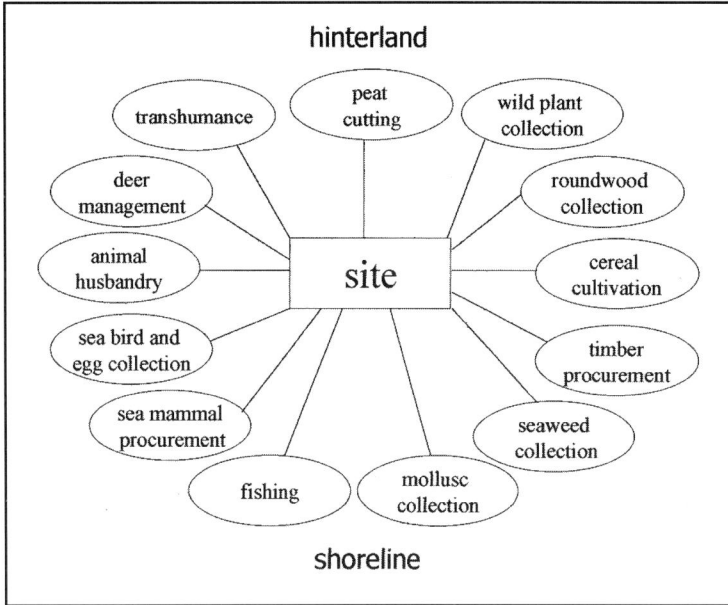

Fig.68 *The theoretical economic landscape.*

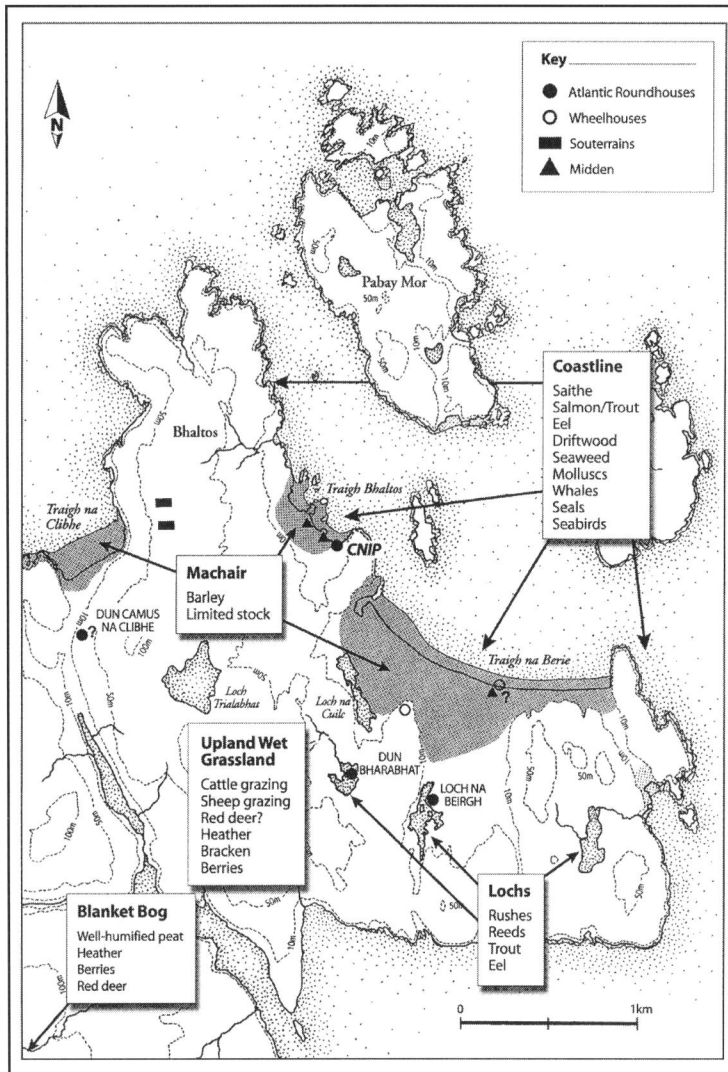

Fig.69 *Landscape reconstruction for the Bhaltos Peninsula. Source: Armit forthcoming.*

pollen. Such integration allows the resources to be placed in their landscape context within the Bhaltos Peninsula and beyond.

Figure 69 demonstrates the likely position for most of the resources within the study area. It can be seen that the rocky shore provides access to many resources: saithe, driftwood, seaweed, molluscs, sea mammals and seabirds would have been harvested from the shoreline. Further inland the machair was used for the cultivation of crops, barley being predominant in the archaeological record, with possible field rotation with limited stock grazing. The numerous lochs could have been harvested for rushes and reeds for bedding and basketwork, as well as being fished for trout and eels. The small copse of mainly Scots Pine near to Dun Bharabhat would have provided some of the structural timber for the sites, with coppiced hazel from an unknown area providing internal furnishings. The upland wet grassland is likely to have provided grazing for stock. These uplands and the moorland provided a wide range of plant resources including heather, various berries, bracken and small shrubs and trees. Movement of red deer is likely to have been restricted to these areas. Finally the moorland provided peat for fuel, and fertiliser from the ash. Although there is no extensive blanket bog on the Bhaltos peninsula itself today, there is easily accessible deep, well-humified peat nearby on the Uig peninsula, which was also the case in the Iron Age (Flitcroft 1997).

The relative contribution of each of these resources to the basic subsistence diet of the inhabitants is impossible to gauge from the palaeoeconomic data alone. This question can only be approached through integration with stable isotope analysis of human remains from the period. For example, measurement of the relative proportions of ^{12}C and ^{13}C gauges the comparative importance of different food types (Richards 2000). Recent work from a small number of burials across Lewis shows a higher proportion of marine foods in the Norse diet compared to that of the Late Iron Age (Montgomery *et al.* 2003.)

The economic landscape as hypothesised above can be regarded as a core area in close proximity to the sites, with a hinterland comprised of the wet upland grassland and the heathland. The core area would have contained most of the staple food sources; the crops, the marine resources and pasture for some of the animal husbandry. The hinterland would not have been as intensively settled and used, but would still have been an important area for peat and plant procurement, summer transhumance and perhaps the management of red deer.

The similarity between the site assemblages suggests a marked degree of continuity of economic practice in the study area, over a period of half a millennium. There is also evidence, from the mineral magnetic analysis of peat ash for example, of repeated localised exploitation throughout this time. This may indicate a formalised division and tenure of the landscape that was established for the Bhaltos Peninsula and which was attached to the site and the region, as opposed to a specific tribal lineage. This continuity of land use and landscape division for both the economic core and hinterland of the sites is consistent with the land inheritance model proposed by Armit (this volume).

This continuity of economic landscape also has implications in terms of the interpretation for the radical changes that occur in the structural and artefactual record from the mid to late Iron Age. Any stimuli that may have been the cause of these fundamental changes are not readily detectable within the palaeoeconomic data. Hence, it may be argued that the reason for such changes must be driven by systems outwith the subsistence based economy. Timber procurement, and any possible associated trade network, is the only area of resource exploitation within the proposed model that could have fluctuated with the changes in structural form. Unfortunately, this topic could not be addressed from the sites investigated due to the nature of the evidence. Whether this timber supply was a cause or effect of the structural change is an important question for future research. The likely presence of *in situ* substantial timber remains from the primary and secondary roundhouses at Loch na Beirgh represents a unique opportunity to address this important issue.

CONCLUSION

An attempt has been made to synthesise the on-site palaeoeconomic evidence from three mid to late Iron Age sites from the Bhaltos Peninsula. A physical landscape and environmental reconstruction has been achieved following integration of landscape proxy records such as that provided by pollen analysis. Four key conclusions can be drawn from this provisional model including;

1. A marked degree of continuity of economic practice existed in the study area, over a period of half a millennium.

2. The relative contribution of each of these resources to the basic subsistence diet of the inhabitants can only be approached through the integration of the palaeoeconomic data with isotopic analysis of human remains from the period.

3. The economic landscape comprised two zones; a core area in close proximity to the sites, with a hinterland of wet upland grassland

and heathland. This suggests, along with other evidence, a formalised division and tenure of the landscape over half a millennium.

4. Any stimuli that may have been the cause of structural changes are not readily detectable within the palaeoeconomic data, except for timber procurement and any possible associated trade network. Therefore, such changes must have been driven by systems outwith the subsistence based economy.

ACKNOWLEDGEMENTS

The authors would like to thank Val Turner for the opportunity to present this paper, Prof. Dennis Harding for the permission to use and amend Fig. 62 and Ian Armit, Finbar McCormick and Tim Lomax for access to unpublished and forthcoming reports. Prof. Dennis Harding and Prof. Ian Ralston, Geraint Coles and Tim Neighbour are also thanked for helpful comments and advice. R.C.C. and J.T. held Historic Scotland Research Studentships and MC held a Caledonian Research Foundation Scholarship. We are also grateful to Historic Scotland for funding the illustrations and Kevin Hicks for illustrating Fig. 69

BIBLIOGRAPHY

Armit, I. (1994) Archaeological field survey of the Bhaltos Peninsula, Lewis. *Proceedings of the Society of Antiquaries of Scotland* 124 (1994), 67-94

Armit, I. (1996) *The Archaeology of Skye and the Western Isles*. Edinburgh, Edinburgh University Press.

Armit, I. (forthcoming) *Anatomy of an Iron Age Roundhouse: the Cnip Wheelhouse Excavations, Lewis.*

Armit, I. and Dunwell, A. (1992) Excavations at Cnip, sites 2 and 3, Lewis. *Proceedings of the Society of Antiquaries of Scotland* 122 (1992), 137-48

Birks, H. J. B. (1994) Floristic and vegetational history of the Outer Hebrides. In Pankhurst, R. J. and Mullin, J. M. (eds) *Flora of the Outer Hebrides*, 32-38. London, HMSO.

Boardman, S. J. and Jones, G. E. M. (1990) Experiments on the effects of charring on cereal plant components. *Journal of Archaeological Science* 17, 1-11

Brayshay, B. A. and Edwards, K. J. (1996) Lateglacial and Holocene vegetational history of South Uist and Barra. In Gilbertson, D. D., Kent, M. and Grattan, J. P. (eds) *The Outer Hebrides: the Last 14000 Years*, 13-26. Sheffield, Sheffield Academic Press.

Campbell, R. N. and Williamson, R. B. (1979) The fishes of inland waters in the Outer Hebrides. *Proceedings of the Royal Society of Edinburgh* 77B, 377-393.

Cerón-Carrasco, R. (forthcoming) The fish and molluscan remains from Cnip. In Armit, I. (forthcoming) *Anatomy of an Iron Age Roundhouse: the Cnip Wheelhouse Excavations, Lewis.*

Cerón-Carrasco, R. (2002) Of fish and men' ('*De iasg agus dhaoine*'): Aspects of the utilization of marine resources as recovered from selected Hebridean archaeological sites. Unpublished PhD thesis, University of Edinburgh.

Church, M. J. (1996) *The Development of a Regional Framework of Archaeobotanical Research for the Island of Lewis, Scotland*. Unpublished B.Sc. (Hons.) Dissertation, University of Edinburgh.

Church, M. J. (2000) Carbonised plant macrofossils and charcoal. In Harding, D. W. and Dixon, T. N. *Dun Bharabhat, Cnip, an Iron Age Settlement in West Lewis: Volume 1, structures and material culture*, 120-130. Calanais Research Monograph No. 2, Edinburgh, University of Edinburgh.

Church, M. J. (2002) Archaeobotanical Considerations of the Conflagration in Dun Bharabhat, Lewis. in Ballin Smith, B. and Banks, I. (eds.), *In the Shadow of the Brochs*, 67-75, Stroud, Tempus.

Church, M. J. (forthcoming a) The physical, chemical and magnetic analysis of the soils. In Armit, I. *Anatomy of an Iron Age Roundhouse: the Cnip Wheelhouse Excavations, Lewis.*

Church, M. J. (forthcoming b) Carbonised plant macrofossils and charcoal. In Armit, I. *Anatomy of an Iron Age Roundhouse: the Cnip Wheelhouse Excavations, Lewis.*

Church, M .J. and Peters, C. (2000) Sedimentary analysis of soil samples. In Harding, D. W. and Dixon, T. N. *Dun Bharabhat, Cnip, an Iron Age Settlement in West Lewis: Volume 1, structures and material culture,* 114-119. Calanais Research Monograph No. 2, Edinburgh, University of Edinburgh.

Flitcroft, C. (1997) *A Preliminary Investigation of the Environmental History of the Loch Ruadh Guinnerso Area, North West Lewis.* Unpublished B.Sc. (Hons.) Dissertation, University of Edinburgh.

Fossit, J. A. (1990) *Holocene Vegetation History of the Western Isles, Scotland.* Unpublished PhD thesis, University of Cambridge.

Gilmour, S. M. D. and Cook, M. (1998) Excavations at Dun Vulan, a reinterpretation of the reappraised Iron Age. *Antiquity* 72 (1998), 327-37.

Harding, D. W. (2000) *The Hebridean Iron Age: Twenty Years' Research.* University of Edinburgh, Dept. of Archaeology, Occasional Paper Series No. 20.

Harding, D. W. and Armit, I. (1990) Survey and excavation in West Lewis. In Armit, I. (ed.) *Beyond the Brochs; Changing Perspectives on the Later Iron Age in Atlantic Scotland*, 71-107. Edinburgh, Edinburgh University Press.

Harding, D. W. and Dixon, T. N. (2000) *Dun Bharabhat, Cnip, an Iron Age Settlement in West Lewis: Volume 1 – The structures and material culture.* Calanais Research Series No. 2. University of Edinburgh, Dept. of Archaeology.

Harding, D. W. and Gilmour, S. M. D. (2000) *The Iron Age Settlement at Beirgh, Riof, Isle of Lewis: Excavations, 1985-1995 – Volume 1: The structures and stratigraphy.* Calanais Research Series No. 1. University of Edinburgh, Dept. of Archaeology.

Jones, M. (1991) Sampling in palaeoethnobotany. In Zeist, W. van, Wasylikowa, K. and Behre, K. E. (eds.) *Progress in Old World Palaeoethnobotany*, 53-62. Rotterdam, Balkema.

Lomax, T. M. (1997) *Holocene Vegetation History and Human Impact in Western Lewis, Scotland.* Unpublished PhD thesis, University of Birmingham

Lomax, T. M. and Edwards, K. J. (2000) Pollen and related studies of human impact at Loch Bharabhat. In Harding, D. W. and Dixon, T. N. *Dun Bharabhat, Cnip, an Iron Age Settlement in West Lewis: Volume 1 – The structures and material culture.* Calanais Research Series No. 2, University of Edinburgh, Dept. of Archaeology, 110-13.

Martin, M. (1716) *A Description of the Western Isles of Scotland.* London, Mercat Press.

McCormick, F. (forthcoming) The mammal bones from Cnip wheelhouse, Lewis. In Armit, I. *Anatomy of an Iron Age Roundhouse: the Cnip Wheelhouse Excavations, Lewis.*

Montgomery, J., Evans, J. A. and Neighbour, T. (2003) Sr isotope evidence for population movement within the Hebridean Norse community of NW Scotland. *Journal of the Geological Society, London* 160, 649-653.

Pankhurst, R. J. and Mullin, J. M. (1994) *Flora of the Outer Hebrides*. London, HMSO.

Peters, C., Church, M. J. and Mitchell, C. (2001) Investigation of domestic fuel sources on Lewis using mineral magnetism. *Archaeological Prospection* 8, 227-237.

Peters, C., Church, M. J. and Batt, C. (2004) Application of mineral magnetism in Atlantic Scotland archaeology 1: techniques, magnetic enhancement and the identification of fuel sources, In Housley, R. and Coles, G. M. (eds.) *Atlantic Connections and Adaptations: Economies, Environments and Subsistence in Lands Bordering the North Atlantic*. Oxford, Oxbow Books.

Richards, M. (2000) Stable isotope analysis in archaeology: a short introduction. *The Archaeologist* 38 (2000), 19-20.

Ritchie, W. (1985) Inter-tidal and sub-tidal organic deposits and sea level changes in the Uists, Outer Hebrides. *Scottish Journal of Geology* 21/2 (1985), 161-176.

Skinner, H. (1995) *An Assessment of the Role of Ethnographic Parallels for the Elucidation of Land Use and Settlement Patterns of the Atlantic Iron Age in Lewis and Harris*, Unpublished MA (Hons.) Dissertation, University of Edinburgh.

Thoms, J. E. (2005) *Aspects of Economy and Environment in North West Lewis in the First Millennium AD: the non-marine faunal evidence from Bostadh and Beirgh considered within the framework of North Atlantic Scotland*, Unpublished PhD thesis, University of Edinburgh.

Animals and Ambiguity in the Iron Age of the Western Isles

JACQUI MULVILLE & JENNIFER THOMS

INTRODUCTION

THE PAPERS in this volume have demonstrated that architecture, chronology and interaction between the different types of Iron Age settlements in the Western Isles remain a source of considerable debate. This paper will use the faunal assemblages from these sites to consider possible cultural and regional variation.

During the Iron Age, there were settlements throughout the Isles and these ranged from the large, tower-like brochs to the semi-subterranean wheelhouses (papers this volume). The individual islands that make up the archipelago all have their own characteristics, varying in size from the large area of Lewis and Harris down to the tiny island of Mingulay. All the islands present a mosaic of habitats from the machair to the peaty moorland, however the sites discussed here are all located on machair land. In this location the calcium rich sediments afford excellent preservation and this has resulted in abundant animal bone evidence.

Zooarchaeological analysis of this evidence provides information on the exploitation and consumption of animals. We can discover if animals were farmed, caught or traded with other sites, identify the season of occupation and the nature of the economic strategies pursued. It is also possible to examine the role that animals played in addition to the provision of food. The use of animals as symbols and metaphors has been discussed by a number of authors (e.g. Douglas 1996) and most recently for the Iron Age by Hill (1995). Animal bones should not be considered in isolation. Their spatial and temporal relationship, both within a site and to other artefacts, can allow us to draw conclusions on the purpose and meaning associated with their use or deposition.

PREVIOUS WORK

Previous faunal work has suggested a difference in food procurement between two of the main types of Iron Age structures in South Uist: wheelhouses and brochs (Parker Pearson *et al.* 1996; 1999). These two distinct types of site had different relative proportions of animals present, suggesting differential access or attitudes to resources. Conversely, Cerón-Carrasco *et al.* (this volume) have proposed that, in the Bhaltos peninsula, north-west Lewis, there was little variation in resource exploitation patterns between the different structural types in that region.

Animals in the Iron Age

Many attempts have been made to characterise Iron Age animal usage; the most recent is Hambleton's review of Britain (1999). On mainland Britain the majority of assemblages from the Neolithic onwards are dominated by domestic species, with very little fish, bird or wild mammal present. This has led to a focus on animal husbandry, with comparisons between sites concentrating on the differing proportions of the main domestic food animals, cattle, sheep and pig (e.g. Hambleton 1999). A similar initial approach is taken here to facilitate comparisons with other British Iron Age sites. Although the Iron Age in Scotland continues much later than that of other parts of Britain, the authors feel it is valid to consider the Western Isle data in this manner to place the islands in context.

The Western Isles however differ from the rest of mainland Britain in the significant contribution made by captured, rather than farmed, animals. The dataset for land mammals is available and we can consider the role of the dominant captured animal, red deer, in addition to the domesticates. The dataset for other major wild resources, the marine mammals, fish and birds, is incomplete, and it is not yet possible to draw firm conclusions on the contribution of these species.

Western Isles data

There are few published animal bone reports from the Western Isles available. To date only eight of the eighteen sites have been published in any form, and four of these very recently (A'Cheardach Mhor, Young and Richardson 1960; A'Cheardach Bheag, Fairhurst 1971; Northton, Finlay 1984; Sollas, Finlay 1991; Dun Vulan, Mulville 1999; Pabbay, Sanday and Mingulay, Mulville 2000).

The data from Beirgh and Bostadh derive from preliminary analysis of faunal material undertaken as part of doctoral research (Thoms 2005). The analysis of data from sites at Cladh Hallan, Kildonan and Bornish is still in progress although preliminary reports dealing with part of these sites are available (Ul Haq 1989; Hanshaw-Thomas 1991; Mulville 1997; 1999 in prep a, b and c; Scales 2001). The remainder of the site data is derived from unpublished specialist reports, some of which should be published soon, for example Baleshare, Hornish Point and Cnip (Halstead in press; McCormick 1991), whilst for others there is no publication timetable at present (Udal, Serjeantson n.d.). With so many of the

sites not yet in a state of published completion the results presented in this paper must be regarded as preliminary.

There are a number of differences between the sites that could be considered. The topography and geology of most of the sites are similar but the date and definition of many of the sites are still under debate (see below). As a result this initial comparison can only focus on regional differences to be found in Iron Age material.

METHODOLOGIES

Quantification

Data obtained from a bone assemblage varies between workers and between sites, but the initial stage of the analysis always involves identifying them to skeletal element and species as far as possible. As the number and nature of further observations vary between workers, this paper focuses on the most basic data category – the relative proportions of the species present at each site. This is quantified as the number of identifiable specimens (NISP) meaning the number of bone fragments that can be identified to a species. Obviously many other questions can be addressed through this data analysis, but these lie outside the scope of this paper.

Analytical strategy

The majority of zooarchaeological analysis is focused on the exploration of catching or farming strategies and has as its focus food production. This approach is problematic when dealing with the material present on site because it could be used for artefact production or be placed in a 'ritual' context. For example, antler is a particular problem. Shed antler is generally collected for tool production and its presence on site cannot be taken to signify the capture of deer, nor the use of their meat, hide etc. The analytical divide between shed/unshed antler and worked/ unworked material can lead to problems in quantifying antler and understanding the contribution that deer make to artefact and food production. The presence of numerous animal burials at Sollas (Campbell 1991), the human and animal burials at Hornish Point (Barber *et al.* 1989) and the deer jawbone kerb at A'Cheardach Bheag (Fairhurst 1971) all influence the relative proportions of species present. In the analysis of sites with a ritual element it is usual to consider such burials separately. Unfortunately the data available to the authors does not allow such exclusion, and the assemblages must be considered as a whole.

Preservation and recovery

The degree to which any assemblage represents animal use is also affected by variation in preservational conditions and recovery between archaeological sites. All the sites mentioned in this paper have excellent preservation, with the fragile bones of very young and very small animals present. Recovery, across many of the sites, has been through a standard approach of blanket sieving. A number of the sites have not had

similar treatment and the implication of this variation is discussed later.

Samples size

Further complications can be brought about by problems with small unrepresentative assemblages. Hambleton (1999) has suggested that the optimum sample size for a comparative study of species proportions in British Iron Age faunal assemblages is a total NISP of greater than 300. A number of the sites included in this survey fall under this number, most notably the sites of Northton, Sollas site B, A'Cheardach Mhor and A'Cheardach Bheag and the tiny site from Mingulay. However as a number of these sites have aspects that are of interest to this debate and fall within the general spread of Iron Age data from the Isles (see below), they will be considered, but with reservations.

RESULTS

Table 16 shows the sites from which the assemblages considered here derive. Many are multi-period sites demonstrating the practice,

	Region	Site type	Date (bones)
Bostadh	Gt Bernera, Lewis	Cellular	400 - 900 AD
Cnip	W Lewis	Wheelhouse	
Beirgh	W Lewis	Cellular	200 - 500 AD
Northton	Harris	Middens	'Iron Age'
Udal	North Uist	Wheelhouses	'Iron Age'
Sollas - A	North Uist	Wheelhouse	c. 100 AD
Sollas - B	North Uist	Wheelhouse	c. 100 AD
Baleshare	North Uist	Wheelhouse	'Late Iron Age'
Hornish Point	South Uist	Wheelhouse & middens	199 BC - 20 AD
A' Cheardach Mhor	South Uist	Wheelhouse	'Late Iron Age'
A' Cheardach Bheag	South Uist	Wheelhouse	'Late Iron Age'
Dun Vulan - midden	South Uist	Midden	100 - 400 AD
Dun Vulan - 'platform'	South Uist	Structures associated with broch	200 - 600 AD
Kildonan	South Uist	Wheelhouse	225 - 1030 AD
Bornish	South Uist	Cellular	400 - 500 AD
Cladh Hallan	South Uist	Domestic structure	'Late Bronze Age'
Pabbay	Pabbay Island	Complex Atlantic roundhouse	100 - 900 AD
Sandray	Sandray Island	Midden	'Iron Age'
Mingulay	Mingulay Island	Midden	'Iron Age'

Table 16 *Sites mentioned in the text.*

common in Atlantic Scotland, of reusing the site, and the building stone, many times. Where dates have been given they relate only to the contexts from which the faunal assemblages have derived. In many cases the authors do not know the precise date of the contexts from which the bones have been retrieved. In such instances an approximate term ('Iron Age') is used. The laxity of this approach is acknowledged, but it seems unavoidable while awaiting the full publication of these sites.

Animal husbandry

Fig. 70 shows the assemblages from the Western Isles within the wider setting of the British Iron Age (after Hambleton 1999). The tripolar graph indicates the relative proportions of cattle, sheep and pig for sites with over 300 NISP. The majority of Western Isles sites fall within the normal range of variation. In Fig. 71 the Western Isles sites are identified by island group. Overall the main difference in domesticates comes from an apparent higher proportion of cattle at the more northerly sites and the predominance of sheep on Pabbay.

The abundance of cattle in the North may be a result of recovery bias. Beirgh was excavated over several seasons and in only one season of excavation was a policy of total bulk sampling employed. In this all material was sieved (mesh sizes of 10 and 2mm) to facilitate the retrieval of small bones. At Bostadh total sampling was undertaken for the entire

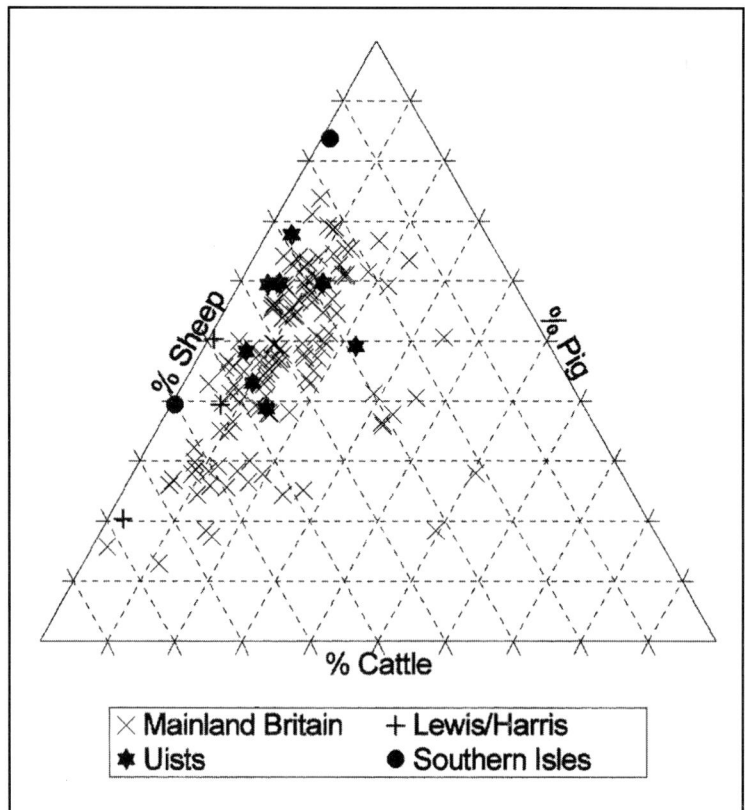

Fig.70 *Percentages of cattle, sheep and pig in faunal samples NISP from Iron Age site in the Western Isles compared with sites in mainland Britain.*

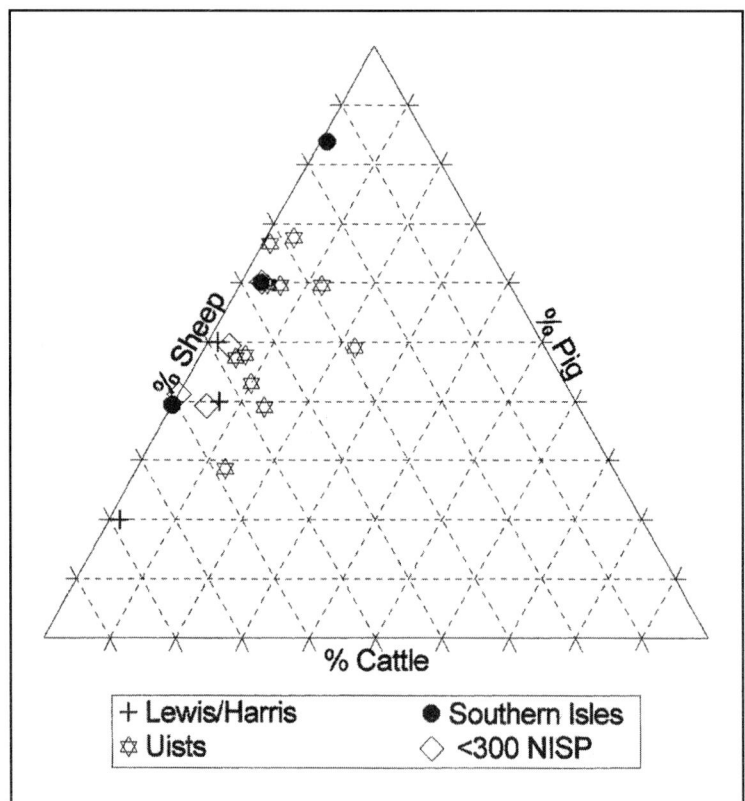

Fig.71 *Percentages of cattle, sheep and pig NISP in faunal samples from Iron Age sites in the Western Isles, by island group.*

assemblage, with a resulting increase in the proportion of smaller material. This could account for the higher proportion of cattle relative to sheep and pig at Beirgh. If we exclude Beirgh from the analysis the difference between the sites falls within the normal range of variation.

The sheep dominated assemblage at Pabbay mostly consists of extremely young sheep and cattle. This has been interpreted as a reflecting only part of the animal economy. The adults are missing from the assemblage suggesting the importation of infants onto the site or the disposal of adults outside the excavated area (Mulville 2000). It is possible that this strange pattern is a result of the small area of land available to farm, however the two other small island sites, Sandray and Mingulay, have proportions of species more similar to those found on other Iron Age sites. This suggests that the size of the island is not the only factor in determining animal husbandry.

Table 17 illustrates the relative proportions of sheep, cattle, pig and deer present on the sites under consideration. In this we can see that the most striking variation in animal exploitation is the strong presence of red deer in the sites on the 'long island' of Lewis and Harris. They are present in smaller numbers on the southern sites and almost completely absent on the very small southernmost islands.

The assemblage from Northton should be treated with caution, due to its small size (Finlay 1984), but it does reflect the larger quantities of red deer present in the north of the

	Sheep	Cattle	Pig	Deer	NISP
Bostadh	37	36	1	27	1273
Berie	12	47	1	39	1337
Cnip	30	40	5	25	1489
Northton	7	10	0	83	259
Udal	59	36	4	1	2305
Baleshare	59	34	6	1	2040
Sollas Site A	67	28	4	1	557
Sollas Site B	38	55	5	2	255
Hornish Point	59	28	12	1	440
A'Cheardach Mhor	59	36	3	2	223
A'Cheardach Bheag	43	41	3	13	68
Kildonan	42	46	10	2	4665
Dun Vulan Midden	48	28	22	3	569
Dun Vulan Platform	39	47	14	1	2313
Bornish	43	41	6	10	732
Cladh Hallen	62	30	1	7	889
Pabbay	83	15	1	0	2278
Mingulay	39	60	0	0	415
Sandray	60	37	3	0	144

	Sheep	Cattle	Pig	Deer	NISP
Bostadh	469	455	7	342	1273
Berie	167	634	19	517	1337
Cnip	442	600	81	366	1489
Northton	19	26	0	214	259
Udal	1362	832	97	14	2344
Baleshare	1206	696	119	19	2040
Sollas Site A	374	158	20	5	558
Sollas Site B	98	139	14	4	257
Hornish Point	260	123	53	4	440
A'Cheardach Mhor	131	81	7	4	223
A'Cheardach Bheag	29	28	2	9	68
Kildonan	1961	2132	460	112	4665
Dun Vulan Midden	272	158	123	16	569
Dun Vulan Platform	892	1080	327	14	2313
Bornish	317	297	43	75	733
Cladh Hallen	555	266	9	59	889
Pabbay	1900	342	29	7	2278
Mingulay	163	249	2	1	415
Sandray	87	53	4		144

Table 17 *Relative Proportions of Species (NISP) from the Western Isles.*

archipelago. Sites further south have demonstrably fewer deer present, with two exceptions – A'Cheardach Bheag and Bornish. At the former the figures for red deer are boosted by the inclusion of the deer jawbone kerb, at the latter there is no such explanation. The deer bone present at Bornish is mostly limb bones, however the wide range of body parts present indicates that complete animals were being brought onto site.

Red deer

The fact that red deer are present at all is worthy of note, as it raises the question of how they got to the Isles. The islands are considered to have been cut off from the mainland of Scotland since before the last Ice Age, which together with their distance from the mainland and inner islands (25km at closest point, using 'island hopping') implies that all mammals have been introduced by humans (Serjeantson 1990). There is some evidence that this may have occurred very early, as pollen analysis has indicated the presence of large herbivores on the Western Isles in the Mesolithic (Edwards and Whittington 1997). Red deer are the most likely grazing animals in this period. Serjeantson (1990) argues convincingly for the introduction of red deer by humans in the early prehistoric period. Antler may have been a vital resource and red deer provided an important backup food reserve in times of scarcity (*ibid.*).

Deer bones are present on all Western Isles sites for which faunal evidence is available, from the Neolithic onwards (McCormick and Buckland 1997). However, early sites are rare and the sparse information available suggests that the number of deer contained within the assemblages increased in the Bronze Age. Evidence from the study of one of the Late Bronze Age sites at Cladh Hallan shows that deer are present at a relatively high proportion for the Uists (Mulville in prep. a; Mulville and Parker Pearson 1997). Further excavation of

the settlement has allowed one of the authors (Mulville) to note that this predominance of deer also occurs in the earlier phases of the settlement.

There is evidence for a breeding population of deer throughout the larger islands, with neonatal deer present on a number of sites. On South Uist this evidence can be found in the Bronze Age, being noted at Cladh Hallan (Mulville in prep. a.). In the Iron Age, sites in the north of the archipelago, Bostadh, Cnip and Beirgh have evidence of red deer breeding locally. Further south, there was little unfused (immature) bone present at Dun Vulan (Mulville 1999), but there is evidence for young and neonatal red deer at the nearby site of Kildonan (Mulville in prep. b.) with more unfused deer bone at Bornish (Mulville in prep. c.). There is no evidence, either in numbers or in age class, for a breeding deer population on the small southerly Isles. These islands are so small it is unlikely that a red deer herd could have existed, and the deer on these sites would have been trade items.

The bones of older deer are also present in the Western Isles assemblages. These, together with the young and neonatal bones, indicate that the procurement of red deer did not focus on prime animals. Young animals in particular provide little meat, and in an optimising model would not be considered worth pursuing for food.

However it is possible that the young animals were not being hunted for the volume of meat they provide and other products, such as their spotted hides, may have made them valuable (Rowley-Conwy 1999). It is possible they provided by-products not available in adult animals, a modern parallel being rennet, obtained from calves. They may have been considered "worth" hunting for sport, or they may have had symbolic value. Alternatively, the presence of the very young and the very old could be the result of population control suggesting the active management of the deer by humans.

Legge (1981) and Clutton-Brock (1984) and most recently Sharples (2000) have discussed deer management in the Neolithic. For the Iron Age the control and use of deer has not been extensively studied, although for the Western Isles various authors have considered the interaction between humans and deer (Serjeantson 1990; Parker Pearson *et al.* 1999; McCormick 1991; Cerón-Carrasco *et al.* this volume).

The extent of human control, or management, of the deer is difficult to ascertain from the archaeological record. The term management can cover a multitude of practices, from keeping herds separate from crops to controlling their numbers by culling or selective breeding. The deer were also a source of antler, and as such could have been closely observed in order to collect the shed antler before destruction (Legge 1981; Clutton Brock 1984). It is notoriously difficult to physically restrict the movement of red deer today, arguably because fences are the main control method used. In the past other methods may have been employed, such as restricting their presence to certain islands or using people and dogs to herd them or drive them away from the crops. The social behaviour of red deer, living in herds segregated by age and sex, and outside the breeding season, being neither territorial nor aggressive, would suit them to living in the relatively restricted environment of an island (e.g. Rhum). In medieval England these same behavioural traits meant the deer were well adapted to royal hunting parks (Clutton-Brock 1987, 183).

SPATIAL DIFFERENCES IN DEER UTILISATION

As noted above we have evidence for a breeding population of deer throughout the larger islands, so deer were available. Until recently it was only on sites on Lewis that appreciable quantities of deer have been recorded. This led to the suggestion that the distribution of deer is related to type of land present on the different islands (McCormick n.d.) with the availability of good grazing on the machair on the Uists and Udal allowing domestic stock to flourish. Conversely, in certain parts of Lewis the inhabitants had to rely on deer. However the site at Bornish throws these conclusions into doubt as at this site there is a relatively high proportion of deer. Additionally much of the bone present is from prime meat bones, similar to the situation prevailing on Lewis.

It has also been suggested that the proportion of deer on different sites reflect regional cultural differences, however as yet we have been unable to find a clear regional pattern. Indeed the different proportions of deer at Dun Vulan and at Bornish, sites very close to each other, argues against regionalism either in cultural choice or economic practice.

We do however have plenty of evidence for the special role deer played in the Western Isles. Deer are the only directly representational motifs found in the islands; found on pottery at Kiphaeder wheelhouse on South Uist (Lethbridge 1952) and on a wooden handle from Dun Bharabhat on Lewis (Armit 1996). The presence of a deer jawbone hearth kerb at A'Cheardach Bheag (Fairhurst 1971) supports a symbolically important role for these animals. These mandibles derive mostly from adults and represent an abundance of prime meat, from at least nine animals. On this site, where little other deer bone was retrieved the placing of deer around the central hearth is of significance. However, without more evidence of the consumption of meat from these animals, understanding the role deer played in food provision is difficult. It is true that on some sites the bone evidence suggests their consumption (e.g. Beirgh, Bostadh, Cnip and Bornish) whilst at others the lack of prime meat bones had led to suggestions that they were consumed away from the site (Dun Vulan).

We know that deer were not treated in the same manner as other domestic species. They are excluded from the several examples of deposits of animals in pits set in or below house floors (Barber *et al.* 1989; Finlay 1984; 1991; Mulville *et al.* 2003). All are domestic species and no deer have yet been found in such contexts, suggesting deer lay outside the domestic context. For example, Ross (1967) brings together evidence that deer were considered in the Iron Age to be capable of shape-shifting, forming a liminal category between the living and the supernatural worlds.

To examine the role of red deer in the wider context of prehistory we have to look outside the Western Isles. We have evidence from Orkney that during the Neolithic deer also held an ambiguous role. Deer bone was excluded from domestic contexts (Sharples 2000), and meat was possibly consumed away from settlements. By the Bronze Age deer bones were present on settlement sites (Smith and Mulville 2004). Sharples (2000) also identified a difference in the treatment of bone and antler on Orkney/Southern Britain and to an extent this is also seen at Cladh Hallan. Here although both bone and antler were present on site, only antler was found in structured deposits. Antler was placed in disused postholes within the house, although deer did not appear in any of the accompanying animal burials. Of course having to compare so few sites over a wide geographical region is unsatisfactory and we need good quality data from more sites. The Iron Age appears to reflect the evidence from the Bronze Age and the Neolithic with deer bone excluded from some Iron Age settlements, but present on others. As in the earlier periods deer are still excluded from structured deposits.

What is most intriguing is the lack of patterning in domesticates or deer relating to settlement type; although with only a few different types of settlement represented and, with problems with dating them, any comparison is problematic. To further explore these ideas we need to undertake a much more detailed contextual comparison of the animal bone between the different sites once analyses are completed. The Iron Age attitude to deer therefore remains unclear. What is of interest is the ambiguity that the various sites reveal, reflecting perhaps the ambiguous nature of deer in Iron Age society. They are neither wild nor truly domestic, managed but not farmed.

CONCLUSION

This paper set out to look at the relationship between animals, architecture and environment in the Iron Age and for a variety of reasons this attempt has failed. We have however begun to draw together the material from all the Western Isles Iron Age sites and to consider them in their geographical and chronological context.

We have found little variation in the use of domestic species seen on the Western Isles sites considered here. If we exclude the smallest isles, for domestic stock management the Western Isles fall within the range of Iron Age sites in the rest of the UK. Instead it is the use of wild resources that defines the Western Isles attitude to animals. It is not yet possible to compare in detail the contribution that the whole range of faunal resources make to an individual site, however as a first step we can look at the differences in one wild species, red deer.

At first glance deer seem to define the island groups, and as such these differences appear to be related to the environment. However a closer reading of the data reveals a far more complex picture. Deer breed throughout the Isles and, although present on all sites examined they are used to a greater extent and lesser extent at different sites. Their ambiguous role sees them managed and controlled, bought on to some sites as food, but featuring in the archaegological remains retrieved from other sites rarely and mostly as antler or waste bone. Although we contest the environmental determinist viewpoint for the role of deer, we cannot as yet exclude a difference related to settlement type, culture or chronological detail due to the lack of suitably precise data for the Iron Age. We also need to undertake detailed contextual analysis of deer, and all other species, at the different sites. By looking in greater detail at the spatial distribution of deer classified by body part, size, age, sex and in their association with other material we should be able to further understand the use of deer in the Iron Age.

By looking back into the archaeological record we find that at least since the Neolithic deer have had held this complex position. Atlantic Scotland is unique in the reliance on red deer in later prehistory and we are only at the beginning of investigating their role. This paper has arguably raised more questions than it has answered. However, the presence of so many large, carefully excavated sites located on similar landscapes will allow us an unprecedented level of analysis. With the full publication of these sites it is anticipated that more data will become available, allowing all lines of evidence more fully integrated.

BIBLIOGRAPHY

Armit, I. (1996) *The Archaeology of Skye and the Western Isles*. Edinburgh, Edinburgh University Press.

Barber, J., Halstead, P., James, H. and Lee, F. (1989) An unusual Iron Age burial at Hornish Point, South Uist. *Antiquity* 63, 773-778.

Campbell, E. (1991) Excavations of a wheelhouse and other Iron Age structures at Sollas, North Uist, by R. J. C. Atkinson in 1957. *Proceedings of the Society of Antiquaries of Scotland* 121, 117-173.

Clutton-Brock, J. (1984) *Excavations at Grimes Graves, Norfolk, 1972-76, fasc. 1: Neolithic Antler Antler Picks from Grames Graves, Norfolk, and Durrington Walls, Wiltshire – a Biometric Analysis*. London, British Museum.

Clutton-Brock, J. (1987) *A Natural History of Domesticated Mammals*. Cambridge, Cambridge University Press and the British Museum.

Douglas, M. (1966) *Purity and Danger: An Analysis of Concepts of Pollution and Taboo*. London, Routledge and Kegan Paul.

Edwards, K. J. and Whittington, G. (1997) Vegetation change. In Edwards, K. J. and Ralston, I. B. M. (eds.) *Scotland: Environment and Archaeology, 8000 BC-AD 1000*, 63-82. Chichester, Wiley.

Fairhurst, H. (1971) The wheelhouse at A'Cheardach Bheag on Drimore machair. *Glasgow Archaeological Journal* 2, 72-110.

Finlay, J. (1984) *Faunal Evidence for Prehistoric Economy and Settlement in the Outer Hebrides to c.400 AD*. Unpublished PhD thesis, University of Edinburgh.

Finlay, J. (1991) The animal bone. In Campbell, E. Excavations of a Wheelhouse and Other Iron Age Structures at Sollas, North Uist by R J. C. Atkinson in 1957. *Proceedings of the Society of Antiquaries of Scotland* 121, 117-173, fiche 1:D-3F10.

Hambleton, E. (1999) *Animal Husbandry Regimes in Iron Age Britain*. British Archaeological Reports British Series 282. Oxford, Archaeopress.

Hanshaw-Thomas, J. R. (1991) *Kildonan, South Uist: faunal analysis*. Unpublished report, University of Sheffield.

Halstead, P. J. (in press) The mammal bones. In Barber, J. *Bronze Age Farms and Iron Age Farm Mounds of the Outer Hebrides.* Edinburgh, Scottish Trust for Archaeological Research Monograph 4.

Hill, J. D. (1995) *Ritual and Rubbish in the Iron Age of Wessex: a Study on the Formation of a Specific Archaeological Record.* Oxford, British Archaeological Reports (British Series) 242.

Legge, T. (1981) The agricultural economy in Grimes Graves, Norfolk. In Mercer, R. J. (ed.) *Excavations at Grimes Graves, Norfolk, 1971-72, vol. I*, 79-103. London, HMSO.

Lethbridge, T.C. (1952) Excavations at Kilphaeder, South Uist and the problem of the brochs and wheel-houses. *Proceedings of the Prehistoric Society* 18, 176-93.

McCormick, F. (1991) *The mammal bones from Cnip wheelhouse, Lewis.* Unpublished report.

McCormick, F. and Buckland, P. C. (1997) Faunal change: the vertebrate fauna. In Edwards, K. J. and Ralston, I. B. M. (eds.) *Scotland: Environment and Archaeology, 8000 BC-AD 1000*, 83-103. Chichester, Wiley.

Mulville, J. (1997) Animal bones. In Sharples, N. *The Iron Age and Norse Settlement at Bornish, South Uist: an interim report on the 1997 excavations.* School of History and Archaeology, University of Wales Cardiff, Cardiff Studies in Archaeology, Specialist Report Number 4.

Mulville, J. (1999) The mammal bone. In Parker Pearson, M. and Sharples, N. with Mulville, J. and Smith, H. *Between Land and Sea: Excavations at Dun Vulan, South Uist.* S.E.A.R.C.H. Volume 3. Sheffield, Sheffield Academic Press.

Mulville, J. (2000) The mammal bone from Pabbay, Mingulay and Sandray. In Brannigan, K and Foster, P (eds.) *From Barra to Berneray: the Archaeology of the Southern Isles of the Outer Hebrides Volume 4.* Sheffield, Sheffield Academic Press.

Mulville, J., Parker Pearson, M., Sharples, N., Smith, H. and Chamberlain, A. (2003) Quarters, Arcs and Squares: Human and Animal Remains in the Hebridean Late Iron Age. In Downes, J. and Ritchie, A. *Sea Change: Orkney and Northern Europe in the Later Iron Age AD 300-800* 20-34. Balgavies, Angus, The Pinkfoot Press.

Mulville, J. (In preparation a.) *The animal bones from Cladh Hallan.*

Mulville, J. (In preparation b.) *The animal bones at Kildonan, South Uist.*

Mulville, J. (In preparation c.) *The animal bones from Bornish.*

Mulville, J. and Parker Pearson, M. (1995) *The Late Bronze Age / Earliest Iron Age house at Cladh Hallan, South Uist: excavations in 1995.* Unpublished report, University of Sheffield.

Mulville, J. and Parker Pearson, M. (1997) *A Late Bronze Age / Early Iron Age roundhouse at Cladh Hallan, South Uist: excavations in 1997.* Unpublished report, University of Sheffield.

Parker Pearson, M., Sharples, N. and Mulville, J. (1996) Brochs and Iron Age Society: a reappraisal. *Antiquity* 70, 57-67.

Parker Pearson, M., Sharples, N. and Mulville, J. (1999) Excavations at Dun Vulan: a correction. *Antiquity* 73, 149-52.

Parker Pearson, M. and Sharples, N. with Mulville, J. and Smith, H. (1999) *Between Land and Sea: Excavations at Dun Vulan, South Uist.* S.E.A.R.C.H. Volume 3. Sheffield, Sheffield Academic Press

Ross, A (1967) *Pagan Celtic Culture*. London, Routledge and Keegan Paul.

Rowley-Conwy, P. (1999) Economic prehistory in Southern Scandinavia. In Coles, J., Bewley, R. and Mellars, P. (eds.) *World Prehistory: Studies in Memory of Grahame Clark*, 125-160. London, British Academy.

Scales, R. (2001) *The study of a Prehistoric Animal Bone Assemblage from Cladh Hallan, South Uist*. Unpublished MSc Dissertation. University of Sheffield.

Serjeantson, D. (n.d). Mammal, bird and fish remains from the Udal (North), N.Uist: Interim. Unpublished report.

Serjeantson, D. (1990) The introduction of mammals to the Outer Hebrides and the role of boats in stock management. *Anthropozoologia* 13, 7-18.

Sharples, N. (2000) Antlers and Orcadian Rituals: An Ambiguous Role for Red Deer in the Neolithic. Ritchie, A. (ed) *Neolithic Orkney in its European context*. Cambridge, McDonald Institute Monograph Series.

Smith, H. and Mulville, J. (2004) Resource Management in the Outer Hebrides: An assessment of the faunal and floral evidence form archaeological investigations. In Housely, R A. and Coles, G. (eds) *Atlantic Connections & Adaptations: Economies, Environments and Subsistence in the North Atlantic*. AEA Symposia No. 21. Oxford: Oxbow Books.

Thoms, J. (2003) *Aspects of Economy and Environment of North West Lewis in the First Millennium AD: the Non-marine Faunal Evidence from Bostadh and Beirgh Considered Within the Framework of North Atlantic Scotland*. Unpublished PhD thesis, University of Edinburgh.

Ul Haq, S. (1989) *Remains of mammalian fauna from Kildonan, South Uist, Outer Hebrides*. Unpublished report, University of Sheffield.

Young, A. and Richardson, K. M. (1960). A'Cheardach Mhor, Drimore, South Uist. *Proceedings of the Society of Antiquaries of Scotland* 93: 135-173.

A Military Assessment of the Defensive Capabilities of Brochs

Ian Blythe

INTRODUCTION

MUCH HAS been written and discussed about the purpose of the brochs, with theories being put forward which include that they were status symbols, strongholds, refuges or domestic accommodation. Some more recent works have sought to establish the broch as just one manifestation of what has come to be known as the Complex Atlantic Roundhouse (see Armit 1990 and this volume) and, since other examples of that form of structure, like the wheelhouse, had little or no potential defensive capability, it could be argued that the broch tower by analogy should be not be considered as a fortification. The archaeological validity of the arguments for such consideration of the brochs' purpose and function are well outside the scope of this paper, but some of the discussions have seemed to be in danger of, what is called in military circles, 'situating the appreciation'. In other words, in their anxiety to establish the broch as a domestic structure, some authorities have ignored the broch's defensive capabilities or even argued that some of the features more usually seen as giving the broch tower defensive strength are in fact weaknesses so serious that they preclude its being considered as any form of fortification.

During this conference the discussions touched on the defensive nature of brochs, but there was insufficient time to develop the arguments to any great extent. The aim of this paper is to take those discussions further forward and to examine, from a military viewpoint, the defensive capabilities of the broch towers in the context of the threats which they would have been likely to have to face when they were built.

DEFENSIVE STRUCTURES

Before looking at brochs specifically, it is necessary to make some general points about defensive structures. Throughout history, fortifications have been constructed to fulfil a wide range of military aims and this diversity of purpose has resulted in differing characteristics being incorporated into their design and location. The applicability of each of these criteria to a specific fortification will depend on what the structure is required to do and what threat it is expected to face. In assessing the defensive capability of any structure, it needs to be recognised that many design features which are essential in other examples of fortification may not be significant in the context under review. This caveat is particularly important when looking at early structures, such as brochs, where the absence of more sophisticated defensive features does not necessarily mean that the structure was not built as a fortification.

The most basic form of fortification is that intended to provide protection to its occupants when faced by a force which is superior in numbers, in armed strength and/or in skill at arms. In terms of modern warfare, the slit-trench is such a structure giving, in its most simple form, some limited protection against artillery, mortar or aerial bombardment. It does not provide invulnerability but does give a greater chance of survival against those threats than would remaining in the open. Despite its obvious shortcomings, the slit-trench is clearly a defensive structure, albeit a simple one whose basic design is capable of considerable development to achieve the sort of complexity that was seen on the Western Front during the First World War. That example is quoted to re-emphasise that simplicity and obvious shortcomings in design do not preclude the primary purpose of a structure having been defensive.

No matter how a fortification is designed it should never be assumed to be totally impregnable; it will, to a greater or lesser extent, have weaknesses which can be exploited by an attacking force and which may result in the structure being overrun or destroyed, given that the potential attacker has the will and the time to achieve his aim. Thus, merely because a particular structure has demonstrable weaknesses, again it should not be assumed that its purpose was not, at least in part, defensive.

Determining the effectiveness of any fortification should include an assessment of the threat which it is intended to meet but, in the case of the broch, the archaeological evidence does not provide any information on what sort of threat had to be faced, or even if any such threat existed. However, there are some indications that conflict was a feature of life in Iron Age Scotland; artefacts such as spears, swords, axes and arrow-heads are all found within Iron Age contexts and all could have been used as weapons. Equally, most of them could have other purposes such as hunting, but the sword has little or no practical purpose other than as a weapon. It can, of course, be a symbol of status but it seems unlikely that it would be chosen for such a purpose in a society that did not have at least a memory of conflict. For the purposes of this paper, which does not seek to establish that the

brochs were built to provide defence, only that their design gave them a defensive capability, it is not necessary to establish either the existence or the nature of any threat but, based on admittedly limited evidence, it does not seem unreasonable to assume that Iron Age society was not entirely pacific. Having made that assumption, it seems more likely that any threat would be from lightly armed marauders rather than highly organised and disciplined forces with the capability of waging prolonged siege operations.

As well as considering the threat, any examination of the defensive potential of the brochs should also take into account the probable military capabilities of those who would form the defending force. As with the attacking force, there is very little available archaeological evidence on which to base such an assessment and, in its absence, it is probably safest not to attribute any great degree of military sophistication to the defenders. On that basis, it is assumed in this paper that the original inhabitants of the brochs and their surrounding areas are unlikely to have been an organised military force, but were farmers with neither the weapons nor the skill in their use to permit more than fairly rudimentary operations probably directed towards self-preservation. Some, perhaps the more important members of their community, would have had swords but the majority would have had little more than improvised weapons or even farm implements similar to the more modern axe or billhook types. In military terms, they would probably have been little more than a disorganised rabble, with very little capability of coordinated defensive action, and for whom offensive operations would have been largely impossible. This assessment has had to be largely conjectural, but attributing a minimal military effectiveness to the defenders means that any inaccuracies in it would result in an under-estimate of how well a broch might be defended, rather than exaggerating the brochs' defensive potential. While not of direct relevance to the aim of this paper, it should perhaps also be noted that the likely deficiencies in the defenders' military skills and equipment would necessitate their finding some form of protection if they were to be able to survive even a very limited attack.

BROCHS AS DEFENSIVE STRUCTURES.

In denigrating the defensive capabilities of the broch, much has sometimes been made of their almost invariably having only one entrance. One of the weak points of any fortification is its entrance or entrances. The mediaeval development of such additional strengthening measures as barbicans, drawbridges, murder holes and portcullises are all examples of the recognition of the vulnerability of the entrance. What then would be the purpose of additional entrances to a broch? Certainly, if counter-attack is seen as a viable tactic in securing a fortification, then alternative exits allowing the defenders to sally forth and launch attacks on the flanks of the besieging force would be important features, as can again be seen in the architecture of mediaeval castles. Assuming the broch defenders to be a group of ill-armed farmers, their emerging from within the broch to launch an attack over open ground would have been more likely to be suicidal than offering any military advantage. If counterattack is not a practicable proposition, could an additional entrance have enabled the defenders to creep away at night leaving the attackers to besiege an empty tower? A few athletic defenders might be able to escape in that way but for the majority which would have presumably included women, children, the old and less agile, to say nothing of livestock and other impedimenta, avoiding detection and massacre would have been impossible, given that the perimeter around a broch, even allowing for the besiegers wishing to remain out of bowshot, would have been little more

than 1000m. If an additional entrance to a broch would have weakened its defensive strength without offering either any compensating practicable tactical advantage or practicable means of escape, it is difficult to see how the absence of such entrances lessens the possibility of the broch having defence as part of its purpose.

Since 1947 some writers have suggested that brochs could not have had a defensive purpose because they are often located on flat ground when better defensive positions are available nearby (Scott, 1947). If a fortification is intended to dominate its neighbourhood, or provide the base from which offensive action against intruders is to be launched, then its positioning on high ground is important. Equally, locating so that its position is not overlooked would have military benefits where bombardment by any form of artillery, even of the most primitive rock projecting kind, is a likely threat. However, if a structure is intended to provide shelter for a population with little offensive military capability against a lightly armed attacking force, then having such shelter as close as possible to the area of daily work may well outweigh the advantages of an apparently better defensive position further away. Thus the location of brochs in inferior defensive positions should perhaps be taken as an indication of the type of threat faced, and the capabilities of their defenders, rather than demonstrating that their purpose could not have been defensive.

The lack of archaeological evidence for any attack on a broch, or of its destruction by offensive action, is often put forward to refute the existence of a threat with the corollary that the purpose of the broch could not have been defensive. In fact, two broch sites do exhibit signs of successful attack, namely Leckie Broch in Stirlingshire (Mackie 1985) and Dun Ardtreck in Skye (Mackie 2002), but this destruction may well be late in the history of the broch and there is no evidence discovered so far of any successful attacks occurring at a time when brochs were first being built. A somewhat simplistic response to this lack of evidence of offensive action has been that the strength of the broch was such that all potential attackers were deterred from making an assault and went off in search of easier objectives, leaving the brochs in peace. Examination of fortifications throughout history tends to undermine confidence in the idea of a defensive strength so great that it acts as a complete deterrent against any form of attack.

The lack of evidence of offensive action against the brochs does not necessarily mean that such attacks never occurred. Had some brochs been successfully attacked but, because the attackers wished to make use of the structures' strength after gaining control, they neither used fire as a weapon, nor burnt the broch after ousting the original occupants, very little archaeological evidence of the attack would be likely to have survived and what there was could have been destroyed by subsequent occupation. There are also numerous examples of defensive structures that have been built to counter a threat which did not, in the event, materialise. Martello Towers built to counter a Napoleonic invasion of England and the pill boxes and other defence structures built around the British coast at the start of the Second World War are but two examples of undoubtedly defensive structures which never came under any form of direct attack. For these reasons, and bearing in mind the relatively small number of brochs which have been fully excavated and the present ruinous state of many examples, the absence of confirmed attacks on brochs should not be considered as conclusive evidence of there having been no threat against them and certainly cannot be a basis for saying that they had no defensive capability.

One way to assess the defensive capability of a fortification is to examine its weaknesses to determine how best an attack might be launched against it. Such an assessment would be the basis of modern military planning and would include an evaluation of the chances of success against the likely costs in terms of casualties and equipment losses. Such a detailed military planning process is beyond the scope of this paper but a simpler examination of the possible weak points of a broch could throw some light on its defensive strengths and weaknesses. In making this assessment, the possible existence of defensive outworks has been ignored since, where they existed, they merely increased the defensive depth of the fortification rather than changing the basic strength of the broch tower itself, although it must be said that the discovery of substantial earthworks and ditches around some broch sites lends weight to the theory that their purpose could have been defensive.

Assuming that time is not of the essence, and a relieving force is not likely to arrive before the broch falls, starving the defenders into submission would allow the broch to be captured with the minimum of casualties in the attacking force. Although a blockading siege has its attractions, it would be a prolonged process given that the defenders could well have pre-stocked the broch with both food and water. Even without such stocks, any animals taken into the broch would be a potential source of food for the defenders while rainfall, which is not an infrequent occurrence in the Atlantic region of Scotland, would help delay thirst driving the defenders into submission, even after any stocks of water had been exhausted. Thus while a broch, like any fortification, is vulnerable to blockading tactics, they are applicable only where the attackers are prepared and able to devote a considerable period of time to achieving their aim, and the arrival of a relieving force is not likely to occur. In the context of the Iron Age, extended siege operations could well be seen as being rather less likely than opportunistic hit and run raids, possibly in search of those traditional incentives for armed conflict – rape and pillage.

It has also been suggested that a broch could not be defended since it could too easily be set on fire and that its structure would result in any such fire being intensified to the point where the broch would behave like a blast furnace (Fojut this volume). Since, with the entrance passage blocked by its door, the broch is effectively a vertical cylinder open only at its top end it is difficult to see how a forced draught would be present to produce anything approaching the conditions required for a blast furnace. It could also be noted that the presence of hearths within many brochs would seem to indicate that fires in the broch's interior were entirely controllable, even with the door opened. Having said that, if any internal wooden structures or roofs could be set on fire, while not necessarily resulting in the immediate incineration of the occupants, falling timbers and blazing debris would be a significant hazard and could make the interior of the broch untenable. Nevertheless, the practicalities of setting the interior of a broch on fire are not without difficulties.

It has been suggested that arrows with some form of burning material attached to them could be shot over the wall and into the interior of the broch (Sharples, this conference) although, it has to be said, without much attention being paid to the problems associated with the procedure. The range of such an arrow would be considerably less than that of its unencumbered counterpart; thus the attacking archers have to be well within bowshot of the defenders before they could launch their projectiles. In addition, the acceleration of the arrow through the air would incur the risk of its fire being extinguished before it reached its target, to say nothing of the possibility of serious burns to the archer's leading hand, ie the one holding the bow and supporting the front end of the

250

arrow. Even those arrows which reached their target would be unlikely to cause a major problem unless they landed in some highly inflammable material, like bone-dry thatch, and even then only if the defenders failed to take any action to extinguish them before the fire could take serious hold. The use of green wood or stone for the broch's internal structures, and turf or skins as roofing rather than thatch, would reduce the risk of a major fire to negligible proportions.

On the basis that any potential attacker is unlikely to have the capability to carry out a prolonged siege, and setting a broch on fire is considered to be difficult with little risk of any resultant conflagration developing into blast furnace proportions, these options are not examined further. The option of gaining entrance through subversion or subterfuge is also ruled out, since the defenders are likely to be members of a close-knit community with a high degree of common purpose and interests, and a Trojan Horse type operation appears to be overly fanciful. Thus any attacking force intent on capturing a broch is faced with getting over, through, or under the walls in order to achieve its aim. The structural strength of the broch precludes any attacker breaching or undermining its walls unless he had siege equipment comparable to that used by the Romans but for which there is no archaeological evidence in the Scottish Iron Age. It would therefore appear that the only viable options for a potential attacker are to gain access through the entrance or to carry out an assault over the walls.

As has already been pointed out, one of the weak points of any fortification is its entrance or entrances; the broch is no exception and its single entrance, even though secured by a wooden door fastened by a substantial bar, represents the most attractive way of gaining access to the interior in force. Having said that, the difficulties of breaching the door and, having done so, assaulting the interior of the broch through the narrow entrance passage should not be under-estimated. The door could be battered down but again the narrowness of the entrance passage will complicate the operation. In addition, the battering force will be vulnerable to attack from above from any defenders on the wallhead using bows and arrows, spears or even stones from the upper courses of the wall itself. Firing the door is assessed as possible but is likely to take a considerable time, not least because much of the heat from a fire lit in the entrance passage will be dissipated outwards and upwards rather than against the door itself. The defenders could also prolong the operation by blocking their side of the entrance passage with stones or earth, cooling the inner face of the door with water, or even attempting to douse the fire with water from either the wallhead or poured through the lintel stones over the entrance passage, although these last courses of action are not without certain practical difficulties from the defenders' point of view. If fire is used to breach the door, the final assault is likely to be complicated by the walls of the entrance passage having reached a very high temperature before the door is burned through.

Whatever means is used to obtain access, the final assault through the entrance passage and into the broch's interior is almost certain to involve heavy casualties in the attacking force. Entry will be impossible for more than one, or possibly two, men at a time, and even a poorly armed and ill-trained defending force will take a severe toll, while access becomes further impeded as the internal end of the passage is blocked by the dead and dying from both sides. This attrition will continue until the defenders can be driven back from the inside end of the entrance passage, thus allowing new waves of attackers to deploy into the interior of the broch before having to engage the defenders. Thereafter, the assumed military

superiority of the attacking force should enable them to subdue the defenders with the minimum of further casualties.

The potentially high cost in terms of casualties of a direct assault through the entrance to the broch necessitates examination of an alternative course, either as the principal means of assault, or as a diversionary tactic. The classic way to capture any fortification is by carrying out an assault over the walls. More recent siege operations usually attempted to facilitate such assault by breaching the wall but without even primitive artillery, or any form of siege train, battering down the walls of a broch is almost certainly not practicable. Nevertheless, an assault over the walls of a broch could be achieved although, given the height of many of the broch towers, some form of climbing equipment or scaling ladders would be essential. The use of ropes attached to grappling hooks, which would be thrown over the wall, is not considered practicable since the dry stone construction of the broch would mean that any such hook would be unlikely to find a secure hold at the wallhead. Some form of scaling ladder is a possibility, but ten metre or longer scaling ladders are not something that a marauding force is likely to carry around with it. A free climb up the broch's walls by individual attackers is also just feasible, although getting sufficient numbers of attackers on to the wallhead to secure it against counter-attacks seems to be problematic. Whatever form of assault is used, such tactics would involve heavy casualties if the defenders made any attempt to man the wallhead and resist the assault by firing arrows or dropping stones on those scaling the walls, but that cost could be considered worthwhile since, once the attackers had gained control of the wallhead, the broch would quickly become indefensible since it would be relatively easy to smoke the defenders out or to facilitate an assault through the entrance passage by firing arrows at, or dropping stones on the defenders.

Of the practicable means of assaulting a broch which have been examined in the foregoing paragraphs, all are greatly simplified if the defenders make no attempt to man and defend the wallhead. It is a well established military principle, that no barrier or defensive structure is likely to be effective in halting an attack unless it is covered by some form of offensive counter-action, and brochs would have been no exception to that rule. No broch retains its upper courses today and any assessment of the existence and nature of wallhead defensive arrangements must be conjectural. The most complete existing broch tower at Mousa in Shetland has an intra-mural staircase extending to its upper courses and evidence of a walkway and parapet, but Mousa has other features which are not common to all brochs and the existence of such defensive features there cannot be read across to argue that all brochs were so designed. Indeed it has been argued that, in many brochs, there would have been insufficient space between the inner and outer walls for an intra-mural staircase to extend to the top of the wall (conference discussion). Such an assessment has to make assumptions about the original height of the broch, and further assume that the angle of batter on the outer wall was continued to the top, rather than the upper courses of the outer wall being of vertical construction. It also begs the question of the purpose of the numerous examples of intra-mural staircases which extend well above the first scarcement level. Such matters are more the realm of an archaeological discussion rather than a military assessment but, even if intra-mural staircases did not in all cases give access to the wallhead, there is no reason to suppose that defenders could not reach that point by using wooden ladders from inside the broch. Quite aside from any possible defensive requirements, access to the wall head from inside the broch would have greatly simplified the building and maintenance of any roof which may have been present.

In summary, a military analysis of the brochs' defensive capabilities shows that, even taking the worst case where the occupants use the broch merely as a shelter and take no active steps to defend themselves, the structure would provide a reasonable measure of protection against lightly armed raiders who were intent on carrying out a hit and run attack but were either not prepared or not able to undertake more complex offensive operations. Assuming that the occupants were outnumbered or faced with a superior force in terms of skill at arms or equipment, sheltering in a broch would significantly improve their chances of survival. If the attackers were more determined and equipped to gain entry through the broch's entrance passage, or by assaulting its walls, the occupants of the broch would have to man and defend the wallhead if they were not to be overwhelmed, but without detailed knowledge of the strength and capabilities of both the attacking and the defending forces, it is not possible to assess accurately the length of time that a defending force would be able to hold out. Given that the defenders, despite lacking military skills and equipment, appreciate the importance of securing the wallhead and are able to man it accordingly, the probable length of time required to take the broch, and the large number of casualties likely to be incurred by the attackers in the process, would probably deter all but the most determined and well-equipped attacking force. The attacking force would also have to consider that taking the broch was of sufficient advantage to justify the effort required. In view of the lack of information available on relative military capabilities, and the aims of any operations against a broch, it is probably safest to restrict conclusions to saying that the strength of a broch would enable its occupants to resist effectively an attack from a force against which they would have stood little chance in open conflict, and thus the broch must be considered as having an effective defensive capability.

While this paper has argued that the broch tower, while certainly not impregnable, had the potential to provide very effective defence against most threats that it was likely to have had to face in the Iron Age, it has quite deliberately not sought to extend those arguments to make a case for the primary purpose of brochs having been defensive. Such an assessment would need to be supported by archaeological evidence obtained from more detailed excavation than most brochs have undergone. The design features, such as the massive construction and probable height of the walls, the narrow entrance passage with a strongly barred door and the frequent occurrence of what appear to be outer defensive works are all entirely consistent with the broch towers having been built as a fortification, but it is also conceivable that they were provided for some other purpose and that their defensive strength is merely fortuitous. What is beyond question is that the builders of

the brochs went to considerable trouble and effort to provide a structure which possessed the features that are seen today and, from a military viewpoint, the need to provide protection would be a convincing reason for such dedication of time and resources.

REFERENCES

Armit, I. (1990) Broch-building in Northern Scotland: the context of innovation. *World Archaeology* 21 (3), 435-445.

MacKie, E. W. (1985) The Leckie broch, Stirlingshire; an interim report, *Glasgow Archaeological Journal* 9, 60-72.

MacKie, E. W. (2002) Excavations at Dun Ardtreck, Skye, in 1964 and 1965. *Proceedings of the Society of Antiquaries of Scotland* 130 (2000), 301-411.

Scott, W.L. (1947) "The problem of the brochs" *Proceedings of the Society of Antiquaries of Scotland* 13 (1947), 1-37.

What Use Are Brochs?

Ian Tait

THEORIES abound as to the use of brochs: defensive castles, strategic lookouts, domiciles. One thing, however, is beyond doubt – they were a very useful source of rubble to plunder in the centuries after the Iron Age.

Brochs fall into ruin – their potential is realised

By the advent of Norse settlement in Shetland around AD 800, a good few brochs had probably been diminished in size by the building of nearby townships. This pattern continued after the Vikings' arrival, as houses came to be larger. There can be little doubt that Mousa was always a superlative broch; it is the only one in Shetland which features in the *Sagas*, and there Moseyarborg merits two mentions. It was used as a shelter by an eloping couple around AD 900, after their ship was damaged en-route from Norway to Iceland (Egil's Saga: Thorsson and Scudder 2001). In AD 1153 *Jarl* Harald Maddadarson wasn't able to take it by attack when an enemy of his named Erlend had eloped with Harald's widowed mother Margaret and stayed in the broch as a stronghold (Orkneyinga Saga: Anderson 1999) (Plate 15).

An inspiration for place names

It is as a root of place names that we have the most enduring evidence of brochs' influence on the Norse. *Borg* signified fortification, and the components Burra-, -broch, -burgh, Burga-, Burgi-, and Bur- are as widespread as the brochs themselves:

Burravoe, Railsbrough, Scousburgh, Burga Water, Burgi Geos, Burland. Not all are necessarily brochs, some are forts.

STOCKPILES OF BUILDING RUBBLE

A broch represented a ready supply of stones for any prospective builder – infinitely preferable to new quarrying. The relative convenience of this rubble can often be judged by the completeness of the broch. Brochs at a place where many buildings were subsequently built have often virtually disappeared. There are many such examples, such as: Brough, Bressay; Scousburgh, Dunrossness; Islesburgh, Northmavine. In the case of the first two, centuries of house and outbuilding construction have completely destroyed the brochs, whereas at Islesburgh many years of development of one farmstead has wiped out the broch. The premium stones sought in erecting a new building were long ones, for use as window, door and fireplace lintels, but the availability of such stones was often very limited if the local geology wasn't right. It has been said that if these stones could be secured, then any project could go ahead (Robbie Arthur pers. comm.). One could be sure that the broch builders would have secured all the best large stones they could, so when a lintel was needed it was often to a local broch that men went to quarry. It is with some dubious pride for me that the handiwork of some of my own ancestors at the East Burrafirth broch in Aithsting was noted by the Royal Commission in the 1930s: "*Of recent years it has been used as a quarry, with the result today it is little more than a site,*

Fig. 72 *Burland, Sandwick, around 1910. A substantial broch surviving in the distance, despite several generations of dwellings, outhouses and dykes being built nearby.*

marked by a heap of debris about 6ft high" (RCAHMS 1946).

There are, however, some paradoxical survivals. Some brochs can be found in remarkably good preservation, despite being near to extensive conglomerations of buildings and dykes, e.g. Burraness, Yell, or Burland, Sandwick (Fig. 72). The latter still stands to 12 feet (4m) at best. Of the broch at Burraness it was written in 1774: *"This Brough is now in the midst of a field of Corn, which surrounds it on all sides, and reaches to the very brink of the rock, not even having a path, so confined are the Schetlanders in soil proper for raising this scarce article"* (Low 1774). A century later there were to be radical changes at Burraness. Nonetheless, such monuments would be all the more impressive today had the later building not taken place. Where the broch was more distant from houses, stones might still be taken from it for smaller vernacular structures, for example the *krø* (sheepfold) at Hawksness, Tingwall, which is sheltered under the lofty broch mound. Even the broch at Burgastu, at Busta Voe in Delting, which consists of little more than a steep-sided islet, was home to an otter trap (in the past this site has been wrongly questioned as an antiquity, but besides the place name evidence for a broch, there is a causeway, and ancient

pottery has been found in the past few years). Most unexpectedly intact is Clickhimin, now hemmed-in by housing and having lost its causeway due to drainage in 1874. Naturally, when houses were being built, stones were taken from various brochs to erect the buildings nearby. However, in one notable case at Dunrossness a house was placed on top of a broch. This was in 1605 when Earl Patrick Stewart had a new wing built onto his mansion at Sumburgh, the new block straddling the broch wall (Hamilton 1956). The broch and wheelhouses here had become entirely subsumed by sand-blow and the builders likely did not know there was a broch under the house.

The scale and form of re-use depending on the type of ancient monument is also of interest. The surviving Neolithic houses in Shetland are usually quite remote from recent settlement, so later structures are often on a small scale (e.g. kale nurseries, *krobbs* or crubs). Brochs, however, are often near to settlement, so, although much larger than houses, they can be more prone to obliteration. One could not, though, say this is a general trend because many a Shetland broch is well out of the way of houses. Nonetheless, it is less common to see a *krobb* built out of a broch site (such as at

Kettlester, Yell) than it is to find one on top of a Stone Age house.

Not all edifices built from broch rubble were secular, for a few churches made use of them too. In medieval times a great many townships had their own chapel, so it could be expected that where houses were built from a ruined broch, so too was the church. At Culbinsbroch in Bressay (evidently, in Norse times, someone called Kolbein held this ruined broch) the St. Mary's Kirk was built next to the broch around the 12th century (Cant 1976). Although the graveyard wall has been subsequently remodelled, doubtless there was also a dyke, similarly made possible because of the broch. A new parish church for Nesting was built in 1790 between Brettabister and Housabister (Plate 16). Here, the broch was an unexpectedly important influence on the siting of a major building; rather than the stones being transported away, it was decided to build the church close to a sizeable broch. This location was away from the pre-Reformation church site, at Kirkabister, and didn't really make the church any more convenient for the populace. As the new church took form, the old broch right behind it diminished accordingly. You couldn't find a better example clearly showing a single-phase destruction of a broch. Nothing is left of the broch at Vidlin, Lunnasting, partly because a Methodist chapel was built there in the 19th century, placing the church in easy sea access.

ECONOMIC DEVELOPMENT – NEW PRESSURE ON BROCHS

The above form of age-old plunder was a gradual affair, as houses and outbuildings were remodelled over the years. I contrast this with a new pattern in the 18th/19th centuries, when the growth of mercantile activity had a knock-on effect on some brochs as they were selected as the source of stones for some project or other, or as an obstacle to be removed.

In 1790 William Mouat, the proprietor of Burravoe, Yell, was anxious to retain the broch there, not out of any antiquarian interest but because it was otherwise useful to him. Mouat was protective of *"The Body of the Picts house called the Brough, which is his Rabbit warren and on which stands his Skeo"* (Sheriff Court papers: Shetland Archives SC12/6/1790/12/4). The most determined efforts to put a broch to use could be the one at Cuppister, Yell. In 1821 many depredations were done, on the orders of the proprietor of Burravoe, Robert Bruce, in order to improve sheep grazings. Bruce *"caused a great quantity of stones that were lying about to be thrown over the banks facing the west in order to allow the grass to grow"* (Thomas Mathewson c.1880: Shetland Archives D1/259/15). This was the most lamentable of pretexts for destruction, but the broch of Cuppister was further damaged when it came in handy for a building project later in the same century. William Pole was the merchant at Burraness, Delting, and he wanted to erect a warehouse there. The nearest large-scale supply of rubble was over Yell Sound, at the broch of Cuppister. Rafts were used to float the stones, which are recorded as being of "a great quantity", over the dangerous Sound to Burraness (T. Mathewson c.1880 *ibid.*).

The commercial fishery which the landowners developed as a policy in the late 18th century involved catching white fish and salting and drying them on beaches. The dried fish needed to be kept inside, so a *bød* (booth) had to be constructed to keep them in. Several boats fished from the Westing, Unst, there not only being *bøds* on Unst proper, but also a large one on the Brough Holm. The broch on that island was so vast that not only was it sensible to put a building there – taking the building to the rubble, as it were – but the boats' crews were still able to plunder hundreds of tons of stones from the unfortunate monument to use as ballast (Spence 1899). At Fethaland, Northmavine, the largest of these fishing stations, an Iron Age site of some kind was virtually eradicated to get stones to build the "lodges" that the crews lived in. At one time it was reputed to be a broch, although this is now dubious, but I mention it nonetheless as the principle of re-use is comparable.

As population grew in the later 18th century, there was more house-building pressure. The landlords of Shetland wanted to earn more money from fish exports, and in order to achieve this they encouraged families to settle on their estates. For the first time settlement spread into peripheral areas, hitherto unattractive for raising crops. A classic example of this is the little croft at Sandsting, beyond the age-old settlements of Culswick and Sotersta. Built under the shelter of the broch, the homestead, naturally enough named Brough, was put up from stones pillaged from the site. The transportation of stone would have been far easier than in most cases – tumbling them down the slope would have sufficed – and because no-one had lived here before, there was an unlimited supply of really useful rock. Low, writing in 1774, notes simply, and with feeling, that the broch would have stood as entire as when it was completed *"had it not been that many of the stones have been removed for house-building"* (Low 1774).

Another broch, the one at Burraness, Yell, unexpectedly fell foul to a different tenurial policy of a landowner – evictions for sheep. During the 19th century some townships had their tenants cleared so that the land could be run as a sheep farm. This usually meant that the centuries-old remodelling of buildings stopped, as the land lay desolate. The Garth estate manager John Walker masterminded several clearances, the evictions at Burraness taking place in 1868. As was the case with other cleared districts, he had a large enclosure built at Burraness to cater for the sheep work. In other clearances of his in Yell he had crofthouses demolished to make an enclosure at the nearby Kirkabister, or cleared buildings

were converted as at Westafirth. At Burraness the houses and outbuildings were remodelled into a large sheepfold, the shortfall of stones being made good by taking from the broch. In the 1770s it survived to around 20 feet (7m) high (and may well still have done today), but in the 1870s only 16 feet (5.5m) was left, not to mention 450 sheep and no people (Gear 1996).

Not all landlords were so cruel – to people that is – but to be cruel to brochs is a different matter. Whilst on some estates people were thrown off for sheep, in other places the proprietor's policies improved the township for the benefit of his tenants. One such was John Scott who found the broch at Estasetter, Sandness a very handy source of rubble for a building project of his - so handy that the location of the broch must have partly dictated the course of his dyke. A local man, Robert Jamieson, wryly wrote that the broch: *"has been in its day a gigantic building, double walled, chambered like a bee-hive and fitted up with every convenience"*. About 1840 the laird of Melby used the stones of it in building about three-quarters of a mile of dyke six feet in height, and left *"as many stones as would build a castle."* Having described how all the artefacts found were thrown away, he continues: *"The stones used in the construction of this castle were of large size, and had to be broken up before they could be removed"* (Spence 1899). All was not lost; what was left of the broch was usefully converted to a *krø* around 1960, by building up an inner face to the wall. Some amends had been done, for it made a far better-looking *krø* than it had latterly done a broch. Far more ambitious was the spate of house building arranged by the proprietor of Whalsay, William Bruce, around the 1850s. At Brough, Bruce had the existing houses and outbuildings knocked down and new dwellings built to improved designs, further uphill. So many houses were built, twelve in all, and larger than their predecessors, that an awful lot more stones were needed. The broch there was so high that one could view the sea on the east side of Whalsay from the top of it, so far that Grøf Skerry and the houses at Huxter were seen (Robbie Simpson pers. comm.). The monument was razed to yield up vital building rubble and you won't find much of a broch at Brough today (Fig. 73). It can be seen that this sudden large-scale programme was different to the age-old gradual plunder of a broch, as previously outlined.

In the late 19th century Shetland benefited from the appearance, and spectacular growth of, a new local industry. This was the herring fishery, and in the 1890s and 1900s herring stations were erected quickly in creeks throughout the islands. Wherever there was a suitably sheltered inlet it was likely to be an ideal location to site the jetties, buildings and curing yards that were needed. At Burgo Taing, Northmavine, the broch remains were removed altogether to provide room for the station's various erections, the larger stones of the broch doubtless coming in handy for the making of the bulwark. So complete was the eradication of the broch that the very existence of one has even been questioned (Fojut 1985). However, the facts that the little promontory where the station was built is called Burgo Taing, and the inlet itself is Burra Voe, show there was something of broch-like nature there once. At Heogan, Bressay, the broch there was also totally demolished around the late 19th century to make way for a herring station. Large quantities of stones were shipped from Brough, Burra, the rocks from this broch going to make a pier at Scalloway (Dryden 1890). Given that herring stations were so well distributed in Shetland, it is truly fortunate no more destruction was done to any brochs.

Mention ought to be made here of the fort at the Loch of Huxter, Whalsay. Although not a broch there are similarities of circumstance, and with no doubt whatsoever the fate of the Huxter site would have been the same had it been a broch instead. The fort lies on the opposite side of the loch to the houses, so all that had been removed from it until the mid 19th century were enough stones to make a few *krobbs*. This unique building survived to about 8 feet (3m) high in the 1860s, and a hundred years before perhaps to 12-15 feet (4-5m). However, disaster was to strike, in the form of compulsory education. Very soon after

Fig.73 *Brough, Whalsay, with not a broch in sight. Re-use at its most efficient.*

this came in, a new school was built at Livister, in 1873. To get the new school, this precious monument had more than half its height demolished, so that the upper storey and chambers were lost forever (John Jamieson pers. comm.).

USE OF THE SITE ITSELF

Besides the constituent stones being useful, to be removed for service elsewhere, the broch site itself was often of use. Such a large expanse of stones was put to good use at Burravoe, Delting, where the broch served the local merchant as a fish-drying beach. The broch at Burravoe in Yell was robbed centuries ago, but the denuded mound stands prominent and is easily accessible (Fig. 74). This was an ideal site to build a *skjo*, a building in which to wind-dry meat and fish, the exposed site being ideally set to the task. The broch at Dalsetter, Dunrossness, has a sheep shelter built on top. These stone walls enabled animals to shelter from blizzards; in this case it was handy to have plenty of rubble in one place, so the structure was built where the quarry was. The broch which gave Burraland, Northmavine, its name proved ultimately to be a good site for the erection of a lime kiln (RCAHMS 1946); in these structures builders' lime was made by burning limestone.

Being on high cliffs and hill tops, as many brochs are, they were ideal lookout posts, not just in prehistory. Watches were, at different times in the past, made out over the open sea to spot vessels in distress, or in wartime to guard against enemy ships. Notwithstanding the perilous access over sheer cliffs to get to the broch at Balta, east of Unst, the very commanding outlook one gets from this site was attractive enough for a watch-house to be erected from the broch remains. In the 20th century a Coastguard hut was built at Eshaness, Northmavine, crews scanning the stormy seas from there, by telescope. The hut required situating at a good vantage point, so naturally the broch at Saebreck was its site – where better? The most unusual building in Shetland to be placed atop a broch is in Fetlar. At the eponymously named Brough, besides having its stones removed to build the rambling eyesore that is Brough Lodge, the broch itself has a Victorian folly planted incongruously on top, the castellated tower also being used as an astronomical observatory (Fig. 75). This has to be the oddest thing to be perched on a Shetland broch. There is no fortification at Sumburgh, Dunrossness, today, although it is marked on a map drawn in the late 16th century, captioned "*The ancient fort of Swenbrugh*" (Hondius 1636). The site there,

Fig.74 *Burravoe, Yell, in 1905. The skjo, a building used in drying fish and flesh, can be seen on top of the broch. An exposed windy site such as this was ideally set to the task.*

Fig.75 *The tasteless sprawl that is Brough Lodge, Fetlar, seen in 1945. All this in part made possible by broch rubble. The broch having played its part, a folly-cum-observatory was perched on top of it.*

which seems not to have been a broch anyway (but something more interesting) was inspected by George Low in 1774, and was eradicated when Shetland's first lighthouse was built in 1821. Not quite so severe was the building, in 1909, of the small unmanned lighthouse at Innfield, Delting. The broch there was already somewhat encroached on by a house, but the lighthouse was less subtly erected right on top of the monument (Fig. 76). It was certainly the best site, guarding the mouth of Firths Voe and being visible form a long way off, just as it had done two thousand years before.

NON-DESTRUCTIVE USE

Not all uses of brochs were destructive. They were, by virtue of their prominence from a long distance off at sea, useful as sea marks.

Fig.76 *The lighthouse at Innfield, Delting, built in 1909, on the broch at the entrance to Firths Voe.*

By lining up a broch with a certain hill, a boat's skipper could lead the vessel to a fishing ground. One such is the Brough Holm, Westing, Unst. This broch was used as a mark so as to find a fishing ground called the Burgaskurs, which, as can be seen, likewise took its name from the broch (Spence 1899). Brochs were aids to navigation too; the broch at Culswick, Sandsting, being used as a mark when entering the safe anchorages of Vaila Sound and Gruting Voe. It is illustrated in profile on a chart of 1781, with the information for the master: "*The old Picts Castle on this Hill is a very good mark to sail into Grueting Voe, the entrance of which you will not discover till you are near to*" (Preston 1781). Being impressive and ancient to locals and tourists alike, walkers have always been attracted to the spectacular broch of Culswick (Plate 17). However, in the 1920s local Sandsting boys sometimes went for a Sunday walk to the broch and whilst there tumbled stones from the top of it, the broch being reckoned fair game for such a stunt (Bertie Gray, pers. comm.). In Low's time this broch had stood 23 feet (8m) high, but by the next time it was comprehensively examined, in the 1930s, it had lost eight feet (3m) off its elevation. This I find the saddest demise of any broch, arguably our most impressive after Mousa, the natural decay being aggravated by wanton ruination.

By the beginning of the 20th century there came to be a wealth of writing about brochs, by such people as the local writer of popular books Fordyce Clark, a native of Unst. Guidebooks to Orkney and Shetland used them as one of their lures to get tourists here, and they feature prominently in holiday-makers' journals, such as the one compiled by one Arthur Oldham, who came here from Norfolk in the 1920s, on the Picts' castles of Shetland (extant in Shetland Archives). Although visitors as a rule drew the line at digging into sites, curiosity could get the better of those interested enough to look, as was the case with soldiers stationed at Tingwall during the Second World War, who did a little digging into the broch at Hawkness in search of relics (Neil Anderson pers. comm.).

SURVEYING, EXCAVATING, SPECULATING

Perhaps the first written description of a Shetland broch was penned by John Brand, who visited in 1700: "*they are round in the form of some Dove-coats, or something like unto an Egg bulging out in the middle, but narrower at the bottom, and yet more narrow at the top. They have a little door for an entry, at which a man of an ordinary stature could not enter without bowing, within which door, there is a Stair going up between two Stone Walls, leading to several Apartments, instead of Windows they have Slits or long narrow Holes in the Wall … they are strongly built, but the conveniency for dwelling hath been but little, for their Diameter is but outside 10 or 12 Foot, and their height scarce 20 or 24.*" The outsider to whom we owe greatest debt was that intelligent observer George Low, who visited the islands in 1774, drawing and describing many ancient monuments during his travels. He commented on the construction, and recognised the defensive nature of brochs. The brochs he left descriptions of are the earliest we have, such as: Snabroch, Unst; Mousa, Sandwick; Hebrista, Aithsting. He was very observant, noticing such things as the round cells at Hebrista. Not all subsequent antiquarian theorising was so sensible. Samuel Hibbert visited Snabroch, Fetlar in 1817, following Low's lead as he so often did. Low had mentioned that this broch was uncharacteristically square, but Hibbert inadvertently set a ball rolling: he postulated that the site represented the remains of a Roman encampment, writing: "*If the antiquary does not fear being contradicted in his conjecture … he may fairly set down this fortress as showing more marks of a Roman construction*", and included a diagram. Although he tempered his idea with caution, the deed was done, and, as happens when things get into print, this erroneous notion endured 150 years. The idea took a while in dying; in a popular booklet in print from the 1950s to '70s was the revelation that "*in the island of Fetlar the ruins of a fortification have been found which Dr Hibbert declared to be those of a Roman camp.*" A few Roman coins have been found in Shetland, and "*in no part of the world is there any evidence of [other] races building fortifications similar to those at Fetlar which are of a kind peculiar to the Romans*" (Irvine 1974). It was a favourite book of mine when I was a boy, and I remember very well being fascinated by the Romans being here, and wished that someone would discover something more than the tantalising Fetlar fort, because there was no question that it was true. The distinguished antiquarian Sir Henry Dryden planned brochs such as Clickhimin, Lerwick and Levenwick, Sandwick in the 1850s, and around this time the first rooting for artefacts by antiquarians began, initially at Clickhimin. It was a local man, Gilbert Goudie, who inaugurated excavation of Shetland brochs. Of the broch of Levenwick in 1869 he wrote: "*My object, in the first place, was merely to lay open the interior of the circle*". The task got larger, and he came back the next two years to continue the work (Goudie 1871). Goudie undertook another such excavation, at the broch of Clumlie, Dunrossness, in 1887. This he called "*bringing to light a structure which for ages had never been exposed to human eye, and whose existence up to this time had been matter of mere conjecture*" (Goudie 1888). Goudie was doing pioneer work; it would be wrong to lament his lack of plans, sections, finds, and so on, because he was better by far than those who preceded him. His was work others could build on, and one can tell by his statement concerning Clumlie the sense of discovery he must have felt. A different kind of sense was what many archaeologists lacked in the later 19th century, as they pained themselves for years with prolonged speculation over the age and purpose of brochs. The ideas ranged from Stone Age

brochs to Viking brochs. All this obsession was pointless and wasteful. Pointless because all along the Shetlanders' terming of them "Pecht's castles" wasn't too far off the mark, and plenty of visitors had come to the same conclusion. As far back as 1700 Brand wrote: "*These have been the Domiciles or Dwellings of the Picts*", going on to explain the defensive nature of them and how the name signifies defence, albeit via some erroneous derivation. I also said wasteful. This is because a broch obsession meant other kinds of sites, such as Neolithic houses, were completely overlooked as a result until into the 20th century. It seems to me, as an interested layman, that as far as archaeologists go, they don't feel like saying anything about brochs unless its radically novel, controversially weird, or somewhere in between. It's the only way to get noticed. What with all the interest in brochs, the more of them that were found, the more that seemed to turn up. Any sizeable site was liable to be identified as a broch, through good intention, for example if there were ramparts extant. But sometimes it seems as if a site could be deemed a broch just because some sort of structure was there, or even no structure of archaeological significance at all (Fojut 1985). To have a broch just seemed good. Remarkably, Noel Fojut has debunked around 30 reputed broch sites – a deed both significant and needful.

At Clickhimin in 1861 the antiquarians did something really useful, by reconstructing the broch, tidying away rubble and replacing dislodged stones. Why not? It was better than dereliction or destruction, it engendered further interest, it was well carried out, and a renovation like this provides a magnet for visitors who wouldn't flock to look at a reconstruction diagram. Again, the adaptable broch has been of some use. In the 1960s schoolboys were taken by their teacher to the perilous broch at Balta, Unst, to "tidy it up". Mousa came into its own after the 1940s as the model for all brochs; archaeologists have been unable to resist reconstructing incomplete brochs to a Mousa-like stature in site reconstruction drawings. The surviving lower courses of the Jarlshof broch were expanded to Mousa size in archaeological illustrations, as was the Clickhimin one, which really isn't all that impressive as it is. One can see these pictures in the respective published reports.

USEFUL BROCHS TODAY

As ought to be known to archaeologists and others besides, the very name "broch" comes in handy for Shetlanders, as it does for Scots, as a shibboleth. The ever-versatile broch finds itself of further use. For good or ill, a person's ability or otherwise to properly pronounce the name of aforementioned building determines in one word who isn't a local or singles out in an instant those who haven't bothered mastering the name. We hear our favourite monument referred to as a "bruff", especially as a "brock", and my favourite, a "brioche" (in this case the Brioche of Mousa). Nowadays, brochs, or the Mousa one at least, have come in very handy as something else – an icon. The image is used here for a school logo, college emblem, a local bakery motif, and fills tourist brochures. It sells Shetland and is among other tired old standards as the Fair Isle jumper, "Up Helly Aa", and the wearisome puffin, when it comes to selling postcards. Some people even busy themselves excavating them.

ACKNOWLEDGEMENTS

All the illustrations within this paper and Plates 15-17 come from the Shetland Museum Collection.

BIBLIOGRAPHY

Anderson, J. (1999) *The Orkneyinga Saga*. 3rd edition. Edinburgh, Mercat Press.

Brand, J. (1703) *Description of Orkney, Zetland, Pightland-Firth and Caithness*. Edinburgh, J. Taylor.

Cant, R. (1976) *The Medieval Churches & Chapels of Shetland*. Lerwick, Shetland Archaeological and Historical Society.

Dryden, Sir H. (1890) Notes on the brochs or "Pictish Towers" of Mousa, Clickhimen &c in Shetland. *Archaeologia Scotica* V, Part 1.

Fojut, N. (1985) Some thoughts on the Shetland Iron Age. In Smith, B (ed.) *Shetland Archaeology*. Lerwick, Shetland Times.

Gear, W. (1996) Walker: A wolf in sheep's clothing? *New Shetlander* 195.

Goudie, G. (1871) Notice of excavations in a broch and adjacent tumuli near Levenwick in the parish of Dunrossness, Zetland. *Proceedings of the Society of Antiquaries of Scotland* (1871), 212-219.

Goudie, G. (1888) Recent Brough Excavations in Shetland. *Proceedings of the Society of Antiquaries of Scotland* (1888-89).

Hamilton, J. (1956) *Excavations at Jarlshof*. Edinburgh, HMSO.

Hibbert, S. (1822) *Description of the Shetland Islands*. Edinburgh, A. Constable and Co.

Hondius, H. (1636) *Orcadum et Schetlandiae Insularum*. Amsterdam.

Irvine, F. (1987) *Pictures From Shetland's Past*. Lerwick, Shetland Times.

Low, G. (1774; pub. 1879). *A Tour Through the Islands of Orkney and Schetland*. Kirkwall, William Peace and Son.

Preston, T. (1781) *New Hydrographical Survey of the Islands of Shetland*.

Royal Commission on the Ancient and Historical Monuments of Scotland (1946) *Inventory of Shetland.* Edinburgh, HMSO.

Shetland Archives, SC12/6/1790/12/4, Defence of W. Mouat, against J.B. Stewart.

Shetland Archives, D.1/259/15, Notebook of T. Mathewson.

Shetland Archives, D.1/150/3, A. Oldham album.

Spence, J. (1899) *Shetland Folk-Lore.* Lerwick, Johnson and Greig.

Thorsson, O. and Scudder, B. (2001) *The Sagas of the Icelanders.* London, Penguin Books Ltd.